Hymns for the Family of God

Hymns for the Family of God

Paragon Associates, Inc.
Nashville, Tennessee 37202

© Copyright 1976 by Paragon Associates, Inc.
Nashville, Tennessee, USA
International copyright secured. All rights reserved.

Printed in the United States of America

10 9 8 7 6 5 4 3

ISBN 0-89477-000-4

Preface

Creating a new hymnal brings many rewards. For two thousand years, Christians have been a singing people. From early chants to sung Scriptures, from versified Psalms to original words and music written in our own time, our musical heritage is as varied as it is long. Different musical styles have spoken the eternal truths of God's Word. The great advantage we have over our forefathers is being able to enjoy the richness of the past together with the creativity of the present. Whereas it used to take decades or centuries for a hymn or song-style to become an established part of the Christian's repertoire, today this can happen in a matter of a few month's time. For example "Alleluia " and "They'll Know We are Christians by our Love" are sung almost everywhere by almost everyone. They stand as a symbol of the legacy we shall leave to future generations.

It was rewarding to all of us who worked on this hymnal to appreciate the work of earlier hymnologists and compilers. The responsibility of accuracy in crediting correct sources of music and text lay heavily upon us as we aimed for a thoroughly researched hymnal in all areas. In compiling the music and reading selections for this book, we sought assistance from over forty pastors, musicians and laymen. We received a wide response, and from these leaders developed a core of hymnody common to us all. As you might expect, the most popular titles were predictable: "Holy, Holy, Holy"; "How Great Thou Art;" "O For a Thousand Tongues;" and "When I Survey the Wondrous Cross." Also from this body of supporters came eclectic denominational, cultural and geographical favorites necessary to make a complete lexicon of music for the Church today. We wanted representation from each member of the family of God. Then came the difficult part: creating a hymnal that would be inspirational and functional to each member of that diverse family of believers.

As we made our list of hymns we found we had music from many sources and many traditions. We had that in the back of our minds all along: our hymnal must have variety. As we began the task of locating the owners of these words and music we found ourselves writing requests all over the world. The composers, authors, publishers, and copyright owners were very cooperative, and we thank them all for their consideration in this venture.

As recently as twenty years ago, there were only two or three major translations of the Scriptures. Hymnals of the past usually chose to use the King James Bible, which dates back to the 1600's. Today there are close to twenty highly regarded versions, paraphrases or new translations of the original Hebrew and Greek. What an enjoyable reward to search for the best possible edition. By comparing each passage in many versions, we were able to select the best one: easiest to understand, and the one that read well when spoken aloud by a congregation.

A major reward was being allowed the freedom to be innovative. From the very beginning, we knew we wanted a hymnal that was like no other. For this, I am greatly indebted to my good friends and colleagues, Robert MacKenzie and William Gaither. They have given loving support and criticism, and as publishers, have made it possible for us to incorporate many new and hitherto untried features. These include numbering each stanza on each staff, and italicizing every other verse for clarity and to help congregations keep their place. We also beamed continuous eighth-notes so that they appear in units of beat, and provided over fifty last-verse harmonizations and/or descants. It is our sincere desire that congregational singing will improve through utilization of these features.

But not only is this hymnal a worship book, it is a devotional tool as well. By interspersing Scripture between hymns of the same topical theme, together with readings by various Christian leaders, a Sunday hymnbook is transformed into a seven-days-a-week devotional book of Scripture, hymnody, and contemporary religious thought. We feel strongly that the readings belong with the hymns, not tucked away in the back of the book.

We have divided our hymnal into four major sections: **God's Love for Us, Our Love for God, Our Love for the Family of God,** and **Our Love for Others.** This seems a logical and theologically oriented sequence. As we are made aware of God's love for us, we respond to His love with our own love. Once we know His love and acknowledge it by giving Him our love, we are then free to love each other and those beyond the family of God. It is our hope that this plan will help us all to know **why** we are singing, and to **whom** we are singing.

Right from the start we set our goals high in the area of quality-control. We wanted the very best music, Scripture sources, readings, music engravings, typefaces, paper, and binding. Our responsibility before God demands excellence, and the family of God deserves excellence. Many people have assisted in the creation of this hymnal, and I want to recognize them properly. Our editorial board of reference, our suppliers, proofreaders, printers, designers and engravers – thank you for your support and interest. Bryan Jeffery Leech, a friend, a minister, a musician, and a very capable Assistant Editor, did his work superbly and also counseled, challenged and admonished us to keep with the task that lay before us; my secretary, Marilyn Powell Austin, who typed, and retyped, and retyped again and again, list after list after list, and briefed us throughout the project on current practices with regard to capitalization and proper use of the semi-colon. I must also share how pleasant it is to be involved in a business where competitors are friends. How good to be able to pick up the phone and call fellow hymnal publishers and find them more than willing to help and share their experience and expertise without reservation. Messrs George and William Shorney, Peter Kladder, James Hawkinson, P.J. Zondervan and Bruce Howe are fine Christian gentlemen. The love of my wife, Lois, and of our family is evidenced in how supportive they've been toward this endeavor, allowing me many hours away from them writing, thinking, phoning, traveling, arranging or planning, while they kept everything running smoothly at home. They love me, I know that, and I love them for giving me this freedom in my work.

Our final reward is not in how many copies of this book are in print, but from the discovery that Christians from many churches will find this a useful tool in their personal lives, the life of their local church, and in the ministries we have as individuals, and as members of His family.

Let the Church continue to be His Church, let God's people rejoice: songs of praise and power, majesty and might, worship and witness, testimony and teaching–let them fill the air. Organs, hymns, readings, drums, guitars, and anthems swell! For His Church is triumphant, alive and well!

FRED BOCK

Acknowledgements

EDITORIAL BOARD: Fred Bock, General Editor; Bryan Jeffery Leech, Assistant Editor; William J. Gaither, Gloria Gaither, Ronn Huff, Wayne Erickson, Robert MacKenzie, Dorothy Sickal.
DESIGN AND LAYOUT: Michael Harris and Illustrated Design, Sherman Oaks, California: Allen D. Eckman, Patricia A. Eckman.
MUSIC TYPOGRAPHY: Musictype, Inc., Omaha, Arkansas: Don Ellingson, Robert Abbott, Jr.
MUSIC ARRANGING, PROOFREADING, and SECRETARIAL ASSISTANTS: Tom Keene, Cinda Goold Redman, Paul Sjolund, John Hall, Fred Bock, Darlene Lawrence, Marilyn Austin, Virginia Watts, Louise Bock, Fred Tulan, Bryan Jeffery Leech, Lois Bock, David Dunham, Diane Zagnoli.

Hymns for the Family of God

The hymns and readings are located together in the following topical areas:

I. God's Love for Us   1-316

begin with selection

God's Hand in Nature	1
God's Love	14
Bible-Word of God	29
Comfort	35
Assurance	65
Grace, Mercy, and Forgiveness	104
Refuge	117
Everlasting Life	123
Trinity	136
Holy Spirit	143
Christmas (including Advent and Epiphany)	165
The Life and Ministry of Jesus Christ	208-302
His Career and Character	
Jesus Christ-Friend	219
Jesus Christ-His Love	222
Jesus Christ-His Name	227
Jesus Christ-Lordship	233
Jesus Christ-Savior	244
Triumphal Entry	248
Cross of Jesus Christ	250
Blood of Jesus Christ	259
Atonement, Crucifixion and Death of Jesus Christ	269
Easter	287
The Second Coming of Jesus Christ	303

II. Our Love for God   317-524

begin with selection

Worship and Adoration	317
Thanksgiving	386
Commitment and Submission	397
Confession and Repentance	415
Invitation	428
Prayer and Intercession	439
Dedication and Devotion	447
Aspiration	468
Inner Peace	489
Discipleship	502
Stewardship	510
Closing Hymns	518

III. Our Love for the Family of God 525-617

begin with selection

Heritage	525
Marriage	529
Family and Home	531
The Church-Family of Believers	543
Communion	562
Dedication Services	568
Renewal and Revival	572
Encouragement	581
Fellowship with God	587
Guidance	594
Loyalty and Courage	612

IV. Our Love for Others 618-699

begin with selection

Testimony, Witness, and Evangelism	618
Missions	658
Concern for Others	675
Brotherhood and World Peace	681
Patriotic	687
Amens: Service Music	696

Indexes

Copyright acknowledgements	703
Scriptural index of readings	704
Alphabetical index of authors (readings)	705
Alphabetical index of readings	706
Scriptural allusions in hymns	707
Topical index of hymns	708
Alphabetical index of titles and first lines of hymns	709

The following indexes are found in the **Hymnal Companion:**
  Alphabetical index of tunes
  Metrical index of tunes
  Composer/author index
  First lines of all stanzas of all hymns

*God's
Love for Us*

A Fair and Glorious Gift

I wish to see all arts, principally music, in the service of Him who gave and created them. Music is a fair and glorious gift of God. I would not for the world forego my humble share of music. Singers are never sorrowful, but are merry, and smile through their troubles in song. Music makes people kinder, gentler, more staid and reasonable. I am strongly persuaded that after theology there is no art than can be placed on a level with music; for besides theology, music is the only art capable of affording peace and joy of the heart . . . the devil flees before the sound of music almost as much as before the Word of God.

—Martin Luther

For the Beauty of the Earth   1

He hath made all things beautiful. — Ecclesiastes 3:11

Folliott S. Pierpoint, alt.

DIX
Adapted by Conrad Kocher

1 For the beau - ty of the earth, For the glo - ry of the skies,
2 *For the won - der of each hour Of the day and of the night,*
3 For the joy of hu - man love, Broth - er, sis - ter, par - ent, child;
4 *For Thy Church that ev - er - more Lift - eth ho - ly hands a - bove,*
5 For Thy-self, best gift di - vine, To our race so free - ly given;

1 For the love which from our birth O - ver and a - round us lies;
2 *Hill and vale and tree and flower, Sun and moon and stars of light:*
3 Friends on earth and friends a - bove; For all gen - tle thoughts and mild:
4 *Off - ering up on ev - ery shore Her pure sac - ri - fice of love:*
5 For that great, great love of Thine, Peace on earth and joy in heaven:

Lord of all, to Thee we raise This our hymn of grate - ful praise. A-men.

GOD'S HAND IN NATURE

2 How Great Thou Art

Great is the Lord and greatly to be praised. — Psalm 48:1

Stuart K. Hine

O STORE GUD
Stuart K. Hine

1. O Lord my God! when I in awe-some won-der Con-sid-er all the worlds Thy hands have made, I see the stars, I hear the roll-ing thun-der, Thy power through-out the u-ni-verse dis-played:
2. When through the woods and for-est glades I wan-der And hear the birds sing sweet-ly in the trees; When I look down from loft-y moun-tain gran-deur And hear the brook and feel the gen-tle breeze:
3. And when I think that God, His Son not spar-ing, Sent Him to die, I scarce can take it in; That on the cross, my bur-den glad-ly bear-ing, He bled and died to take a-way my sin:
4. When Christ shall come with shout of ac-cla-ma-tion And take me home, what joy shall fill my heart! Then I shall bow in hum-ble ad-o-ra-tion, And there pro-claim, my God, how great Thou art!

Then sings my soul, my Sav-ior God, to Thee;

© Copyright 1953 by Stuart K. Hine, Assigned to Manna Music, Inc. © Copyright 1955 by Manna Music, Inc. International copyright secured. All rights reserved. Used by permission.

GOD'S HAND IN NATURE

(music: How great Thou art, how great Thou art! Then sings my soul, my Sav-ior God, to Thee; How great Thou art, how great Thou art!)

Praise Hymn

3

Praise the Lord!
    Praise the Lord from the heavens!
        Praise Him from the skies!
Praise the Lord!
    Praise the Lord, O heavens!
        Praise Him from the skies!
All of His angels,
All of the armies of heaven,
        Praise Him! Praise Him!
Praise Him, sun, and moon, and shining stars.
    Let everything He has made give thanks to Him;
    Let everything God has made give praise to Him!
        Mountains and hills, the fruit trees and cedars,
        Beasts of the fields, and fish of the oceans;
        Fire and hail, and snow and rain,
            And wind and weather obey Him.
The young men and women,
    The old men and children
All praise the Lord together!
        Sing out your thanks to Him,
        Sing praises to God!
        Sing out your thanks to Him,
        Sing praises to God!
        Sing out your praises with cymbals and harp,
        And with timbrel and voices and organ!
Let them praise the name of the Lord,
    For His name alone is exalted;
        His glory is above earth and heaven.
He raised up a horn for His people,
    Praise for all His saints.
Praise the Lord! Praise the Lord!

                —Psalm 148. Fred Bock, alt.

GOD'S HAND IN NATURE

4   God, Who Made the Earth and Heaven

Let the sea roar, let the floods clap their hands, let the hills be joyful together. — Psalm 98: 7-8

Reginald Heber, stanza 1   AR HYD Y NOS
Frederick L. Hosmer, stanza 2   Traditional Welsh Melody

1. God, who made the earth and heav-en, Dark-ness and light,
Who the day for toil has giv-en, For rest the night,
May Your an-gels guard, de-fend us, Slum-ber sweet Your mer-cy send us;
Ho-ly dreams and hopes at-tend us, All through the night.

2. *When the con-stant sun re-turn-ing Un-seals our eyes,*
May we, born a-new like morn-ing, To la-bor rise;
Fit us for the task that calls us, Let not ease and self en-thrall us,
Strong through You what-e'er be-fall us, O God most wise!

GOD'S HAND IN NATURE

Morning Has Broken

This is the day that the Lord hath made; we shall rejoice.... — Psalm 118:24

Eleanor Farjeon

BUNESSAN
Traditional Gaelic Melody
Arranged by David Evans

1. Morning has broken Like the first morning,
   Blackbird has spoken Like the first bird.
   Praise for the singing! Praise for the morning!
   Praise for them, springing Fresh from the Word!

2. *Sweet the rain's new fall Sunlit from heaven,*
   Like the first dewfall On the first grass.
   Praise for the sweetness Of the wet garden,
   Sprung in completeness Where His feet pass.

3. Mine is the sunlight! Mine is the morning
   Born of the one light Eden saw play!
   Praise with elation, Praise every morning,
   God's recreation Of the new day! A-men.

Words copyright used by permission David Higham Associates, Ltd., London.
Music from "Revised Church Hymnary" by permission of Oxford University Press.

GOD'S HAND IN NATURE

6 This Is My Father's World

The earth is the Lord's and the fullness thereof.... — Psalm 24:1

Maltbie D. Babcock

TERRA BEATA
English Melody
Adapted by Franklin L. Sheppard

1. This is my Father's world, And to my listening ears
   All nature sings, and 'round me rings The music of the spheres.
   This is my Father's world: I rest me in the thought
   Of rocks and trees, of skies and seas— His hand the wonders wrought.

2. *This is my Father's world, The birds their carols raise,*
   The morning light, the lily white, Declare their Maker's praise.
   This is my Father's world: He shines in all that's fair;
   In the rustling grass I hear Him pass, He speaks to me everywhere.

3. This is my Father's world, O let me ne'er forget
   That though the wrong seems oft so strong, God is the ruler yet.
   This is my Father's world: The battle is not done;
   Jesus who died shall be satisfied, And earth and heaven be one.

GOD'S HAND IN NATURE

Alternate Last Verse Harmonization
Arranged by Richard Purvis

3 This is my Father's world, O let me ne'er forget That though the wrong seems oft so strong, God is the ruler yet. This is my Father's world: The battle is not done; Jesus who died shall be satisfied, And earth and heaven be one.

© Copyright 1976 by Paragon Associates, Inc. All rights reserved.

GOD'S HAND IN NATURE

7 Great God, We Sing Your Mighty Hand

Even there shall Thy hand lead me, and Thy right hand shall hold me. — Psalm 139:10

Philip Doddridge, alt.

GERMANY
William Gardiner's *Sacred Melodies*

1. Great God, we sing Your mighty hand By which supported still we stand; The opening year Your mercy shows, That mercy crowns it 'til its close.
2. By day, by night, at home, abroad, Still are we guarded by our God, By His incessant bounty fed, By His unerring counsel led.
3. In scenes exalted or depressed, You are our joy, and You our rest; Your goodness all our hopes shall raise, Adored through all our changing days.
4. When death shall interrupt our songs And seal in silence mortal tongues, In fairer realms, O God, shall we Your praises sing eternally. A-men.

8 Psalm 24

The earth is the Lord's and the fulness thereof, *the world and those who dwell therein;* for He has founded it upon the seas, *and established it upon the rivers.*

Who shall ascend the hill of the Lord? And who shall stand in His holy place? *He who has clean hands and a pure heart, who does not lift up his soul to what is false, and does not swear deceitfully.* He will receive blessings from the Lord, *and vindication from the God of his salvation.* Such is the generation of those who seek Him, *who seek the face of the God of Jacob.*

GOD'S HAND IN NATURE

Lift up your heads, O gates! and be lifted up, O ancient doors! *that the King of glory may come in.* Who is the King of glory? *The Lord, strong and mighty, the Lord, mighty in battle!* Lift up your heads, O gates! and be lifted up, O ancient doors! *that the King of glory may come in.* Who is this King of glory? *The Lord of hosts, He is the King of glory!*

—(RSV)

Teach Us What We Yet May Be   9

We then, as workers together with Him . . . — II Corinthians 6:1

Catherine C. Arnott

HYMN TO JOY
Arranged by Ludwig van Beethoven

1. God, who stretched the span-gled heav-ens In - fi - nite in time and place,
2. *We have con-quered worlds un-dreamed of Since the child-hood of our race,*
3. As Thy new ho - ri - zons beck - on, Fa - ther, give us strength to be

1. Flung the suns in burn - ing ra-diance Through the si - lent fields of space,
2. *Known the ec - sta - cy of wing-ing Through un-chart-ed realms of space,*
3. Chil - dren of cre - a - tive pur-pose, Serv - ing man and hon-oring Thee,

1. We, Thy chil - dren, in Thy like - ness, Share in - ven-tive powers with Thee—
2. *Probed the se - crets of the a - tom, Yield-ing un - im - ag-ined power—*
3. 'Til our dreams are rich with mean-ing— Each en - deav - or Thy de-sign—

1. Great Cre - a - tor, still cre - a - ting, Teach us what we yet may be.
2. *Fac - ing us with life's de-struc-tion Or our most tri-um-phant hour.*
3. Great Cre - a - tor, lead us on - ward 'Til our work is one with Thine. A-men.

Words by permission of Catherine Cameron.

GOD'S HAND IN NATURE

10 Earth and All Stars

*Let the sea roar, let the floods clap their hands,
let the hills be joyful together.* — Psalm 98:7,8

Herbert F. Brokering

DEXTER
David N. Johnson
Harmonized by Jan Bender

1 Earth and all stars, Loud rushing planets, Sing to the Lord a new song! O victory, Loud shouting army, Sing to the Lord a new song!
2 *Hail, wind and rain, Loud blowing snowstorms, Sing to the Lord a new song! Flowers and trees, Loud rustling dry leaves, Sing to the Lord a new song!*
3 Trumpet and pipes, Loud clashing cymbals, Sing to the Lord a new song! Harp, lute and lyre, Loud humming 'cellos, Sing to the Lord a new song!
4 *Engines and steel, Loud pounding hammers, Sing to the Lord a new song! Limestone and beams, Loud building workmen, Sing to the Lord a new song!*
5 Knowledge and truth, Loud sounding wisdom, Sing to the Lord a new song! Daughter and son, Loud praising members, Sing to the Lord a new song!

Words and music reprinted from "Twelve Folksongs and Spirituals", compiled and arranged by David N. Johnson, 1968, by permission of Augsburg Publishing House, Minneapolis, Minnesota, copyright owner. Harmonization by Jan Bender, from "Contemporary Worship 1–Hymns", © 1969 revised edition, by permission of the publishers for the Inter-Lutheran Commission on Worship, representing the cooperating churches, the copyright owners.

GOD'S HAND IN NATURE

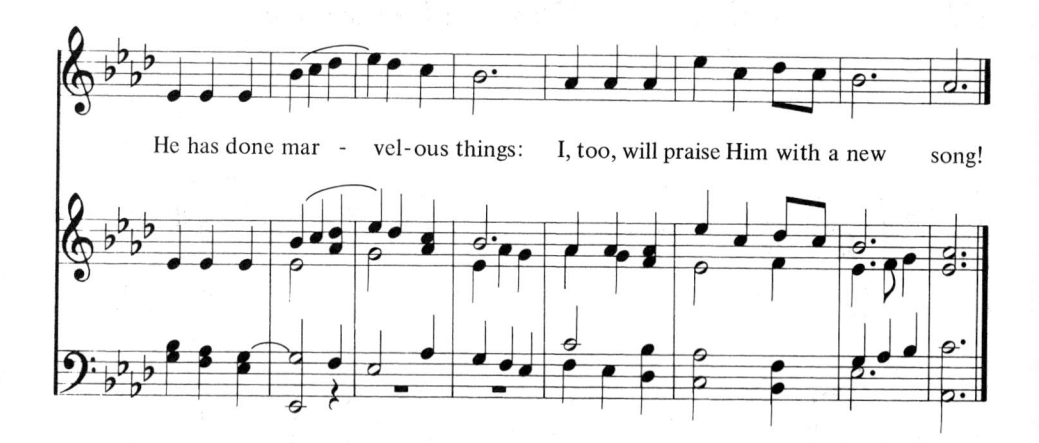

He has done mar - vel-ous things: I, too, will praise Him with a new song!

Psalm 104

O Lord, how great and all-powerful You are!
And how beautiful is the world You created for our habitation!

Even before man was brought forth from the dust,
    You prepared for him a place in which to live and grow.
    And everything man saw about him
        reflected the beauty and power of the living God.

There was clean air.
Pure water from snowcapped mountains flowed through green valleys
        and gathered together to become great lakes.
The skies shone with a million lights.
The land brought forth flowers and fruits
    to delight the eye and palate of God's creature.
And every part of the land
        and the waters that covered the land
        and the skies that looked down upon the land
        were filled with uncountable forms of life;
    and the world was vibrant and alive.

Your power and Your beauty were spread throughout the universe,
    but it was only upon the heart of man
        that You imprinted Your image.
And this creature,
    in his short stay upon this world,
        was destined to be Your son and co-worker
            in the ever-continuing process of creation.

—Leslie Brandt

GOD'S HAND IN NATURE

12. O Day of Rest and Gladness

Upon the first day of the week . . . the disciples came together, — Acts 20:7

MENDEBRAS
Traditional German Melody
Arranged by Lowell Mason

Christopher Wordsworth

1. O day of rest and gladness, O day of joy and light,
O balm of care and sadness, Most beautiful, most bright:
On thee the high and lowly, Through ages joined in tune,
Sing "Holy, holy, holy," To the great God Triune.

2. On thee, at the creation, The light first had its birth;
On thee, for our salvation, Christ rose from depths of earth;
On thee our Lord victorious The Spirit sent from heaven;
And thus on thee most glorious A triple light was given.

3. Today on weary nations The heavenly manna falls;
To holy convocations The silver trumpet calls,
Where gospel light is glowing With pure and radiant beams,
And living water flowing With soul-refreshing streams.

4. New graces ever gaining From this our day of rest,
We reach the rest remaining To spirits of the blest;
To Holy Ghost be praises, To Father and to Son;
The Church her voice upraises To Thee, blest Three in One. A-men.

GOD'S HAND IN NATURE

The Wonder of It All

13

For we are His workmanship created in Christ Jesus unto good works. — Ephesians 2:10

WONDER OF IT ALL
George Beverly Shea
George Beverly Shea

1. There's the won-der of sun-set at eve-ning, The won-der as sun-rise I see; But the won-der of won-ders that thrills my soul Is the won-der that God loves me.
2. *There's the won-der of spring-time and har-vest, The sky, the stars, the sun; But the won-der of won-ders that thrills my soul Is a won-der that's on-ly be-gun.*

O, the won-der of it all! The won-der of it all! Just to think that God loves me. O the won-der of it all! The won-der of it all! Just to think that God loves me.

© Copyright 1956 by Chancel Music, Inc. International copyright secured. All rights reserved. Used by permission.

GOD'S LOVE

14 A Celebration for Family People

Leader: God has called us to live within the privilege of family life.
He has gifted us with mothers, fathers, sisters, brothers, aunts and uncles, and grandparents, and beyond this with friends who become equally precious to us.
People: PRAISE GOD FOR THE GIFT OF FAMILY LIFE!
Leader: Lord,
We thank you for older folk who link us with the past and who enrich us with their experience.
We thank you for the newborn so rich in potential greatness and goodness.
We thank you for the gifts we see emerging in our children.
We thank you for the excitement of living with those who are on the brink of adulthood, even though this is sometimes a time of struggle for all of us.
People: PRAISE GOD FOR THE GIFT OF FAMILY LIFE!
Leader: Eternal Father of us all,
Enter our homes,
not as the occupant of a guest room,
but as the senior member of each household,
that we may live out your love in the most ordinary parts of life.
Keep us human as you make us holy. Amen.
People: PRAISE GOD FOR THE GIFT OF FAMILY LIFE!
IT IS ALL YOUR DOING, LORD. IT IS WONDERFUL IN OUR EYES.

—Bryan Jeffery Leech

15 Jesus Loves the Little Children

"Suffer little children... to come unto Me." — Matthew 19:14

CHILDREN
Unknown
George F. Root

Je-sus loves the lit-tle chil-dren, All the chil-dren of the world. Red and yel-low, black and white, They are pre-cious in His sight — Je-sus loves the lit-tle chil-dren of the world.

GOD'S LOVE

Tell Me the Old, Old Story

16

Of which salvation the prophets have enquired . . . who prophesied of the grace that should come . . . . — I Peter 1:10

Katherine Hankey

EVANGEL
William H. Doane

1. Tell me the old, old story Of unseen things above, Of Jesus and His glory, Of Jesus and His love. Tell me the story simply, As to a little child; For I am weary and weary, And helpless and defiled.
2. Tell me the story slowly, That I may take it in— That wonderful redemption, God's remedy for sin. Tell me the story often, For I forget so soon; The early dew of morning Has passed away at noon.
3. Tell me the same old story When you have cause to fear, That this world's empty glory Is costing me too dear. Yes, and when that world's glory Is dawning on my soul, Tell me the old, old story: "Christ Jesus makes thee whole."

Tell me the old, old story. Tell me the old, old story. Tell me the old, old story, Of Jesus and His love.

GOD'S LOVE

17 Psalm 89

I feel like singing this morning, O Lord.
I feel like telling everyone about me
    how great You are.
If only they could know the depths of Your love
    and Your eternal concern for those who
    will follow You!
But my songs are so often off-key.
My speech is so inadequate.
I simply cannot express what I feel,
    what I know to be true about Your love
    for Your creatures upon this world.

But even the songs of the birds
    proclaim Your praises.
The heavens and the earth beneath them,
    the trees that reach toward You,
    the flowers that glow in colorful beauty,
    the green hills and soaring mountains,
    the valleys and the plains,
    the lakes and the rivers,
    the great oceans that pound our shores,
    they proclaim Your greatness, O God,
    and Your love for the sons of men.

How glorious it is to be alive, O Lord!
May every breath of my body,
    every beat of my heart,
    be dedicated to Your praise and glory.

—Leslie Brandt

18 The Love of God

Who shall separate us from the love of Christ? — Romans 8:35

F. M. Lehman
Arranged by Claudia Lehman Mays

F. M. Lehman

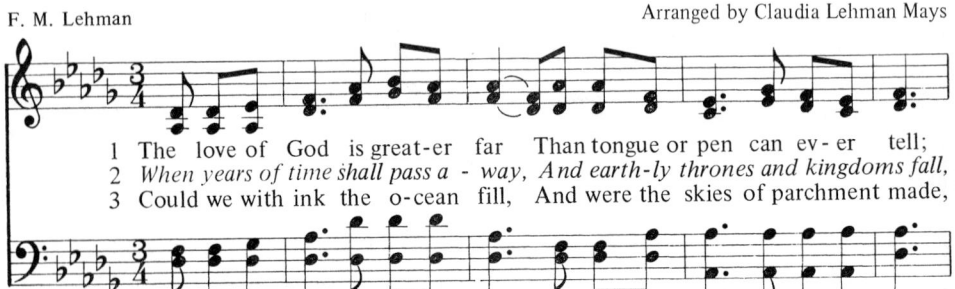

1 The love of God is great-er far Than tongue or pen can ev-er tell;
2 *When years of time shall pass a-way, And earth-ly thrones and kingdoms fall,*
3 Could we with ink the o-cean fill, And were the skies of parchment made,

Copyright 1917. Renewed 1945 by Nazarene Publishing House. All rights reserved. Used by permission.

GOD'S LOVE

1. It goes beyond the highest star, And reaches to the lowest hell;
2. *When men, who here refuse to pray, On rocks and hills and mountains call,*
3. Were every stalk on earth a quill, And every man a scribe by trade,

1. The guilty pair, bowed down with care, God gave His Son to win;
2. *God's love so sure, shall still endure, All measureless and strong;*
3. To write the love of God above Would drain the ocean dry.

1. His erring child He reconciled, And pardoned from his sin.
2. *Redeeming grace to Adam's race—The saints' and angels' song.*
3. Nor could the scroll contain the whole, Though stretched from sky to sky.

O love of God, how rich and pure! How measureless and strong!

It shall for evermore endure The saints' and angels' song.

GOD'S LOVE

19 John 3:14-21

"And as Moses lifted up the serpent in the wilderness, so must the Son of man be lifted up, that whoever believes in Him may have eternal life."

For God so loved the world that He gave His only Son, that whoever believes in Him should not perish but have eternal life. For God sent the Son into the world, not to condemn the world, but that the world might be saved through Him. He who believes in Him is not condemned; he who does not believe is condemned already, because He has not believed in the name of the only Son of God. And this is the judgment, that the light has come into the world, and men loved darkness rather than light, because their deeds were evil. For every one who does evil hates the light, and does not come to the light, lest his deeds should be exposed. But he who does what is true comes to the light, that it may be clearly seen that his deeds have been wrought in God.

—(RSV)

20 God So Loved the World

...He gave His only begotten Son.... — John 3:16

John 3:16, 17

STAINER
John Stainer

[Musical score with lyrics:]

God so loved the world, God so loved the world, that He gave His on-ly be-got-ten Son, that who-so be-liev-eth, be-liev-eth in Him should not per-ish, should not per-ish but have ev-er-last-ing life. For God sent not His

GOD'S LOVE

GOD'S LOVE

21. Love Divine, All Loves Excelling

For the law of the Spirit of Life, . . . hath made us free from the law of sin and death.
— Romans 8:2 (Read Romans 7:24, 25; 8:1-5)

Charles Wesley

BEECHER
John Zundel

1. Love divine, all loves excelling, Joy of heaven to earth come down,
Fix in us Thy humble dwelling, All Thy faithful mercies crown.
Jesus, Thou art all compassion, Pure, unbounded love Thou art;
Visit us with Thy salvation, Enter every trembling heart.

2. Breathe, O breathe Thy loving Spirit Into every troubled breast;
Let us all in Thee inherit, Let us find Thy promised rest.
Take away our bent to sinning, Alpha and Omega be;
End of faith, as its beginning, Set our hearts at liberty.

3. Come, Almighty to deliver, Let us all Thy life receive;
Suddenly return, and never, Nevermore Thy temples leave.
Thee we would be always blessing, Serve Thee as Thy hosts above,
Pray, and praise Thee without ceasing, Glory in Thy perfect love.

4. Finish then Thy new creation, Pure and spotless let us be;
Let us see Thy great salvation Perfectly restored in Thee.
Changed from glory into glory, 'Til in heaven we take our place,
'Til we cast our crowns before Thee, Lost in wonder, love, and praise. A-men.

GOD'S LOVE

Alternate Last Verse Harmonization Arranged by Robert J. Powell

4 Finish then Thy new creation, Pure and spotless let us be;
Let us see Thy great salvation Perfectly restored in Thee.
Changed from glory into glory, 'Til in heaven we take our place,
'Til we cast our crowns before Thee, Lost in wonder, love and praise.

© Copyright 1976 by Paragon Associates, Inc. All rights reserved.

GOD'S LOVE

22. One Day

When the fullness of time was come, God sent forth His son.... — Galatians 4:4

J. Wilbur Chapman
ONE DAY
Charles H. Marsh

1. One day when heav-en was filled with His prais-es, One day when sin was as black as could be, Je-sus came forth to be born of a vir-gin, Dwelt a-mong men—my ex-am-ple is He!
2. One day they led Him up Cal-va-ry's moun-tain, One day they nailed Him to die on the tree; Suf-fer-ing an-guish, de-spised and re-ject-ed, Bear-ing our sins, my Re-deem-er is He!
3. One day they left Him a-lone in the gar-den, One day He rest-ed, from suf-fer-ing free; An-gels came down o'er His tomb to keep vig-il— Hope of the hope-less, my Sav-ior is He!
4. One day the grave could con-ceal Him no long-er, One day the stone rolled a-way from the door; Then He a-rose, o-ver death He had con-quered, Now is as-cend-ed, my Lord ev-er-more!
5. One day the trum-pet will sound for His com-ing, One day the skies with His glo-ry will shine; Won-der-ful day, my be-lov-ed ones bring-ing! Glo-ri-ous Sav-ior, this Je-sus is mine!

Liv-ing, He loved me! dy-ing, He saved me! Bur-ied, He

Copyright 1910 by C. H. Marsh. Copyright renewed 1938 by C. H. Marsh. Assigned to The Rodeheaver Co. Used by permission.

GOD'S LOVE

car - ried my sins far a - way! Ris - ing, He jus - ti - fied free - ly, for - ev - er! One day He's com - ing— O glo - ri - ous day!

Hosea 14:4b-9   23

I will love them with all my heart,
    for my anger has turned from them.
I will fall like dew on Israel.
    He shall bloom like the lily,
and thrust out roots like the poplar,
    his shoots will spread far;
he will have the beauty of the olive
    and the fragrance of Lebanon.
They will come back to live in my shade;
    they will grow corn that flourishes,
they will cultivate vines
    as renowned as the wine of Helbon.
What has Ephraim to do with idols any more
    when it is I who hear his prayer and care for him?
I am like a cypress ever green,
    all your fruitfulness comes from me.

Let the wise men understand these words.
    Let the intelligent man grasp their meaning.
For the ways of Jehovah are straight,
    and virtuous men walk in them,
but sinners stumble.

                                                                                         –(JB)

24 O the Deep, Deep Love of Jesus

Who shall separate us from the love of Jesus? Romans 8:35

Samuel Trevor Francis

EBENEZER
Thomas J. Williams

1. O the deep, deep love of Jesus, Vast, unmeasured, boundless, free! Rolling as a mighty ocean In its fullness over me! Underneath me, all around me, Is the current of Thy love— Leading onward, leading homeward, To my glorious rest above!

2. O the deep, deep love of Jesus— Spread His praise from shore to shore! How He loveth, ever loveth, Changeth never, nevermore! How He watches o'er His loved ones, Died to call them all His own; How for them He intercedeth, Watcheth o'er them from the throne!

3. O the deep, deep love of Jesus, Love of every love the best! 'Tis an ocean full of blessing, 'Tis a haven giving rest! O the deep, deep love of Jesus— 'Tis a heaven of heavens to me; And it lifts me up to glory, For it lifts me up to Thee!

Music copyright by Gwenlyn Evans Ltd. Used by permission.

GOD'S LOVE

1 lead-ing	home-ward,	To Thy	glo-rious	rest	a-bove!	
2 in-ter-	ced-eth,	Watch-eth	o'er them	from	the throne!	
3 up to	glo-ry,	For it	lifts me	up	to Thee!	A-men.

God, Thou Art Love 25

If I forget,
    Yet God remembers! If these hands of mine
Cease from their clinging, yet the hands divine
    Hold me so firmly that I cannot fall;
And if sometimes I am too tired to call
    For Him to help me, then He reads the prayer
Unspoken in my heart, and lifts my care.

I dare not fear, since certainly I know
    That I am in God's keeping, shielded so
From all that else would harm, and in the hour
    Of stern temptation strengthened by His power;
I tread no path in life to Him unknown;
    I lift no burden, bear no pain, alone:
My soul a calm, sure hiding-place has found:
    The everlasting arms my life surround.

God, Thou art love! I build my faith on that.
    I know Thee who has kept my path, and made
Light for me in the darkness, tempering sorrow
    So that it reached me like a solemn joy;
It were too strange that I should doubt Thy love.

—Robert Browning

GOD'S LOVE

26. Why Should He Love Me So?

Robert Harkness

I am not worthy of the least of Thy mercies. — Genesis 32:10

LOVE ME
Robert Harkness

1. Love sent my Sav-ior to die in my stead — Why should He love me so?
2. *Nails pierced His hands and His feet for my sin — Why should He love me so?*
3. O how He ag-o-nized there in my place — Why should He love me so?

1. Meek-ly to Cal-va-ry's cross He was led — Why should He love me so?
2. *He suf-fered sore my sal-va-tion to win — Why should He love me so?*
3. Noth-ing with-hold-ing my sin to ef-face — Why should He love me so?

Why should He love me so? Why should He love me so?

Why should my Sav-ior to Cal-va-ry go? Why should He love me so?

© Copyright 1925. Renewed 1952, Broadman Press. All rights reserved. Used by permission.

27. Psalm 110

God spoke to me today. He broke through my childish doubts with words of comfort and assurance. "Hang in there; sit tight; stick to My course for your life," He said, "I will not let you down."

He reminded me of how He cared for past saints, how He watched over them and kept them through their hours of suffering and uncertainty. He reviewed for me my own life, His loving concern through the days of my youth. He restated for me my commission and appointment, His trust in me as His servant in this sorry world. He reiterated His gracious promises to stand by me, to empower and support me in the conflicts that await me.

I know that God is with me today — just as surely as He was with His saints of old. I have neither to fear nor to doubt the eternal love and presence of my Lord.

—Leslie Brandt

GOD'S LOVE

Love Was When

28

John E. Walvoord — *And the Word became flesh and dwelt among us....* — John 1:14

DALSEM
Don Wyrtzen

1. Love was when God became a man Locked in time and space without rank or place; Jesus walked in history— Lovingly He brought a new life that's free; Love was God nailed to bleed and die To reach and love one such as I.
   Love was God born of Jewish kin, Just a carpenter with some fishermen. Love was when

2. Love was when God became a man Down where I could see love that reached to me; Jesus rose to walk with me— Lovingly He brought a new life that's free; Love was God— only He would try To reach and love one such as I.
   Love was God dying for my sin— And so trapped was I my whole world caved in. Love was when

© Copyright 1970 by Singspiration, Inc. Arr. © 1974 by Singspiration, Division of The Zondervan Corporation. All rights reserved. Used by permission.

GOD'S LOVE

29 Wonderful Words of Life

Lord, to whom shall we go? Thou hath the words of eternal life. — John 6:68

Philip P. Bliss, alt.

WORDS OF LIFE
Philip P. Bliss

1. Sing them o-ver a-gain to me, Won-der-ful words of life;
2. *Christ, the bless-ed One, gives to all Won-der-ful words of life;*
3. Sweet-ly ech-o the gos-pel call, Won-der-ful words of life;

1. Let me more of their beau-ty see, Won-der-ful words of life.
2. *Lis-ten well to the lov-ing call, Won-der-ful words of life.*
3. Of-fer par-don and peace to all, Won-der-ful words of life.

1. Words of life and beau-ty, Teach me faith and du-ty:
2. *All the won-drous sto-ry, Show-ing us His glo-ry:*
3. Je-sus, on-ly Sav-ior, Sanc-ti-fy for-ev-er:

Beau-ti-ful words, won-der-ful words, Won-der-ful words of Life. Life.

BIBLE—WORD OF GOD

Break Thou the Bread of Life 30

Based on Matthew 14:19 — *For the bread of God is He which cometh down from Heaven, and giveth life unto the world.* — John 6:33

Mary A. Lathbury, stanzas 1, 2
Alexander Groves, stanzas 3, 4

BREAD OF LIFE
William F. Sherwin

1. Break Thou the bread of life, Dear Lord, to me, As Thou didst break the loaves Beside the sea; Beyond the sacred page I seek Thee, Lord; My spirit pants for Thee, O living Word.
2. *Bless Thou the truth, dear Lord, To me, to me, As Thou didst bless the bread By Galilee; Then shall all bondage cease, All fetters fall; And I shall find my peace, My all in all.*
3. Thou art the bread of life, O Lord, to me; Thy holy Word the truth That saveth me; Give me to eat and live With Thee above; Teach me to love Thy truth, For Thou art love.
4. *O send Thy Spirit, Lord, Now unto me, That He may touch my eyes And make me see; Show me the truth concealed Within Thy word, For in Thy book revealed I see Thee, Lord.* A-men.

Proverbs 3:13-26 31

Happy is the man who finds wisdom, and the man who gets understanding, for the gain from it is better than gain from silver and its profit better than gold. She is more precious than jewels, and nothing you desire can compare with her. Long life is in her right hand; in her left hand are riches and honor. Her ways are ways of pleasantness, and all her paths are peace. She is a tree of life to those who lay hold of her; those who hold her fast are called happy.

The Lord by wisdom founded the earth; by understanding He established the heavens; by His knowledge the deeps broke forth, and the clouds drop down the dew.

My son, keep sound wisdom and discretion; let them not escape from your sight, and they will be life for your soul and adornment for your neck. Then you will walk on your way securely and your foot will not stumble. If you sit down, you will not be afraid; when you lie down, your sleep will be sweet. Do not be afraid of sudden panic, or of the ruin of the wicked, when it comes; for the Lord will be your confidence and will keep your foot from being caught.

—(RSV)

BIBLE—WORD OF GOD

32 How Firm a Foundation

... And my God is the rock of my refuge. — Psalm 94:22

Based on II Timothy 2:19; Hebrews 13:5; Isaiah 43:1-2
"K" in Rippon's *Selection*, 1787

FOUNDATION
Early American Melody

1. How firm a foundation, ye saints of the Lord,
   Is laid for your faith in His excellent Word!
   What more can He say than to you He hath said,
   To you who for refuge to Jesus have fled?

2. "Fear not, I am with thee; O be not dismayed,
   For I am thy God, and will still give thee aid;
   I'll strengthen thee, help thee, and cause thee to stand,
   Upheld by My righteous, omnipotent hand.

3. "When through fiery trials thy pathway shall lie,
   My grace, all sufficient, shall be thy supply:
   The flame shall not hurt thee; I only design
   Thy dross to consume and thy gold to refine.

4. "The soul that on Jesus hath leaned for repose
   I will not, I will not desert to its foes;
   That soul, though all hell should endeavor to shake,
   I'll never, no, never, no, never forsake!"

BIBLE—WORD OF GOD

Not by Bread Alone 33

Man does not live by bread alone,
  but by beauty and harmony,
    truth and goodness,
      work and recreation,
        affection and friendship,
          aspiration and worship.

Man does not live by bread alone,
  but by the splendor of the starry firmament at midnight,
    the glory of the heavens at dawn,
      the gorgeous blending of colors at sunset,
        the luxuriant loveliness of magnolia trees,
          the sheer magnificence of mountains.

Man does not live by bread alone,
  but by the lyrics and sonnets of poets,
    the mature wisdom of sages,
      the holiness of saints,
        the biographies of great souls,
          the life-giving words of Holy Scripture.

Man does not live by bread alone,
  but by being faithful in prayer,
    responding to the guidance of the Holy Spirit,
      taking up the cross and following the living Christ,
        finding and doing the loving will of God now and eternally.

—Kirby Page

Holy Bible, Book Divine 34

Thy word is a lamp unto my feet, and a light unto my path. — Psalm 119:105

John Burton
ALETTA
William B. Bradbury

1. Holy Bible, book divine, Precious treasure, thou art mine;
   Mine to tell me whence I came; Mine to teach me which I am;
2. *Mine to chide me when I rove; Mine to show a Savior's love;*
   Mine thou art to guide and guard; Mine to punish or reward;
3. Mine to comfort in distress, Suffering in this wilderness;
   Mine to show, by living faith, Man can triumph over death;
4. *Mine to tell of joys to come, And the rebel sinner's doom;*
   O thou holy book divine, Precious treasure, thou art mine. A-men.

BIBLE—WORD OF GOD

35 Near to the Heart of God

Draw nigh to God and He will draw nigh to you. — James 4:8

Cleland B. McAfee

McAFEE
Cleland B. McAfee

1. There is a place of qui-et rest, Near to the heart of God;
   A place where sin can-not mo-lest, Near to the heart of God.
2. *There is a place of com-fort sweet, Near to the heart of God;*
   A place where we our Sav-ior meet, Near to the heart of God.
3. There is a place of full re-lease, Near to the heart of God;
   A place where all is joy and peace, Near to the heart of God.

O Je-sus, blest Re-deem-er, Sent from the heart of God,
Hold us, who wait be-fore Thee, Near to the heart of God.

COMFORT

No One Understands Like Jesus

... But He knoweth the way that I take. — Job 23:10

John W. Peterson

ARIZONA
John W. Peterson

1. No one understands like Jesus, He's a friend beyond compare;
2. *No one understands like Jesus, Every woe He sees and feels;*
3. No one understands like Jesus, When the foes of life assail;
4. *No one understands like Jesus, When you falter on the way,*

1. Meet Him at the throne of mercy, He is waiting for you there.
2. *Tenderly He whispers comfort, And the broken heart He heals.*
3. You should never be discouraged, Jesus cares and will not fail.
4. *Tho you fail Him, sadly fail Him, He will pardon you today.*

No one understands like Jesus, When the days are dark and grim;

No one is so near, so dear as Jesus— Cast your every care on Him.

© Copyright 1952 by Norman J. Clayton, Norman Clayton Publishing Co., owner. Used by permission.

COMFORT

37 The Hiding Place

He shall cover thee with His feathers, and under His wings shalt thou trust...
— Psalm 91:4

Bryan Jeffery Leech

HIDING PLACE
Bryan Jeffery Leech

In a time of trou-ble, in a time for-lorn, There is a hid-ing place where hope is born.
In a time of dan-ger, when our faith is proved, There is a hid-ing place where we are loved.

There is a hid-ing place, a strong pro-tec-tive space, where God pro-vides the grace to per-se-vere; For noth-ing can re-move us from the Father's love, Tho' all may change, yet nothing changes here.

In a time of sor-row, in a time of grief, There is a hid-ing place to give re-lief.
In a time of weak-ness, in a time of fear, There is a hid-ing place where God is near. A-men.

© Copyright 1973, 1974 by Fred Bock Music Company. All rights reserved. Used by permission.
COMFORT

The Great Physician

38

Bless the Lord, O my soul . . . who forgiveth all thine iniquities and healeth all thy diseases. — Psalm 103:1,3

William Hunter

GREAT PHYSICIAN
John H. Stockton

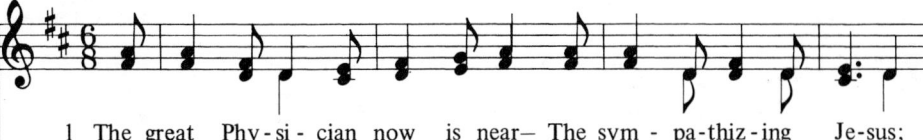

1. The great Physician now is near— The sympathizing Jesus;
2. *Your many sins are all forgiven— O hear the voice of Jesus;*
3. All glory to the dying Lamb— I now believe in Jesus;
4. *And when to that bright world above We rise to be with Jesus,*

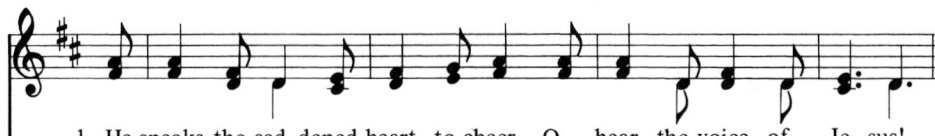

1. He speaks the saddened heart to cheer— O hear the voice of Jesus!
2. *Go on your way in peace to heaven And wear a crown with Jesus.*
3. I love the blessed Savior's name, I love the name of Jesus.
4. *We'll sing around the throne of love His name, the name of Jesus.*

Sweetest note in angels' song! Sweetest name on mortal tongue!

Sweetest carol ever sung— Jesus, blessed Jesus!

COMFORT

39 Blessed Jesus

Sing unto the Lord, Bless His Name, ... — Psalm 96:2

Gloria Gaither

BLESSED JESUS
William J. Gaither

1. O Jesus, You're so at the center of things,
   Our lives are all wrapped up in You;
   Like children we run to the arms that we know,
   You love us, what else could we do?

2. It was Your name, sweet Jesus, our baby's first word,
   Our old folks died praising Your name;
   And all in between the beginning and end,
   Our joy, our salvation, our Friend.

3. When those who have stolen their piece of our heart,
   Fail, disappointing us so;
   You whisper, "My child, will you too go away?"
   O Lord, to whom should we go?

© Copyright 1972 by William J. Gaither. All rights reserved. Used by permission.

COMFORT

Blessed Jesus, blessed Jesus,
Where could we go but to You?
Blessed Jesus, blessed Jesus, You love us, what else could we do?

COMFORT

40 The Lord's My Shepherd, I'll Not Want

He shall feed His flock like a shepherd.   Isaiah 40:11

Based on Psalm 23
Scottish Psalter

(FIRST TUNE)

CRIMOND
Jessie S. Irvine

1. The Lord's my shep-herd, I'll not want; He makes me down to lie In pas-tures green; He lead-eth me The qui-et wa-ters by.
2. *My soul He doth re-store a-gain,* And me to walk doth make With-in the paths of right-eous-ness, E'en for His own name's sake.
3. Yea, though I walk in death's dark vale, Yet will I fear no ill, For Thou art with me, and Thy rod And staff me com-fort still.
4. *My ta-ble Thou hast fur-nish-ed* In pres-ence of my foes; My head Thou dost with oil a-noint, And my cup o-ver-flows.
5. Good-ness and mer-cy all my life Shall sure-ly fol-low me, And in God's house for-ev-er-more My dwell-ing place shall be. A-men.

41   Psalm 23

The Lord is my shepherd; I shall not want.
> He maketh me to lie down in green pastures:
He leadeth me beside the still waters.
> He restoreth my soul:
He leadeth me in the paths of righteousness for His name's sake.
> Yea, though I walk through the valley of the shadow of death,
I will fear no evil: for Thou art with me;
> Thy rod and Thy staff, they comfort me.
Thou preparest a table before me in the presence of mine enemies:
> Thou annointest my head with oil;
My cup runneth over!
> Surely goodness and mercy shall follow me all the days of my life:
And I will dwell in the house of the Lord forever.

—Psalm 23 (KJV)

COMFORT

The Lord's My Shepherd, I'll Not Want

The Lord Is My Shepherd — Psalm 23

42

Based on Psalm 23
Scottish Psalter

(SECOND TUNE)

BROTHER JAMES' AIR
Traditional

1 The Lord's my Shep-herd, I'll not want, He makes me down to lie
2 My soul He doth re - store a - gain, And me to walk doth make
3 Yea, though I walk through shad-owed vale, Yet will I fear no ill,
4 My ta - ble Thou hast fur - nished In pres-ence of my foes.
5 Good - ness and mer - cy all my days Shall sure - ly fol - low me,

1 In pas-tures green; He lead-eth me The si - lent wa - ters by;
2 With - in the paths of bless - ed - ness, E'en for His own name's sake;
3 For Thou art with me and Thy rod And staff me com - fort still;
4 My head with oil Thou dost a - noint, And my cup o - ver - flows;
5 And in my Fa - ther's house al - ways My dwell - ing place shall be;

1 He lead - eth me, He lead - eth me The si - lent wa - ters by.
2 With - in the paths of bless - ed - ness E'en for His own name's sake.
3 Thy rod and staff me com - fort still, Me com - fort still.
4 My head with oil Thou dost a - noint, And my cup o - ver - flows.
5 And in my heart for - ev - er - more Thy dwell - ing place shall be.

© Copyright 1926 by Oxford University Press. Used by permission.

COMFORT

43 Through It All

He delivereth me ... therefore shall I give thanks. — Psalm 18:48,49

Andraé Crouch

THROUGH IT ALL
Andraé Crouch

1. I've had man-y tears and sor-rows, I've had ques-tions for to-mor-row, There've been times I did-n't know right from wrong; But in ev-ery sit-u-a-tion God gave bless-ed con-so-la-tion That my tri-als come to on-ly make me strong.

2. I've been to lots of plac-es, And I've seen a lot of fac-es, There've been times I felt so all a-lone; But in my lone-ly hours, Yes, those pre-cious lone-ly hours, Je-sus let me know that I was His own.

3. I thank God for the moun-tains, And I thank Him for the val-leys, I thank Him for the storms He brought me through; For if I'd nev-er had a prob-lem I would-n't know that He could solve them, I'd nev-er know what faith in God could do.

Through it all, Through it all, I've learned to trust in

© Copyright 1971 by Manna Music, Inc. International copyright secured. All rights reserved. Used by permission.
COMFORT

Je-sus, I've learned to trust in God; Through it all,

Through it all, I've learned to de-pend up-on His Word.

Prayer for Comfort 44

Jesus, our Master, whose heart was moved with compassion toward the weak and oppressed, and who was more willing to serve than to be served; we pray for all conditions of people:
> for those lacking food, shelter, or clothing;
> for the sick and all who are wasting away by disease;
> for the blind, deaf, and lame;
> for prisoners;
> for those oppressed by injustice;
> for those who have lost their way in society;
> for the corrupted and morally fallen;
> for the lonely and depressed;
> for the worried and anxious;
> for all living faithfully in obscurity;
> for those fighting bravely in unpopular wars or causes;
> for all who are serving diligently and dependably;
> for those who stand in the valley of decision;
> for those who are suffering the consequences of misdeeds repented of;
> for all family circles broken by death;
> for those faced by tasks too great for their powers.

Let the power of Jesus' spirit be strong within us, and those for whom we pray. Amen.

—James L. Christensen

45 For Loneliness in Bereavement

Father, I am only human. I need the touch of human companionship. Sorely I miss those I love who are with Thee.

I pray, O Jesus, that Thou wilt reveal to me unseen presences. Help me to know how close my loved ones are. For if they are with Thee, and Thou art with me, I know that they cannot be far away.

Make real for me that contact of spirit with spirit that will re-establish the lost fellowship for which my heart yearns.
Give to me faith shining through my tears.
Plant peace and hope within my heart.
Point me with joy to the great reunion.

But until then, enable me to live happily and worthily of those who are with Thee. In the Name of Him who is the Lord of Life, I pray, Amen.

—Peter Marshall

46 They That Sow in Tears

Gloria Gaither
William J. Gaither

They that sow in tears shall reap in joy. — Psalm 126:5

THEY THAT SOW IN TEARS
William J. Gaither

1. Though it seems that your prayers have been in vain, Though your faith the world would destroy, Though your heart should ache 'til it breaks in two, They that sow in tears shall reap in joy.
2. Though the mists of despair cloud the sky above, Do you pray 'til His face appears? In your heart do you know that you've touched the throne? They shall reap in joy who sow in tears.
3. Does your heart fill with doubt when alone you pray? Does the world your soul annoy? Lift your sights! Look beyond! God is standing near! They that sow in tears shall reap in joy.

© Copyright 1964 by William J. Gaither. All rights reserved. Used by permission.

COMFORT

They that sow in tears shall reap in joy, For God is on His throne, Though you've prayed 'til it seems that your heart would break, They that sow in tears shall reap in joy!

Joy at All Times 47

We must recognize that there is all the difference in the world between rejoicing and feeling happy. The Scripture tells us that we should always rejoice. Take the lyrical Epistle of Paul to the Philippians where he says: "Rejoice in the Lord always and again I say rejoice". He goes on saying it. To rejoice is a command, yes, but there is all the difference in the world between rejoicing and being happy. You cannot make yourself happy, but you can make yourself rejoice, in the sense that you will always rejoice in the Lord. Happiness is something within ourselves, rejoicing is "in the Lord". How important it is then, to draw the distinction between rejoicing in the Lord and feeling happy. Take the fourth chapter of the Second Epistle to the Corinthians. There you will find that the great Apostle puts it all very plainly and clearly in that series of extraordinary contrasts which he makes: "We are troubled on every side (I don't think he felt very happy at the moment) yet not distressed", "we are perplexed (he wasn't feeling happy at all at that point) but not in despair", "persecuted but not forsaken", "cast down, but not destroyed"—and so on. In other words the Apostle does not suggest a kind of happy person in a carnal sense, but he was still rejoicing. That is the difference between the two conditions.

—Martin Lloyd-Jones

48 There Is a Balm in Gilead

Go up to Gilead and take balm.... — Jeremiah 46:11

Jeremiah 8:22

BALM IN GILEAD
Traditional Spiritual

There is a balm in Gil-e-ad to make the wound-ed whole;

Fine

There is a balm in Gil-e-ad to heal the sin-sick soul.

1 Some-times I feel dis-cour-aged, And think my work's in vain,
2 If you can't preach like Pe-ter, If you can't pray like Paul,

D.C. al Fine

1 But then the Ho-ly Spir-it Re-vives my soul a-gain.
2 Just tell the love of Je-sus, And say He died for all.

COMFORT

I Must Tell Jesus

49

... by prayer ... with thanksgiving let your requests be made known unto God.
— Philippians 4:6

Elisha A. Hoffman

ORWIGSBURG
Elisha A. Hoffman

1. I must tell Jesus all of my trials, I cannot bear these burdens alone; In my distress He kindly will help me, He always loves and cares for His own.
2. *I must tell Jesus all of my troubles, He is a kind, compassionate friend; If I but ask Him, He will deliver, Make of my troubles quickly an end.*
3. Tempted and tried, I need a great Savior, One who can help my burdens to bear; I must tell Jesus, I must tell Jesus, He all my cares and sorrows will share.
4. *O how the world of evil allures me! O how my heart is tempted to sin! I must tell Jesus, and He will help me Over the world the victory to win.*

I must tell Jesus! I must tell Jesus! I cannot bear my burdens alone; I must tell Jesus! I must tell Jesus! Jesus can help me, Jesus alone.

COMFORT

50   God Is For Us

Minister: *What can we ever say to such wonderful things as these?*

People: If God is on our side, who can ever be against us?

Minister: *Since He did not spare even His own Son for us*
but gave Him up for us all,
won't He also surely give us everything else?
Who dares accuse us whom God has chosen for His own?
Will God?

People: No!
He is the one who has forgiven us
and given us right standing with Himself.

Minister: *Who then will condemn us?*
Will Christ?

People: No!
For He is the one who died for us
and came back to life again for us
and is sitting at the place of highest honor next to God,
pleading for us there in Heaven.

Minister: *Who then can ever keep Christ's love from us?*
When we have trouble or calamity,
when we are hunted down or destroyed,
is it because He doesn't love us anymore?
And if we are hungry, or penniless, or in danger, or threatened with death,
has God deserted us?

People: No,
for the Scriptures tell us that for His sake
we must be ready to face death at every moment of the day—
we are like sheep awaiting slaughter;
but despite all this,
the overwhelming victory is ours through Christ who loved us enough to die for us.

All: For I am convinced that nothing can ever separate us from His love.
Death can't, and life can't.
The angels won't, and all the powers of hell itself cannot keep God's love away!
Our fears for today,
our worries about tomorrow,
or where we are—high above the sky, or in the deepest ocean—
nothing will ever be able to separate us from the love of God
demonstrated by our Lord Jesus Christ when He died for us.

—Romans 8:28-39 (LB)

COMFORT

I Heard the Voice of Jesus Say

51

*Come unto Me, all ye who labor and are heavy laden
and I will give you rest.* — Matthew 11:28

Horatius Bonar

VOX DILECTI
John B. Dykes

1. I heard the voice of Jesus say, "Come unto me and rest;
Lay down, thou weary one, lay down Thy head upon my breast."
I came to Jesus as I was, Weary, and worn, and sad;
I found in Him a resting place, And He has made me glad.

2. *I heard the voice of Jesus say, "Behold, I freely give
The living water—thirsty one, Stoop down, and drink, and live."
I came to Jesus, and I drank Of that life-giving stream;
My thirst was quenched, my soul revived, And now I live in Him.*

3. I heard the voice of Jesus say, "I am this dark world's light;
Look unto me—thy morn shall rise, And all thy day be bright."
I looked to Jesus, and I found In Him my star, my sun;
And in that light of life I'll walk, 'Til traveling days are done.

COMFORT

52 They that Wait upon the Lord

*They that wait upon the Lord . . .
shall mount up with wings as eagles . . . . — Isaiah 40:31*

Isaiah 40:31
Stuart Hamblen

TEACH ME LORD
Stuart Hamblen

They that wait up-on the Lord shall re-new their strength;

They shall mount up with wings like ea - gles;

They shall run, and not be wea - ry; They shall walk, and not faint.

Teach me, Lord, teach me, Lord, to wait.

© Copyright 1953 by Hamblen Music Co., Inc. All rights reserved. Used by permission.

COMFORT

Cast Thy Burden upon the Lord 53

Cast thy burden upon the Lord.... — Psalm 55:22

CAST THY BURDEN
From *Elijah*
Felix Mendelssohn

Based on Psalm 55:22

Cast thy bur-den up-on the Lord, and He shall sus-tain thee; He nev-er will suf-fer the right-eous to fall: He is at thy right hand. Thy mer-cy, Lord, is great and far a-bove the heav'ns: Let none be made a-sham-ed that wait up-on Thee. A-men.

COMFORT

54   There Has to Be a Song

There has to be a song —

    There are too many dark nights,
        too many troublesome days,
        too many wearisome miles,

There has to be a song—

    To make our burdens bearable,
    To make our hopes believable,
    To transform our successes into praise,
    To release the chains of past defeats,
  Somewhere—down deep in a forgotten corner of each man's heart—

There has to be a song —

    Like a cool, clear drink of water,
    Like the gentle warmth of sunshine,
    Like the tender love of a child,

          There has to be a song.

                        —Robert Benson

55   A Prayer for Strength

    O God, You have given us life through Your Son, Jesus Christ. You have given us the security of faith in a world that longs for something on which to rely. We thank You for Your gifts to us.

    Teach us to stand strong for Your Kingdom: to be free in this world in order to be Christ's men and women.

    Help us to know Your love and the love of each other. Set us free to become our true selves because we are loved, and to free others because we love.

Give us enough tests to make us strong;
    enough vision and endurance to follow Your way;
    enough patience to persist when the going is difficult;
    enough of reality to know our weaknesses;
    and enough humility to know these gifts come from You.

Go before us to prepare the way;
    walk behind us to be our protection;
    and walk beside us to be our companion,
          through Christ our Lord, Amen.

                        —Richard Langford

God Will Take Care of You

56

... I will never leave thee or forsake thee. — Hebrews 13:5

Civilla D. Martin, alt.

GOD CARES
W. Stillman Martin

1. Be not dis-mayed what-e'er be-tide, God will take care of you;
2. *Through days of toil when your heart doth fail, God will take care of you;*
3. All you may need He will pro-vide, God will take care of you;
4. *No mat-ter what may be the test, God will take care of you;*

1. Be-neath His wings of love a-bide, God will take care of you.
2. *When dan-gers fierce your path as-sail, God will take care of you.*
3. Noth-ing you ask will be de-nied, God will take care of you.
4. *Lean, wea-ry one, up-on His breast, God will take care of you.*

God will take care of you, Through ev-ery day, o'er all the way;
He will take care of you, God will take care of you.

COMFORT

57   John 14:1-12

"Do not let your hearts be troubled.
Trust in God still, and trust in Me.
There are many rooms in my Father's house;
if there were not, I should have told you.
I am going now to prepare a place for you,
and after I have gone and prepared you a place,
I shall return to take you with Me;
so that where I am
you may be too.
You know the way to the place where I am going."

Thomas said,
"Lord, we do not know where You are going,
so how can we know the way?"

Jesus said:
"I am the Way, the Truth and the Life.
No one can come to the Father except through Me.
If you know Me,
you know my Father too.
From this moment you know Him and have seen Him."

Philip said,
"Lord, let us see the Father
and then we shall be satisfied".
"Have I been with you all this time, Philip," said Jesus to him, "and you still do not know me?"
"To have seen me is to have seen the Father,
so how can you say, 'Let us see the Father'?
Do you not believe that I am in the Father and the Father is in Me?

The words I say to you I do not speak as from Myself:
it is the Father, living in Me, who is doing this work.
You must believe Me when I say that I am in the Father and the Father is in Me;
believe it on the evidence of this work, if for no other reason.

I tell you most solemnly,
whoever believes in Me will perform the same works as I do Myself,
he will perform even greater works."

—(JB)

58   Sitting at the Feet of Jesus

... Mary hath chosen the good part which shall not be taken away from her. — Luke 10:42

Author Unknown

COMFORT
Asa Hull

1. Sit-ting at the feet of Je-sus, Won-drous words I hear Him say!
2. Sit-ting at the feet of Je-sus, Is there an-y-where more blest?
3. Bless me, O my Fa-ther, bless me, All my in-ner life re-new;

Text revision © Copyright 1976 by Fred Bock Music Co. All rights reserved. Used by permission.

COMFORT

1. Hap-py place! so near, so pre-cious! May it find me there each day.
2. *There I lay my sins and sor-rows,* And when wea-ry, find His rest.
3. Now look down in love up-on me, Let me catch a glimpse of You.

1. Sit-ting at the feet of Je-sus, I re-flect up-on the past;
2. *Sit-ting at the feet of Je-sus,* There I wor-ship and I pray,
3. Give me, Lord, the mind of Je-sus, Make me ho-ly through His Word.

1. For His love has been so gra-cious, It has won my heart at last.
2. *While I from His full-ness gath-er* Grace and com-fort for to-day.
3. May I prove I've been with Je-sus, Been with Him, my ris-en Lord.

Plans While in Prison 59

"The most important part of our task will be to tell everyone who will listen that Jesus is the only answer to the problems that are disturbing the hearts of men and nations. We shall have the right to speak because we can tell from our experience that His light is more powerful than the deepest darkness... How wonderful that the reality of His presence is greater than the reality of the hell about us."

—Betsie ten Boom, to her sister, Corrie

COMFORT

60 Burdens Are Lifted at Calvary

For when we were yet without strength Christ died for the ungodly. — Romans 5:6

John M. Moore

BURDENS LIFTED
John M. Moore

Slowly

1. Days are filled with sor-row and care, Hearts are lone-ly and drear;
2. *Cast your care on Je-sus to-day, Leave your wor-ry and fear;*
3. Trou-bled soul, the Sav-ior can see Ev - ery heart-ache and tear;

1. Bur-dens are lift-ed at Cal - va-ry, Je-sus is ver - ry near.
2. *Bur-dens are lift-ed at Cal - va-ry, Je-sus is ver - ry near.*
3. Bur-dens are lift-ed at Cal - va-ry, Je-sus is ver - ry near.

Bur-dens are lift-ed at Cal - va-ry, Cal - va-ry, Cal - va-ry;

Bur-dens are lift-ed at Cal - va-ry, Je-sus is ver - y near.

© Copyright 1952 by Singspiration, Inc. All rights reserved. Used by permission.

COMFORT

Like a Lamb Who Needs the Shepherd   61

He shall feed His flock like a shepherd; He shall gather His lambs with His arms.
— Isaiah 40:11

Ralph Carmichael

LIKE A LAMB
Ralph Carmichael

1. Where He leads me I must fol-low, With-out Him I'd lose my way. I will see a bright to-mor-row If I fol-low Him to-day. Like a lamb who needs the Shep-herd, At His side I'll al-ways stay. Through the night His strength I'll bor-row, Then I'll see an-oth-er day.

2. *Life is like a wind-ing path-way, Who can tell what lies a-head? Will it lead to shad-y pas-tures, Or to wild-er-ness in-stead? Like a lamb who needs the Shep-herd, When in-to the night I go, Help me find the path that's nar-row, While I trav-el here be-low.*

3. Though you walk through dark-est val-leys And the sky is cold and gray, Though you climb the steep-est moun-tains He will nev-er let you stray. Like a lamb who needs the Shep-herd, By your side He'll al-ways stay. 'Til the end of life's long jour-ney He will lead you all the way.

© Copyright 1964, 1976 by Lexicon Music, Inc. All rights reserved. International copyright secured. Used by permission.

COMFORT

62   Sun of My Soul

The darkness and the light are the same to Thee. — Psalm 139:12

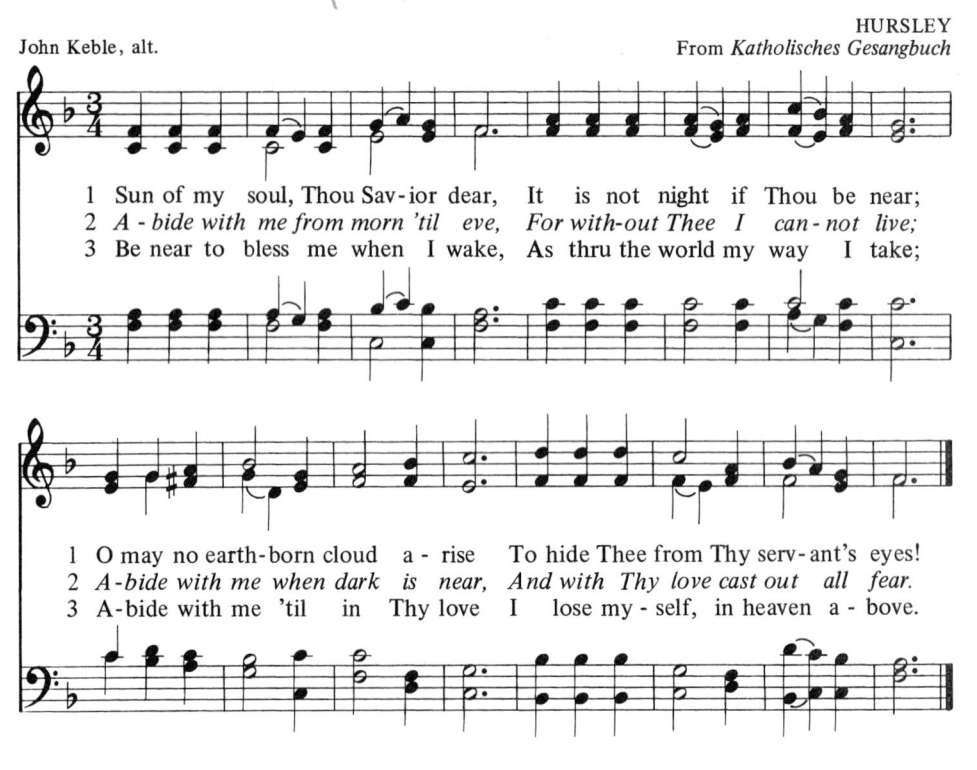

John Keble, alt.

HURSLEY
From *Katholisches Gesangbuch*

1. Sun of my soul, Thou Sav-ior dear, It is not night if Thou be near;
2. A-bide with me from morn 'til eve, For with-out Thee I can-not live;
3. Be near to bless me when I wake, As thru the world my way I take;

1. O may no earth-born cloud a-rise To hide Thee from Thy serv-ant's eyes!
2. A-bide with me when dark is near, And with Thy love cast out all fear.
3. A-bide with me 'til in Thy love I lose my-self, in heaven a-bove.

63   II Corinthians 4:6-12

For God who said, "Let light shine out of darkness," made His light shine in our hearts to give us the light of the knowledge of the glory of God in the face of Christ.

But we have this treasure in jars of clay to show that this all-surpassing power is from God and not from us. We are hard pressed on every side, but not crushed;

> perplexed, but not in despair;
>
> persecuted, but not abandoned;
>
> struck down, but not destroyed.

We always carry around in our body the death of Jesus, so that the life of Jesus may also be revealed in our body. For we who are alive are always being given over to death for Jesus' sake, so that His life may be revealed in our mortal body. So then, death is at work in us, but life is at work in you.

—(NIV)

COMFORT

Peace I Leave with You

Thou wilt keep him in perfect peace whose mind is stayed on Thee. — Isaiah 26:3

Richard Maxwell

PEACE I GIVE
William Wirges

64

1. Peace I leave with you; My peace I give unto you. Not as the world giveth, give I unto you; Not as the world giveth, give I unto you. Let not your heart be troubled; Neither let it be afraid. Peace I leave with you; My peace I give unto you.

2. *Peace I leave with you; My peace I give unto you. Keep my commandments if you love me; Keep my commandments, if you love Me. For I will not leave you comfortless; I will come unto you. Peace I leave with you; My peace I give unto you.* A-men.

© Copyright 1943, by Shawnee Press, Inc. U.S. copyright renewed 1971. International copyright secured. All rights reserved. Used by permission.

COMFORT

65 Moment by Moment

But the Lord is faithful, who shall stablish you and keep you....
— II Thessalonians 3:3

Daniel W. Whittle

WHITTLE
May W. Moody

1. Dy-ing with Je-sus, by death reck-oned mine, Liv-ing with Je-sus a new life di-vine, Look-ing to Je-sus 'til glo-ry doth shine,—Mo-ment by mo-ment, O Lord, I am Thine.
2. Nev-er a tri-al that He is not there, Nev-er a bur-den that He doth not bear, Nev-er a sor-row that He doth not share,—Mo-ment by mo-ment, I'm un-der His care.
3. Nev-er a heart-ache and nev-er a groan, Nev-er a tear-drop and nev-er a moan; Nev-er a dan-ger, but there on the throne, Mo-ment by mo-ment, He thinks of His own.
4. Nev-er a weak-ness that He doth not feel, Nev-er a sick-ness that He can-not heal; Mo-ment by mo-ment, in woe or in weal, Je-sus, my Sav-ior, a-bides with me still.

Mo-ment by mo-ment I'm kept in His love, Mo-ment by mo-ment I've life from a-bove; Look-ing to Je-sus 'til glo-ry doth shine, Mo-ment by mo-ment, O Lord, I am Thine.

ASSURANCE

My Shepherd Will Supply My Need

My beloved is mine and I am his; he feedeth among the lilies.
— Song of Solomon 2:16

Psalm 23, paraphrased
Isaac Watts

RESIGNATION
Traditional American Melody
Arranged by Fred Bock

1. My Shepherd will supply my need: Jehovah is His name; In pastures fresh He makes me feed, Beside the living stream. He brings my wandering spirit back When I forsake His ways, And leads me, for His mercy's sake, In paths of truth and grace.

2. When I walk through the shades of death His presence is my stay; One word of His supporting grace Drives all my fears away. His hand, in sight of all my foes, Doth still my table spread; My cup with blessings overflows, His oil anoints my head.

3. The sure provisions of my God Attend me all my days; O may Thy house be my abode, And all my work be praise. There would I find a settled rest, While others go and come; No more a stranger, nor a guest, But like a child at home. A-men.

© Copyright 1976 by Fred Bock Music Co. All rights reserved. Used by permission.

ASSURANCE

67 Blessed Assurance, Jesus Is Mine

.... Whereof He hath given assurance unto all men that He hath raised Him from the dead. — Acts 17:31

Fanny J. Crosby

ASSURANCE
Phoebe P. Knapp

1. Bless-ed as-sur-ance, Je-sus is mine! O what a fore-taste of glo-ry di-vine! Heir of sal-va-tion, pur-chase of God, Born of His Spir-it, washed in His blood.
2. *Per-fect sub-mis-sion, per-fect de-light, Vi-sions of rap-ture now burst on my sight; An-gels de-scend-ing bring from a-bove Ech-oes of mer-cy, whis-pers of love.*
3. Per-fect sub-mis-sion, all is at rest, I in my Sav-ior am hap-py and blest; Watch-ing and wait-ing, look-ing a-bove, Filled with His good-ness, lost in His love.

This is my sto-ry, this is my song, Prais-ing my Sav-ior all the day long; This is my sto-ry, this is my song, Prais-ing my Sav-ior all the day long.

ASSURANCE

Alternate Last Chorus Harmonization — Arranged by Ovid Young

This is my story, this is my song, Praising my Savior all the day long; This is my story, this is my song, Praising my Savior, all the day long.

© Copyright 1976 by Paragon Associates, Inc. All rights reserved.

II Corinthians 12:1-10 — 68

It is not expedient for me doubtless to glory. I will come to visions and revelations of the Lord. I knew a man in Christ above fourteen years ago, (whether in the body, I cannot tell; or whether out of the body, I cannot tell: God knoweth;) such a one caught up to the third heaven. And I knew such a man, (whether in the body, or out of the body, I cannot tell: God knoweth;) How that he was caught up into paradise, and heard unspeakable words which it is not lawful for a man to utter. Of such a one will I glory; yet of myself I will not glory, but in mine infirmities. For though I would desire to glory, I shall not be a fool; for I will say the truth: but *now* I forbear, lest any man should think of me above that which he seeth me *to be,* or *that* he heareth of me. And lest I should be exalted above measure through the abundance of the revelations, there was given to me a thorn in the flesh, the messenger of Satan to buffet me, lest I should be exalted above measure. For this thing I besought the Lord thrice, that it might depart from me. And He said unto me, My grace is sufficient for thee: for My strength is made perfect in weakness. Most gladly therefore will I rather glory in my infirmities, that the power of Christ may rest upon me. Therefore I take pleasure in infirmities, in reproaches, in necessities, in persecutions, in distresses for Christ's sake: for when I am weak, then am I strong.

—(KJV)

ASSURANCE

69 Standing on the Promises

For all the promises of God are "yes," and in him "Amen".... — II Corinthians 1:20

R. Kelso Carter

TURLOCK
Norman E. Johnson

Unison

1. Stand-ing on the prom-is-es of Christ my King,
2. Stand-ing on the prom-is-es that can-not fail,
3. Stand-ing on the prom-is-es of Christ the Lord,
4. Stand-ing on the prom-is-es I can-not fall,

1. Through e-ter-nal a-ges let His prais-es ring! Glo-ry in the
2. When the howl-ing storms of doubt and fear as-sail; By the liv-ing
3. Bound to Him e-ter-nal-ly by love's strong cord, O-ver-com-ing
4. Lis-tening ev-ery mo-ment to the Spir-it's call, Rest-ing in my

1. high-est I will shout and sing— Stand-ing on the prom-is-es of
2. word of God I shall pre-vail— Stand-ing on the prom-is-es of
3. dai-ly with the Spir-it's sword— Stand-ing on the prom-is-es of
4. Sav-ior as my all in all— Stand-ing on the prom-is-es of

1. God, Stand-ing on the prom-is-es of God!
2. God, Stand-ing on the prom-is-es of God!
3. God, Stand-ing on the prom-is-es of God!
4. God, Stand-ing on the prom-is-es of God!

© Copyright 1973 by Covenant Press. All rights reserved. Used by permission.
ASSURANCE

Hiding in Thee

70

For Thou has been a shelter for me, and a strong tower from the enemy.
— Psalm 61:3

William O. Cushing

HIDING IN THEE
Ira D. Sankey

1. O safe to the Rock that is high-er than I, My
2. *In the calm of the noon-tide, in sor-row's lone hour, In*
3. How oft-en in con-flict, when pressed by the foe, I have

1. soul in its con-flicts and sor-rows would fly; So sin-ful, so
2. *times when temp-ta-tion casts o'er me its power, In the tem-pests of*
3. fled to my Ref-uge and breathed out my woe; How oft-en, when

1. wea-ry—Thine, Thine would I be: Thou blest "Rock of A-ges," I'm
2. *life, on its wide, heav-ing sea, Thou blest "Rock of A-ges," I'm*
3. tri-als like sea-bil-lows roll, Have I hid-den in Thee, O Thou

1. hid-ing in Thee.
2. *hid-ing in Thee.* Hid-ing in Thee, Hid-ing in
3. Rock of my soul.

Thee, Thou blest "Rock of A-ges," I'm hid-ing in Thee.

ASSURANCE

71 Faith Is the Victory

. . . . for this is the victory that overcometh the world, even our faith. — I John 5:4

John H. Yates

FAITH IS THE VICTORY
Ira D. Sankey

1. En-camped a-long the hills of light, Ye Chris-tian sol-diers, rise, And press the bat-tle ere the night Shall veil the glow-ing skies. A-gainst the foe in vales be-low Let all our strength be hurled; Faith is the vic-to-ry, we know, That o-ver-comes the world.

2. *His ban-ner o-ver us is love, Our sword the Word of God; We tread the road the saints a-bove With shouts of tri-umph trod. By faith they like a whirlwind's breath, Swept on o'er ev-ery field; The faith by which they conquer'd death Is still our shin-ing shield.*

3. On ev-ery hand the foe we find Drawn up in dread ar-ray; Let tents of ease be left be-hind, And on-ward to the fray. Sal-va-tion's hel-met on each head, With truth all girt a-bout, The earth shall trem-ble 'neath our tread, And ech-o with our shout.

4. To him that o-ver-comes the foe, White rai-ment shall be-given; Be-fore the an-gels he shall know His name con-fessed in heaven. Then onward from the hills of light, Our hearts with love a-flame; We'll van-quish all the hosts of night, In Je-sus' con-qu'ring name.

Faith is the vic-to-ry! Faith is the

ASSURANCE

vic-to-ry! O glo-ri-ous vic-to-ry, That o-ver-comes the world.

He the Pearly Gates Will Open 72

They that do His commandments . . . may enter through the gates into the city. — Revelation 22:14

Fred Blom
Tr. by Nathaniel Carlson

PEARLY GATES
Elsie Ahlwen

1. Love di-vine, so great and won-drous, Deep and might-y, pure, sub-lime,
2. Like a dove when hunt-ed, frightened, As a wound-ed fawn was I;
3. Love di-vine, so great and won-drous! All my sins He then for-gave.
4. In life's e-ven-tide, at twi-light, At His door I'll knock and wait;

1. Com-ing from the heart of Je-sus, Just the same through tests of time!
2. Bro-ken-heart-ed, yet He healed me. He will heed the sin-ner's cry.
3. I will sing His praise for-ev-er, For His blood, His power to save.
4. By the pre-cious love of Je-sus, I shall en-ter heav-en's gate.

He the pear-ly gates will o-pen, So that I may en-ter in;

For He pur-chased my re-demp-tion, And for-gave me all my sin.

ASSURANCE

73 I Am Trusting Thee, Lord Jesus

Trust in the Lord and do good, so shall thou dwell in the land . . . . and be fed. — Psalm 37:3

Frances Ridley Havergal

BULLINGER
Ethelbert W. Bullinger

1. I am trust-ing Thee, Lord Je-sus— Trust-ing on-ly Thee;
2. I am trust-ing Thee to guide me— Thou a-lone shalt lead,
3. I am trust-ing Thee for pow-er— Thine can nev-er fail;
4. I am trust-ing Thee, Lord Je-sus— Nev-er let me fall;

1. Trust-ing Thee for full sal-va-tion, Great and free.
2. Ev-ery day and hour sup-ply-ing All my need.
3. Words which Thou Thy-self shalt give me Must pre-vail.
4. I am trust-ing Thee for-ev-er, And for all. A-men.

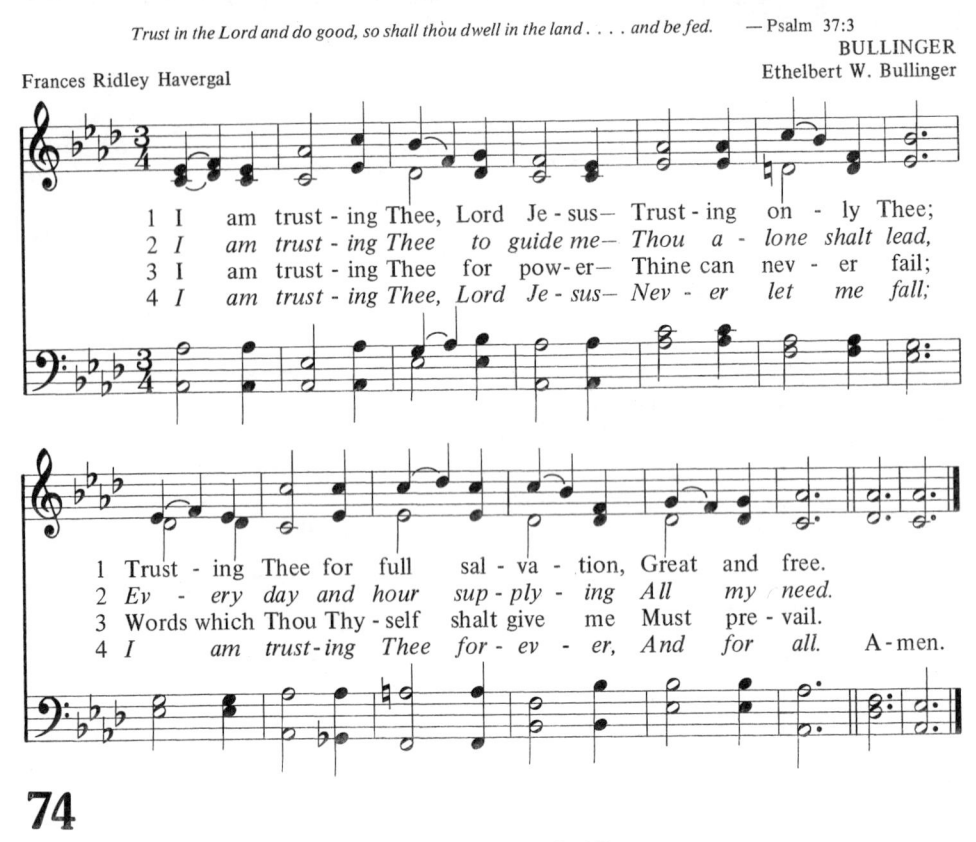

74 A Pledge of Trust

Father, during this coming week there may be times when I shall not be able to sense Your presence or to be aware of Your nearness.

When I am lonely and by myself
I TRUST YOU TO BE MY COMPANION.

When I am tempted to sin
I TRUST YOU TO KEEP ME FROM IT.

When I am depressed and anxious
I TRUST YOU TO LIFT MY SPIRITS.

When I am crushed by responsibility and overwhelmed by the demands of people on my time,
I TRUST YOU TO GIVE ME POISE AND A SENSE OF PURPOSE.

When I am rushed and running
I TRUST YOU TO MAKE ME STILL INSIDE.

When I forget You
I TRUST THAT YOU WILL NEVER FORGET ME.

When I forget others
I TRUST YOU TO PROMPT ME TO THINK OF THEM.

When You take something or someone from me that I want to keep; when You remove the props I lean on for comfort in place of You; when You refuse to respond to my questions and to answer my too-selfish prayers, I will trust You even then. Amen.

—Bryan Jeffery Leech

ASSURANCE

My Faith Has Found a Resting Place 75

Let us labor, therefore, to enter into that rest. — Hebrews 4:11

Lidie H. Edmunds

NO OTHER PLEA
Norwegian Melody

1 My faith has found a rest-ing place, Not in a man-made creed;
2 E-nough for me that Je-sus saves, This ends my fear and doubt;
3 My soul is rest-ing on the Word, The liv-ing Word of God:
4 The great Phy-si-cian heals the sick, The lost He came to save;

1 I trust the ev-er liv-ing One, That He for me will plead.
2 A sin-ful soul I come to Him, He will not cast me out.
3 Sal-va-tion in my Sav-ior's name, Sal-va-tion through His blood.
4 For me His pre-cious blood He shed, For me His life He gave.

I need no oth-er ev-i-dence, I need no oth-er plea;

It is e-nough that Je-sus died And rose a-gain for me.

ASSURANCE

76 Yesterday, Today, and Tomorrow

Jack Wyrtzen

Jesus Christ, the same yesterday, today, and forever.
- Hebrews 13:8

YESTERDAY-TODAY-TOMORROW
Don Wyrtzen

Yesterday He died for me, yesterday, yesterday,
Yesterday He died for me, yesterday, Yesterday He died for me, died for me— This is his-to-ry.

Today He lives for me, today, today, Today He lives for me, today, Today He lives for me, lives for me— This is vic-to-ry.

Tomorrow He comes for me,

ASSURANCE © Copyright 1966 by Singspiration, Inc. Arr. © 1970 by Singspiration, Inc. All rights reserved.

He comes, He comes, To-mor-row He comes for me, He comes, To-mor-row He comes for me, comes for me— This is mys-ter-y. O friend, do you know Him? know Him? know Him? O friend, do you know Him? know Him? O friend, do you know Him? do you know Him? Je-sus Christ the Lord, Je-sus Christ the Lord, Je-sus Christ the Lord.

ASSURANCE

77 Be Still My Soul

Be still and know that I am God. — Psalm 46:10

Katharina von Schlegel
Tr. by Jane L. Borthwick

FINLANDIA
Jean Sibelius

1. Be still, my soul! the Lord is on thy side; Bear patiently the cross of grief or pain; Leave to thy God to order and provide; In every change He faithful will remain. Be still, my soul! thy best, thy heavenly Friend Through thorny ways leads to a joyful end.

2. *Be still, my soul! thy God doth undertake To guide the future as He has the past. Thy hope, thy confidence let nothing shake; All now mysterious shall be bright at last. Be still, my soul! the waves and winds still know His voice who ruled them while He dwelt below.*

3. Be still, my soul! the hour is hastening on When we shall be forever with the Lord, When disappointment, grief, and fear are gone, Sorrow forgot, love's purest joys restored. Be still, my soul! when change and tears are past, All safe and blessed we shall meet at last.

Melody used by permission of Breitkoph & Härtel, Wiesbaden. Arrangement © Copyright 1933 by Presbyterian Board of Christian Education, renewed 1961; from "The Hymnbook": used by permission of The Westminster Press.

ASSURANCE

My Hope Is in the Lord

Christ, in you the hope of Glory. — Colossians 1:27

Norman J. Clayton

WAKEFIELD
Norman J. Clayton

1. My hope is in the Lord Who gave Himself for me,
2. *No merit of my own His anger to suppress,*
3. And now for me He stands Before the Father's throne,
4. *His grace has planned it all, 'Tis mine but to believe,*

1. And paid the price of all my sin at Calvary.
2. *My only hope is found in Jesus' righteousness.*
3. And shows His wounded hands, and names me as His own.
4. *And recognize His work of love and Christ receive.*

For me He died, For me He lives,
And everlasting life and light He freely gives.

Copyright 1945 by Norman J. Clayton in "Word of Life Melodies No. 2." Assigned to Norman Clayton Publishing Co. © Renewal 1973 by Norman Clayton Publishing Co. Used by permission.

ASSURANCE

79 Trusting Jesus

Commit thy way into the Lord; trust also in Him . . . . — Psalm 37:5

Edgar P. Stites

TRUSTING JESUS
Ira D. Sankey

1. Sim-ply trust-ing ev-ery day, Trust-ing through a storm-y way;
2. Bright-ly doth His Spir-it shine In-to this poor heart of mine;
3. Sing-ing if my way is clear, Pray-ing if the path be drear;
4. Trust-ing Him while life shall last, Trust-ing Him 'til earth be past;

1. E-ven when my faith is small, Trust-ing Je-sus— that is all.
2. While He leads I can-not fall, Trust-ing Je-sus— that is all.
3. If in dan-ger, for Him call, Trust-ing Je-sus— that is all.
4. 'Til I hear His fi-nal call, Trust-ing Je-sus— that is all.

Trust-ing as the mo-ments fly, Trust-ing as the days go by;

Trust-ing Him what-e'er be-fall, Trust-ing Je-sus— that is all.

ASSURANCE

Problems 80

So be glad—yes, actually *be glad* that you have problems. Be grateful for them as implying that God has confidence in your ability to handle these problems with which He has entrusted you. Adopt this attitude toward problems and it will tend to syphon off the depression you may have developed from a negative reaction to them. And as you develop the habit of thinking in hopeful terms about your problems, you will find yourself doing much better with them.

This will add to your enjoyment of life too, for one of the few greatest satisfactions of this life is to handle problems efficiently and well. Morover, this successful handling tends to build up your faith that, through God's help and guidance, you have what it takes to deal with anything that may ever face you.

—Norman Vincent Peale

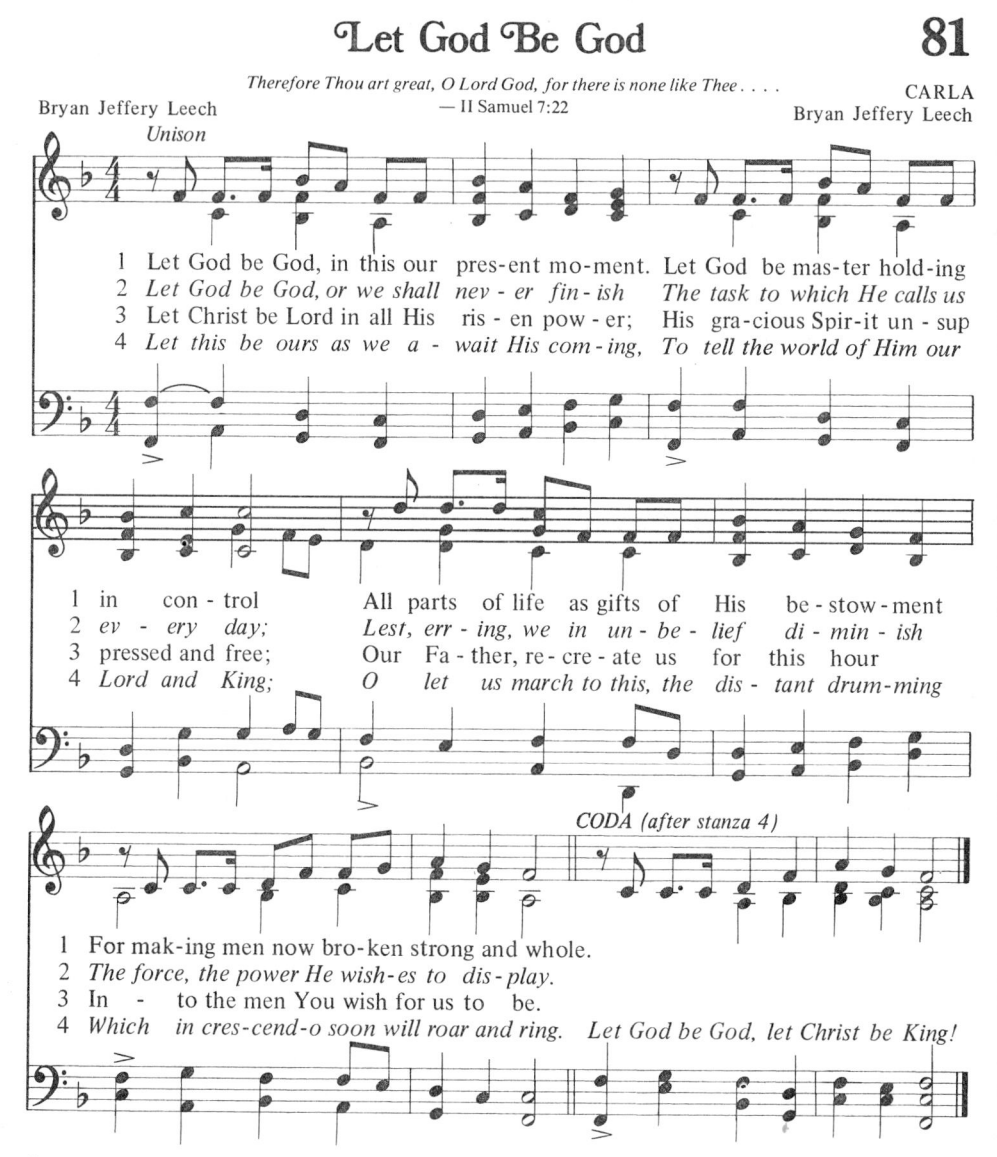

Let God Be God 81

Therefore Thou art great, O Lord God, for there is none like Thee....
— II Samuel 7:22

Bryan Jeffery Leech

CARLA
Bryan Jeffery Leech

Unison

1. Let God be God, in this our pres-ent mo-ment. Let God be mas-ter hold-ing in con-trol. All parts of life as gifts of His be-stow-ment For mak-ing men now bro-ken strong and whole.
2. *Let God be God, or we shall nev-er fin-ish The task to which He calls us ev-ery day; Lest, err-ing, we in un-be-lief di-min-ish The force, the power He wish-es to dis-play.*
3. Let Christ be Lord in all His ris-en pow-er; His gra-cious Spir-it un-sup-pressed and free; Our Fa-ther, re-cre-ate us for this hour In-to the men You wish for us to be.
4. *Let this be ours as we a-wait His com-ing, To tell the world of Him our Lord and King; O let us march to this, the dis-tant drum-ming Which in cres-cend-o soon will roar and ring.* Let God be God, let Christ be King!

CODA (after stanza 4)

© Copyright 1972 by Fred Bock Music Co. All rights reserved. Used by permission.

ASSURANCE

82. Victory in Jesus

And this is the victory that overcometh the world, even our faith. — I John 5:4

Eugene M. Bartlett

HARTFORD
Eugene M. Bartlett

1. I heard an old, old story, how a Savior came from glory,
2. *I heard about His healing, of His cleansing power revealing,*
3. I heard about a mansion He has built for me in glory,

1. How He gave His life on Calvary to save a wretch like me;
2. *How He made the lame to walk again and caused the blind to see;*
3. And I heard about the streets of gold beyond the crystal sea;

1. I heard about His groaning, of His precious blood's atoning,
2. *And then I cried, "Dear Jesus, come and heal my broken spirit,"*
3. About the angels singing and the old redemption story,

1. Then I repented of my sins and won the victory.
2. *And somehow Jesus came and brought to me the victory.*
3. And some sweet day I'll sing up there the song of victory.

O victory in Jesus, my Savior, forever! He sought me and

Copyright 1939 by E. M. Bartlett. © 1967 by Mrs. E. M. Bartlett, renewal. Assigned to Albert E. Brumley and Sons. All rights reserved. Used by permission.

ASSURANCE

bought me with His re-deem-ing blood; He loved me ere I knew Him, and all my love is due Him—He plunged me to vic-to-ry be-neath the cleans-ing flood.

Yesterday, Today, Forever 83

... A chief cornerstone, elect, precious; and he that believeth on Him shall not be confounded. — I Peter 2:6

Albert B. Simpson

NYACK
J. H. Burke

Yes-ter-day, to-day, for-ev-er, Je-sus is the same; All may change, but Je-sus nev-er! Glo-ry to His name! Glo-ry to His name! Glo-ry to His name! All may change, but Je-sus nev-er! Glo-ry to His name!

ASSURANCE

84. My Faith Looks Up to Thee

Then Peter said unto him, Lord .... Thou hast the words of eternal life. — John 6:68

Ray Palmer

OLIVET
Lowell Mason

1. My faith looks up to Thee, Thou Lamb of Cal-va-ry, Sav-ior di-vine! Now hear me while I pray, Take all my guilt a-way, O let me from this day Be whol-ly Thine!

2. May Thy rich grace im-part Strength to my faint-ing heart, My zeal in-spire; As Thou has died for me, O may my love to Thee Pure, warm, and change-less be, A liv-ing fire!

3. While life's dark maze I tread And griefs a-round me spread, Be Thou my guide; Bid dark-ness turn to day, Wipe sor-row's tears a-way, Nor let me ev-er stray From Thee a-side.

4. When ends life's pass-ing dream, When death's cold, threat-ening stream Shall o'er me roll, Blest Sav-ior, then, in love, Fear and dis-trust re-move; O lift me safe a-bove, A ran-somed soul! A-men.

85. Song of Ascent

I lift my eyes to the mountains:
    where is help to come from?
Help comes to me from Jehovah,
    who made heaven and earth.

No letting our footsteps slip!
    This guard of yours, He does not doze!
The guardian of Israel
    does not doze or sleep.

Jehovah guards you, shades you.
    With Jehovah at your right hand
sun cannot strike you down by day,
    nor moon at night.

Jehovah guards you from harm,
    He guards your lives,
He guards you leaving, coming back,
    now and for always.

—Psalm 121 (JB)

ASSURANCE

Jesus, I Am Resting, Resting

86

There remaineth . . . . a rest for the people of God. — Hebrews 4:9

Jean Sophia Pigott

TRANQUILITY
James Mountain

1. Je - sus, I am rest - ing, rest - ing In the joy of what Thou art;
2. *Sim - ply trust - ing Thee, Lord Je - sus, I be - hold Thee as Thou art,*
3. Ev - er lift Thy face up - on me As I work and wait for Thee;

1. I am find - ing out the great - ness Of Thy lov - ing heart.
2. *And Thy love, so pure, so change - less, Sat - is - fies my heart—*
3. Rest - ing 'neath Thy smile, Lord Je - sus, Earth's dark shad - ows flee.

1. Thou hast bid me gaze up - on Thee, And Thy beau - ty fills my soul,
2. *Sat - is - fies its deep - est long - ings, Meets, sup - plies its ev - ery need,*
3. Bright - ness of my Fa - ther's glo - ry, Sun - shine of my Fa - ther's face,

1. For by Thy trans - form - ing pow - er Thou hast made me whole.
2. *And sur - rounds me with its bless - ings: Thine is love in - deed!*
3. Keep me ev - er trust - ing, rest - ing, Fill me with Thy grace. A - men.

ASSURANCE

87 Leaning on the Everlasting Arms

The eternal God is our refuge and underneath are the everlasting arms. — Deuteronomy 33:27

Elisha A. Hoffman
SHOWALTER
Anthony J. Showalter

1. What a fel-low-ship, what a joy di-vine, Lean-ing on the ev-er-last-ing arms; What a bless-ed-ness, what a peace is mine, Lean-ing on the ev-er-last-ing arms.
2. *O how sweet to walk in this pil-grim way, Lean-ing on the ev-er-last-ing arms; O how bright the path grows from day to day, Lean-ing on the ev-er-last-ing arms.*
3. What have I to dread, what have I to fear, Lean-ing on the ev-er-last-ing arms? I have bless-ed peace with my Lord so near, Lean-ing on the ev-er-last-ing arms.

Lean-ing, lean-ing, Safe and se-cure from all a-larms; Lean-ing, lean-ing, Lean-ing on the ev-er-last-ing arms.

Lean-ing on Je-sus, lean-ing on Je-sus, Lean-ing on Je-sus, lean-ing on Je-sus,

ASSURANCE

When We Feel Forsaken — 88

Our Father, sometimes Thou dost seem so far away, as if Thou art a God in hiding, as if Thou art determined to elude all who seek Thee.

Yet we know that Thou art far more willing to be found than we are to seek. Thou hast promised "If with all your heart ye truly seek me, ye shall ever surely find me." And hast Thou not assured us that Thou art with us always?

Help us now to be as aware of Thy nearness as we are of the material things of every day. Help us to recognize Thy voice with as much assurance as we recognize the sounds of the world around us.

We would find Thee now in the privacy of our hearts, in the quiet of this moment. We would know, our Father, that Thou art near us and beside us; that Thou dost love us and art interested in all that we do, art concerned about all our affairs.

May we become aware of Thy companionship, of Him who walks beside us.

At times when we feel forsaken, may we know the presence of the Holy Spirit who brings comfort to all human hearts when we are willing to surrender ourselves.

May we be convinced that even before we reach up to Thee, Thou art reaching down to us. These blessings, together with the unexpressed longing in our hearts, we ask in the strong name of Jesus Christ, Our Lord. Amen.

—Peter Marshall

Children of the Heavenly Father — 89

As a father pitieth his children, so the Lord pitieth.... — Psalm 103:13

Lina Sandell
Tr. by Ernst W. Olson

TRYGGARE KAN INGEN VARA
Swedish Folk Melody

1. Children of the heavenly Father Safely in His bosom gather;
   Nestling bird nor star in heaven Such a refuge e'er was given.

2. *God His own doth tend and nourish, In His holy courts they flourish;*
   From all evil things He spares them, In His mighty arms He bears them.

3. Neither life nor death shall ever From the Lord His children sever;
   Unto them His grace He showeth, And their sorrows all He knoweth.

4. *Praise the Lord in joyful numbers, Your Protector never slumbers;*
   At the will of your Defender Ev'ry foeman must surrender.

5. Though He giveth or He taketh, God His children ne'er forsaketh;
   His the loving purpose solely To preserve them pure and holy.

ASSURANCE

Hope

Worship Leader: *Praise be to the God and Father of our Lord Jesus Christ, who in His great mercy gave us new birth into a living hope by the resurrection of Jesus Christ from the dead![1]*

People: Death be not proud, though some have called thee
Mighty and dreadful, for thou art not so:
For those whom thou thinkest thou dost overthrow
Die not, poor death; nor yet canst thou kill me.[2]

Worship Leader: *So be truly glad! There is wonderful joy ahead, even though the going is rough for a while down here. These trials are only to test your faith, to see whether or not it is strong and pure. It is being tested as fire tests gold and purifies it— and your faith is far more precious to God than mere gold.[3]*

People: Yet, in the maddening maze of things,
And tossed by storm and flood,
To one fixed trust my spirit clings;
I know that God is good![4]
And we know that all things work together for good to them that love God . . . [5]

Worship Leader: *You must therefore be mentally stripped for action, perfectly self-controlled. Fix your hopes on the gift of grace which is to be yours when Jesus Christ is revealed. The One who called you is holy; like Him, be holy in all your behavior, because Scripture says, "You shall be holy, for I am holy."[6]*

People: There are men who can't be bought.
There are women beyond purchase.
The fireborn are at home in fire.
The stars make no noise.
You can't hinder the wind from blowing.
Time is a great teacher.
Who can live without hope?[7]

Worship Leader: *We rejoice, then, in the hope we have of sharing God's glory! And we also rejoice in our troubles, because we know that troubles produce endurance, endurance brings God's approval, and His approval creates hope.[8]*

People: This hope does not disappoint us, because God has poured out His love into our hearts by means of His Holy Spirit, who is God's gift to us.

— Gloria Gaither

1. I Peter 1:30 (NEB)
2. John Donne from "Death Be Not Proud"
3. I Peter 1:6-7 (LB)
4. John Greenleaf Whittier from "The Eternal Goodness"
5. Romans 8:28a
6. I Peter 1:13, 15, 16 (NEB)
7. Carl Sandburg from "The People Speak"
8. Romans 5:2b-5 (TEV)

'Tis So Sweet to Trust in Jesus   91

... because we trust in the living God, who is the Savior of all men. — I Timothy 4:10

Louisa M. R. Stead

TRUST IN JESUS
William J. Kirkpatrick

1. 'Tis so sweet to trust in Je - sus, Just to take Him at His word,
2. *How I love to trust in Je - sus, Just to trust His cleans-ing blood,*
3. Yes, I've learned to trust in Je - sus, And from sin and self to cease,
4. *I'm so glad I learned to trust Him, Pre - cious Je - sus, Sav - ior, Friend;*

1. Just to rest up - on His prom - ise, Just to know, "Thus saith the Lord."
2. *Just in sim - ple faith to plunge me 'Neath the heal - ing, cleans - ing flood!*
3. Now from Je - sus sim - ply tak - ing Life and rest and joy and peace.
4. *And I know that He is with me, He'll be with me to the end.*

Je - sus, Je - sus, how I trust Him! How I've proved Him o'er and o'er!

Je - sus, Je - sus, pre - cious Je - sus! O for grace to trust Him more!

ASSURANCE

92 The Solid Rock

*They who trust in the Lord shall be as Mount Zion,
which cannot be moved...* —Psalm 125:1

Edward Mote

SOLID ROCK
William B. Bradbury

1. My hope is built on nothing less Than Jesus' blood and righteousness; I dare not trust the sweetest frame, But wholly lean on Jesus' name.
2. *When darkness veils His lovely face, I rest on His unchanging grace; In every high and stormy gale, My anchor holds within the veil.*
3. His oath, His covenant, His blood, Support me in the whelming flood; When all around my soul gives way, He then is all my hope and stay.
4. *When He shall come with trumpet sound, O may I then in Him be found; Dressed in His righteousness alone, Faultless to stand before the throne.*

On Christ, the solid Rock, I stand; All other ground is sinking sand, All other ground is sinking sand.

ASSURANCE

Alternate Last Verse Harmonization Arranged by Ronn Huff

4 When He shall come with trum-pet sound, O may I then in Him be found; Dressed in His right-eous-ness a-lone, Fault-less to stand be-fore the throne. On Christ the sol-id Rock I stand; All oth-er ground is sink-ing sand, All oth-er ground is sink-ing sand.

© Copyright 1976 by Paragon Associates, Inc. All rights reserved.

93 My God Is There Controlling

The fool hath said in his heart, there is no God. — Psalm 14:1

We search the starlit Milky Way,
A million worlds in rhythmic sway,
Yet in our blindness some will say,
"There is no God controlling!"

But as I grope from sphere to sphere,
New wonders crowd the eye, the ear,
And faith grows firmer every year:
"My God is there, controlling!"

We probe the atoms for their cause,
Explore the earth for nature's laws,
Yet seldom in our searching pause
To think of God controlling.

Each flash of fact from out the night,
Each burst of truth upon my sight
That quickens awe or adds delight,
Reveals my God controlling.

© Copyright 1963 by the Hymn Society of America. Used by permission.

William H. Reid

94 I Am Not Skilled to Understand

But where shall wisdom be found? — Job 28:12

Dora Greenwell

EWHURST
Cecil J. Allen

1. I am not skilled to understand
What God hath willed, what God hath planned;
I only know at His right hand
Stands One who is my Savior.

2. I take Him at His word and deed:
"Christ died to save me," this I read;
And in my heart I find a need
Of Him to be my Savior.

3. That He should leave His place on high
And come for sinful man to die,
You count it strange? so once did I
Before I knew my Savior.

4. And O that He fulfilled may see
The travail of His soul in me,
And with His work contented be,
As I with my dear Savior!

5. Yes, living, dying, let me bring
My strength, my solace, from this spring,
That He who lives to be my King
Once died to be my Savior!

Music used by permission of Cecil J. Allen.
ASSURANCE

At the Cross

95

*For the preaching of the cross is . . . . unto us who are saved
the power of God.* — 1 Corinthians 1:18

Isaac Watts
Refrain added by Ralph E. Hudson

HUDSON
Ralph E. Hudson

1. A - las, and did my Sav - ior bleed? And did my Sov-ereign die?
2. *Was it for crimes that I have done, He suf-fered on the tree?*
3. Well might the sun in dark - ness hide And shut his glo - ries in,
4. *But drops of grief can ne'er re - pay The debt of love I owe:*

1. Would He de - vote that sa - cred head For some - one such as I?
2. *A - maz - ing pit - y! grace un-known! And love be - yond de - gree!*
3. When Christ, the might - y Mak - er, died For man the crea - ture's sin.
4. *Here, Lord, I give my - self a - way, 'Tis all that I can do!*

At the cross, at the cross where I first saw the light, And the bur - den of my heart rolled a - way, It was there by faith I re - ceived my sight, And now I am hap - py all the day!

ASSURANCE

96. I Know Who Holds Tomorrow

Fear ye not . . ye are of more value than many sparrows . . . . — Matthew 10:31

Ira F. Stanphill

I KNOW
Ira F. Stanphill

1. I don't know a-bout to-mor-row, I just live from day to day; I don't bor-row from its sun-shine, For its skies may turn to gray. I don't wor-ry o'er the fu-ture, For I know what Je-sus said; And to-day I'll walk be-side Him, For He knows what is a-head.

2. *Ev-ery step is get-ting bright-er, As the gold-en stairs I climb; Ev-ery bur-den's get-ting light-er, Ev-ery cloud is sil-ver-lined. There the sun is al-ways shin-ing, There no tear will dim the eye; At the end-ing of the rain-bow, Where the moun-tains touch the sky.*

3. I don't know a-bout to-mor-row, It may bring me pov-er-ty; But the one who feeds the spar-row, Is the one who stands by me. And the path that is my por-tion, May be through the flame or flood; But His pres-ence goes be-fore me, And I'm cov-ered with His blood.

© Copyright 1950 by Singspiration, Inc. All rights reserved. Used by permission.
ASSURANCE

Many things about tomorrow I don't seem to understand; But I know who holds tomorrow, And I know who holds my hand.

Assurance

How easy for me to live with You, O Lord!
How easy for me to believe in You!
When my mind parts in bewilderment or falters,
then the most intelligent people see no further
than this day's end
and do not know what must be done tomorrow,
You grant me the serene certitude
that You exist and that You will take care
that not all the paths of good be closed.
Atop the ridge of earthly fame,
I look back in wonder at the path
which I alone could never have found,
a wondrous path through despair to this point
from which I, too, could transmit to mankind
a reflection of Your rays.
And as much as I must still reflect
You will give me.
But as much as I cannot take up
You will have already assigned to others.

—Aleksandr Solzhenitsyn

98 Great Is Thy Faithfulness

... For He is faithful that promised. — Hebrews 10:23

Based on Lamentations 3:22, 23
Thomas O. Chisholm

FAITHFULNESS
William M. Runyan

1. Great is Thy faith-ful-ness, O God my Fa-ther! There is no shad-ow of turn-ing with Thee; Thou chang-est not, Thy com-pas-sions, they fail not: As Thou hast been Thou for-ev-er wilt be.
2. Sum-mer and win-ter, and spring-time and har-vest, Sun, moon, and stars in their cours-es a-bove, Join with all na-ture in man-i-fold wit-ness To Thy great faith-ful-ness, mer-cy, and love.
3. Par-don for sin and a peace that en-dur-eth, Thine own dear pres-ence to cheer and to guide, Strength for to-day and bright hope for to-mor-row— Bless-ings all mine, with ten thou-sand be-side!

Great is Thy faith-ful-ness, Great is Thy faith-ful-ness, Morn-ing by

© Copyright 1923. Renewal 1951. Hope Publishing Company. All rights reserved. Used by permission.

morn - ing new mer - cies I see; All I have need - ed Thy hand hath pro - vid - ed—Great is Thy faith - ful - ness, Lord, un - to me! A - men.

Lamentations 3 : 22-33　　　　　　99

The steadfast love of the Lord never ceases, His mercies never come to an end; they are new every morning; great is Thy faithfulness.

"The Lord is my portion," says my soul, "therefore I will hope in Him."

The Lord is good to those who wait for Him, to the soul that seeks Him. It is good that one should wait quietly for the salvation of the Lord. It is good for a man that he bear the yoke in his youth.

Let him sit alone in silence when He has laid it on him; let him put his mouth in the dust—there may yet be hope; let him give his cheek to the smiter, and be filled with insults.

For the Lord will not cast off forever, but, though He cause grief, He will have compassion according to the abundance of His steadfast love; for He does not willingly afflict or grieve the sons of men.

—(RSV)

FAITHFULNESS

100 Satisfied

As the heart panteth after the waterbrook so panteth my soul after Thee, O God.
— Psalm 42:1

Clara T. Williams

SATISFIED
Ralph E. Hudson

1. All my life long I had pant-ed For a drink from some cool spring
2. *Feed-ing on the food a-round me 'Til my strength was al-most gone,*
3. Well of wa-ter, ev-er spring-ing, Bread of life, so rich and free,

1. That I hoped would quench the burn-ing Of the thirst I felt with-in.
2. *Longed my soul for some-thing bet-ter, On-ly still to hun-ger on.*
3. Un-told wealth that nev-er fail-eth, My Re-deem-er is to me.

Hal-le-lu-jah! I have found Him—Whom my soul so long has craved!
Je-sus sat-is-fies my long-ings; Through His blood I now am saved.

ASSURANCE

The Haven of Rest   101

I will put thee in a cleft of the rock, and I will cover thee with my hand. — Exodus 33:22

H. L. Gilmour

GOOD SHIP
George D. Moore

1. My soul, in sad ex-ile, was out on life's sea. So bur-dened with sin and dis-tressed, 'Til I heard a sweet voice saying, "Make me your choice," And I en-tered the ha-ven of rest.
2. *I yield-ed my-self to His ten-der em-brace, And, faith tak-ing hold of the Word, My fet-ters fell off, and I an-chored my soul, The ha-ven of rest is my Lord.*
3. The song of my soul, since the Lord made me whole, Has been the old sto-ry so blest Of Je-sus, who'll save who-so-ev-er will have A home in the ha-ven of rest.

I've an-chored my soul in the ha-ven of rest, I'll sail the wide seas no more; The tem-pest may sweep o'er the wild, storm-y deep, In Je-sus I'm safe ev-er-more.

ASSURANCE

102 Day By Day and With Each Passing Moment

Lina Sandell
Tr. by A. L. Skoog

As thy days so shall thy strength be. — Deuteronomy 33:25

BLOTT EN DAG
Oscar Ahnfelt

1. Day by day and with each pass-ing mo-ment, Strength I find to meet my tri-als here; Trust-ing in my Fa-ther's wise be-stow-ment, I've no cause for wor-ry or for fear. He whose heart is kind be-yond all meas-ure Gives un-to each day what He deems best— Lov-ing-ly, its part of pain and

2. Ev-ery day the Lord Him-self is near me With a spe-cial mer-cy for each hour; All my cares He fain would bear, and cheer me, He whose name is Coun-sel-lor and Power. The pro-tec-tion of His child and treas-ure Is a charge that on Him-self He laid; "As thy days, thy strength shall be in

3. Help me then in ev-ery trib-u-la-tion So to trust Thy prom-is-es, O Lord, That I lose not faith's sweet con-so-la-tion Of-fered me with-in Thy ho-ly word. Help me Lord, when toil and trou-ble meet-ing, E'er to take, as from a fa-ther's hand, One by one, the days, the mo-ments

ASSURANCE

1 pleas - ure,	Min - gling toil with peace and	rest.	
2 meas - ure,"	This the pledge to me He	made.	
3 fleet - ing,	'Til I reach the prom - ised	land.	A - men.

Morning Prayer

103

O God,
Early in the morning do I cry unto Thee.
Help me to pray,
And to think only of Thee.
I cannot pray alone.

In me there is darkness,
But with Thee there is light.
I am lonely, but Thou leavest me not.
I am feeble in heart, but Thou leavest me not.
I am restless, but with Thee there is peace.
In me there is bitterness, but with Thee there is patience;
Thy ways are past understanding, but
Thou knowest the way for me.

O heavenly Father,
I praise and thank Thee
For the peace of the night.
I praise and thank Thee for this new day.
I praise and thank Thee for all Thy goodness
and faithfulness throughout my life.
Thou hast granted me many blessings:
Now let me accept tribulation
from Thy hand.
Thou wilt not lay on me more
than I can bear.
Thou makest all things work together for good
for Thy children.

—Dietrich Bonhoeffer

ASSURANCE

104   Great God of Wonders

. . . And I will pardon all their iniquities . . — Jeremiah 33:8

Samuel Davies   WONDERS
                                        John Newton

1. Great God of wonders! all Thy ways Are matchless, Godlike, and divine; But the fair glories of Thy grace More Godlike and unrivaled shine, More Godlike and unrivaled shine.
2. *In wonder lost, with trembling joy, We take the pardon of our God: Pardon for crimes of deepest dye, A pardon bought with Jesus' blood, A pardon bought with Jesus' blood.*
3. O may this strange, this matchless grace, This Godlike miracle of love, Fill the whole earth with grateful praise, And all th'angelic choirs above, And all th'angelic choirs above.

(Use after last stanza)

Who is a pardoning God like Thee? Or who has grace so rich and free? Or who has grace so rich and free?

Fine

GRACE, MERCY, AND FORGIVENESS

Grace Greater Than Our Sin

105

... But where sin abounded, grace did much more abound. — Romans 5:20

Julia H. Johnston

MOODY
Daniel B. Towner

1. Mar-vel-ous grace of our lov-ing Lord, Grace that ex-ceeds our sin and our guilt! Yon-der on Cal-va-ry's mount out-poured— There where the blood of the Lamb was spilt.
2. Sin and de-spair, like the sea-waves cold, Threat-en the soul with in-fi-nite loss; Grace that is great-er— yes, grace un-told— Points to the Ref-uge, the might-y Cross.
3. Dark is the stain that we can-not hide, What can a-vail to wash it a-way? Look! There is flow-ing a crim-son tide— Whit-er than snow you may be to-day.
4. Mar-vel-ous, in-fi-nite, match-less grace, Free-ly be-stowed on all who be-lieve! You that are long-ing to see His face, Will you this mo-ment His grace re-ceive?

Grace, grace, God's grace, Grace that will par-don and cleanse with-in; Grace, grace, God's grace, Grace that is great-er than all our sin!

Copyright 1910. Renewal 1938 extended. Hope Publishing Company. All rights reserved. Used by permission.

GRACE, MERCY, AND FORGIVENESS

106   We're Hungry, Lord

We're hungry for something, Lord.

We have so much rich food and cake and candy for ourselves,
*   but we're hungry.*

People around us are so stiff and tight and hard to reach.

And they make us that way.

But we're hungry for something more.

People we know keep talking about great ideas, brilliant questions,
*   and the problem of God's existence.*

But we're hungry for You, not ideas or theories.

We want You to touch us, to reach inside us and turn us on.

There are so many people who will counsel us to death.

But we're hungry for someone who really knows You and has
*   You, someone who can get so close to us that we can see You*
*   there.*

We have so many things, but we're hungry for You.

Deep, deep down inside we're hungry, even if we appear to be
*   silly, lazy, or unconcerned at times.*

We're hungry for Your kind of power and love and joy.

Feed us, Lord, feed us with Your rich food.

                                   – Anonymous

107   Amazing Grace! How Sweet the Sound

For by grace are ye saved through faith . . . — Ephesians 2:8

AMAZING GRACE
American Melody
Carrell and Clayton's *Virginia Harmony*
Harmonized by Edwin O. Excell

John Newton
John P. Rees, stanza 5

1. A-mazing grace! How sweet the sound—That saved a wretch like me!
2. 'Twas grace that taught my heart to fear, And grace my fears re-lieved;
3. The Lord has prom-ised good to me, His word my hope se-cures;
4. Through man-y dan-gers, toils, and snares, I have al-read-y come;
5. When we've been there ten thou-sand years, Bright shin-ing as the sun,

GRACE, MERCY, AND FORGIVENESS

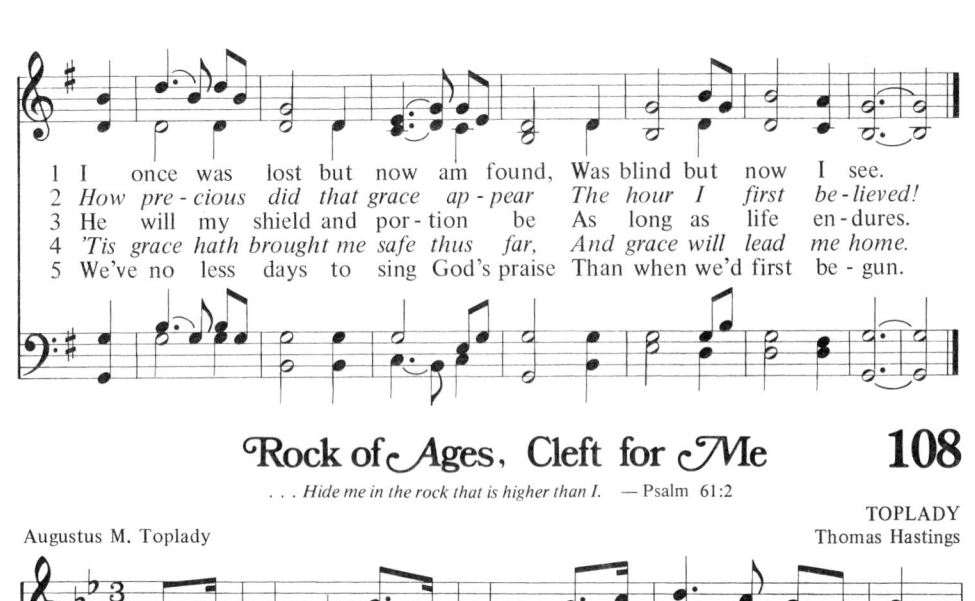

1. I once was lost but now am found, Was blind but now I see.
2. *How pre-cious did that grace ap-pear The hour I first be-lieved!*
3. He will my shield and por-tion be As long as life en-dures.
4. *'Tis grace hath brought me safe thus far, And grace will lead me home.*
5. We've no less days to sing God's praise Than when we'd first be-gun.

Rock of Ages, Cleft for Me 108

... Hide me in the rock that is higher than I. — Psalm 61:2

Augustus M. Toplady

TOPLADY
Thomas Hastings

1. Rock of A-ges, cleft for me, Let me hide my-self in Thee;
2. *Could my tears for-ev-er flow, Could my zeal no lan-guor know,*
3. While I draw this fi-nal breath, When my eyes shall close in death,

1. Let the wa-ter and the blood, From Thy wound-ed side which flowed,
2. *These for sin could not a-tone— Thou must save, and Thou a-lone:*
3. When I rise to worlds un-known, And be-hold Thee on Thy throne,

1. Be of sin the dou-ble cure, Save from wrath and make me pure.
2. *In my hand no price I bring, Sim-ply to Thy cross I cling.*
3. Rock of A-ges, cleft for me, Let me hide my-self in Thee. A-men.

GRACE, MERCY, AND FORGIVENESS

109 Whiter Than Snow

*Purge me . . . and I shall be clean;
wash me and I shall be whiter than snow.* — Psalm 51:7

James Nicholson

FISCHER
William G. Fischer

1. Lord Jesus, I long to be perfectly whole; I want Thee forever to live in my soul. Break down every idol, cast out every foe— Now wash me and I shall be whiter than snow.
2. Lord Jesus, look down from Your throne in the skies And help me to make a complete sacrifice. I give up myself and whatever I know— Now wash me and I shall be whiter than snow.
3. Lord Jesus, for this I most humbly entreat; I wait, blessed Lord, at Thy crucified feet. By faith, for my cleansing I see Your blood flow— Now wash me and I shall be whiter than snow.
4. Lord Jesus, You see as I patiently wait; Come now and within me a new heart create. To those who have sought You, You never said, "No"— Now wash me and I shall be whiter than snow.

Whiter than snow, yes, whiter than snow— Now wash me and I shall be whiter than snow.

GRACE, MERCY, AND FORGIVENESS

Thank God for the Promise of Spring

110

While the earth remaineth, seed time and harvest . . . shall not cease. — Genesis 8:22

Gloria Gaither
William J. Gaither

SPRINGTIME
William J. Gaither

1. Though the skies be gray a-bove me And I can't see the light of day, There's a ray break-ing through the shad-ows, And His smile can't be far a-way.
2. Though the earth seemed bleak and bar-ren And the seeds lay brown and dead, Yet the prom-ise of life throbbed with-in them, And I knew spring was just a-head.

Thank God for the prom-ise of spring-time, Once a-gain my heart will sing; There's a brand new day that is dawn-ing, Thank God for the prom-ise of spring.

© Copyright 1973 by William J. Gaither. All rights reserved. Used by permission.

GRACE, MERCY, AND FORGIVENESS

111 A Certain Uncertain Future

"Wisely enough,
God does not let us skip ahead in the story of our lives,
but rather leads us page by page
to its understandable conclusion in Him.
And so, as each of us faces an uncertain future,
we can trust in God's promise as expressed by Jeremiah:
'For I know the plans I have for you,' saith the Lord,
'They are plans for good and not for evil,
to give a future and a hope.'"

—Pann Baltz

112 He Giveth More Grace

God is able to make all grace abound toward you — II Corinthians 9:8

HE GIVETH MORE GRACE

Annie Johnson Flint
Hubert Mitchell

1. He giv-eth more grace when the burdens grow greater, He send-eth more strength when the la-bors in-crease; To add-ed af-flic-tion He add-eth His mer-cy, To mul-ti-plied tri-als, His mul-ti-plied peace.

2. When we have ex-haust-ed our store of en-dur-ance, When our strength has failed ere the day is half done, When we reach the end of our hoard-ed re-sourc-es, Our Fa-ther's full giv-ing is on-ly be-gun.

© Copyright 1941. Renewed 1969 by Lillenas Publishing Co. All rights reserved. Used by permission.

GRACE, MERCY, AND FORGIVENESS

His love has no lim-it, His grace has no meas-ure, His power has no bound-a-ry known un-to men; For out of His in-fi-nite rich-es in Je-sus, He giv-eth, and giv-eth, and giv-eth a-gain!

A Prayer for Our World   113

ALMIGHTY GOD: You have called us together, and by Your Holy Spirit, make us one with Your Son our Lord. We thank You for the church, for the power of Your word, and for our life together in Christ. Give us a heart to love the loveless, the lonely, the hungry, and the hurt, without pride or a calculating spirit, so that we may serve You with integrity and joy.

GOD OF GRACE: In Your world there are fields to seed and harvest. We thank You for men and women who farm the land, and for workers who prepare and distribute food. While we struggle with the problem of overweight, millions are dying from hunger. Help us to find the wisdom and the commitment to bring hope and health to our brothers and sisters throughout the world. May no one starve because of our greed or neglect, and may we all hunger and thirst for righteousness alone; through Jesus Christ our Lord. Amen.

—Gary W. Demarest

GRACE, MERCY, AND FORGIVENESS

114 Wonderful Grace of Jesus

For by grace are ye saved, through faith.... — Ephesians 2:8

Haldor Lillenas

WONDERFUL GRACE
Haldor Lillenas

1. Won-der-ful grace of Je-sus, Great-er than all my sin;
2. *Won-der-ful grace of Je-sus, Reach-ing to all the lost,*
3. Won-der-ful grace of Je-sus, Reach-ing the most de-filed,

1. How shall my tongue de-scribe it, Where shall its praise be-gin?
2. *By it I have been par-doned, Saved to the ut-ter-most;*
3. By its trans-form-ing pow-er Mak-ing him God's dear child,

1. Tak-ing a-way my bur-den, Set-ting my spir-it free,
2. *Chains have been torn a-sun-der, Giv-ing me lib-er-ty,*
3. Pur-chas-ing peace and heav-en For all e-ter-ni-ty—

1. For the won-der-ful grace of Je-sus reach-es me.
2. *For the won-der-ful grace of Je-sus reach-es me.*
3. And the won-der-ful grace of Je-sus reach-es me.

Copyright 1918. Renewal 1946 extended. Hope Publishing Company. All rights reserved. Used by permission.

GRACE, MERCY, AND FORGIVENESS

Won-der-ful the matchless grace of Jesus, Deep-er than the might-y roll-ing sea; High-er than the moun-tain, spark-ling like a foun-tain, All suf-fi-cient grace for e-ven me; Broad-er than the scope of my trans-gres-sions, Great-er far than all my sin and shame; O mag-ni-fy the pre-cious name of Jesus, Praise His name!

GRACE, MERCY, AND FORGIVENESS

115   There's a Wideness in God's Mercy

And they sang together . . . because He is good, for His mercy endureth forever. . . . — Ezra 3:11

Frederick W. Faber

WELLESLEY
Lizzie S. Tourjée

1. There's a wide-ness in God's mer-cy Like the wide-ness of the sea; There's a kind-ness in His jus-tice Which is more than lib-er-ty.
2. *There is wel-come for the sin-ner And more grac-es for the good; There is mer-cy with the Sav-ior; There is heal-ing in His blood.*
3. For the love of God is broad-er Than the meas-ure of man's mind; And the heart of the E-ter-nal Is most won-der-ful-ly kind.
4. *If our love were but more sim-ple We should take Him at His word, And our lives would be all sun-shine In the sweet-ness of our Lord.* A-men.

116   Psalm 32

    Blessed is he whose transgression is forgiven, *whose sin is covered.* Blessed is the man to whom the Lord imputes no iniquity, *and in whose spirit there is no deceit.*

    When I declared not my sin, *my body wasted away through my groaning all day long.* For day and night Thy hand was heavy upon me, *my strength was dried up as by the heat of summer.*

    I acknowledge my sin to Thee, and I did not hide my iniquity; *I said, "I will confess my transgressions to the Lord";* then Thou didst forgive the guilt of my sin. Therefore let every one who is godly offer prayer to Thee; *at a time of distress, in the rush of great waters, they shall not reach Him.* Thou art a hiding place for me, Thou preservest me from trouble; *Thou dost encompass me with deliverance.*

    I will instruct you and teach you the way you should go; *I will counsel you with my eye upon you.* Be not like a horse or a mule, without understanding, *which must be curbed with bit and bridle, else it will not keep with you.*

    Many are the pangs of the wicked; *but steadfast love surrounds him who trusts in the Lord.* Be glad in the Lord, and rejoice, O righteous, *and shout for joy, all you upright in heart!*

                                                                 –(RSV)

GRACE, MERCY, AND FORGIVENESS

A Shelter in the Time of Storm 117

*There is none as holy as the Lord, . . .
neither is there any rock like our God.* — I Samuel 2:2

Vernon J. Charlesworth
Adapted by Ira D. Sankey

SHELTER
Ira D. Sankey

1. The Lord's our rock, in Him we hide, A shelter in the time of storm;
   Secure whatever ill betide, A shelter in the time of storm.
2. *A shade by day, defense by night, A shelter in the time of storm;
   No fears alarm, no fears affright, A shelter in the time of storm.*
3. The raging storms may 'round us beat, A shelter in the time of storm;
   We'll never leave our safe retreat, A shelter in the time of storm.
4. *O Rock divine, O Refuge dear, A shelter in the time of storm;
   Be Thou our helper ever near, A shelter in the time of storm.*

O Jesus is a rock in a weary land, A weary land, a weary land; O, Jesus is a rock in a weary land, A shelter in the time of storm.

REFUGE

118 A Mighty Fortress Is Our God

The Lord is my rock, my fortress, and my deliverer . . . — Psalm 18:2

Based on Psalm 46
Martin Luther
Tr. by Frederick H. Hedge

EIN' FESTE BURG
Martin Luther
Descant by Mary E. Caldwell

Descant: That word a-bove all, a-bid - eth;

1. A might-y for-tress is our God, A bul-wark nev-er fail - ing;
2. Did we in our own strength con-fide, Our striv-ing would be los - ing,
3. And though this world with dev-ils filled, Should threat-en to un - do us,
4. That word a-bove all earth-ly powers, No thanks to them, a-bid - eth;

Descant: The gifts are ours, Who with us sid - eth.

1. Our help-er He a-mid the flood Of mor-tal ills pre-vail - ing.
2. Were not the right man on our side, The man of God's own choos - ing.
3. We will not fear, for God hath willed His truth to tri-umph through us.
4. The Spir-it and the gifts are ours Through Him who with us sid - eth.

Descant: Let goods and kin-dred go, This mor-tal life al - so— The bod-y

1. For still our an-cient foe Doth seek to work us woe— His craft and power are
2. Dost ask who that may be? Christ Je-sus, it is He— Lord Sab-a-oth His
3. The prince of dark-ness grim, We trem-ble not for him— His rage we can en -
4. Let goods and kin-dred go, This mor-tal life al - so— The bod-y they may

© Copyright 1976 by Paragon Associates, Inc. All rights reserved.
REFUGE

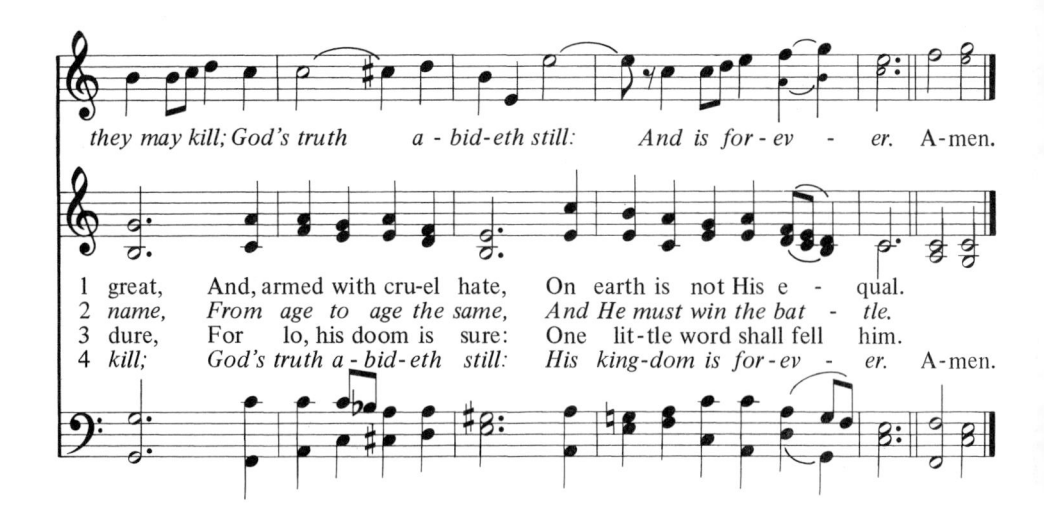

they may kill; God's truth	*a - bid-eth still:*	*And is for - ev - er.*	*A-men.*

1 great,	And, armed with cru-el hate,	On earth is not His e -	qual.
2 name,	From age to age the same,	And He must win the bat -	tle.
3 dure,	For lo, his doom is sure:	One lit-tle word shall fell	him.
4 kill;	God's truth a - bid-eth still:	His king-dom is for - ev - er.	A-men.

A Contemporary Te Deum   119

You are God: we praise You;
You are the Lord: we acclaim You;
You are the eternal Father:
All creation worships You.
To You all angels, all the powers of heaven,
Cherubim and Seraphim, sing in endless praise:
Holy, holy, holy Lord, God of power and might,
heaven and earth are full of your glory.
The glorious company of apostles praises You.
The noble fellowship of prophets praises You.
The white-robed army of martyrs praises You.
Throughout the world the holy Church acclaims You:
Father, of majesty unbounded,
Your true and only Son, worthy of all worship,
and the Holy Spirit, advocate and guide.
You, Christ, are the king of glory,
eternal Son of the Father.
When You became man to set us free
You did not disdain the Virgin's womb.
You overcame the sting of death,
and opened the kingdom of heaven to all believers.
You are seated at God's right hand in glory.
We believe that You will come, and be our judge.
Come then, Lord, sustain Your people,
bought with the price of Your own blood,
and bring us with Your saints
to everlasting glory.

REFUGE

120 He Hideth My Soul

I will put thee in a cleft of the Rock, and will cover thee with My hand. — Exodus 33:22

Fanny J. Crosby

HE HIDETH MY SOUL
William J. Kirkpatrick

1. A wonderful Savior is Jesus my Lord, A wonderful Savior to me; He hideth my soul in the cleft of the rock, Where rivers of pleasure I see.
2. *A wonderful Savior is Jesus my Lord, He taketh my burden away; He holdeth me up, and I shall not be moved, He giveth me strength for each day.*
3. With numberless blessings each moment He crowns, And, filled with His fullness divine, I sing in my rapture, "O glory to God For such a Redeemer as mine!"
4. *When clothed in His brightness transported I rise To meet Him in clouds of the sky, His perfect salvation, His wonderful love, I'll shout with the millions on high.*

He hideth my soul in the cleft of the rock That shadows a...

REFUGE

dry, thirst-y land; He hid-eth my life in the depths of His love,

And cov-ers me there with His hand, And cov-ers me there with His hand.

How Good Is God — 121

How good is God for Israel,
for the pure of heart!

> *As for me, my feet had almost stumbled;*
> *my steps had well-nigh slipped.*
> *I was jealous of the arrogant*
> *and envied the prosperity of the wicked.*

My mind is embittered:
my thoughts, irritating.
I am so stupid, so ignorant!
I am but a dumb brute before You.

> *And yet I am always before You:*
> *You keep me in Your hand.*
> *With counsel You lead me;*
> *You take me by the hand behind You.*

I have but You in the heavens
and nothing more on earth.
My flesh and my brain may fail
but my Rock, the desire of my mind, is God evermore.

> *Those who avoid You will perish;*
> *You exterminate all those who stray.*
> *God's presence is good for me;*
> *I make the Lord my refuge*
> *and I will witness to His deeds.*

—Psalm 73:1-3, 21-28
(Psalms in Modern Speech)

REFUGE

122 In the Hour of Trial

He ever liveth to make intercession for them. — Hebrews 7:25

James Montgomery, alt.

PENITENCE
Spencer Lane

1. In the hour of trial, Jesus, plead for me,
Lest, by base denial, I depart from Thee;
When Thou seest me waver, With a look recall;
Nor for fear or favor Suffer me to fall.

2. With forbidden pleasures Would this vain world charm,
Or its sordid treasures Spread to work me harm;
Bring to my remembrance Sad Gethsemane,
Or, in darker semblance, Rugged Calvary.

3. Should Thy mercy send me Sorrow, toil, and woe,
Or should pain attend me On my path below,
Grant that I may never Fail Thy hand to see;
Grant that I may ever Cast my care on Thee. A-men.

REFUGE

When We All Get to Heaven

*Then we, . . . shall be caught up together with the Lord . . .
and so shall we ever be with the Lord.* — I Thessalonians 4:17

Eliza E. Hewitt

HEAVEN
Emily D. Wilson

1 Sing the won-drous love of Je-sus, Sing His mer-cy and His grace;
2 While we walk the pil-grim path-way Clouds will o-ver-spread the sky;
3 Let us then be true and faith-ful, Trust-ing, serv-ing ev-ery day;
4 On-ward to the prize be-fore us! Soon His beau-ty we'll be-hold;

1 In the man-sions bright and bless-ed He'll pre-pare for us a place.
2 But when trav-eling days are o-ver Not a shad-ow, not a sigh.
3 Just one glimpse of Him in glo-ry Will the toils of life re-pay.
4 Soon the pearl-y gates will o-pen— We shall tread the streets of gold.

When we all get to heav-en, What a day of re-joic-ing that will be! When we all see Je-sus, We'll sing and shout the vic-to-ry!

EVERLASTING LIFE

124   Revelation 7:9-17

Minister: *After this I looked, and behold, a great multitude which no man could number, from every nation, from all tribes and peoples and tongues, standing before the throne and before the Lamb, clothed in white robes, with palm branches in their hands, and crying out with a loud voice,*

People: "Salvation belongs to our God who sits upon the throne and to the Lamb!"

Minister: *And all the angels stood 'round the throne and 'round the elders and the four living creatures, and they fell on their faces before the throne and worshiped God, saying,*

People: "Amen! Blessing and glory and wisdom and thanksgiving and honor and power and might be to our God for ever and ever!

Minister and People: "Amen!"

Minister: *Then one of the elders addressed me, saying,*

Women of the Congregation: "Who are these, clothed in white robes, and whence have they come?"

Minister: *I said to him, "Sir, you know." And he said to me,*

Men of the Congregation: "These are they who have come out of the great tribulation;

Women of the Congregation: they have washed their robes and made them white in the blood of the Lamb.

People (Men and Women): Therefore are they before the throne of God, and serve Him day and night within His temple; and He who sits upon the throne will shelter them with His presence.

Men of the Congregation: They shall hunger no more, neither thirst any more;

Women of the Congregation: the sun shall not strike them, nor any scorching heat.

Minister: *For the Lamb in the midst of the throne will be their shepherd,*

Women of the Congregation: and He will guide them to springs of living water;

Men of the Congregation: and God shall wipe away every tear from their eyes."

—(RSV)

EVERLASTING LIFE

Is My Name Written There?

125

And another Book was opened which is the Book of Life... — Revelation 20:12

Mary A. Kidder

IS MY NAME
Frank M. Davis

1. Lord, I care not for rich-es, Nei-ther sil-ver nor gold, I would make sure of heav-en, I would en-ter the fold. In the book of Thy king-dom, With its pag-es so fair, Tell me, Je-sus, my Sav-ior, Is my name writ-ten there? Is my name writ-ten there On the page white and fair? In the book of Thy king-dom, Is my name writ-ten there?

2. *Lord, my sins they are man-y, Like the sands of the sea, But Thy blood, O my Sav-ior, Is suf-fi-cient for me; For Thy prom-ise is writ-ten In bright let-ters that glow, "Though your sins be as scar-let, I will make them like snow." Is my name writ-ten there On the page white and fair? In the book of Thy king-dom, Is my name writ-ten there?*

3. O that beau-ti-ful cit-y With its man-sions of light, With its glo-ri-fied be-ings In pure gar-ments of white; Where no e-vil thing com-eth To de-spoil what is fair; Where the an-gels are watch-ing, Yes, my name's writ-ten there. Yes, my name's writ-ten there On the page white and fair! In the book of Thy king-dom, Yes, my name's writ-ten there!

EVERLASTING LIFE

126   I John 3:1-6

See how much the Father has loved us! His love is so great that we are called God's children—and so, in fact, we are. This is why the world does not know us: it has not known God. My dear friends, we are now God's children, but it is not yet clear what we shall become. But we know that when Christ appears, we shall become like Him, because we shall see Him as He really is. Everyone who has this hope in Christ keeps himself pure, just as Christ is pure.

Whoever sins is guilty of breaking God's law; because sin is a breaking of the law. You know that Christ appeared in order to take away men's sins, and that there is no sin in Him. So everyone who lives in Christ does not continue to sin; but whoever continues to sin has never seen Him or known Him.

—(TEV)

127   Beyond the Sunset

For now we see through a glass darkly; but then face to face. — I Corinthians 13:12

SUNSET

Virgil P. Brock   Blanche Kerr Brock

1. Be-yond the sun-set, O bliss-ful morn-ing, When with our Sav-ior heaven is be-gun; Earth's toil-ing end-ed, O glo-rious dawn-ing, Be-yond the sun-set, when day is done.
2. Be-yond the sun-set no clouds will gath-er, No storms will threat-en, no fears an-noy; O day of glad-ness, O day un-end-ing, Be-yond the sun-set, e-ter-nal joy!
3. Be-yond the sun-set a hand will guide me To God the Fa-ther, whom I a-dore; His glo-rious pres-ence, His words of wel-come, Will be my por-tion on that fair shore.
4. *Be-yond the sun-set, O glad re-un-ion, With our dear loved ones who've gone be-fore; In that fair home-land we'll know no part-ing, Be-yond the sun-set, for-ev-er-more!*

Copyright 1936 by The Rodeheaver Co. © Renewed 1964 by The Rodeheaver Co., owner. All rights reserved. Used by permission.

EVERLASTING LIFE

Face to Face

128

For now we see through a glass darkly; . . .
—I Corinthians 13:12

Carrie E. Breck

FACE TO FACE
Grant C. Tullar

1. Face to face with Christ my Sav-ior, Face to face—what will it be—
   When with rap-ture I be-hold Him, Je-sus Christ who died for me?
2. On - ly faint-ly now I see Him, With the dark-ened veil be-tween,
   But a bless-ed day is com - ing When His glo - ry shall be seen.
3. What re-joic-ing in His pres - ence When are ban-ished grief and pain,
   When the crook-ed ways are straight-ened And the dark things shall be plain.
4. Face to face! O bliss-ful mo - ment! Face to face— to see and know;
   Face to face with my Re-deem - er, Je-sus Christ who loves me so.

Refrain:
Face to face I shall be - hold Him, Far be-yond the star-ry sky;
Face to face in all His glo - ry, I shall see Him by and by!

EVERLASTING LIFE

129 When We See Christ

. . . We shall be like Him for we shall see Him as He is.
— I John 3:2

Esther Kerr Rusthoi

WHEN WE SEE CHRIST
Esther Kerr Rusthoi

1. Oft-times the day seems long, our trials hard to bear, We're tempt-ed to com-plain, to mur-mur and de-spair; But Christ will soon ap-pear to catch His Bride a-way, All tears for-ev-er o-ver in God's e-ter-nal day.

2. *Some-times the sky looks dark with not a ray of light, We're tossed and driv-en on, no hu-man help in sight; But there is One in heaven who knows our deep-est care, Let Je-sus solve your prob-lem—just go to Him in prayer.*

3. Life's day will soon be o'er, all storms for-ev-er past, We'll cross the great di-vide to glo-ry, safe at last. We'll share the joys of heaven— a harp, a home, a crown, The tempt-er will be ban-ished, we'll lay our bur-den down.

It will be worth it all when we see Jesus, Life's trials will seem so small when we see Christ;

Copyright 1941. Renewal 1969 by Howard Rusthoi. Assigned to Singspiration, Inc. All rights reserved. Used by permission.

EVERLASTING LIFE

One glimpse of His dear face all sor-row will e-rase,
So brave-ly run the race 'til we see Christ.

I'll Be There

Being justified . . . through the redemption that is in Christ Jesus.
— Romans 3:24

130

Tim Spencer

I'LL BE THERE
Tim Spencer

I'll be there, I'll be there, When the Sav-ior calls my name, I'll be there; I'll be there, I'll be there, By His a-maz-ing grace and mer-cy I'll be there.

Optional Coda *pp*

By His a-maz-ing grace and mer-cy I'll be there.

© Copyright 1960 by Manna Music, Inc. All rights reserved. Used by permission.

EVERLASTING LIFE

131 In Heaven Above

Mine eyes have seen the King, the Lord of hosts - Isaiah 6:5

Laurentius L. Laurinus
Revised by John Åstrom
Tr. by William Maccall

HAUGE
Norwegian Folk Melody

1. In heaven above, in heaven above, Where God our Father dwells, How boundless there the blessedness! No tongue its greatness tells; There face to face, and full and free, Forever, evermore we see Our God, the Lord of hosts!

2. *In heaven above, in heaven above, What glory deep and bright! The splendor of the noonday sun Grows pale before its light: The heavenly light that ne'er goes down, Around whose radiance clouds ne'er frown, Is God, the Lord of hosts!*

3. In heaven above, in heaven above, God hath a joy prepared Which mortal ear had never heard Nor mortal vision shared. Which never entered mortal breast, By mortal lips was ne'er expressed: 'Tis God, the Lord of hosts!

EVERLASTING LIFE

O, That Will be Glory for Me

132

But when the multitude saw it, they marvelled and glorified God – Matthew 9:8

Charles H. Gabriel

GLORY SONG
Charles H. Gabriel

1. When all my la-bors and tri-als are o'er, And I am safe on that beau-ti-ful shore, Just to be near the dear Lord I a-dore Will through the a-ges be glo-ry for me.
2. When by the gift of His in-fi-nite grace, I am ac-cord-ed in heav-en a place, Just to be there and to look on His face Will through the a-ges be glo-ry for me.
3. Friends will be there I have loved long a-go; Joy like a riv-er a-round me will flow; Yet, just a smile from my Sav-ior, I know, Will through the a-ges be glo-ry for me.

O, that will be glo-ry for me, Glo-ry for me, glo-ry for me; When by His grace I shall look on His face, That will be glo-ry, be glo-ry for me.

EVERLASTING LIFE

133 Until Then

*Because Thy lovingkindness is better than life,
my lips shall praise Thee.*
— Psalm 63:3

Stuart Hamblen

UNTIL THEN
Stuart Hamblen

1. My heart can sing when I pause to remember
A heart-ache here is but a stepping stone
A-long a trail that's winding always upward,
This troubled world is not my final home.

2. *The things of earth will dim and lose their value
If we recall they're borrowed for a while;
And things of earth that cause the heart to tremble,
Remembered there will only bring a smile.*

3. This weary world with all its toil and struggle
May take its toll of misery and strife;
The soul of man is like a waiting falcon;
When it's released, it's destined for the skies.

© Copyright 1958 by Hamblen Music Co., Inc. All rights reserved. Used by permission.

EVERLASTING LIFE

But un-til then my heart will go on sing-ing,

Un-til then with joy I'll car-ry on

Un-til the day my eyes be-hold the cit-y,

Un-til the day God calls me home.

EVERLASTING LIFE

134 When I Can Read My Title Clear

"In My Father's house are many mansions." — John 14:2

Isaac Watts

PISGAH
Traditional American Melody
Kentucky Harmony

1. When I can read my title clear To mansions in the skies,
I'll bid farewell to every fear And wipe my weeping eyes,
And wipe my weeping eyes, And wipe my weeping eyes,
I'll bid farewell to every fear And wipe my weeping eyes.

2. *Should earth against my soul engage And fier-y darts be hurled,*
Then I can smile at Satan's rage And face a frowning world;
And face a frowning world, And face a frowning world,
Then I can smile at Satan's rage And face a frowning world.

3. Let cares like a wild deluge come And storms of sorrow fall!
May I but safely reach my home, My God, my heaven, my all;
My God, my heaven, my all, My God, my heaven, my all,
May I but safely reach my home, My God, my heaven, my all.

EVERLASTING LIFE

It Will Be Worth It All

135

Let us run with patience the race that is set before us.
— Hebrews 12:1

William J. Gaither

WORTH IT ALL
William J. Gaither

1. There's a prom-ised land made for all the free, When our race on earth is run, Where no bro-ken dreams will mar our mem-o-ry; It will be worth it all when we get home. It will be worth it all just to see His face, When He claims us for His own; Then ten mil-lion years to sing a-maz-ing grace; It will be worth it all when we get home.

2. There no sad fare-wells, there no tear-stained eyes, There no heart-ache, grief, or woe, There no shat-tered hopes will ev-er cloud the skies; It will be worth it all when we get home.

© Copyright 1966 by William J. Gaither. All rights reserved. Used by permission.

EVERLASTING LIFE

136 Praise Ye the Triune God

. . . The Father, the Word, and the Holy Spirit, and these three are one. — 1 John 5:8

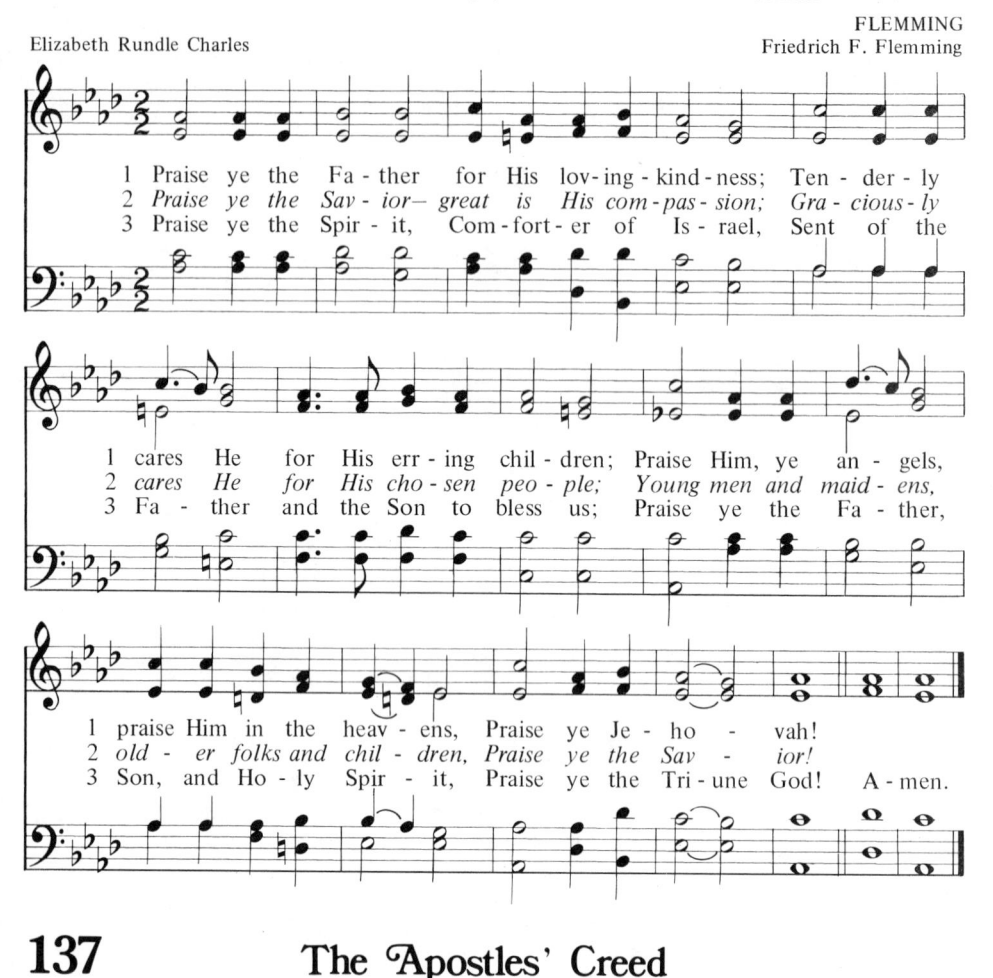

Elizabeth Rundle Charles

FLEMMING
Friedrich F. Flemming

1. Praise ye the Fa-ther for His lov-ing-kind-ness; Ten-der-ly cares He for His err-ing chil-dren; Praise Him, ye an-gels, praise Him in the heav-ens, Praise ye Je-ho-vah!
2. *Praise ye the Sav-ior— great is His com-pas-sion; Gra-cious-ly cares He for His cho-sen peo-ple; Young men and maid-ens, old-er folks and chil-dren, Praise ye the Sav-ior!*
3. Praise ye the Spir-it, Com-fort-er of Is-rael, Sent of the Fa-ther and the Son to bless us; Praise ye the Fa-ther, Son, and Ho-ly Spir-it, Praise ye the Tri-une God! A-men.

137 The Apostles' Creed

I believe in God the Father Almighty, maker of heaven and earth:

And in Jesus Christ His only Son, our Lord; Who was conceived by the Holy Spirit, born of the Virgin Mary, suffered under Pontius Pilate, was crucified, dead, and buried; He descended into hades; the third day He rose again from the dead; He ascended into heaven, and sitteth on the right hand of God, the Father Almighty; from thence He shall come to judge the quick and the dead.

I believe in the Holy Spirit, the holy Christian church, the communion of saints, the forgiveness of sins, the resurrection of the body, and the life everlasting.

Amen.

TRINITY

The Nicene Creed

I believe in one God
the Father Almighty,
maker of heaven and earth,
and of all things visible and invisible:

And in one Lord Jesus Christ, the only-begotten Son of God,
begotten of His Father before all worlds,
God of God, Light of Light, very God of very God,
begotten,
not made,
being of one substance with the Father,
by whom all things were made;
Who for us men and for our salvation came down from heaven,
and was incarnate by the Holy Spirit of the Virgin Mary,
and was made man,
and crucified also for us under Pontius Pilate;

He suffered and was buried, and the third day He rose again
according to the Scriptures,
and ascended into heaven, and sitteth on the right hand of the Father;
And He shall come again with glory
to judge both the quick and the dead;
Whose kingdom shall have no end.

And I believe in the Holy Spirit, the Lord and giver of life,
who proceedeth from the Father and the Son,
who with the Father and the Son together is worshiped and glorified;
who spoke by the prophets.

And I believe in one universal and apostolic church;
I acknowledge one baptism for the remission of sins,
and I look for the resurrection of the dead, and the life of the world to come.

Amen.

139 An Affirmation

WE BELIEVE IN JESUS CHRIST THE LORD,
    Who was promised to the people of Israel,
    Who came in the flesh to dwell among us,
    Who announced the coming of the rule of God,
    Who gathered disciples and taught them,
    Who died on the cross to free us from sin,
    Who rose from the dead to give us life and hope,
    Who reigns in heaven at the right hand of God,
    Who comes to judge and bring justice to victory.
WE BELIEVE IN GOD HIS FATHER,
    Who raised Him from the dead,
    Who created and sustains the universe,
    Who acts to deliver His people in times of need,
    Who desires all men everywhere to be saved.
WE BELIEVE IN THE HOLY SPIRIT,
    Who is the form of God present in the church,
    Who is the guarantee of our deliverance,
    Who leads us to find God's will in the Word,
    Who guides us in discernment,
    Who impels us to act together.

—The Mennonite Hymnal, 1967

140 Hymn to the Trinity

*There are three that bear record in heaven;
the Father, the Word, and the Holy Spirit,
and these three are one.* 1 John 5:6

Paul Sjolund

HYMN TO THE TRINITY
Paul Sjolund

Praise we the Father and the Son, and the Holy Spirit. Thanks be to Thee whose living Word doth lead and guide us. Praise we Thy majesty, O blessed Trinity! Amen, Amen.

© Copyright 1966 by Sacred Songs (A Division of Word, Inc.). Arr. © 1973 by Word Music, Inc. International copyright secured. All rights reserved. Used by permission.

We Believe in a Triune God 141

We believe in God, the Eternal Spirit, Father of our Lord Jesus Christ and our Father, and to His deeds we testify:
    He calls the worlds into being,
        creates man in His own image,
        and sets before him the ways of life and death.
    He seeks in holy love to save all people from aimlessness and sin.
    He judges men and nations by His righteous will declared through prophets and apostles.
    In Jesus Christ, the man of Nazareth, our crucified and risen Lord,
        He has come to us and shared our common lot,
            conquering sin and death,
            and reconciling the world to Himself.
    He bestows upon us His Holy Spirit,
        creating and renewing the Church of Jesus Christ,
        binding in covenant faithful people of all ages, tongues, and races.
    He calls us into His Church,
        to accept the cost and joy of discipleship,
        to be His servants in the service of men,
        to proclaim the gospel to all the world,
        to resist the powers of evil,
        to share in Christ's baptism and eat at His table,
        to join Him in His passion and victory.
    He promises to all who trust Him:
        forgiveness of sins and fulness of grace,
        courage in the struggle for justice and peace,
        His presence in trial and rejoicing,
        and eternal life in His kingdom which has no end.
Blessing and honor, glory and power be unto Him. Amen.

                —Statement of Faith of the United Church of Christ,
                    adopted by the General Synod at Oberlin in 1959.

Gloria Patri 142

And He said unto them, . . . how much more shall your heavenly Father give the Holy Spirit . . .   Luke 11:13

Source unknown

GLORIA PATRI
Henry W. Greatorex

Glo-ry be to the Fa-ther, and to the Son, and to the Ho-ly Ghost: as it was in the be-gin-ning, is now and ev-er shall be, world with-out end. A-men, A-men.

TRINITY

143 The Comforter Has Come

I will pray the Father and He will give you another Comforter. — John 14:16

Frank Bottome
COMFORTER
William J. Kirkpatrick

1. O spread the tidings 'round wherever man is found, Wherever human hearts and human woes abound; Let every Christian tongue proclaim the joyful sound: The Comforter has come!

2. *The long, long night is past, the morning breaks at last, And hushed the dreadful sound and fury of the blast, As over golden hills the day advances fast!* The Comforter has come!

3. Lo, the great King of kings, with healing in His wings, To every captive soul a full deliverance brings; And through the vacant cells the song of triumph rings: The Comforter has come!

4. O boundless love divine! How shall this tongue of mine To wondering mortals tell the matchless grace divine— That I, a child of hell, should in His image shine? The Comforter has come!

The Comforter has come, the Comforter has come! The

HOLY SPIRIT

Ho-ly Ghost from Heaven, the Fa-ther's pro-mise given; O spread the ti-dings 'round wher-ev-er man is found—The Com-fort-er has come!

Come, Holy Spirit, Heavenly Dove 144

And I saw the Spirit, descending like a dove and it abode upon Him. John 1:32

GRÄFENBERG
Praxis Pietatis Melica
Johann Crüger

Isaac Watts

1 Come, Ho-ly Spir-it, heaven-ly Dove, With all Thy quick-ening powers;
2 *Dear Lord, and shall we ev-er live At this poor, dy-ing rate?*
3 Come, Ho-ly Spir-it, heaven-ly Dove, With all Thy quick-ening powers;

1 Kin-dle a flame of sa-cred love In these cold hearts of ours.
2 *Our love so faint, so cold to Thee, And Thine to us so great!*
3 Come, shed a-broad the Sav-ior's love, And that shall kin-dle ours. A-men.

HOLY SPIRIT

145 Blessed Quietness

He shall give you another comforter that He may abide with you forever. — John 14:16

BLESSED QUIETNESS
W. S. Marshall
Arranged by James M. Kirk

Manie P. Ferguson

1. Joys are flow-ing like a riv-er Since the Com-fort-er has come;
2. *Bring-ing life and health and glad-ness All a-round this heav'n-ly Guest*
3. Like the rain that falls from heav-en, Like the sun-light from the sky,
4. *See, a fruit-ful field is grow-ing, Bless-ed fruit of right-eous-ness;*
5. What a won-der-ful sal-va-tion, Where we al-ways see His face!

1. He a-bides with us for-ev-er, Makes the trust-ing heart His home.
2. *Ban-ished un-be-lief and sad-ness, Changed our wea-ri-ness to rest.*
3. So the Ho-ly Ghost is giv-en, Com-ing on us from on high.
4. *And the streams of life are flow-ing In the lone-ly wil-der-ness.*
5. What a per-fect hab-i-ta-tion, What a qui-et rest-ing place!

Bless-ed qui-et-ness, ho-ly qui-et-ness, What as-sur-ance in my soul!

On the storm-y sea He speaks peace to me, How the bil-lows cease to roll!

HOLY SPIRIT

The Holy Spirit 146

MINISTER: O God! How great You are! On the first day of the week we commemorate Your creation of the world and all that is in it.
PEOPLE: *Thank You for the light which wakes us morning by morning, and for that greater light which shines in Jesus Christ.*
MINISTER: O God! How great You are! On the first day of the week You raised Jesus from the dead.
PEOPLE: *Raise us with Him to a new quality of faith and life.*
MINISTER: O God! How great You are! Again on the first day of the week You sent Your Spirit on Your disciples.
PEOPLE: *Do not deprive us of Your Spirit, but renew Him in us day by day.*

—Caryl Michlem

Spirit of God, Descend upon My Heart 147

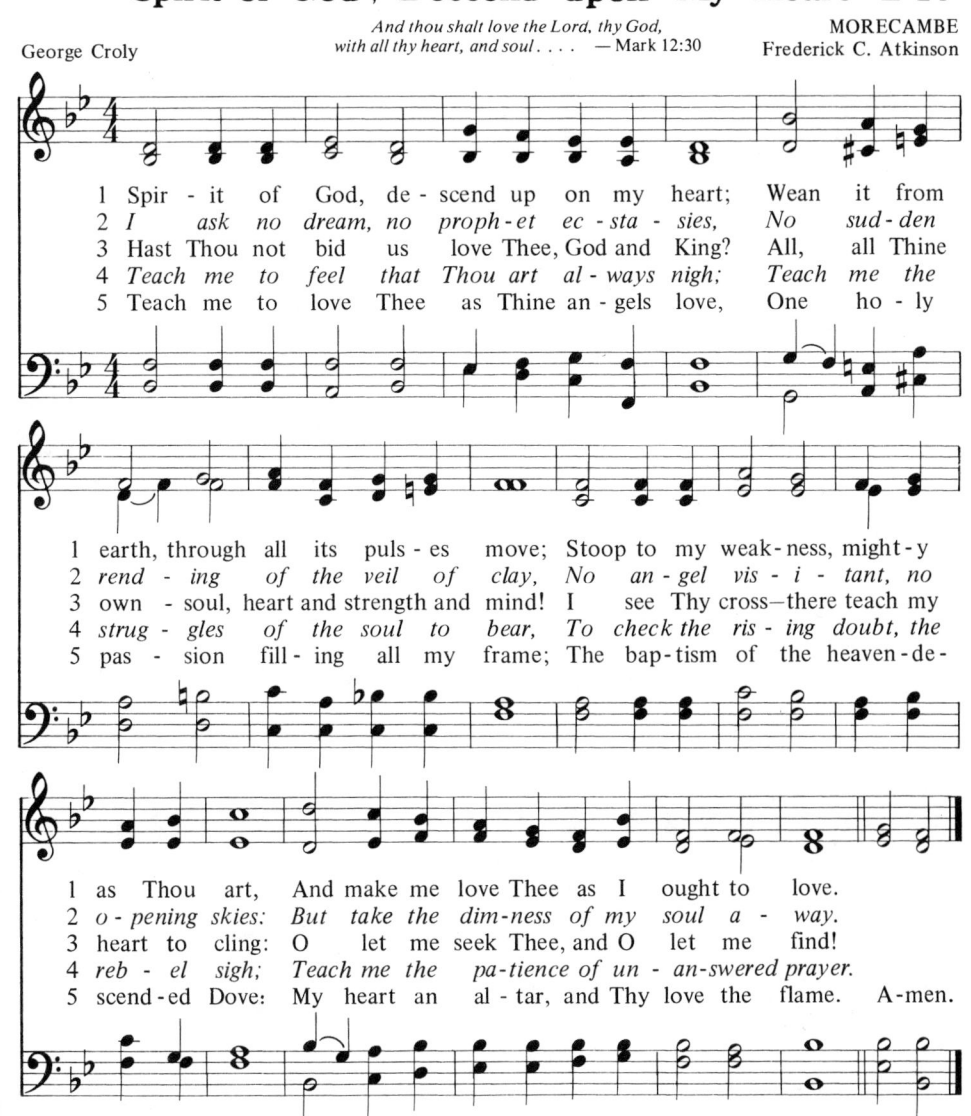

George Croly

And thou shalt love the Lord, thy God, with all thy heart, and soul.... — Mark 12:30

MORECAMBE
Frederick C. Atkinson

1. Spirit of God, descend upon my heart; Wean it from earth, through all its pulses move; Stoop to my weakness, mighty as Thou art, And make me love Thee as I ought to love.
2. I ask no dream, no prophet ecstasies, No sudden rending of the veil of clay, No angel visitant, no opening skies: But take the dimness of my soul away.
3. Hast Thou not bid us love Thee, God and King? All, all Thine own—soul, heart and strength and mind! I see Thy cross—there teach my heart to cling: O let me seek Thee, and O let me find!
4. Teach me to feel that Thou art always nigh; Teach me the struggles of the soul to bear, To check the rising doubt, the rebel sigh; Teach me the patience of unanswered prayer.
5. Teach me to love Thee as Thine angels love, One holy passion filling all my frame; The baptism of the heaven-descended Dove: My heart an altar, and Thy love the flame. A-men.

HOLY SPIRIT

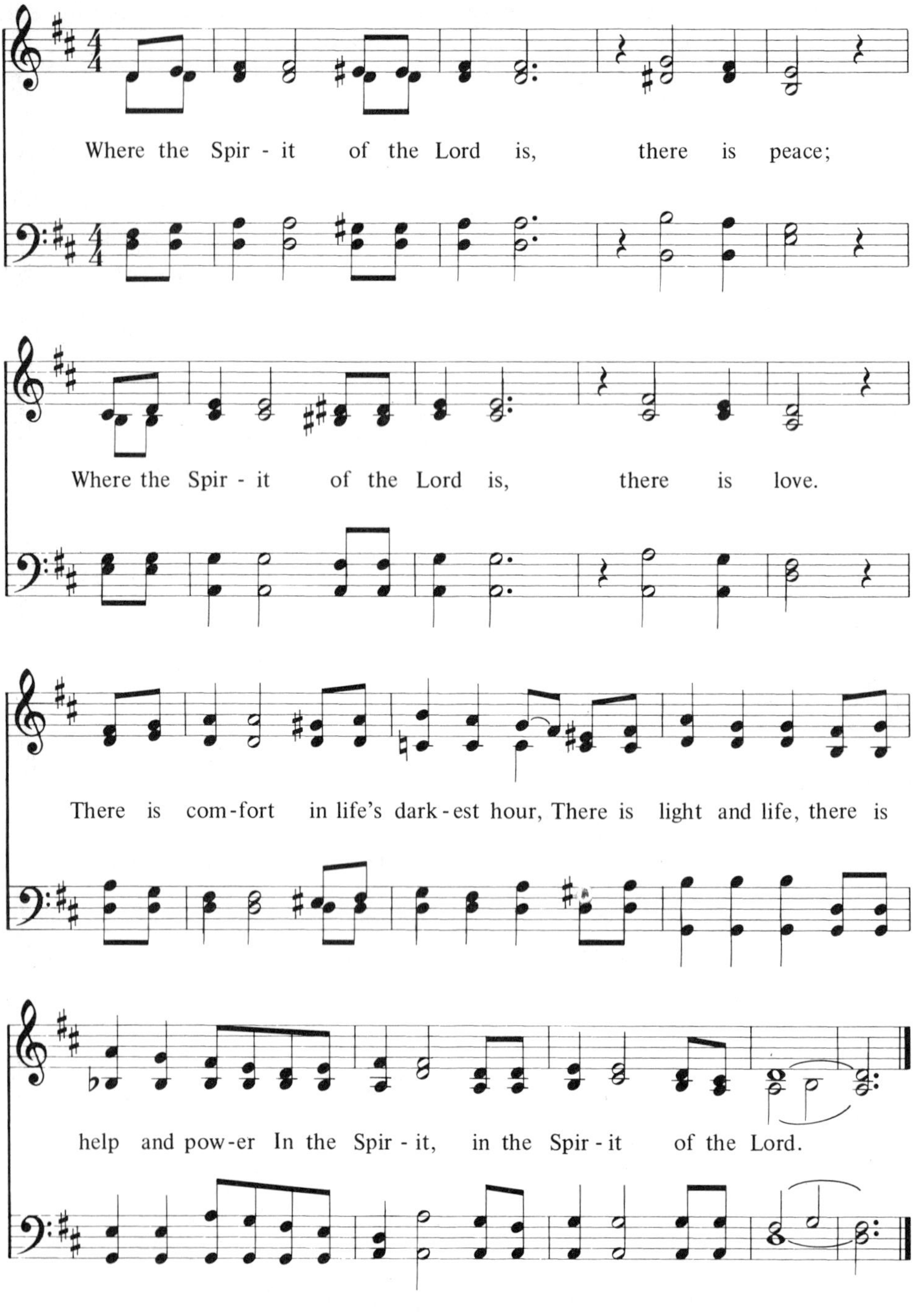

Holy, Holy

149

*They rest not day and night,
saying holy, holy, holy, Lord God almighty.*
— Revelation 4:8

Jimmy Owens

HOLY, HOLY
Jimmy Owens

1 Ho - ly, ho - ly, ho - ly, ho - ly, Ho - ly, ho - ly,
2 *Gra - cious Fa - ther, gra - cious Fa - ther, We're so blest to be your*
3 Pre - cious Je - sus, pre - cious Je - sus, We're so glad that You've re -
4 *Ho - ly Spir - it, Ho - ly Spir - it, Come and fill our hearts a -*
5 Ho - ly, ho - ly, ho - ly ho - ly, Ho - ly, ho - ly,
6 *Hal - le - lu - jah, hal - le - lu - jah, Hal - le - lu - jah,*

1   Lord God Al - might - y; And we lift our hearts be - fore You as a
2 *chil - dren, gra - cious Fa - ther; And we lift our heads be - fore You as a*
3 deemed us, pre - cious Je - sus; And we lift our hands be - fore You as a
4 *new, Ho - ly Spir - it; And we lift our voice be - fore You as a*
5   Lord God Al - might - y; And we lift our hearts be - fore You as a
6   *hal - le - lu - jah; And we lift our hearts be - fore You as a*

1 to - ken of our love, Ho - ly, ho - ly, ho - ly, ho - ly.
2 *to - ken of our love, Gra - cious Fa - ther, gra - cious Fa - ther.*
3 to - ken of our love, Pre - cious Je - sus, pre - cious Je - sus.
4 *to - ken of our love, Ho - ly Spir - it, Ho - ly Spir - it.*
5 to - ken of our love, Ho - ly, ho - ly, ho - ly, ho - ly.
6 *to - ken of our love, Hal - le - lu - jah, hal - le - lu - jah.*

© Copyright 1972 by Lexicon Music, Inc. All rights reserved. International copyright secured. Used by permission.

HOLY SPIRIT

150 Come, Holy Spirit

My grace is sufficient for thee; for my strength is made perfect in weakness. — II Corinthians 12:9

Gloria Gaither
William J. Gaither

COME, HOLY SPIRIT
William J. Gaither

1. Come as a wisdom to children, Come as new sight to the blind, Come, Lord, as strength to my weakness, Take me: soul, body and mind.
2. *Come as a rest to the weary, Come as a balm for the sore, Come as a dew to my dryness: Fill me with joy evermore,*
3. Come like a spring in the desert, Come to the withered of soul; O let Your sweet healing power Touch me and make me whole.

Come, Holy Spirit, I need You, Come, sweet Spirit, I pray; Come in Your strength and Your power, Come in Your own gentle way. A-men.

© Copyright 1964 by William J. Gaither. All rights reserved. Used by permission.
HOLY SPIRIT

Spirit, Now Live in Me 151

... How much more shall your Heavenly Father give the Holy Spirit to them that ask Him. — Luke 11:13

Bryan Jeffery Leech

LOIS
Bryan Jeffery Leech

Unison

1. O ho-ly Dove of God de-scend-ing, You are the love that knows no end-ing,
2. O ho-ly Wind of God now blow-ing, You are the seed that God is sow-ing,
3. O ho-ly Rain of God now fall-ing, You make the Word of God en-thrall-ing,
4. O ho-ly Flame of God now burn-ing, You are the power of Christ re-turn-ing,

1. All of our shattered dreams You're mending: Spir-it, now live in me.
2. You are the life that starts us grow-ing: Spir-it, now live in me.
3. You are that in-ner voice now call-ing: Spir-it, now live in me.
4. You are the an-swer to our yearn-ing: Spir-it, now live in me. A-men.

© Copyright 1976 by Fred Bock Music Company. All rights reserved. Used by permission.

The Day of Pentecost 152

When the day of Pentecost had come, they were all together in one place. And suddenly a sound came from heaven like the rush of a mighty wind, and it filled all the house where they were sitting. And there appeared to them tongues as of fire, distributed and resting on each one of them. And they were all filled with the Holy Spirit and began to speak in other tongues, as the Spirit gave them utterance.

But Peter, standing with the eleven, lifted up his voice and addressed them, "Men of Judea and all who dwell in Jerusalem, let this be known to you, and give ear to my words.

"Jesus of Nazareth, a man attested to you by God with mighty works and wonders and signs which God did through Him in your midst, as you yourselves know—this Jesus, delivered up according to the definite plan and foreknowledge of God, you crucified and killed by the hands of lawless men. But God raised Him up, having loosed the pangs of death, because it was not possible for Him to be held by it.

"Let all the house of Israel therefore know assuredly that God has made Him both Lord and Christ, this Jesus whom you crucified."

Now when they heard this they were cut to the heart, and said to Peter and the rest of the apostles, "Brethren, what shall we do?" And Peter said to them, "Repent, and be baptized every one of you in the name of Jesus Christ for the forgiveness of yours sins; and you shall receive the gift of the Holy Spirit. For the promise is to you and to your children and to all that are far off, everyone whom the Lord our God calls to Him." And he testified with many other words and exhorted them, saying, "Save yourselves from this crooked generation." So those who received his word were baptized, and there were added that day about three thousand souls. And they devoted themselves to the apostles' teaching and fellowship, to the breaking of bread and the prayers.

—Acts 2:1-4; 14; 22b-24; 36-42. (RSV)

HOLY SPIRIT

153 Fill Me Now

And to know the love of Christ, . . . that ye might be filled . . .
— Ephesians 3:19

Elwood R. Stokes
FILL ME NOW
John R. Sweney

1. Hover o'er me, Holy Spirit, Bathe my trembling heart and brow;
   Fill me with Thy hallowed presence, Come, O come and fill me now.
2. Thou canst fill me, gracious Spirit, Though I cannot tell Thee how;
   But I need Thee, greatly need Thee, Come, O come and fill me now.
3. I am weakness, full of weakness, At Thy sacred feet I bow;
   Blest, divine, eternal Spirit, Fill with power, and fill me now.
4. Cleanse and comfort, bless and save me, Bathe, O bathe my heart and brow;
   Thou art comforting and saving, Thou art sweetly filling now.

Refrain:
Fill me now, fill me now, Jesus, come and fill me now;
Fill me with Thy hallowed presence—Come, O come and fill me now.

154 The Promise Fulfilled

We want to be as full of the Holy Spirit as the sea is full of water, as the sky is full of air, as the air is full of oxygen, as the continent is full of land, and as the fire is full of flame. His purpose is to animate our spirits for the doing of God's will, to calm our souls and claim our comfort and recall Christ's promises.

The Holy Spirit is the witness of God's Presence and Power for good. He is the rush of Heaven's wind, the fire of Divine communication, and He does not rest until He has revealed Christ as the Son of God, Redeemer of believing men and inseparable Companion of the committed soul. The Holy Spirit never fails. He is imperturbable in tribulation, indomitable in spiritual action and invincible in evangelism.

—Raymond Lindquist

HOLY SPIRIT

Spirit of the Living God

The Holy Spirit fell on us as on them in the beginning.
— Acts 11:15

Daniel Iverson

LIVING GOD
Daniel Iverson

155

Spir - it of the Liv - ing God, Fall a - fresh on me,

Spir - it of the Liv - ing God, Fall a - fresh on me.

Melt me, mold me, Fill me, use me.

Spir - it of the Liv - ing God, Fall a - fresh on me.

I Corinthians 2:10-16

156

The Spirit searches all things, even the deep things of God. For who among men knows the thoughts of a man except the man's spirit within him? In the same way no one knows the thoughts of God except the Spirit of God. We have not received the spirit of the world but the Spirit who is from God, that we may understand what God has freely given us. This is what we speak, not in words taught us by human wisdom but in words taught by the Spirit, expressing spiritual truths in spiritual words. The man without the Spirit does not accept the things that come from the Spirit of God, for they are foolishness to him, and he cannot understand them, because they are spiritually discerned. The spiritual man makes judgments about all things, but he himself is not subject to any man's judgment:

"For who has known the mind of the Lord that he may instruct him?" But we have the mind of Christ.

—(NIV)

HOLY SPIRIT

157 The Spirit of Jesus Is in This Place

Gloria Gaither
William J. Gaither

SPIRIT OF JESUS
William J. Gaither

O, the Spir-it of Je-sus is in this place,

I can see the change He's mak-ing on each face;

When the power of Heaven is tapped, then, some-thing good is bound to

hap-pen, for the Spir-it of Je-sus is in this place.

O my friend, He is so near that we could touch Him,

© Copyright 1972 by William J. Gaither. All rights reserved. Used by permission.

HOLY SPIRIT

His sweet pres-ence this old world could ne'er re - place;
Won't you let His Spir - it warm you, let His might - y love trans-form you, while the Spir - it of Je - sus is in this place.

The Outpouring of the Spirit 158

"After this I will pour out my spirit on all mankind.
Your sons and daughters shall prophesy,
    your old men shall dream dreams,
    and your young men see visions.
Even on the slaves, men and women, will I pour out my spirit in those days.
I will display portents in heaven and on earth,
    blood and fire
    and columns of smoke."
The sun will be turned into darkness, and the moon into blood,
    before the day of Jehovah dawns, that great and terrible day.
All who call on the name of Jehovah will be saved,
    for on Mount Zion there will be some who have escaped,
    as Jehovah has said,
    and in Jerusalem some survivors whom Jehovah will call.

—Joel 3:1-5 (JB)

159 Sweet, Sweet Spirit

I will not leave you comfortless; I will come to you. — John 14:18

Doris Akers

SWEET, SWEET SPIRIT
Doris Akers

1. There's a sweet, sweet Spir-it in this place, And I know that it's the Spir-it of the Lord; There are sweet ex-pres-sions on each face, And I know they feel the pres-ence of the Lord.
2. *There are bless-ings you can-not re-ceive 'Til you know Him in His full-ness and be-lieve; You're the one to prof-it when you say, "I am going to walk with Je-sus all the way."*
3. If you say He saved you from your sin, Now you're weak, you're bound and can-not en-ter in; You can make it right if you will yield— You'll en-joy the Ho-ly Spir-it that we feel.

Sweet Ho-ly Spir-it, Sweet heav-en-ly Dove, Stay right here with us, Fill-ing us with Your love; And for these

© Copyright 1962 by Manna Music, Inc. International copyright secured. All rights reserved. Used by permission.
HOLY SPIRIT

bless-ings   We   lift   our   hearts   in   praise: With-out a doubt we'll know

that we have been re-vived, When we shall leave this place.

Give Us Your Holy Spirit   160

Leader: Make us one, Lord, in our eagerness to speak good news and set all captives free.

People: *Give us Your Holy Spirit.*

Leader: Make us one, Lord, in concern for the poor, the hurt, and the downtrodden, to show them Your love.

People: *Give us Your Holy Spirit.*

Leader: Make us one, Lord, in worship, breaking bread together and singing Your praise with single voice.

People: *Give us Your Holy Spirit.*

Leader: Make us one, Lord, in faithfulness to Jesus Christ who never fails us, and who will come again in triumph.

People: *Give us Your Holy Spirit.*

Leader: Give us Your Holy Spirit, God our Father, so we may have among us the same mind that was in Christ Jesus; and proclaim Him to the world. May every knee bow down and every tongue confess Him Lord, to the glory of Your name.

People: *Amen.*

—Gary W. Demarest

161 Breathe On Me, Breath of God

Edwin Hatch
... that the love wherewith Thou hath loved me, may be in them, and I in them — John 17:26

TRENTHAM
Robert Jackson

1. Breathe on me, Breath of God, Fill me with life a-new,
That I may love what Thou dost love, And do what Thou wouldst do.
2. *Breathe on me, Breath of God, Un-til my heart is pure,*
Un-til with Thee I will one will To do and to en-dure.
3. Breathe on me, Breath of God, Till I am whol-ly Thine,
Un-til this earth-ly part of me Glows with Thy fire di-vine.
4. *Breathe on me, Breath of God, So shall I nev-er die,*
But live with Thee the per-fect life Of Thine e-ter-ni-ty. A-men.

162 Holy Ghost, With Light Divine

Andrew Reed
... ye do well that ye heed, as unto a light that shineth in a dark place ... — II Peter 1:19

MERCY
Louis M. Gottschalk
Adapted by Edwin P. Parker

1. Ho-ly Ghost, with light di-vine, Shine up-on this heart of mine;
Chase the shades of night a-way, Turn my dark-ness in-to day.
2. *Ho-ly Ghost, with power di-vine, Cleanse this guilt-y heart of mine;*
Long hath sin with-out con-trol Held do-min-ion o'er my soul.
3. Ho-ly Ghost, with joy di-vine, Cheer this sad-dened heart of mine;
Bid my man-y woes de-part, Heal my wound-ed, bleed-ing heart.
4. *Ho-ly Spir-it, all di-vine, Dwell with-in this heart of mine;*
Cast down ev-ery i-dol-throne, Reign su-preme and reign a-lone. A-men.

HOLY SPIRIT

Life in Two Ages 163

Our ascended Lord gives hope for two ages.
In the age to come, He is the judge, rejecting unrighteousness,
isolating His enemies to hell, blessing His new creation in Christ.
In this age, His Holy Spirit is with us, calling nations to follow Christ's path,
uniting people through Christ's love.

—*"Our song of hope"—a confessional of faith.*

Holy Spirit, Flow Through Me 164

Walt Mills

... But if ye through the Spirit do mortify the deeds of the body, ye shall live. — Romans 8:13

MILLS
Walt Mills

1 Ho - ly Spir - it, flow through me,
2 Ho - ly Spir - it, rest on me,
3 Ho - ly Spir - it, flow out from me,

1 Ho - ly Spir - it, flow through me, And
2 Ho - ly Spir - it, rest on me, And
3 Ho - ly Spir - it, flow out through me, That

1 make my life what it ought to be,
2 use me, Lord, win the lost to Thee,
3 oth - ers, Lord, may see You in me,

1 Ho - ly Spir - it, flow through me.
2 Ho - ly Spir - it, rest on me.
3 Ho - ly Spir - it, flow out through me.

© Copyright 1974 by Heart Warming Music. All rights reserved. Used by permission.

HOLY SPIRIT

165 Beginning

In the beginning was the Word:
the Word was with God
and the Word was God.

He was with God in the beginning.

Through Him all things came to be,
not one thing had its being but through Him.

All that came to be had life in Him
and that life was the light of men,
a light that shines in the dark,
a light that darkness could not overpower.

A man came, sent by God.

His name was John.

He came as a witness,
as a witness to speak for the light,
so that everyone might believe through him.

He was not the light,
only a witness to speak for the light.

The Word was the true light
that enlightens all men;
and He was coming into the world.

He was in the world
that had its being through Him,
and the world did not know Him.

He came to His own domain
and His own people did not accept Him.

But to all who did accept Him
He gave power to become children of God,
to all who believe in the name of Him
who was born not out of human stock
or urge of the flesh
or will of man
but of God Himself.

The Word was made flesh,
He lived among us,
and we saw His glory,
the glory that is His as the only Son of the Father,
full of grace and truth.

—John 1:1-14 (JB)

CHRISTMAS

Let All Mortal Flesh Keep Silence

Let all mortal flesh keep silent.
— Habakkuk 2:20

Liturgy of St. James
Tr. by Gerard Moultrie

PICARDY
French Carol

167 The Incarnation

The Son of God became a man to enable men to become sons of God.
—C. S. Lewis

168 Come, Thou Long-Expected Jesus

HYFRYDOL

And we declare unto you glad tidings how that the promise . . . God hath fulfilled. — Acts 13: 32,33

Charles Wesley   Rowland Hugh Prichard
Descant by Paul Sjolund

2 Come, Lord, born to deliver, Born a child, born a child and a King, born to reign, reign in us forever,

1 Come, Thou long-expected Jesus, Born to set Thy people free;
From our fears and sins release us;
Let us find our rest in Thee. Israel's

2 Born Thy people to deliver, Born a child and yet a King,
Born to reign in us forever,
Now Thy gracious Kingdom bring. By Thine

Now Thy gracious Kingdom bring. By Thy Spirit,

© Copyright 1976 by Paragon Associates, Inc. All rights reserved.

CHRISTMAS

2 Thine eternal Spirit Rule in all our hearts a-
1 Strength and Con-so-la-tion, Hope of all the earth Thou
2 own eternal Spirit Rule in all our hearts a-

lone; Al-le-lu-ia, Al-le-lu-ia, Al-le-lu-ia,
1 art; Dear Desire of every nation,
2 lone; By Thine all-sufficient merit

Al-le-lu-ia, to Thy glorious throne. A-men. A-men.
1 Joy of every longing heart.
2 Raise us to Thy glorious throne. A-men.

CHRISTMAS

169 O Come, O Come, Emmanuel

Behold, a virgin shall... bear a Son and shall call His name Immanuel.
— Isaiah 7:14

Latin: c. 9th Century
Tr. by John M. Neale, stanzas 1, 2, alt.
Tr. by Henry S. Coffin, stanzas 3, 4, alt.

VENI EMMANUEL
Adapted from Plainsong, Mode I
Thomas Helmore

1. O come, O come, Emmanuel, And ransom captive Israel, That mourns in lonely exile here, Until the Son of God appear. Rejoice! Rejoice! Emmanuel Shall come to thee, O Israel! Amen.

2. *O come, Thou Day-spring, come and cheer Our spirits by Thine advent here; Disperse the gloomy clouds of night, And death's dark shadows put to flight.*

3. *O come, Thou Wisdom from on high, And order all things, far and nigh; To us the path of knowledge show, And cause us in her ways to go.*

4. *O come, Desire of nations, bind In one the hearts of all mankind; Bid Thou our sad divisions cease, And be Thyself our King of peace.*

CHRISTMAS

Alternate Last Verse Harmonization Descant and Arrangement by Richard Purvis

Unison

4 O come, De-sire of na - tions, bind In one the hearts of all man-kind; Bid Thou our sad di - vi - sions cease, And be Thy-self our King of peace. Re - joice! Re - joice! Em-man - u - el Shall come to thee, O Is - ra - el! A - men!

Descant

Re-joice! Re-joice! Em-man-u-el Shall come to thee, O Is - ra - el! A - men!

© Copyright 1976 by Paragon Associates, Inc. All rights reserved.

CHRISTMAS

170 Thou Didst Leave Thy Throne

He came unto His own and His own received Him not.
— John 1:11

Emily E. S. Elliott

MARGARET
Timothy R. Matthews

1. Thou didst leave Thy throne and Thy king-ly crown When Thou cam-est to earth for me, But in Beth-le-hem's home there was found no room For Thy ho-ly na-tiv-i-ty. O come to my heart, Lord Je-sus: There is room in my heart for Thee!

2. Heav-en's arch-es rang when the an-gels sang, Pro-claim-ing Thy roy-al de-gree, But in low-ly birth didst Thou come to earth And in great hu-mil-i-ty. O come to my heart, Lord Je-sus: There is room in my heart for Thee!

3. The fox-es found rest, and the birds their nest In the shade of the for-est tree, But Thy couch was the sod, O Thou Son of God, In the des-erts of Gal-i-lee. O come to my heart, Lord Je-sus: There is room in my heart for Thee!

4. Thou cam-est, O Lord, with the liv-ing word That should set Thy peo-ple free, But with mock-ing scorn and with crown of thorn They bore Thee to Cal-va-ry. O come to my heart, Lord Je-sus: There is room in my heart for Thee!

5. When the heavens shall ring and the an-gels sing At Thy com-ing to vic-to-ry, Let Thy voice call me home, say-ing, "Yet there is room, There is room at my side for thee." And my heart shall re-joice, Lord Je-sus, When Thou com-est and call-est me. A-men.

CHRISTMAS

Joy to the World! 171

For unto you is born this day . . . a Savior. . . .
— Luke 2:11

Psalm 98
Adapted by Isaac Watts

ANTIOCH
George Friedrich Handel
Arranged by Fred Bock
and Ralph Carmichael

1. Joy to the world! the Lord is come: Let earth receive her King; Let every heart prepare Him room, And heaven and nature sing, And heaven and nature sing, And heaven, and heaven and nature sing.

2. Joy to the world! the Savior reigns: Let men their songs employ; While fields and floods, rocks, hills, and plains Repeat the sounding joy, Repeat the sounding joy, Repeat, repeat the sounding joy.

3. No more let sins and sorrows grow, Nor thorns infest the ground; He comes to make His blessings flow Far as the curse is found, Far as the curse is found, Far as, far as the curse is found.

4. He rules the world with truth and grace, And makes the nations prove The glories of His righteousness, And wonders of His love, And wonders of His love, And wonders, wonders of His love. A-men.

© Copyright 1976 by Lexicon Music, Inc. All rights reserved. Used by permission.

CHRISTMAS

172 Of the Father's Love Begotten

I am Alpha and Omega — the beginning and the end, which is, and which was, and which is to come.
— Revelation 1:8

Aurelius Clemens Prudentius
Tr. by John M. Neale, stanza 1
Tr. by Henry W. Baker, stanzas 2, 3

DIVINUM MYSTERIUM
13th Century Plainsong, Mode V

Unison

1. Of the Father's love begotten, Ere the worlds began to be,
   He is Alpha and Omega, He the source, the ending He,
   Of the things that are, that have been, And that future years shall see,
   Evermore and evermore!

2. O ye heights of heaven adore Him; Angel hosts, His praises sing;
   Powers, dominions, bow before Him, And extol our God and King;
   Let no tongue on earth be silent, Every voice in concert ring,
   Evermore and evermore!

3. Christ, to Thee with God the Father And, O Holy Ghost, to Thee,
   Hymn and chant and high thanksgiving And unwearied praises be.
   Honor, glory, and dominion, And eternal victory,
   Evermore and evermore! Amen.

CHRISTMAS

The Birth of Jesus

Now when Jesus was born in Bethlehem of Judea
in the days of Herod the king,
behold, wise men from the East came to Jerusalem, saying,
"Where is He who has been born king of the Jews?
For we have seen His star in the East,
and have come to worship Him."

When Herod the king heard this, he was troubled,
and all Jerusalem with him;
and assembling all the chief priests and scribes of the people,
he inquired of them where the Christ was to be born.

They told him, "In Bethlehem of Judea;
for so it is written by the prophet:
'And you, O Bethlehem, in the land of Judah,
are by no means least among the rulers of Judah,
for from you shall come a ruler who will govern my people Israel.' "

Then Herod summoned the wise men secretly
and ascertained from them what time the star appeared;
and he sent them to Bethlehem, saying,
"Go and search diligently for the child,
and when you have found Him bring me word,
that I too may come and worship Him."

When they had heard the king they went their way;
and lo, the star which they had seen in the East went before them,
'til it came to rest over the place where the child was.

When they saw the star, they rejoiced exceedingly with great joy;
and going into the house they saw the child with Mary His mother,
and they fell down and worshiped Him.

Then, opening their treasures, they offered Him gifts,
gold
frankincense
and myrrh.

And being warned in a dream not to return to Herod,
they departed to their own country by another way.

—Matthew 2:1-12 (RSV)

CHRISTMAS

174 Lo! How a Rose E'er Blooming

I am the rose of Sharon, the lily of the valley. — Song of Solomon 2:1

German Carol
Tr. by Theodore Baker, stanzas 1,2
Tr. by Harriet Krauth Spaeth, stanza 3

ES IST EIN ROS'
Geistliche Kirchengesäng
Harmonized by Michael Praetorius

1. Lo, how a rose e'er bloom-ing From ten-der stem hath sprung! Of Jes-se's lin-eage com-ing As men of old have sung. It came, a flow-er bright, A-mid the cold of win-ter, When half-gone was the night.

2. *I - sa-iah 'twas fore-told it, The rose I have in mind; With Mar-y we be-hold it, The vir-gin moth-er kind. To show God's love a - right She bore to men a Sav - ior, When half-gone was the night.*

3. This flower, whose fra-grance ten-der With sweet-ness fills the air, Dis - pels with glo-rious splen-dor The dark-ness ev - ery-where. True man, yet ver - y God, From sin and death He saves us And light-ens ev - ery load.

CHRISTMAS

While Shepherds Watched Their Flocks by Night

175

Nahum Tate

Fear not, for I bring you good tidings of great joy. — Luke 2:10

CHRISTMAS
Arranged from George Friedrich Handel

1. While shepherds watched their flocks by night, All seated on the ground, The angel of the Lord came down, And glory shone around, And glory shone around.
2. "Fear not!" said he, for mighty dread Had seized their troubled mind; "Glad tidings of great joy I bring To you and all mankind, To you and all mankind.
3. "To you in David's town this day Is born, of David's line, The Savior, who is Christ the Lord, And this shall be the sign— And this shall be the sign:
4. "The heavenly Babe you there shall find To human view displayed, All meanly wrapt in swathing-bands And in a manger laid, And in a manger laid.
5. "All glory be to God on high, And to the earth be peace: Good will henceforth from heaven to men Begin and never cease! Begin and never cease!"

Luke 1:46b-55

176

"My soul magnifies the Lord, and my spirit rejoices in God my Savior, for He has regarded the low estate of His handmaiden. For behold, henceforth all generations will call me blessed; for He who is mighty has done great things for me, and holy is His name. And His mercy is on those who fear Him from generation to generation. He has shown strength with His arm, He has scattered the proud in the imagination of their hearts, He has put down the mighty from their thrones, and exalted those of low degree; He has filled the hungry with good things, and the rich He has sent empty away. He has helped His servant Israel, in remembrance of His mercy, as He spoke to our fathers, to Abraham and to his posterity for ever."

—(RSV)

177 Good Christian Men, Rejoice

When they saw the star they rejoiced. — Matthew 2:10

Latin Carol
Tr. by John M. Neale

IN DULCI JUBILO
German Melody

1. Good Christian men, rejoice With heart and soul and voice;
Give ye heed to what we say: News! news! Jesus Christ is born today!
Ox and ass before Him bow, And He is in the manger now.
Christ is born today! Christ is born today!

2. *Good Christian men, rejoice With heart and soul and voice;*
Now ye hear of endless bliss: Joy! joy! Jesus Christ was born for this!
He has opened heaven's door, And man is blessed evermore.
Christ was born for this! Christ was born for this!

3. Good Christian men, rejoice With heart and soul and voice;
Now ye need not fear the grave: Peace! peace! Jesus Christ was born to save!
Calls you one and calls you all To gain His everlasting hall.
Christ was born to save! Christ was born to save!

CHRISTMAS

O Little Town of Bethlehem

178

But thou, Bethlehem, out of thee shall come He forth . . . a ruler in Israel. — Micah 5:2

Phillips Brooks

ST. LOUIS
Lewis H. Redner

1. O little town of Bethlehem, How still we see thee lie!
2. *For Christ is born of Mary, And gathered all above,*
3. How silently, how silently, The wondrous gift is given!
4. *O holy Child of Bethlehem! Descend to us, we pray;*

1. Above thy deep and dreamless sleep The silent stars go by;
2. *While mortals sleep, the angels keep Their watch of wondering love.*
3. So God imparts to human hearts The blessings of His heaven.
4. *Cast out our sin and enter in, Be born in us today.*

1. Yet in thy dark streets shineth The everlasting Light:
2. *O morning stars, together Proclaim the holy birth!*
3. No ear may hear His coming, But in this world of sin,
4. *We hear the Christmas angels The great glad tidings tell;*

1. The hopes and fears of all the years Are met in thee tonight.
2. *And praises sing to God the King, And peace to men on earth.*
3. Where meek souls will receive Him still, The dear Christ enters in.
4. *O come to us, abide with us, Our Lord Emmanuel!* A-men.

CHRISTMAS

179 The First Noel

And there were in that same country, Shepherds . . . in the field . . . .
— Luke 2:8

English Carol

THE FIRST NOEL
English Melody
From Sandys' *Christmas Carols*

1. The first no-el the an-gel did say Was to cer-tain poor shep-herds in fields as they lay— In fields where they lay keep-ing their sheep, On a cold win-ter's night that was so deep.
2. *They look-ed up and saw a star Shin-ing in the east, be-yond them far; And to the earth it gave great light, And so it con-tin-ued both day and night.*
3. And by the light of that same star, Three wise men came from coun-try far; To seek for a king was their in-tent, And to fol-low the star wher-ev-er it went.
4. *This star drew nigh to the north-west, O-ver Beth-le-hem it took its rest; And there it did both stop and stay, Right o-ver the place where Je-sus lay.*
5. Then en-tered in those wise men three, Full rev-erent-ly up-on their knee, And of-fered there, in His pres-ence, Their gold and myrrh and frank-in-cense.
6. *Then let us all with one ac-cord Sing prais-es to our heaven-ly Lord, That hath made heaven and earth of naught, And with His blood man-kind hath bought.*

No-el, no-el! No-el, no-el! Born is the King of Is-ra-el!

CHRISTMAS

Alternate Last Verse Harmonization

Descant and arrangement by Jan Sanborn

180 What Child Is This, Who, Laid to Rest?

... What manner of child shall this be? — Luke 1:66

William C. Dix

GREENSLEEVES
English Melody
Harmonized by John Stainer

1. What child is this, who, laid to rest, On Mary's lap is sleeping?
Whom angels greet with anthems sweet, While shepherds watch are keeping?
This, this is Christ the King, Whom shepherds guard and angels sing:
Haste, haste to bring Him laud, The Babe, the son of Mary.

2. *Why lies He in such mean estate Where ox and ass are feeding?*
Good Christian, fear: for sinners here The silent Word is pleading.
This, this is Christ the King, Whom shepherds guard and angels sing:
Haste, haste to bring Him laud, The Babe, the son of Mary.

3. So bring Him incense, gold, and myrrh, Come peasant, king, to own Him;
The King of kings salvation brings, Let loving hearts enthrone Him.
This, this is Christ the King, Whom shepherds guard and angels sing:
Haste, haste to bring Him laud, The Babe, the son of Mary.

CHRISTMAS

Some Children See Him

181

Blessed are the pure in heart for they shall see God. — Matthew 5:8

Wihla Hutson

SOME CHILDREN
Alfred S. Burt

1. Some children see Him lil-y white, The ba-by Je-sus born this night,
2. *Some children see Him al-mond-eyed, This Sav-ior whom we kneel be-side,*
3. The children in each dif-ferent place Will see the ba-by Je-sus' face

1. Some children see Him lil-y white, With tress-es soft and fair.
2. *Some children see Him al-mond-eyed, With skin of yel-low hue.*
3. Like theirs, but bright with heaven-ly grace, And filled with ho-ly light.

1. Some children see Him bronzed and brown, The Lord of heaven to earth come down;
2. *Some children see Him dark as they, Sweet Mary's Son, to whom we pray;*
3. O lay a-side each earth-ly thing, And with thy heart as of-fer-ing,

1. Some children see Him bronzed and brown, With dark and heav-y hair.
2. *Some children see Him dark as they, And ah! they love Him, too!*
3. Come wor-ship now the in-fant King, 'Tis love that's born to-night!

© Copyright 1954, 1957 by Hollis Music, Inc. International copyright secured. All rights reserved. Used by permission.
Choral arrangements of this selection available from Shawnee Press, Inc., Delaware Water Gap, PA 18327.

CHRISTMAS

182 How Great Our Joy!

Therefore with joy shall they draw water out of the wells of salvation.... — Isaiah 12:3

German Carol

JUNGST
German Melody
Arranged by Hugo Jungst

1. While by the sheep we watched at night, Glad tidings brought an angel bright. How great our joy! Great our joy! Joy, joy, joy! Joy, joy, joy! Praise we the Lord in heaven on high! Praise we the Lord in heaven on high!
2. *There shall be born, so he did say, In Bethlehem a Child today.* How great our joy! Great our joy! Joy, joy, joy! Joy, joy, joy! Praise we the Lord in heaven on high! Praise we the Lord in heaven on high!
3. There shall the Child lie in a stall, This Child who shall redeem us all. How great our joy! Great our joy! Joy, joy, joy! Joy, joy, joy! Praise we the Lord in heaven on high! Praise we the Lord in heaven on high!
4. *This gift of God we'll cherish well, That ever joy our hearts shall fill.* How great our joy! Great our joy! Joy, joy, joy! Joy, joy, joy! Praise we the Lord in heaven on high! Praise we the Lord in heaven on high!

CHRISTMAS

I Wonder As I Wander 183

*As He spake by His Holy Prophets
which have been since the world began.*
— Luke 1:70

Appalachian carol
Collected by John Jacob Niles

I WONDER
Appalachian Folksong
Adapted by John Jacob Niles
Arranged by Fred Bock

1. I wonder as I wander out under the sky, How Jesus, the Savior, did come for to die. For poor, ornery people like you and like I— I wonder as I wander, Out under the sky.
2. When Mary birthed Jesus, 'twas in a cows' stall, With wise-men and farmers and shepherds and all. But high from God's heaven a star's light did fall, And the promise of ages It then did recall.
3. If Jesus had wanted for any wee thing: A star in the sky, or a bird on the wing; Or all of God's angels in heaven to sing, He surely could have had it, 'Cause He was the King!
4. I wonder as I wander out under the sky, How Jesus, the Savior did come for to die. For poor, ornery people like you and like I— I wonder as I wander, Out under the sky.

© Copyright 1934, 1944 by G. Schirmer, Inc. This arrangement © Copyright 1976 by G. Schirmer, Inc. All rights reserved. Used by permission.

CHRISTMAS

184 Hark! the Herald Angels Sing

And suddenly there was with the Angel a multitude of the Heavenly Host praising God. . . .
— Luke 2:13

Charles Wesley

MENDELSSOHN
Felix Mendelssohn
Descant by Paul Liljestrand

Descant
3 All hail the Sun of Right-eous-ness!

1 Hark! the her-ald an-gels sing, "Glo-ry to the new-born King:
2 Christ, by high-est heaven a-dored; Christ, the ev-er-last-ing Lord!
3 Hail the heaven-born Prince of Peace! Hail the Sun of Right-eous-ness!

He is risen with heal-ing

1 Peace on earth, and mer-cy mild, God and sin-ners
2 Late in time be-hold Him come, Off-spring of the
3 Light and life to all He brings, Risen with heal-ing

in His wings. His glo-ry by, No

1 rec-on-ciled!" Joy-ful, all ye na-tions, rise, Join the tri-umph
2 Vir-gin's womb. Veiled in flesh the God-head see; Hail th' in-car-nate
3 in His wings. Mild He lays His glo-ry by, Born that man no

© Copyright 1976 by Paragon Associates, Inc. All rights reserved.
CHRISTMAS

CHRISTMAS

185 Away in a Manger

Source unknown, stanzas 1, 2
John Thomas McFarland, stanza 3

... there was no room for them in the inn.
— Luke 2:7

AWAY IN A MANGER
James R. Murray

(FIRST TUNE)

1. A-way in a manger, no crib for a bed, The little Lord Jesus laid down His sweet head. The stars in the sky all looked down where He lay, The little Lord Jesus, asleep on the hay.
2. The cattle are lowing, the baby awakes, The little Lord Jesus, no crying He makes. I love Thee, Lord Jesus! Look down from the sky, And stay by my side until morning is nigh.
3. Be near me, Lord Jesus! I ask Thee to stay Close by me forever, and love me, I pray. Bless all the dear children in Thy tender care, And fit us for heaven, to live with Thee there.

186 Luke 2:1-12

At that time Emperor Augustus sent out an order for all the citizens of the Empire to register themselves for the census. When this first census took place, Quirinius was the governor of Syria. Everyone went to register himself, each to his own town.

Joseph went from the town of Nazareth, in Galilee, to Judea, to the town named Bethlehem, where King David was born. Joseph went there because he was a descendant of David. He went to register himself with Mary, who was promised in marriage to him. She was pregnant, and while they were in Bethlehem, the time came for her to have her baby. She gave birth to her first son, wrapped Him in cloths and laid Him in a manger—there was no room for them to stay in the inn.

There were some shepherds in that part of the country who were spending the night in the fields, taking care of their flocks. An angel of the Lord appeared to them, and the glory of the Lord shone over them. They were terribly afraid, but the angel said to them, "Don't be afraid! I am here with good news for you, which will bring great joy to all the people. This very day in David's town your Savior was born—Christ the Lord! What will prove it to you is this: you will find a baby wrapped in cloths and lying in a manger."

— (TEV)

CHRISTMAS

Away in a Manger 187

"Ye shall find the babe ... lying in a manger." — Luke 2:12

Source unknown, stanzas 1, 2
John Thomas McFarland, stanza 3

(SECOND TUNE)

CRADLE SONG
William J. Kirkpatrick

1. A-way in a man-ger, no crib for a bed, The lit-tle Lord Je-sus laid down His sweet head. The stars in the bright sky looked down where He lay, The lit-tle Lord Je-sus, a-sleep on the hay.
2. The cat-tle are low-ing, the ba-by a-wakes, But lit-tle Lord Je-sus, no cry-ing He makes. I love Thee, Lord Je-sus! Look down from the sky, And stay by my side un-til morn-ing is nigh.
3. Be near me, Lord Je-sus! I ask Thee to stay Close by me for-ev-er, and love me, I pray. Bless all the dear chil-dren in Thy ten-der care, And fit us for heav-en, to live with Thee there.

Christmas 188

We yearn, our Father, for the simple beauty of Christmas—for all the old familiar melodies and words that remind us of that great miracle when He who had made all things was one night to come as a Babe, to lie in the crook of a woman's arm.

Before such mystery we kneel, as we follow the Shepherds and Wise Men to bring Thee the gift of our love—a love we confess that has not always been as warm or sincere or real as it should have been. But now, on this Christmas Day, that love would find its Beloved, and from Thee receive the grace to make it pure again, warm and real.

We bring Thee our gratitude for every token of Thy love.

—*Peter Marshall*

CHRISTMAS

189 How Proper It Is

How proper it is that Christmas should follow Advent.
—For him who looks toward the future, the Manger is situated on Golgotha,
and the Cross has already been raised in Bethlehem.

—Dag Hammarskjöld

190 Angels from the Realms of Glory

... We have come to worship Him. — Matthew 2:2

James Montgomery

REGENT SQUARE
Henry T. Smart

1 An - gels, from the realms of glo - ry, Wing your flight o'er all the earth;
2 Shep - herds, in the fields a - bid - ing, Watch - ing o'er your flocks by night,
3 Wise men, leave your con - tem - pla - tion, Bright - er vi - sions beam a - far;
4 Saints be - fore the al - tar bend - ing, Watch - ing long in hope and fear,

1 Ye who sang cre - a - tion's sto - ry, Now pro - claim Mes - si - ah's birth:
2 God with man is now re - sid - ing, Yon - der shines the in - fant light:
3 Seek the great De - sire of na - tions, Ye have seen His na - tal star:
4 Sud - den - ly the Lord, de - scend - ing, In His tem - ple shall ap - pear:

Come and wor - ship, come and wor - ship, Wor - ship Christ, the new - born King. A - men.

CHRISTMAS

Alternate Last Verse Harmonization   *Arranged by Fred Bock*

4. Saints be-fore the al-tar bend-ing, Watch-ing long in hope and fear,
Sud-den-ly the Lord, de-scend-ing, In His tem-ple shall ap-pear:
Come and wor-ship, come and wor-ship, Wor-ship Christ, the new-born King. A-men.

© Copyright 1968 by Fred Bock Music Company. All rights reserved. Used by permission.

Luke 1:68-79   191

"Blessed be the Lord God of Israel, for He has visited and redeemed His people, and has raised up a horn of salvation for us in the house of His servant David, as He spoke by the mouth of His holy prophets from of old, that we should be saved from our enemies, and from the hand of all who hate us; to perform the mercy promised to our fathers, and to remember His holy covenant, the oath which He swore to our father Abraham, to grant us that we, being delivered from the hand of our enemies, might serve Him without fear, in holiness and righteousness before Him all the days of our life. And you, child, will be called the prophet of the Most High; for You will go before the Lord to prepare His ways, to give knowledge of salvation to His people in the forgiveness of their sins, through the tender mercy of our God, when the day shall dawn upon us from on high to give light to those who sit in darkness and in the shadow of death, to guide our feet into the way of peace."

—(RSV)

CHRISTMAS

192 Angels We Have Heard On High

... Glory to God in the highest. — Luke 2:14

French Carol

GLORIA
French Carol

1. Angels we have heard on high Sweetly singing o'er the plains,
And the mountains in reply Echo back their joyous strains.
2. *Shepherds, why this jubilee? Why your joyous strains prolong?*
Say what may the tidings be, Which inspire your heavenly song?
3. Come to Bethlehem and see Him whose birth the angels sing;
Come adore, on bended knee, Christ, the Lord, the newborn King.

Gloria in excelsis Deo, Gloria in excelsis Deo.

CHRISTMAS

O Come, All Ye Faithful

193

Let us go even unto Bethlehem. — Luke 2:15

Latin: John F. Wade
Tr. by Frederick Oakeley

ADESTE FIDELES
John F. Wade's *Cantus Diversi*
Descant by Fred Bock

1. O come, all ye faithful, joyful and triumphant, O come ye, O come ye to Bethlehem; Come and behold Him, born the King of angels;
2. *Sing, choirs of angels, sing in exultation, O sing, all ye citizens of heaven above; Glory to God, all glory in the highest;*
3. Yea, Lord, we greet Thee, born this happy morning, O Jesus, to Thee be all glory given; Word of the Father, now in flesh appearing;

Descant
O come, O come,

O come, let us adore Him, O come, let us adore Him,

O come, let us adore Him, Christ, the Lord. A-men.

O come, let us adore Him, Christ, the Lord. A-men.

© Copyright 1976 by Fred Bock Music Company. All rights reserved. Used by permission.

CHRISTMAS

194 Infant Holy, Infant Lowly

For He is Lord of lords, and King of kings...
and they that are with Him are called, chosen, and faithful.
— Revelation 17:14

Paraphrase by Edith M. G. Reed

W ZLOBIE LEZY
Polish Carol

1. In-fant ho-ly, in-fant low-ly, for His bed a cat-tle stall;
Ox-en low-ing, lit-tle know-ing Christ, the babe, is Lord of all.
Swift are wing-ing an-gels sing-ing, no-els ring-ing,
tid-ings bring-ing: Christ the babe is Lord of all.

2. *Flocks were sleep-ing: shep-herds keep-ing vig-il till the morn-ing new*
Saw the glo-ry, heard the sto-ry, ti-dings of a gos-pel true.
Thus re-joic-ing, free from sor-row, Prais-es voic-ing
greet the mor-row: Christ the babe was born for you.

Taken with permission from the "Kingsway Carol Book". Published by Evans Brothers, London.

CHRISTMAS

Silent Night, Holy Night 195

Joseph Mohr
Tr. by John F. Young

And they . . . found Mary and Joseph, and the baby . . . .
— Luke 2:16

STILLE NACHT
Franz Gruber

1. Si - lent night, ho - ly night, All is calm, all is bright
2. *Si - lent night, ho - ly night, Shep-herds quake at the sight.*
3. Si - lent night, ho - ly night, Son of God, love's pure light

1. Round yon vir - gin moth-er and child. Ho - ly in-fant so ten-der and mild,
2. *Glo - ries stream from heav-en a - far, Heaven-ly hosts sing al - le - lu - ia;*
3. Ra - diant beams from Thy ho - ly face, With the dawn of re - deem - ing grace,

1. Sleep in heav - en - ly peace, Sleep in heav - en - ly peace.
2. *Christ the Sav - ior, is born! Christ, the Sav - ior, is born!*
3. Je - sus, Lord, at Thy birth, Je - sus, Lord, at Thy birth.

For Unto Us 196

For unto us a Child is born, unto us a Son is given:
> *and the government shall be upon His shoulder:*

and His name shall be called Wonderful, Counsellor, The mighty God,
The everlasting Father, The Prince of Peace.
> *Of the increase of His government and peace there shall be no end, upon the throne of David, and upon His kingdom, to order it, and to establish it with judgment and with justice from henceforth even for ever.*

With righteousness shall He judge the poor,
and reprove with equity for the meek of the earth:
> *and He shall smite the earth with the rod of His mouth, and with the breath of His lips shall He slay the wicked.*

—Isaiah 9:6-7; 11:4 (KJV)

197 It Came upon the Midnight Clear

Through the tender mercies of our God . . . the dayspring from on high hath visited us. — Luke 1:78

Edmund H. Sears

CAROL
Richard S. Willis

1 It came up-on the mid-night clear, That glo-rious song of old,
2 *And ye, be-neath life's crush-ing load, Whose forms are bend-ing low,*
3 For lo, the days are has-tening on, By proph-et seen of old,

1 From an-gels bend-ing near the earth To touch their harps of gold:
2 *Who toil a-long the climb-ing way With pain-ful steps and slow,*
3 When, with the ev-er-cir-cling years, Shall come the time fore-told,

1 "Peace on the earth, good-will to men, From heaven's all-gra-cious King":
2 *Look now! for glad and gold-en hours Come swift-ly on the wing:*
3 When the new heaven and earth shall own The Prince of Peace their King,

1 The world in sol-emn still-ness lay To hear the an-gels sing.
2 *O rest be-side the wea-ry load, And hear the an-gels sing.*
3 And the whole world send back the song Which now the an-gels sing.

CHRISTMAS

Child in the Manger

198

And this shall be a sign unto you; you shall find the child . . . lying in a manger. — Luke 2:12

Mary MacDonald
Fred Bock

BUNESSAN
Traditional Gaelic Melody
Arranged by Fred Bock

1. Child in the manger, Infant of Mary,
Came as a stranger born in the stall;
Sweet little Jesus sent down from heaven,
God's gift of new life offered to all.

2. Prophets foretold Him, Infant of wonder,
Angels behold Him there on His throne;
Worthy the Savior of all our praises,
Happy and ever blest are His own. Amen.

© Copyright 1974, 1976 by Fred Bock Music Company. All rights reserved. Used by permission.

CHRISTMAS

199 Redeeming Love

Surely He hath borne our griefs and carried our sorrows. — Isaiah 53:4

REDEEMING LOVE
William J. Gaither
Adapted by Ronn Huff

Gloria Gaither

1. From God's heav-en to a man-ger, From great rich-es to the poor, Came the ho-ly Son of God, a lit-tle Child; From the a-zure halls of heav-en To a low-ly man-ger stall, Je-sus came, and here He gave His life for all.

2. From a lov-ing heaven-ly Fa-ther, To a world that knew Him not, Came a man of sor-rows, Je-sus Christ, the Lord; In my wan-dering Je-sus found me, Touched my life with His great love, And this Babe has grown to be my sov-ereign Lord.

Re-deem-ing love, a love that knows no lim-it; Re-deem-ing

© Copyright 1963, 1976 by William J. Gaither. All rights reserved. Used by permission.
CHRISTMAS

love, a love that nev-er dies; My soul shall sing through-out the end-less a - ges The ad-o-ra-tion of this great love on high.

His Love......Reaching   200

Right from the beginning God's love has reached, and from the beginning man has refused to understand. But love went on reaching, offering itself. Love offered the eternal . . . we wanted the immediate. Love offered deep joy . . . we wanted thrills. Love offered freedom . . . we wanted license. Love offered communion with God Himself . . . we wanted to worship at the shrine of our own minds. Love offered peace . . . we wanted approval for our wars. Even yet, love went on reaching. And still today, after two thousand years, patiently, lovingly, Christ is reaching out to us today. Right through the chaos of our world, through the confusion of our minds. He is reaching . . . longing to share with us . . . the very being of God.

His love still is longing, His love still is reaching, right past the shackles of my mind. And the Word of the Father became Mary's little Son. And His love reached all the way to where I was.

–Gloria Gaither

CHRISTMAS

201 The Star Carol

When they saw the star, they rejoiced... — Matthew 2:10

Wihla Hutson

STAR CAROL
Alfred S. Burt

1. Long years a-go on a deep win-ter night,
High in the heavens a star shone bright,
While in a man-ger a wee Ba-by lay,
Sweet-ly a-sleep on a bed of hay.

2. *Je-sus, the Lord, was that Ba-by so small,
Laid down to sleep in a hum-ble stall;
Then came the star and it stood o-ver-head,
Shed-ding its light 'round His lit-tle bed.*

3. Dear Ba-by Je-sus, How ti-ny Thou art,
I'll make a place for Thee in my heart,
And when the stars in the heav-ens I see,
Ev-er and al-ways I think of Thee.

© Copyright 1954, 1957 by Hollis Music, Inc. International copyright secured. All rights reserved. Choral arrangements available from Shawnee Press, Inc., Delaware Water Gap, PA 18327. Used by permission.

CHRISTMAS

As with Gladness Men of Old

202

And they sang praises with gladness and bowed their heads and worshipped.
— II Chronicles 29:30

William C. Dix

DIX
Conrad Kocher

1. As with gladness men of old Did the guiding star behold, As with joy they hailed its light, Leading onward, beaming bright, So, most gracious Lord, may we Evermore be led to Thee.

2. As with joyful steps they sped To that lowly manger bed, There to bend the knee before Him whom heaven and earth adore, So, may we with willing feet Ever seek the mercy seat.

3. As they offered gifts most rare At that manger rude and bare, So may we with holy joy, Pure and free from sin's alloy, All our costliest treasures bring, Christ, to Thee, our heavenly King.

4. Holy Jesus, every day Keep us in the narrow way; And when earthly things are past, Bring our ransomed souls at last Where they need no star to guide, Where no clouds Thy glory hide. A-men.

CHRISTMAS

203 All My Heart Today Rejoices

When they saw the star they rejoiced with exceeding great joy. — Matthew 2:10

Paul Gerhardt
Tr. by Catherine Winkworth

WARUM SOLLT ICH
Johann G. Ebeling

1. All my heart to-day re-joic-es As I hear, Far and near,
Sweet-est an-gel voic-es. "Christ is born," their choirs are sing-ing,
'Til the air Ev-ery-where Now with joy is ring-ing.

2. Hark! a voice from yon-der man-ger, Soft and sweet, Doth en-treat:
"Flee from woe and dan-ger! Breth-ren, come! from all that grieves you,
You are freed— All you need I will sure-ly give you."

3. Come, then, let us has-ten yon-der! Here let all, Great and small,
Kneel in awe and won-der! Love Him who with love is yearn-ing!
Hail the star That from far Bright with hope is burn-ing!

204 Peace on Earth

This is God's Christmas greeting.
In the beautiful story of Jesus' birth,
  it was sung by a chorus of angelic voices.
Heard at first only by Judean shepherds outside the town of Bethlehem,
  nevertheless, it is a message that the whole world should hear.
  On each Christmas Day,
    God repeats His greeting.

—Anonymous

CHRISTMAS

Go, Tell It on the Mountains 205

They made known abroad the saying . . . concerning this child.
— Luke 2:17

Traditional

GO TELL IT ON THE MOUNTAINS
American Folk Song

Unison

Go, tell it on the moun-tains, O-ver the hills and ev-ery-where;

Go, tell it on the moun-tains That Je-sus Christ is born!

Fine

Harmony

1 While shep-herds kept their watch-ing O'er si-lent flocks by night, Be-
2 *The shep-herds feared and trem-bled When lo! A-bove the earth Rang*
3 Down in a low-ly man-ger The hum-ble Christ was born, And

1 hold through-out the heav-ens There shone a ho-ly light.
2 *out the an-gel cho-rus That hailed our Sav-ior's birth.*
3 brought us God's sal-va-tion That bless-ed Christ-mas morn.

D.C.

CHRISTMAS

206 We Three Kings of Orient Are

*Now when Jesus was born in Bethlehem
... there came wise men from the East....* — Matthew 2:1

John H. Hopkins, Jr.

KINGS OF ORIENT
John H. Hopkins, Jr.

1. We three kings of O-ri-ent are, Bear-ing gifts we trav-erse a-far
2. Born a King on Beth-le-hem's plain, Gold I bring to crown Him a-gain,
3. Frank-in-cense to of-fer have I, In-cense owns a De-i-ty nigh;
4. Myrrh is mine, its bit-ter per-fume Breathes a life of gath-er-ing gloom:
5. Glo-rious now be-hold Him a-rise, King and God and Sac-ri-fice;

1. Field and foun-tain, moor and moun-tain, Fol-low-ing yon-der star.
2. King for-ev-er, ceas-ing nev-er O-ver us all to reign.
3. Prayer and prais-ing all men rais-ing, Wor-ship Him, God on high.
4. Sor-row-ing, sigh-ing, bleed-ing, dy-ing, Sealed in the stone-cold tomb.
5. Al-le-lu-ia, Al-le-lu-ia! Sounds thru the earth and skies.

O star of won-der, star of night, Star with roy-al beau-ty bright,

West-ward lead-ing, still pro-ceed-ing, Guide us to Thy per-fect light. A-men.

CHRISTMAS

Break Forth, O Beauteous Heavenly Light 207

Johann Rist
Tr. by John Troutbeck, stanza 1
Norman E. Johnson, stanza 2

*For He is our peace who hath . . .
broken down the middle wall
of partition between us.* — Ephesians 2:14

ERMUNTRE DICH
Johann Schop
Harmonized by J. S. Bach

1. Break forth, O beauteous heavenly light, And usher in the morning; Ye shepherds, shrink not with affright, But hear the angel's warning. This Child, now weak in infancy, Our confidence and joy shall be, The power of Satan breaking, Our peace eternal making.

2. Break forth, O beauteous heavenly light, To herald our salvation; He stoops to earth— the God of might, Our hope and expectation. He comes in human flesh to dwell, Our God with us, Immanuel, The night of darkness ending, Our fallen race befriending.

Second stanza Copyright 1973 by Covenant Press. Used by permission.

CHRISTMAS

208 O Sing a Song

To this end was I born, and for this cause came I into the world. — John 18:37

Louis F. Benson

KINGSFOLD
Melody collected by Lucy Broadman
Arranged by Ralph Vaughan Williams

1. O sing a song of Beth-le-hem, Of shep-herds watch-ing there,
2. *O sing a song of Naz-a-reth, Of sun-ny days of joy,*
3. O sing a song of Gal-i-lee, Of lake and woods and hill,
4. *O sing a song of Cal-va-ry, Its glo-ry and dis-may,*

1. And of the news that came to them From an-gels in the air:
2. *O sing of fra-grant flow-ers' breath, And of the sin-less Boy:*
3. Of Him who walked up-on the sea And bade the waves be still:
4. *Of Him who hung up-on the tree, And took our sins a-way:*

1. The light that shone on Beth-le-hem Fills all the world to-day;
2. *For now the flowers of Naz-a-reth In ev-ery heart may grow;*
3. For though like waves on Gal-i-lee, Dark seas of trou-ble roll,
4. *For He who died on Cal-va-ry Is ris-en from the grave,*

1. Of Je-sus' birth and peace on earth The an-gels sing al-way.
2. *Now spreads the fame of His dear name On all the winds that blow.*
3. When faith has heard the Mas-ter's word, Falls peace up-on the soul.
4. *And Christ, our Lord, by heaven a-dored, Is might-y now to save.* A-men.

Music from "The English Hymnal", by permission of Oxford University Press.

THE LIFE AND MINISTRY OF JESUS CHRIST

God's Nature

If you have any encouragement
from being united with Christ,
if any comfort from His love,
if any fellowship with the Spirit,
if any tenderness and compassion,
then make my joy complete
by being like-minded,
having the same love,
being one in spirit and purpose.

Do nothing out of selfish ambition or vain conceit,
but in humility
consider others better than yourselves.

Each of you should look not only to your own interests,
but also to the interests of others.

Your attitude should be the same as that of Christ Jesus:

Who, being in very nature God,
did not consider equality with God
something to be grasped,
but made Himself nothing, taking the very
nature of a servant,
being made in human likeness.
And being found in appearance as a man, He
humbled Himself
and became obedient to death—
even death on a cross!
Therefore God exalted Him to the highest place
and gave Him the name that is above every name,
that at the name of Jesus every knee should bow,
in heaven and on earth and under the earth,
and every tongue confess that Jesus Christ is Lord,
to the glory of God the Father.

—Philippians 2:1-11 (NIV)

210 I Cannot Tell

The righteous shall be glad in the Lord, and shall trust in Him . . . — Psalm 64:10

W. Y. Fullerton

LONDONDERRY AIR
Traditional Irish Melody

1. I cannot tell why He, whom angels worship Should set His love upon the sons of men, Or why, as Shepherd, He should seek the wanderers To bring them back, they know not how or when. But this I know, that He was born of Mary When Bethlehem's

2. I cannot tell how silently He suffered As with His peace He graced this place of tears, Or how His heart upon the cross was broken, The crown of pain to three and thirty years. But this I know, He heals the broken hearted And stays our

3. I cannot tell how He will win the nations, How He will claim His earthly heritage, Or satisfy the needs and aspirations Of east and west, of sinner and of sage. But this I know, all flesh shall see His glory, And He shall

4. I cannot tell how all the lands shall worship When at His bidding every storm is stilled, Or who can say how great the jubilation When all the hearts of men with love are filled. But this I know, the skies will thrill with rapture, And countless

Words used by permission of Carey Kingsgate Press, Ltd.

THE LIFE AND MINISTRY OF JESUS CHRIST

1. man-ger was His on-ly home, And that He lived at Naz-a-reth and la-bored, And so the Sav-ior, Sav-ior of the world, is come.
2. *sin and calms our lurk-ing fear, And lifts the bur-den from the heav-y la-den, For yet the Sav-ior, Sav-ior of the world, is here.*
3. *reap the har-vest He has sown, And some glad day His sun will shine in splen-dor When He the Sav-ior, Sav-ior of the world, is known.*
4. *voic-es then will join to sing, And earth to heaven, and heaven to earth will an-swer: "At last the Sav-ior, Sav-ior of the world, is King!"*

Jesus and the Children — 211

Leader: *And they brought young children to Him, that He should touch them: and His disciples rebuked those that brought them.*

People: But when Jesus saw it, He was much displeased, and said unto them, Suffer the little children to come unto Me, and forbid them not: for of such is the kingdom of God.

Leader: *Verily I say unto you, Whosoever shall not receive the kingdom of God as a little child, he shall not enter therein.*

People: And He took them up in His arms, put His hands upon them, and blessed them.[1]

Leader: *And He took a child, and set him in the midst of them: and when He had taken him in His arms, He said unto them, Whosoever shall receive one of such children in My name, receiveth Me: and whosoever shall receive Me, receiveth not Me, but Him that sent Me.*[2]

People: Verily I say unto you, Except ye be converted, and become as little children, ye shall not enter the kingdom of heaven.

Leader: *Whosoever therefore shall humble himself as this little child, the same is greatest in the kingdom of heaven.*

People: And whoso shall receive one such little child in My name, receiveth Me.[3]

1. Mark 10:14-16
2. Mark 9:35-37
3. Matthew 18:3-6 (KJV)

212 Tell Me the Stories of Jesus

. . . I count all things but loss for the excellency of the knowledge of Christ Jesus. . . . —Philippians 3:8

William H. Parker
STORIES OF JESUS
Frederic A. Challinor

Unison or duet

1. Tell me the sto-ries of Je-sus I love to hear;
2. *First let me hear how the chil-dren Stood 'round His knee,*
3. In-to the cit-y I'd fol-low The chil-dren's band,

1. Things I would ask Him to tell me If He were here:
2. *I shall im-ag-ine His bless-ing Rest-ing on me;*
3. Wav-ing a branch of the palm-tree High in my hand;

1. Scenes by the way-side, Tales of the sea,
2. *Words full of kind-ness, Deeds full of grace,*
3. One of His her-alds, Yes, I would sing

1. Sto-ries of Je-sus, Tell them to me.
2. *All in the bright-ness Of Jesus' face.*
3. Loud-est ho-san-nas, "Je-sus is King!"

THE LIFE AND MINISTRY OF JESUS CHRIST

I Think, When I Read That Sweet Story — 213

Then were there brought little children, that He should put His hands on them . . .
— Matthew 19:13

Based on Mark 10:13-15
Jemima T. Luke

SWEET STORY
Greek Melody
Adapted by William B. Bradbury

1. I think, when I read that sweet story of old, When Jesus was here among men, How He called little children as lambs to His fold— I should like to have been with Him then.
2. *I wish that His hands had been placed on my head, That His arms had been thrown around me, And that I might have seen His kind look when He said, "Let the little ones come unto Me."*
3. Yet still to His footstool in prayer I may go And ask for a share in His love; And if I thus earnestly seek Him below, I shall see Him and hear Him above.

I Timothy 3:16b — 214

He appeared in a body,
was vindicated by the Spirit,
was seen by angels,
was preached among the nations,
was believed on in the world,
was taken up in glory.

—(NIV)

THE LIFE AND MINISTRY OF JESUS CHRIST

215 Tell Me the Story of Jesus

Did not our hearts burn within us when He talked to us?
— Luke 24:32

Fanny J. Crosby

STORY OF JESUS
John R. Sweney

1. Tell me the story of Jesus, Write on my heart every word;
   Tell me the story most precious, Sweetest that ever was heard.
   Tell how the angels in chorus Sang as they welcomed His birth,
   "Glory to God in the highest! Peace and good tidings to earth."

2. Fasting alone in the desert, Tell of the days that are past,
   How for our sins He was tempted, Yet was triumphant at last.
   Tell of the years of His labor, Tell of the sorrow He bore,
   He was despised and afflicted, Homeless, rejected and poor.

3. Tell of the cross where they nailed Him, Writhing in anguish and pain;
   Tell of the grave where they laid Him, Tell how He liveth again.
   Love in that story so tender, Clearer than ever I see:
   Lord, may I always remember Love paid the ransom for me.

Refrain: Tell me the story of Jesus, Write on my heart every word;
Tell me the story most precious, Sweetest that ever was heard.

THE LIFE AND MINISTRY OF JESUS CHRIST

Strong, Righteous Man of Galilee 216

All things are delivered to Me of My Father.
— Luke 10:22

Harry Webb Farrington

MELITA
John Bacchus Dykes

1. Strong, right-eous Man of Gal-i-lee, With bor-rowed peace we fol-low Thee: In tem-ple court Thy cleans-ing rod, On Phar-i-sees the scorn of God. With bor-rowed peace we fol-low Thee, Strong, right-eous Man of Gal-i-lee.

2. *Firm, peace-ful Man of Gal-i-lee, With bor-rowed strength we fol-low Thee: Not to re-venge but heal and pray, To turn the cheek and trib-ute pay. With bor-rowed strength we fol-low Thee, Firm, peace-ful Man of Gal-i-lee.*

3. Calm, suf-fering Man of Gal-i-lee, With bor-rowed grace we fol-low Thee: Love at the well, share Mar-tha's loss, For-give the nails and take the cross. With bor-rowed grace we fol-low Thee, Calm, suf-fering Man of Gal-i-lee.

4. God's peace-ful Man of Gal-i-lee, Love's tri-umph, we shall fol-low Thee: To crum-ble ev-ery boun-dary wall, Build high-ways to the hearts of all. Love's tri-umph, we shall fol-low Thee, God's peace-ful Man of Gal-i-lee. A-men.

THE LIFE AND MINISTRY OF JESUS CHRIST

217 Jesus Walked This Lonesome Valley

He was in all points tempted as we are, yet without sin. — Hebrews 4:15

Traditional
Erna Moorman, 2nd stanza

LONESOME VALLEY
Traditional Spiritual

1. Jesus walked this lonesome valley, He had to walk it by Himself; O nobody else could walk it for Him, He had to walk it by Himself.
2. As we walk our lonesome valley, We do not walk it by ourselves; For God sent His Son to walk it with us, We do not walk it by ourselves.

Second stanza © Copyright 1976 by Fred Bock Music Co. All rights reserved. Used by permission.

218 The Humanity of Jesus

May our prayer, O Christ, awaken all Thy human reminiscences, that we may feel in our hearts the sympathizing Jesus.

    Thou hast walked this earthly vale and hast not forgotten what it is to be tired, what it is to know aching muscles, as Thou didst work long hours at the carpenter's bench.

    Thou hast not forgotten what it is to feel the sharp stabs of pain, or hunger, or thirst.

    Thou knowest what it is to be forgotten, to be lonely.

    Thou dost remember the feel of hot and scalding tears running down Thy cheeks. O we thank Thee that Thou wert willing to come to earth and share with us the weakness of the flesh, for now we know that Thou dost understand all that we are ever called upon to bear.

    We know that Thou, our God, art still able to do more than we ask or expect. So bless us, each one, not according to our deserving, but according to the riches in glory of Christ Jesus, our Lord. Amen.

Peter Marshall

Jesus Is the Friend of Sinners

They that are whole need not a physician, but they that are sick.
— Matthew 9:12

FRIEND OF SINNERS

John W. Peterson John W. Peterson

220 I've Found a Friend, O Such a Friend

A friend loveth at all times. — Proverbs 17:17

James G. Small

FRIEND
George C. Stebbins

1. I've found a Friend, O such a Friend! He loved me ere I knew Him; He drew me with the cords of love, And thus He bound me to Him. And 'round my heart still close-ly twine Those ties which can't be sev-ered. For I am His, and He is mine, For-ev-er and for-ev-er.

2. *I've found a Friend, O such a Friend! He bled, He died to save me: And not a-lone the gift of life, But His own self He gave me. Naught that I have my own I call, I hold it for the giv-er; My heart, my strength, my life, my all Are His, and His for-ev-er.*

3. I've found a Friend, O such a Friend! So kind, and true, and ten-der, So wise a Coun-se-lor and Guide, So might-y a De-fend-er! From Him who loves me now so well, What power my soul can sev-er? Shall life or death, shall earth or hell? No! I am His for-ev-er.

JESUS CHRIST—FRIEND

No, Not One! 221

There is a friend that sticketh closer than a brother. — Proverbs 18:24

Johnson Oatman, Jr.
NO, NOT ONE
George C. Hugg

1. There's not a friend like the lowly Jesus, No, not one! no, not one!
2. *No friend like Him is so high and holy,* No, not one! no, not one!
3. There's not an hour that He is not near us, No, not one! no, not one!
4. *Did ever saint find this friend forsake him?* No, not one! no, not one!
5. Was e'er a gift like the Savior given? No, not one! no, not one!

1. None else could heal all our soul's diseases, No, not one! no, not one!
2. *And yet no friend is so meek and lowly,* No, not one! no, not one!
3. No night so dark but His love can cheer us, No, not one! no, not one!
4. *Or sinner find that He would not take him?* No, not one! no, not one!
5. Will He refuse us a home in heaven? No, not one! no, not one!

Jesus knows all about our struggles, He will guide 'til the day is done;

There's not a friend like the lowly Jesus, No, not one! no, not one!

JESUS CHRIST—FRIEND

222 Jesus, Lover of My Soul

For Thou hath been a shelter for me and a strong tower....
— Psalm 61:3

Charles Wesley

ABERYSTWYTH
Joseph Parry

1. Jesus, lover of my soul, Let me to Thy bosom fly,
While the nearer waters roll, While the tempest still is high.
Hide me, O my Savior, hide, 'Til the storm of life is past;
Safe into the haven guide, O receive my soul at last!

2. *Other refuge have I none, Hangs my helpless soul on Thee;*
Leave, O leave me not alone, Still support and comfort me.
All my trust on Thee is stayed, All my help from Thee I bring;
Cover my defenseless head With the shadow of Thy wing.

3. Plenteous grace with Thee is found, Grace to cover all my sin;
Let the healing streams abound, Make and keep me pure within.
Thou of life the fountain art, Freely let me take of Thee;
Spring Thou up within my heart, Rise to all eternity. A-men.

JESUS CHRIST—HIS LOVE

I Stand Amazed

223

God, who is rich in mercy, for His great love wherewith He loved us . . .

— Ephesians 2:4

Charles H. Gabriel

MY SAVIOR'S LOVE
Charles H. Gabriel

1. I stand a-mazed in the pres-ence Of Je-sus the Naz-a-rene,
2. *For me it was in the gar-den He prayed, "Not my will, but Thine;"*
3. In pit-y an-gels be-held Him, And came from the world of light
4. *He took my sins and my sor-rows, He made them His ver-y own;*
5. When with the ran-somed in glo-ry His face I at last shall see,

1. And won-der how He could love me, A sin-ner, con-demned, un-clean.
2. He had no tears for His own griefs, But sweat drops of blood for mine.
3. To com-fort Him in the sor-rows He bore for my soul that night.
4. He bore the bur-den to Cal-vary, And suf-fered and died a-lone.
5. 'Twill be my joy through the a-ges To sing of His love for me.

How mar-vel-ous! how won-der-ful! And my song shall ev-er be:

How mar-vel-ous! how won-der-ful Is my Sav-ior's love for me!

JESUS CHRIST—HIS LOVE

224 If That Isn't Love

So Christ was once offered to bear the sins of many. . . . Hebrews 9:28

Dottie Rambo

LOVE
Dottie Rambo

1. He left the splen-dor of heav-en, Know-ing His des-ti-ny Was the lone-ly hill of Gol-goth-a, There to lay down His life for me.
2. E-ven in death He re-mem-bered The thief hang-ing by His side; He spoke with love and com-pas-sion Then He took him to Par-a-dise.

If that is-n't love the o-cean is dry, There's no star in the sky and the spar-row can't fly! If that is-n't love then heav-en's a myth, There's no feel-ing like this, if that is-n't love.

© Copyright 1969 by Heart Warming Music Company. All rights reserved. Used by permission.
JESUS CHRIST—HIS LOVE

Jesus Loves Even Me

225

Christ came into the world to save sinners of whom I am chief.
— I Timothy 1:15

Philip P. Bliss

GLADNESS
Philip P. Bliss

1. I am so glad that my Father in heaven Tells of His love in the Book He has given; Wonderful things in the Bible I see— This is the dearest, that Jesus loves me.
2. *Though I forget Him and wander away, Still Jesus loves me wherever I stray; Back to His dear loving arms I would flee, When I remember that Jesus loves me.*
3. O if there's only one song I can sing, When in His beauty I see the great King, This shall my song in eternity be: O, what a wonder that Jesus loves me!"

I am so glad that Jesus loves me, Jesus loves me, Jesus loves me;
I am so glad that Jesus loves me, Jesus loves even me.

JESUS CHRIST—HIS LOVE

226 Jesus Loves Me, This I Know

I love them that love Me, and those who seek Me early shall find Me.
— Proverbs 8:17

Anna B. Warner

JESUS LOVES ME
William B. Bradbury

1. Je-sus loves me! this I know, For the Bi-ble tells me so;
2. *Je-sus loves me! He who died Heav-en's gate to o-pen wide;*
3. Je-sus, take this heart of mine, Make it pure and whol-ly Thine;

1. Lit-tle ones to Him be-long, They are weak but He is strong.
2. *He will wash a-way my sin, Let His lit-tle child come in.*
3. On the cross You died for me, I will try to live for Thee.

Yes, Je-sus loves me! Yes, Je-sus loves me!

Yes, Je-sus loves me! The Bi-ble tells me so.

JESUS CHRIST—HIS LOVE

There's Something About That Name 227

The Spirit and the bride say, Come. And let him that heareth say, Come . . . . and whosoever will let him take of the water of life freely . . . . — Revelation 22:17

Gloria Gaither
William J. Gaither

THAT NAME
William J. Gaither

Je - sus, Je - sus, Je - sus! There's just some-thing a - bout that name! Mas - ter, Sav - ior, Je - sus! Like the fra - grance af - ter the rain; Je - sus, Je - sus, Je - sus! Let all Heav - en and earth pro - claim: Kings and king - doms will all pass a - way, But there's some-thing a - bout that name!

© Copyright 1970 by William J. Gaither. All rights reserved. Used by permission.

JESUS CHRIST—HIS NAME

228 I Will Sing of My Redeemer

For I know that my Redeemer liveth . . . — Job 19:25

Philip P. Bliss

MY REDEEMER
James McGranahan

*1. I will sing of my Redeemer And His won-drous love to me;
2. I will tell the won-drous sto-ry, How my lost es-tate to save,
3. I will praise my dear Re-deem-er, His tri-um-phant power I'll tell,
4. I will sing of my Re-deem-er, And His heaven-ly love to me;

1. On the cru-el cross He suf-fered From the curse to set me free.
2. In His bound-less love and mer-cy, He the ran-som free-ly gave.
3. How the vic-to-ry He giv-eth O-ver sin and death and hell.
4. He from death to life hath brought me, Son of God, with Him to be.

Sing, O sing of my Re-deem-er, With His blood He pur-chased me; On the
sing of my Re-deem-er, Sing, O sing of my Re-deem-er, He pur-chased me, He pur-chased me,

*These words may also be sung to the hymn-tune HYFRYDOL.

JESUS CHRIST—HIS NAME

cross   He sealed my par - don,   Paid the
He sealed my par - don, On the cross He sealed my par - don,

debt   and made me free.
and made me free,   and made me free.

How Sweet the Name of Jesus Sounds 229

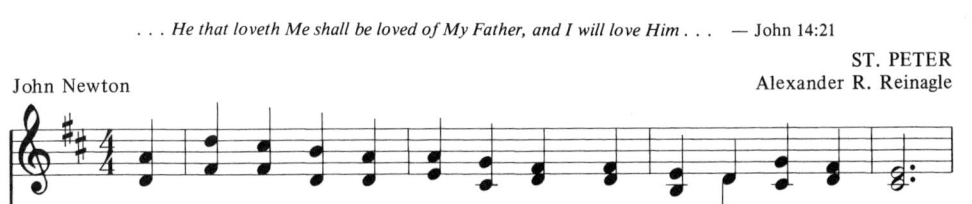

. . . He that loveth Me shall be loved of My Father, and I will love Him . . . — John 14:21

John Newton

ST. PETER
Alexander R. Reinagle

1. How sweet the name of Je-sus sounds In a be-liev-er's ear!
2. *It makes the wound-ed spir-it whole And calms the trou-bled breast;*
3. Je-sus! my Sav-ior, Shep-herd, Friend, My Proph-et, Priest, and King,
4. *Weak is the ef-fort of my heart, And cold my warm-est thought;*

1. It soothes his sor-rows, heals his wounds, And drives a-way his fear.
2. *'Tis nour-ish-ment to hun-gry souls, And to the wea-ry rest.*
3. My Lord, my Life, my Way, my End, Ac-cept the praise I bring.
4. *But when I see Thee as Thou art, I'll praise Thee as I ought.* A-men.

JESUS CHRIST—HIS NAME

230 His Name Is Wonderful

... Which is, and which was, and which is to come, the Almighty.
— Revelation 1:8

Audrey Mieir

MIEIR
Audrey Mieir

His name is Wonderful, His name is Wonderful, His name is Wonderful, Jesus, my Lord; He is the mighty King, Master of everything, His name is Wonderful, Jesus, my Lord.

He's the great Shepherd, the Rock of all ages, Almighty God is He; Bow down before Him, Love and a-

© Copyright 1959 by Manna Music, Inc. International copyright secured. All rights reserved. Used by permission.

JESUS CHRIST—HIS NAME

dore Him, His name is Won-der-ful, Je - sus, my Lord.

Take the Name of Jesus with You 231

Neither is there salvation in any other.... — Acts 4:12

Lydia Baxter

PRECIOUS NAME
William H. Doane

1. Take the name of Je-sus with you, Child of sor-row and of woe.
2. *Take the name of Je-sus ev - er As pro-tec-tion ev-ery-where;*
3. At the name of Je-sus bow-ing, When in heav-en we shall meet,

1. It will joy and com-fort give you, Take it then wher-e'er you go.
2. *If temp-ta-tions 'round you gath-er, Breathe that ho-ly name in prayer.*
3. King of kings, we'll glad-ly crown Him When our jour-ney is com-plete.

Pre-cious name, O how sweet! Hope of earth and joy of heaven,

Pre-cious name, O how sweet— Hope of earth and joy of heaven.

JESUS CHRIST—HIS NAME

232 Join All the Glorious Names

Wonderful, Counselor, The Almighty God, Everlasting Father, Prince of Peace....
— Isaiah 9:6

Isaac Watts

DARWALL'S 148th
John Darwall

1. Join all the glo-rious names Of wis-dom, love, and power,
   That ev-er mor-tals knew, That an-gels ev-er bore:
   All are too poor to speak His worth,
   Too poor to set my Sav-ior forth.

2. *Great Proph-et of my God, My life would bless Thy name;*
   By Thee the joy-ful news Of our sal-va-tion came:
   The joy-ful news of sins for-given,
   Of hell sub-dued, and peace with heaven.

3. Di-vine, al-might-y Lord, My Con-queror and my King,
   Thy scep-ter and Thy sword, Thy reign-ing grace I sing;
   Thine is the power! Be-hold I sit
   And to Your lord-ly power sub-mit.

4. *Now let my soul a-rise And tread the tempt-er down;*
   My cap-tain leads me forth To con-quest and a crown:
   A fee-ble saint shall win the day,
   Though death and hell ob-struct the way.

JESUS CHRIST—HIS NAME

The Supremacy of Christ   233

He is the image of the invisible God, the firstborn over all creation. For by Him all things were created: things in heaven and on earth, visible and invisible, whether thrones or powers or rulers or authorities; all things were created by Him and for Him. He is before all things, and in Him all things hold together. And He is the head of the body, the church; He is the beginning and the firstborn from among the dead, so that in everything He might have the supremacy. For God was pleased to have all His fullness dwell in Him, and through Him to reconcile to Himself all things, whether things on earth or things in heaven, by making peace through His blood, shed on the cross.

Once you were alienated from God and were enemies in your minds because of your evil behavior. But now He has reconciled you by Christ's physical body through death to present you holy in His sight, without blemish and free from accusation—if you continue in your faith, established and firm, not moved from the hope held out in the gospel. This is the gospel that you heard and that has been proclaimed to every creature under heaven, and of which I, Paul, have become a servant.

—Colossians 1:15-23 (NIV)

He Is Lord   234

And that every tongue should confess that Jesus Christ is Lord. — Philippians 2:11

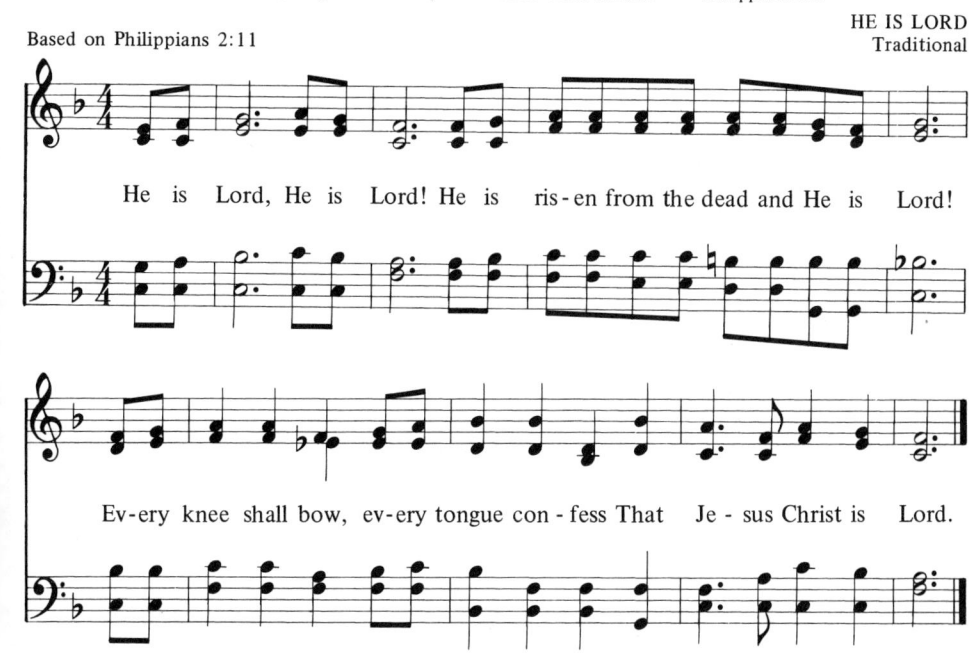

Based on Philippians 2:11

HE IS LORD
Traditional

He is Lord, He is Lord! He is ris-en from the dead and He is Lord!

Ev-ery knee shall bow, ev-ery tongue con-fess That Je-sus Christ is Lord.

JESUS CHRIST–LORDSHIP

235 Jesus Is Lord of All

No man can serve two masters; . . . he will hold to one . . . . — Matthew 6:24

Gloria Gaither
William J. Gaither

LORD OF ALL
William J. Gaither

1. All my tomorrows, all my past, Jesus is Lord of all. I've quit my struggles, contentment at last, Jesus is Lord of all.
2. *All of my conflicts, all my thoughts, Jesus is Lord of all. His love wins the battles I could not have fought, Jesus is Lord of all.*
3. All of my longings, all my dreams, Jesus is Lord of all. All of my failures His power redeems, Jesus is Lord of all.

King of kings, Lord of lords, Jesus is Lord of all; All my possessions and all my life, Jesus is Lord of all.

© Copyright 1973 by William J. Gaither. All rights reserved. Used by permission.

JESUS CHRIST–LORDSHIP

The Unveiled Christ 236

*And Jesus . . . gave up the ghost.
And the veil of the temple was rent from the top to the bottom.*
— Mark 15:37, 38

N. B. Herrell

UNVEILED CHRIST
N. B. Herrell

1. Once our bless-ed Christ of beau-ty Was veiled off from hu-man view;
2. *Yes, He is with God, the Fa-ther, In-ter-ced-ing there for you;*
3. Ho-ly an-gels bow be-fore Him, Men of earth give prais-es due;

1. But through suf-fering, death, and sor-row He has rent the veil in two.
2. *For He is the Well-be-lov-ed Since He rent the veil in two.*
3. For He is the might-y Con-queror Since He rent the veil in two.

O be-hold the Man of Sor-rows! O be-hold Him in plain view!

Lo! He is the might-y Con-queror Since He rent the veil in two;

Lo! He is the might-y Con-queror Since He rent the veil in two.

Copyright 1916. Renewed 1944 by Nazarene Publishing House. Used by permission.

JESUS CHRIST—LORDSHIP

237 Revelation 15:3b-4

Great and wonderful are Thy deeds,
O Lord God the Almighty!
Just and true are Thy ways,
O, King of the ages!
Who shall not fear and glorify Thy name, O Lord?
For Thou alone art holy.
All nations shall come and worship Thee,
For Thy judgments have been revealed.

—(RSV)

238 Jesus Shall Reign Where'er the Sun

Based on Psalm 72
Isaac Watts

His kingdom is an everlasting kingdom, and His dominion from generation to generation. — Daniel 4:3

DUKE STREET
John Hatton

1. Jesus shall reign where'er the sun Does His successive journeys run, His kingdom spread from shore to shore, 'Til moons shall wax and wane no more.
2. To Him shall endless prayer be made, And endless praises crown His head; His name like sweet perfume shall rise With every morning sacrifice.
3. People and realms of every tongue Dwell on His love with sweetest song; And infant voices shall proclaim Their early blessings on His name. (name.)
4. Let every creature rise and bring His grateful honors to our King; Angels descend with songs again, And earth repeat the loud "Amen!"

JESUS CHRIST—LORDSHIP

Alternate Last Verse Harmonization Arranged by Steven R. Quesnel

4 Let every creature rise and bring
His grateful honors to our King:
Angels descend with songs again,
And earth repeat the loud "A-men!"

© Copyright 1976 by Paragon Associates, Inc. All rights reserved.

JESUS CHRIST—LORDSHIP

239 Lift Up Your Heads, Ye Mighty Gates

Give unto the Lord the glory due His name.
— I Chronicles 16:29

Based on Psalm 24:7
Georg Weissel
Tr. by Catherine Winkworth

TRURO
Psalmodia Evangelica

1. Lift up your heads, ye might-y gates: Be-hold, the King of glo-ry waits! The King of kings is draw-ing near, The Sav-ior of the world is here.
2. *O blest the land, the cit-y blest, Where Christ the rul-er is con-fessed! O hap-py hearts and hap-py homes To whom this King of tri-umph comes!*
3. Fling wide the por-tals of your heart: Make it a tem-ple, set a-part From earth-ly use for heaven's em-ploy, A-dorned with prayer and love and joy.
4. *Re-deem-er, come! I o-pen wide My heart to Thee: here, Lord, a-bide! Let me Thy in-ner pres-ence feel: Thy grace and love in me re-veal.*
5. So come, my Sov-ereign, en-ter in! Let new and no-bler life be-gin! Thy Ho-ly Spir-it guide us on, Un-til the glo-rious crown be won. A-men.

JESUS CHRIST—LORDSHIP

Fairest Lord Jesus 240

Thou art fairer than the children of men.
— Psalm 45:2

From *Münster Gesangbuch*

CRUSADERS' HYMN
Silesian Folk Melody

1. Fair-est Lord Je-sus, Rul-er of all na-ture,
O Thou of God and man the Son: Thee will I cher-ish,
Thee will I hon-or, Thou my soul's glo-ry, joy, and crown.

2. *Fair are the mead-ows, Fair-er still the wood-lands,*
Robed in the bloom-ing garb of spring: Je-sus is fair-er,
Je-sus is pur-er, Who makes the woe-ful heart to sing.

3. Fair is the sun-shine, Fair-er still the moon-light,
And all the twin-kling star-ry host: Je-sus shines bright-er,
Je-sus shines pur-er Than all the an-gels heaven can boast.

4. Beau-ti-ful Sav-ior! Lord of the na-tions!
Son of God and Son of Man! Glo-ry and hon-or,
Praise, ad-o-ra-tion, Now and for-ev-er-more be Thine! A-men.

No Distant Lord 241

No distant Lord have I,
    Loving afar to be;
Made flesh for me He cannot rest
    Until He rests in me.

I need not journey far
    This dearest friend to see;
Companionship is always mine,
    He makes His home with me.

I envy not the twelve,
    Nearer to me is He;
The life He once lived here on earth
    He lives again in me.

Ascended now to God
    My witness there to be,
His witness here am I because
    His Spirit dwells in me.

    O glorious Son of God,
        Incarnate Deity,
    I shall forever be with Thee
        Because Thou art with me.

—Maltbie D. Babcock

JESUS CHRIST—LORDSHIP

242 He's Still the King of Kings

Gloria Gaither
William J. Gaither
Ronn Huff

... And of His kingdom there shall be no end.
— Luke 1:33

KING OF KINGS
William J. Gaither

1. Hear the voice of your ser-vant, a man sent of God
2. He is light that is come to a world that is dark,

1. To bear wit-ness of hope for the na-tions;
2. He is love and a-round Him is ha-tred;

1. "There will be One come af-ter, Whose mes-sage to us
2. E-ven few of His own ev-er saw Him as truth,

1. Will bring life from the Fa-ther in Heav-en."
2. But He comes e-ven now to for-give them.

Ho-san-na! Ho-san-na! The whole world is sing-ing! The hope of all

© Copyright 1971, 1973 by William J. Gaither. All rights reserved. Used by permission.
JESUS CHRIST–LORDSHIP

a - ges is come; Sing His praise, sing His great-ness, Let ev - ery-one know He's still the King of kings, and Lord of lords.

Who Is This Man?   243

Worship Leader:	*Jesus asked His disciples, "Who do men say that I the Son of man am?"*
Choir:	And they said, "Some say that Thou art John the Baptist; some, Elias; and others Jeremias, or one of the prophets."
Worship Leader:	*Who do men say that I am?*
Men:	I have looked far and wide, inside and outside my own head and heart, and I have found nothing other than this Man and His words which offer any answers to the dilemmas of this tragic, troubled time. If His light has gone out, then, as far as I am concerned, there is no light.[1]
Worship Leader:	*Who do men say that I am?*
Women:	He is the one Person in this world who is always present to me. When others only half-listen, He hears. When others are preoccupied with problems of their own, He is tuned in to my pain or joy. Yet it is this very presence in my life that strangely turns my attentions to the needs of others.
Worship Leader:	*Who do men say that I am?*
Choir:	Some say Jesus was an impressive personality, a strong leader and a great teacher. The world needs such men.
Worship Leader:	*Who do men say that I am?*
Youth (ages 12-25):	There are those who say, "Every person needs to believe in *something* or *someone*. Christ was a good person, a good pattern for our lives."
Worship Leader:	*He said to them, "But, who do **you** say that I am?"*
All:	You are the Christ, the Son of the Living God![2]

—Compiled by Gloria Gaither

1. Malcolm Muggeridge
2. Matthew 16:13b-16 (KJV)

JESUS CHRIST–LORDSHIP

244 Jesus! What a Friend for Sinners

Behold, . . . a friend of publicans and sinners.
— Luke 7:34

J. Wilbur Chapman

HYFRYDOL
Rowland H. Prichard
Arranged by Robert Harkness

1. Jesus! what a friend for sinners! Jesus! lover of my soul!
2. *Jesus! what a strength in weakness!* Let me hide myself in Him;
3. Jesus! what a help in sorrow! While the billows o'er me roll;
4. *Jesus! what a guide and keeper!* While the tempest still is high;
5. Jesus! I do now receive Him, More than all in Him I find;

1. Friends may fail me, foes assail me, He, my Savior, makes me whole.
2. *Tempted, tried, and sometimes failing,* He, my strength, my victory wins.
3. Even when my heart is breaking, He, my comfort, helps my soul.
4. *Storms about me, night o'ertakes me,* He, my pilot, hears my cry.
5. He hath granted me forgiveness, I am His, and He is mine.

Hallelujah! what a Savior! Hallelujah! what a friend!
Saving, helping, keeping, loving, He is with me to the end.

Copyright 1910. Renewal 1938 extended, Hope Publishing Company. All rights reserved. Used by permission.

JESUS CHRIST—SAVIOR

Christ Is Crucified Anew　　245

Not only once, and long ago,
There on Golgotha's side,
Has Christ, the Lord, been crucified
Because He loved a lost world so.
But hourly souls, sin-satisfied,
Mock His great love, flout His commands.
And I drive nails deep in His hands,
You thrust the spear within His side.

—John Richard Moreland

"Man of Sorrows," What a Name!　　246

Who hath believed our report? And to whom is the arm of the Lord revealed? — Isaiah 53:1

HALLELUJAH! WHAT A SAVIOR
Philip P. Bliss

1. "Man of sor-rows!" what a name For the Son of God who came
   Ru-ined sin-ners to re-claim! Hal-le-lu-jah, what a Sav-ior!
2. *Bear-ing shame and scoff-ing rude, In my place con-demned He stood,*
   Sealed my par-don with His blood; Hal-le-lu-jah, what a Sav-ior!
3. Guilt-y, vile, and help-less we, Spot-less Lamb of God was He;
   Full a-tone-ment! Can it be? Hal-le-lu-jah, what a Sav-ior!
4. *Lift-ed up was He to die, "It is fin-ished," was His cry;*
   Now in heaven ex-alt-ed high, Hal-le-lu-jah, what a Sav-ior!
5. When He comes, our glo-rious King, All His ran-somed home to bring,
   Then a-new this song we'll sing, Hal-le-lu-jah, what a Sav-ior!

JESUS CHRIST—SAVIOR

247 He's the Savior of My Soul

. . . My soul shall be joyful in my God . . .

— Isaiah 61:10

SAVIOR OF MY SOUL
Spanish Melody

Adapted

He's the Sav-ior of my soul, My Je-sus, My Je-sus, He's the Sav-ior of my soul, He's the Sav-ior of my soul. Je-sus, Je-sus, Je-sus, Je-sus. He's the Sav-ior of my soul, He's the Sav-ior of my soul.

JESUS CHRIST–SAVIOR

Hosanna, Loud Hosanna

248

Blessed is He that cometh in the name of the Lord; Hosanna in the highest.
— Matthew 21:9

Based on Matthew 21:15, 16
Jennette Threlfall
Jeff Redd, stanza 2

ELLACOMBE
Gesangbuch der Herzogl, Wirtemberg

1. Ho - san - na, loud ho - san - na, The lit - tle chil - dren sang;
   Through pil - lared court and tem - ple The love - ly an - them rang:
   To Je - sus, who had blessed them Close fold - ed to His breast,
   The chil - dren sang their prais - es, The sim - plest and the best.

2. *From Ol - i - vet they fol - lowed, A hap - py, joy - ous crowd,*
   Their large palm branch - es wav - ing, And sing - ing clear and loud;
   The Lord of men and an - gels Rode on in sim - ple joy,
   And wel - comed all the chil - dren: Each lit - tle girl and boy.

3. "Ho - san - na in the high - est!" That an - cient song we sing,
   For Christ is our Re - deem - er, The Lord of heaven our King;
   O may we ev - er praise Him With heart and life and voice,
   And in His ho - ly pres - ence E - ter - nal - ly re - joice!

© Copyright 1976 by Fred Bock Music Co. All rights reserved. Used by permission.

THE TRIUMPHAL ENTRY OF JESUS CHRIST

249 All Glory, Laud and Honor

... Hosanna; Blessed is the King of Israel that cometh in the name of the Lord.
— John 12:13

Theodulph of Orleans
Tr. by John M. Neale

ST. THEODULPH
Melchior Teschner

1. All glo-ry, laud, and hon-or To Thee, Re-deem-er, King, To whom the lips of chil-dren Made sweet ho-san-nas ring: Thou art the King of Is-ra-el, Thou Da-vid's roy-al Son, Who in the Lord's name com-est, The King and bless-ed one!

2. *The com-pa-ny of an-gels Are prais-ing Thee on high, And mor-tal men and all things Cre-at-ed make re-ply: The peo-ple of the He-brews With palms be-fore Thee went; Our praise and prayer and an-thems Be-fore Thee we pre-sent.*

3. To Thee, be-fore Thy pas-sion, They sang their hymns of praise; To Thee, now high ex-alt-ed, Our mel-o-dy we raise: Thou didst ac-cept their prais-es— Ac-cept the praise we bring, Who in all good de-light-est, Thou good and gra-cious King! A-men.

THE TRIUMPHAL ENTRY OF JESUS CHRIST

Alternate Last Verse Harmonization — Descant and arranged by A. Royce Eckhardt

3 Be-fore Thy pas - sion they sang their hymns of praise;
Now high ex - alt - ed, our mel - o - dy we raise.

3 Ac-cept their prais - es; ac - cept the praise we bring,

3 Who in all good de - light - est, Thou good and gra-cious King. A - men.

Free accompaniment and descant © Copyright 1973 by Covenant Press. Used by permission.

THE TRIUMPHAL ENTRY OF JESUS CHRIST

250 Calvary Covers It All

And that He might reconcile unto God . . . by the cross . . .
— Ephesians 2:16

Mrs. Walter G. Taylor

CALVARY COVERS IT
Mrs. Walter G. Taylor

1. Far dearer than all that the world can impart Was the message that came to my heart; How that Jesus alone for my sin did atone, And Calvary covers it all.

2. *The stripes that He bore and the thorns that He wore Told His mercy and love evermore;* And my heart bowed in shame as I called on His name, And Calvary covers it all.

3. How matchless the grace, when I looked in the face Of this Jesus, my crucified Lord; My redemption complete I then found at His feet, And Calvary covers it all.

4. How blessed the thought, that my soul by Him bought, Shall be His in the glory on high, Where with gladness and song I'll be one of the throng, And Calvary covers it all.

Calvary covers it all, My past with its sin and stain; My guilt and despair Jesus took on Him there, and Calvary covers it all.

© Copyright 1934 by Mrs. Walter G. Taylor. © Copyright renewed 1962, The Rodeheaver Company, owner. All rights reserved. Used by permission.

THE CROSS OF JESUS CHRIST

In the Cross of Christ I Glory 251

God forbid that I should glory, save in the Cross....
— Galatians 6:14

John Bowring

RATHBUN
Ithamar Conkey

1. In the cross of Christ I glory, Towering o'er the wrecks of time; All the light of sacred story Gathers round its head sublime.
2. *When the woes of life o'er-take me, Hopes deceive, and fears annoy, Never shall the cross forsake me: Lo! it glows with peace and joy.*
3. When the sun of bliss is beaming Light and love upon my way, From the cross the radiance streaming Adds more luster to the day.
4. *Bane and blessing, pain and pleasure, By the cross are sanctified; Peace is there that knows no measure, Joys that through all time abide.* A-men.

1 Corinthians 2:1-5 252

When I came to you, brothers, I did not come with eloquence or superior wisdom as I proclaimed to you the testimony about God. For I resolved to know nothing while I was with you except Jesus Christ and Him crucified. I came to you in weakness and fear, and with much trembling. My message and my preaching were not with wise and persuasive words, but with a demonstration of the Spirit's power, so that your faith might not rest on men's wisdom, but on God's power.

—(NIV)

253 Beneath the Cross of Jesus

Now there stood by the cross of Jesus....
— John 19:25

Elizabeth C. Clephane

ST. CHRISTOPHER
Frederick C. Maker

1. Be-neath the cross of Je-sus I glad-ly take my stand:
   The shad-ow of a might-y rock With-in a wea-ry land,
   A home with-in the wil-der-ness, A rest up-on the way,
   From the burn-ing of the noon-tide heat And the bur-den of the day.

2. Up-on that cross of Je-sus My eyes at times can see
   The ver-y dy-ing form of One Who suf-fered there for me;
   And from my smit-ten heart, with tears, Two won-ders I con-fess—
   The won-ders of His glo-rious love And my un-wor-thi-ness.

3. I take, O cross, thy shad-ow For my a-bid-ing place;
   I ask no oth-er sun-shine than The sun-shine of His face,
   Con-tent to let the world go by, To know no gain or loss,
   My sin-ful self my on-ly shame, My glo-ry all the cross.

THE CROSS OF JESUS CHRIST

Near the Cross

254

I will open rivers in high places, and fountains . . .
− Isaiah 41:18

Fanny J. Crosby

NEAR THE CROSS
William H. Doane

1. Je - sus, keep me near the cross— There a pre - cious foun - tain,
   Free to all, a heal - ing stream, Flows from Cal - vary's moun - tain.
2. *At the cross I stood one day. Love and mer - cy found me;*
   There the bright and morn - ing star Shed its beams a - round me.
3. Near the cross! O Lamb of God, Bring its scenes be - fore me;
   Help me walk from day to day With its shad - ow o'er me.
4. *Near the cross I'll watch and wait, Hop - ing, trust - ing ev - er,*
   'Til I reach the gold - en strand Just be - yond the riv - er.

In the cross, in the cross, Be my glo - ry ev - er,
'Til my rap - tured soul shall find Rest be - yond the riv - er. A - men.

THE CROSS OF JESUS CHRIST

255 Down at the Cross

I am crucified with Christ; Nevertheless I live...
— Galatians 2:20

Elisha A. Hoffman
GLORY TO HIS NAME
John H. Stockton

1. Down at the cross where my Savior died, Down where for cleansing from sin I cried, There to my heart was the blood applied; Glory to His name. Glory to His name, Glory to His name! There to my heart was the blood applied; Glory to His name.

2. *I am so wondrously saved from sin, Jesus so sweetly abides within; There at the cross where He took me in;*

3. O, precious fountain that saves from sin, I am so glad I have entered in; There Jesus saves me and keeps me clean;

4. *Come to this fountain so rich and sweet; Cast your poor soul at the Savior's feet; Plunge in today, and be made complete;*

THE CROSS OF JESUS CHRIST

The Old Rugged Cross

Who for the joy that was set before Him endured the cross....
— Hebrews 12:2

256

RUGGED CROSS

George Bennard
George Bennard

1. On a hill far a-way stood an old rug-ged cross, The em-blem of suf-fering and shame; And I love that old cross where the dear-est and best For a world of lost sin-ners was slain.
2. *O that old rug-ged cross, so de-spised by the world, Has a won-drous at-trac-tion for me; For the dear Lamb of God left His glo-ry a-bove To bear it to dark Cal-va-ry.*
3. In the old rug-ged cross, stained with blood so di-vine, A won-drous beau-ty I see; For 'twas on that old cross Je-sus suf-fered and died To par-don and sanc-ti-fy me.
4. *To the old rug-ged cross I will ev-er be true, Its shame and re-proach glad-ly bear; Then He'll call me some day to my home far a-way, Where His glo-ry for-ev-er I'll share.*

So I'll cher-ish the old rug-ged cross, 'Til my tro-phies at last I lay down; I will cling to the old rug-ged cross, And ex-change it some day for a crown.

Copyright 1913 by George Bennard. © renewed 1941 (extended). The Rodeheaver Co., owner. Used by permission.

THE CROSS OF JESUS CHRIST

257 Good Friday

We acknowledge, O Lord, that there is so little in us that is lovable. So often we are not lovely in our thoughts, in our words, or in our deeds. And yet Thou dost love us still, with a love that neither ebbs nor flows, a love that does not grow weary, but is constant—year after year, age after age.

O God, may our hearts be opened to that love today. With bright skies above us, the fields and woods and gardens bursting with new life and beauty, how can we fail to respond? With the clear notes of bird songs challenging us to praise, with every lowly shrub and blooming tree catching new life and beauty, our hearts indeed would proclaim Thee Lord, and we would invite Thee to reign over us and make us truly Thine own. May Thy healing love invade our inmost hearts, healing sorrow, pain, frustration, defeat, and despair.

May this day create within us a love for Thee of stronger stuff than vague sentimentality—a love which seeks to know Thy will and do it. So grant that this day of hallowed remembrance may be the beginning of a new way of life for each of us, a new kind of living that shall be the best answer to the confusion and to the challenge of evil in our day. This we ask in Jesus' name. Amen.

—Peter Marshall

258 When I Survey the Wondrous Cross

HAMBURG

What things were gain to me, those I counted loss for Christ.
— Philippians 3:7

Isaac Watts
Based on Gregorian Chant
Arr. by Lowell Mason

1. When I survey the wondrous cross On which the Prince of glory died, My richest gain I count but loss, And pour contempt on all my pride.
2. Forbid it, Lord, that I should boast, Save in the death of Christ my God; All the vain things that charm me most, I sacrifice them to His blood.
3. See, from His head, His hands, His feet, Sorrow and love flow mingled down: Did e'er such love and sorrow meet, Or thorns compose so rich a crown?
4. Were the whole realm of nature mine, That were a present far too small; Love so amazing, so divine, Demands my soul, my life, my all. A-men.

THE CROSS OF JESUS CHRIST

Are You Washed in the Blood? 259

But if we walk in the light . . . the blood of Jesus Christ cleanses us . . .
— I John 1:7

Elisha A. Hoffman

WASHED IN THE BLOOD
Elisha A. Hoffman

1. Have you been to Je-sus for the cleans-ing power? Are you washed in the blood of the Lamb? Are you ful-ly trust-ing in His grace this hour? Are you washed in the blood of the Lamb?
2. *Are you walk-ing dai-ly by the Sav-ior's side? Are you washed in the blood of the Lamb? Do you rest each mo-ment in the Cru - ci - fied? Are you washed in the blood of the Lamb?*
3. When the Bride-groom com-eth, will your robes be white, Pure and white in the blood of the Lamb? Will your souls be read-y for the man-sions bright And be washed in the blood of the Lamb?
4. *Lay a - side the gar-ments that are stained with sin And be washed in the blood of the Lamb? There's a foun-tain flow-ing for the soul un-clean; O be washed in the blood of the Lamb?*

Are you washed in the blood, In the soul-cleans-ing blood of the Lamb? Are your garments spotless? Are they white as snow? Are you washed in the blood of the Lamb?

THE BLOOD OF JESUS CHRIST

260 And Can It Be That I Should Gain?

For God hath not appointed us to wrath, but . . . salvation, by our Lord Jesus Christ.
— I Thessalonians 5:9

Charles Wesley

SAGINA
Thomas Campbell

1. And can it be that I should gain An interest in the Savior's blood? Died He for me, who caused His pain? For me, who Him to death pursued? Amazing love! how can it be That Thou, my God, shouldst die for me?

2. He left His Father's throne above, So free, so infinite His grace! Emptied Himself of all but love, And bled for Adam's helpless race! 'Tis mercy all, immense and free, For, O my God, it found out me.

3. Long my imprisoned spirit lay Fast bound in sin and nature's night. Thine eye diffused a quickening ray; I woke—the dungeon flamed with light! My chains fell off, my heart was free, I rose, went forth, and followed Thee.

4. No condemnation now I dread: Jesus, and all in Him, is mine! Alive in Him, my living Head, And clothed in righteousness divine, Bold I approach th'eternal throne, And claim the crown, through Christ my own.

THE BLOOD OF JESUS CHRIST

A - maz - ing love! how can it be
A - maz - ing love! how can it be
That Thou, my God, shouldst die for me! A - men.

Luke 4:14-22

261

And Jesus returned in the power of the Spirit into Galilee: and there went out a fame of Him through all the region round about. And He taught in their synagogues, being glorified of all.

And He came to Nazareth, where He had been brought up: and, as His custom was, He went into the synagogue on the sabbath day, and stood up for to read. And there was delivered unto Him the book of the prophet Esaias. And when He had opened the book, He found the place where it was written, The Spirit of the Lord is upon me, because He hath annointed me to preach the gospel to the poor; He hath sent me to heal the brokenhearted, to preach deliverance to the captives, and recovering of sight to the blind, to set at liberty them that are bruised, to preach the acceptable year of the Lord. And He closed the book, and He gave it again to the minister, and sat down. And the eyes of all them that were in the synagogue were fastened on Him. And He began to say unto them, This day is this Scripture fulfilled in your ears. And all bare Him witness, and wondered at the gracious words which proceeded out of His mouth.

–(KJV)

THE BLOOD OF JESUS CHRIST

262 The Blood Will Never Lose Its Power

Now the God of peace . . . through the everlasting covenant, make you perfect . . . .
— Hebrews 13:20, 21

Andraé Crouch

THE BLOOD
Andraé Crouch

1. The blood that Jesus shed for me, Way back on Calvary, The blood that gives me strength from day to day, It will never lose its power.

2. It soothes my doubts and calms my fears, And it dries all my tears; The blood that gives me strength from day to day, It will never lose its power.

It reaches to the highest mountain. It flows to the lowest valley The blood that gives me strength from

© Copyright 1966 by Manna Music, Inc. International copyright secured. All rights reserved. Used by permission.
THE BLOOD OF JESUS CHRIST

day to day, It will never lose its power.

There Is a Fountain Filled with Blood 263

For in Thee is the fountain of life: in Thy light shall we see light – Psalm 36:9

William Cowper
BELMONT
William Gardiner

1. There is a foun-tain filled with blood Drawn from Em-man-uel's veins; And sin-ners, plunged be-neath that flood, Lose all their guilt-y stains.
2. *The dy-ing thief re-joiced to see That foun-tain in his day; And there may I, though sin-ful, too, Wash all my sins a-way.*
3. Dear dy-ing Lamb, Thy pre-cious blood Shall nev-er lose its power, 'Til all the ran-somed Church of God Be saved, to sin no more.
4. *And since, by faith, I saw the stream Thy flow-ing wounds sup-ply, Re-deem-ing love has been my theme, And shall be 'til I die.* A-men.

THE BLOOD OF JESUS CHRIST

264   I Peter 1:18-21

You know that you were ransomed from the futile ways inherited from your fathers,
not with perishable things,
such as silver or gold,
but with the precious blood of Christ,
like that of a lamb without spot or blemish.
Through Him you have confidence in God who raised Him from the dead
and gave Him glory, so that your faith and hope are in God.

—(RSV)

265   I Know a Fount

O. Cooke

In that day there shall be a fountain opened . . . for sin and for uncleanness.
— Zechariah 13:1

I KNOW A FOUNT
O. Cooke

I know a fount where sins are washed a-way,
I know a place where night is turned to day;
Bur-dens are lift-ed, blind eyes made to see; There's a
won-der work-ing power in the blood of Cal-va-ry.

THE BLOOD OF JESUS CHRIST

Nothing but the Blood

266

*Christ died for us, much more then,
being now justified by His blood, we shall be saved.*

— Romans 5:8, 9

Robert Lowry

PLAINFIELD
Robert Lowry

1 What can wash a-way my sin? Noth-ing but the blood of Je-sus;
2 *For my par-don this I see—* *Noth-ing but the blood of Je-sus;*
3 Noth-ing can for sin a-tone— Noth-ing but the blood of Je-sus;
4 *This is all my hope and peace—* *Noth-ing but the blood of Je-sus;*

1 What can make me whole a-gain? Noth-ing but the blood of Je-sus.
2 *For my cleans-ing this my plea—* *Noth-ing but the blood of Je-sus.*
3 Naught of good that I have done— Noth-ing but the blood of Je-sus.
4 *This is all my right-eous-ness—* *Noth-ing but the blood of Je-sus.*

O! pre-cious is the flow That makes me white as snow;
No oth-er fount I know, Noth-ing but the blood of Je-sus.

THE BLOOD OF JESUS CHRIST

267 I John 1:6-9

So if we say we are His friends,
    but go on living in spiritual darkness and sin,
        we are lying.
But if we are living in the light of God's presence,
    just as Christ does,
then we have wonderful fellowship and joy with each other,
    and the blood of Jesus, His Son, cleanses us from every sin.
        If we say that we have no sin,
            we are only fooling ourselves,
            and refusing to accept the truth.
But if we confess our sins to Him, He can be depended on to forgive us
        and to cleanse us from every wrong.
                              — (LB)

268 Jesus, Thy Blood and Righteousness

... our Lord Jesus Christ, by whom we have now received the atonement.
                        — Romans 5:11

Nicolaus L. von Zinzendorf
Tr. by John Wesley

GERMANY
William Gardiner's *Sacred Melodies*

1. Jesus, Thy blood and righteousness My beauty are, my glorious dress; 'Midst flaming worlds, in these arrayed, With joy shall I lift up my head.

2. *Bold shall I stand in that great day, For who aught to my charge shall lay? Fully absolved through these I am, From sin and fear, from guilt and shame.*

3. Lord, I believe Thy precious blood, Which, at the mercy seat of God, Forever doth for sinners plead, For me, e'en for my soul was shed.

4. *Lord, I believe were sinners more Than sands upon the ocean shore, Thou hast for all a ransom paid, For all a full atonement made.* A-men.

THE BLOOD OF JESUS CHRIST

Jesus, the Son of God 269

Believe me that I am in the Father, and the Father in me. — John 14:11

G. T. Haywood

SWEET WONDER
G. T. Haywood

1. Do you know Jesus, Our Lord, our Savior, Jesus, the Son of God? Have you ever seen Him, Or shared of His favor?
2. *God gave Him, a ransom, Our souls to recover; Jesus, the Son of God; His blood made us worthy His Spirit to hover:*
3. O who would reject Him, Despise, or forsake Him, Jesus, the Son of God? O who ever sought Him, And He would not take him?
4. *If you will accept Him And trust and believe Him, Jesus, the Son of God. Your soul will exalt Him, And never will leave Him;*
5. Then someday from heaven, On clouds of bright glory, Jesus, the Son of God, Will come for His jewels, Most precious and holy,

Jesus, the Son of God. O sweet Wonder! O sweet Wonder! Jesus, the Son of God; How I adore Thee! O how I love Thee! Jesus, the Son of God.

THE ATONEMENT, CRUCIFIXION AND DEATH OF JESUS CHRIST

270 I Believe in a Hill Called Mount Calvary

And when they came to the place called Calvary, they crucified Him – Luke 23:33

Dale Oldham
Gloria Gaither
William J. Gaither

MOUNT CALVARY
William J. Gaither

1. There are things as we travel this earth's shifting sands
That transcend all the reason of man;
But the things that matter the most in this world,
They can never be held in our hand.

2. *I believe that the Christ who was slain on that cross
Has the power to change lives today;
For He changed me completely, a new life is mine,
That is why by the cross I will stay.*

3. I believe that this life with its great mysteries
Surely someday will come to an end;
But faith will conquer the darkness and death
And will lead me at last to my friend.

I believe in a hill called Mount Calvary— I'll believe what-

© Copyright 1968 by William J. Gaither. All rights reserved. Used by permission.
THE ATONEMENT, CRUCIFIXION AND DEATH OF JESUS CHRIST

ev - er the cost; And when time has sur - ren - dered and earth is no more, I'll still cling to that old rug - ged cross.

The Good Shepherd 271

I am the good shepherd;
> I know my own
>> and my own know me,
> just as the Father knows me
> and I know the Father;
>> and I lay down my life for my sheep.

And there are other sheep I have
> that are not of this fold,
and these I have to lead as well.
> They too will listen to my voice,
> and there will be only one flock,
>> and one shepherd.

The Father loves me,
> because I lay down my life
> in order to take it up again.
No one takes it from me;
I lay it down of my own free will,
> And as it is in my power to lay it down,
> so it is in my power to take it up again;
> and this is the command I have been given by my Father.

—John 10:14-18 (JB)

THE ATONEMENT, CRUCIFIXION AND DEATH OF JESUS CHRIST

See, My Servant shall prosper; He shall be highly exalted. Yet many shall be amazed when they see Him—yes, even far-off foreign nations and their kings; they shall stand dumbfounded, speechless in His presence. For they shall see and understand what they had not been told before. They shall see My Servant beaten and bloodied, so disfigured one would scarcely know it was a person standing there. So shall He cleanse many nations.

But, oh, how few believe it! Who will listen? To whom will God reveal His saving power? In God's eyes He was like a tender green shoot, sprouting from a root in dry and sterile ground. But in our eyes there was no attractiveness at all, nothing to make us want Him. We despised Him and rejected Him—a man of sorrows, acquainted with bitterest grief. We turned our backs on Him and looked the other way when He went by. He was despised and we didn't care.

Yet it was *our* grief He bore, *our* sorrows that weighed Him down. And we thought His troubles were a punishment from God, for His *own* sins! But He was wounded and bruised for *our* sins. He was chastised that we might have peace; He was lashed—and we were healed! *We* are the ones who strayed away like sheep! *We,* who left God's paths to follow our own. Yet God laid on *Him* the guilt and sins of every one of us!

He was oppressed and He was afflicted, yet He never said a word. He was brought as a lamb to the slaughter; and as a sheep before her shearers is dumb, so He stood silent before the ones condemning Him. From prison and trial they led Him away to His death. But who among the people of that day realized it was their sins that He was dying for—that He was suffering their punishment? He was buried like a criminal in a rich man's grave; but He had done no wrong, and had never spoken an evil word.

Yet it was the Lord's good plan to bruise Him and fill Him with grief. But when His soul has been made an offering for sin, then He shall have a multitude of children, many heirs. He shall live again and God's program shall prosper in His hands. And when He sees all that is accomplished by the anguish of His soul, He shall be satisfied; and because of what He had experienced, My righteous Servant shall make many to be counted righteous before God, for He shall bear all their sins. Therefore I will give Him the honors of one who is mighty and great, because He has poured out His soul unto death. He was counted as a sinner, and He bore the sins of many, and He pled with God for sinners.

—Isaiah 52:13-53:12 (LB)

Jesus Paid It All

273

Ye are bought with a price; be ye not servants of men.
— I Corinthians 7: 23

Elvina M. Hall

ALL TO CHRIST
John T. Grape

1. I hear the Sav-ior say, "Thy strength in-deed is small!
Child of weak-ness watch and pray, Find in me thine all in all."

2. For noth-ing good have I Where-by Thy grace to claim—
I will wash my gar-ments white In the blood of Cal-vary's Lamb.

3. And when be-fore the throne I stand in Him com-plete,
"Je-sus died my soul to save," My lips shall still re-peat.

Refrain:
Je-sus paid it all, All to Him I owe;
Sin had left a crim-son stain— He washed it white as snow.

THE ATONEMENT, CRUCIFIXION AND DEATH OF JESUS CHRIST

274 Alas! and Did My Savior Bleed

He was bruised for our iniquities. — Isaiah 53:5

Isaac Watts
MARTYRDOM
Hugh Wilson

1. Alas! and did my Savior bleed And did my sovereign die? Would He devote that sacred Head For sinners such as I?
2. Was it for sins that I have done He suffered on the tree? Amazing pity! grace unknown! And love beyond degree!
3. Well might the sun in darkness hide And shut his glories in, When Christ, the great Redeemer, died For man the creature's sin.
4. Thus might I hide my blushing face While His dear cross appears, Dissolve my heart in thankfulness, And melt mine eyes to tears.
5. But drops of grief can ne'er repay The debt of love I owe: Here, Lord, I give myself away— 'Tis all that I can do. A-men.

THE ATONEMENT, CRUCIFIXION AND DEATH OF JESUS CHRIST

Blessed Redeemer

275

Avis B. Christiansen

*And the Redeemed shall come to Zion,
and unto them that turn from transgression...* — Isaiah 59:20

REDEEMER
Harry Dixon Loes

1. Up Cal-vary's moun-tain, one dread-ful morn, Walked Christ my Sav-ior,
2. "Fa-ther, for-give them!" thus did He pray, E'en while His life-blood
3. O how I love Him, Sav-ior and Friend! How can my prais-es

1. wea-ry and worn; Fac-ing for sin-ners death on the cross,
2. flowed fast a-way; Pray-ing for sin-ners while in such woe—
3. ev-er find end! Thru years un-num-bered on heav-en's shore,

1. That He might save them from end-less loss.
2. No one but Je-sus ev-er loved so.
3. My tongue shall praise Him for-ev-er-more.

Bless-ed Re-deem-er, pre-cious Re-deem-er! Seems now I see Him on Cal-va-ry's tree Wound-ed and bleed-ing, for sin-ners plead-ing—Blind and un-heed-ing—dy-ing for me!

© Copyright 1921. Renewal 1949, by H. D. Loes. Assigned to John T. Benson, Jr. All rights reserved. Used by permission.

THE ATONEMENT, CRUCIFIXION AND DEATH OF JESUS CHRIST

276 Come to Calvary's Holy Mountain

And this voice ... we heard when we were ... in the holy mount.
— II Peter 1:18

James Montgomery
HOLY MOUNTAIN
Ludwig M. Lindeman

1. Come to Calvary's holy mountain, Sinners ruined by the fall; Here a pure and healing fountain Flows to you, to me, to all, In a full, perpetual tide, Opened when our Savior died.

2. Come in poverty and meanness, Come defiled, without, within; From infection and uncleanness, From the leprosy of sin, Wash your robes and make them white: Ye shall walk with God in light.

3. Come in sorrow and contrition, Wounded, impotent, and blind; Here the guilty free remission, Here the troubled peace may find: Health this fountain will restore; He that drinks shall thirst no more.

4. He that drinks shall live forever— 'Tis a soul-renewing flood; God is faithful, God will never Break His covenant of blood, Signed when our Redeemer died, Sealed when He was glorified.

THE ATONEMENT, CRUCIFIXION AND DEATH OF JESUS CHRIST

Jesus, Priceless Treasure 277

Like a merchantman, . . . who, when he had found a pearl of great price, went and . . . bought it. — Matthew 13:45, 46

Johann Franck
Tr. by Catherine Winkworth

JESU, MEINE FREUDE
German Melody
Adapted by Johann Crüger

1. Jesus, priceless treasure, Source of purest pleasure, Truest friend to me: Long my heart hath panted, 'Til it well-nigh fainted, Thirsting after Thee. Thine I am, O spotless Lamb, I will suffer nought to hide Thee, Ask for naught beside Thee.

2. *In Thy strength I rest me; Foes who would molest me Cannot reach me here. Though the earth be shaking, Every heart be quaking, God dispels our fear. Sin and hell in conflict fell With their heaviest storms assail us: Jesus will not fail us.*

3. Banished is our sadness! For the Lord of gladness, Jesus, enters in. Those who love the Father, Though the storms may gather, Still have peace within. Yea, what-e'er we here must bear, Still in Thee lies purest pleasure, Jesus, priceless treasure! A-men.

THE ATONEMENT, CRUCIFIXION AND DEATH OF JESUS CHRIST

278 There Is a Green Hill Far Away

Wherefore ... Jesus also suffered outside the gate ...
— Hebrews 13:12

Cecil Frances Alexander

GREEN HILL
George C. Stebbins
Arranged by A. Royce Eckhardt

1. There is a green hill far away, Outside a city wall, Where the dear Lord was cru-ci-fied, Who died to save us all.
2. *We may not know, we can-not tell What pains He had to bear, But we be-lieve it was for us He hung and suf-fered there.*
3. He died that we might be for-given, He died to make us good, That we might go at last to heaven, Saved by His pre-cious blood.
4. *There was no oth-er good e-nough To pay the price of sin; He on-ly could un-lock the gate Of heaven and let us in.*

O dear-ly, dear-ly has He loved, And we must love Him too, And trust in His re-deem-ing blood, And try His works to do.

© Copyright 1973 by Covenant Press. Used by permission.

THE ATONEMENT, CRUCIFIXION AND DEATH OF JESUS CHRIST

Savior, Thy Dying Love

279

It was the third hour and they crucified Him
— Mark 15:25

S. Dryden Phelps, alt.

SOMETHING FOR JESUS
Robert Lowry

1. Savior, Thy dying love Thou gavest me,
   Nothing should I withhold, Dear Lord, from Thee;
   In love my soul would bow, My heart fulfill its vow,
   Some offering bring Thee now, Something for Thee.

2. *Give me a faithful heart, Guided by Thee,*
   That each departing day Henceforth may see
   Some work of love begun, Some deed of kindness done,
   Some wanderer sought and won, Something for Thee.

3. All that I am and have, Thy gifts so free,
   Ever in joy or grief, My Lord, for Thee;
   And when Thy face I see, My ransomed soul shall be,
   Through all eternity, Something for Thee. A-men.

THE ATONEMENT, CRUCIFIXION AND DEATH OF JESUS CHRIST

280 Justified by Faith

Therefore, since we are justified by faith,
  we have peace with God through our Lord Jesus Christ.
      Through Him
          we have obtained access to this grace in which we stand,
          and we rejoice in our hope of sharing the glory of God.
  More than that, we rejoice in our sufferings,
      knowing that suffering produces endurance,
          and endurance produces character,
          and character produces hope,
          and hope does not disappoint us,
          because God's love has been poured into our hearts
          through the Holy Spirit which has been given to us.

While we were still weak,
  at the right time Christ died for the ungodly.
    Why, one will hardly die for a righteous man—
    though perhaps for a good man one will dare even to die.
        But God shows His love for us in that while we were yet sinners
        Christ died for us.
            Since, therefore, we are now justified by His blood,
    much more shall we be saved by Him from the wrath of God.
For if while we were enemies we were reconciled to God by the death of His Son,
    much more, now that we are reconciled,
    shall we be saved by His life.
        Not only so, but we also rejoice in God through our Lord Jesus Christ,
    through whom we have now received our reconciliation.

—Romans 5:1-11 (RSV)

281 Go to Dark Gethsemane

That I might know Him, . . ., and the fellowship of His suffering.
— Philippians 3:10

James Montgomery

REDHEAD No. 76
Richard Redhead

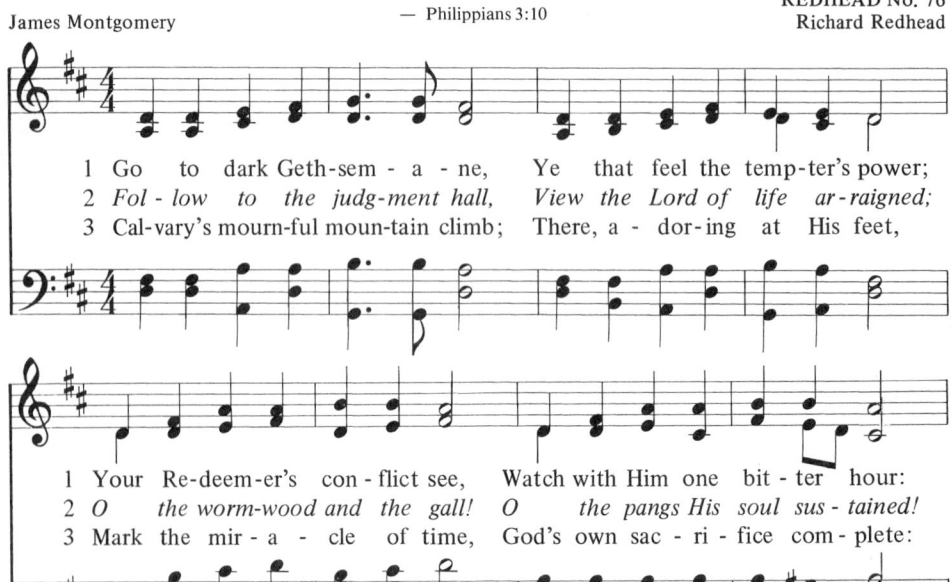

1. Go to dark Geth-sem-a-ne, Ye that feel the temp-ter's power;
   Your Re-deem-er's con-flict see, Watch with Him one bit-ter hour:
2. *Fol-low to the judg-ment hall, View the Lord of life ar-raigned;*
   O the worm-wood and the gall! O the pangs His soul sus-tained!
3. Cal-vary's mourn-ful moun-tain climb; There, a-dor-ing at His feet,
   Mark the mir-a-cle of time, God's own sac-ri-fice com-plete:

THE ATONEMENT, CRUCIFIXION AND DEATH OF JESUS CHRIST

1. Turn not from His griefs a-way— Learn from Jesus Christ to pray.
2. *Shun not suf-fering, shame or loss— Learn from Him to bear the cross.*
3. "It is fin-ished!" hear Him cry— Learn from Jesus Christ to die.

Wounded for Me 282

But He was wounded for our transgressions.... — Isaiah 53:5

W. G. Ovens, stanza 1
Gladys Westcott Roberts, stanzas 2-5

FOR ME
W. G. Ovens

1. Wound-ed for me, wound-ed for me, There on the cross
2. *Dy-ing for me, dy-ing for me, There on the cross*
3. Ris-en for me, ris-en for me, Up from the grave
4. *Liv-ing for me, liv-ing for me, Up in the skies*
5. Com-ing for me, com-ing for me, One day to earth

1. He was wound-ed for me; Gone my trans-gres-sions, and now I am
2. *He was dy-ing for me; Now in His death my re-demp-tion I*
3. He has ris-en for me; Now ev-er-more from death's sting I am
4. *He is liv-ing for me; Dai-ly He's plead-ing and pray-ing for*
5. He is com-ing for me; Then with what joy His dear face I shall

1. free, All be-cause Je-sus was wound-ed for me.
2. *see, All be-cause Je-sus was dy-ing for me.*
3. free, All be-cause Je-sus has ris-en for me.
4. *me, O how I praise Him, He's liv-ing for me.*
5. see, O how I praise Him— He's com-ing for me!

THE ATONEMENT, CRUCIFIXION AND DEATH OF JESUS CHRIST

283 What Wondrous Love Is This?

We all like sheep have gone astray...
and the Lord hath laid on Him the iniquity of us all
— Isaiah 53:6

American Folk Hymn

WONDROUS LOVE
Southern Harmony

1. What wondrous love is this, O my soul, O my soul, What wondrous love is this, O my soul! What wondrous love is this that caused the Lord of bliss To bear the dreadful curse for my soul, for my soul, To bear the dreadful curse for my soul!

2. To God and to the Lamb I will sing, I will sing, To God and to the Lamb I will sing; To God and to the Lamb, who is the great "I Am," While millions join the theme, I will sing, I will sing, While millions join the theme, I will sing!

3. And when from death I'm free, I'll sing on, I'll sing on, And when from death I'm free, I'll sing on; And when from death I'm free, I'll sing and joyful be, And through eternity I'll sing on, I'll sing on, And through eternity I'll sing on!

THE ATONEMENT, CRUCIFIXION AND DEATH OF JESUS CHRIST

O Sacred Head, Now Wounded

284

When they had platted a crown of thorns they put it upon His head.
— Matthew 27:29

Latin: 12th Century
German: Paul Gerhardt
Tr. by James W. Alexander, alt.

PASSION CHORALE
Hans Leo Hassler
Harmonized by J. S. Bach

1. O sacred Head, now wounded, With grief and shame weighed down,
Now scornfully surrounded With thorns, Thy only crown,
How art Thou pale with anguish, With sore abuse and scorn!
How does that visage languish Which once was bright as morn!

2. *What Thou, my Lord, hast suffered Was all for sinners' gain;*
Mine, mine was the transgression, But Thine the deadly pain.
Lo, here I fall, my Savior! 'Tis I deserve Thy place;
Look on me with Thy favor, Vouchsafe to me Thy grace.

3. What language shall I borrow To thank Thee, dearest friend,
For this Thy dying sorrow, Thy pity without end?
O make me Thine forever; And, should I fainting be,
Lord, let me never, never Outlive my love for Thee! A-men.

THE ATONEMENT, CRUCIFIXION AND DEATH OF JESUS CHRIST

285 Worthy the Lamb

Gloria Gaither
William J. Gaither

Thou art worthy, O Lord, to receive glory, and honor, and power....
— Revelation 4:11

WORTHY
William J. Gaither

1. Hear the cries of the shack-led from the on-set of time— For the chains of de-feat there's no key; See the tears of the bro-ken, the cries of the slaves— "Is there no one worth-y to set us free?" Worth-y, worth-y, Worth-y the Lamb that was slain; slain.

2. Then the cry-ing is stilled as the cho-rus rings out— The shack-led re-leased from their chains; And thou-sands of voic-es are swell-ing the song— *"Worth-y the Lamb that was slain."* Worth-y,

3. Then all the arch-an-gels, the saints of all time, Hold-ing their crowns in their hands, Fall down be-fore Him, join-ing the song— "Worth-y, worth-y the Lamb."

© Copyright 1974 by William J. Gaither. All rights reserved. Used by permission.
THE ATONEMENT, CRUCIFIXION AND DEATH OF JESUS CHRIST

If We Had Been There — 286

Minister: *If we had been Jews, would we have spoken out for Him*
   when the Sanhedrin accused Him of blasphemy?
If we had been Gentiles, would we have defended Him
   when the Romans condemned Him to death?
If we had been disciples, would we have stayed with Him
   when the crowd became a crucifying mob?
Or would we have been like Peter—
   who followed Him and loved Him
   and denied Him three times before the dawn?

Choir *(sings)*: Were you there when they crucified my Lord?
O! Sometimes it causes me to tremble, tremble, tremble.

Minister: *And the Christ who was crucified there, once said:*
   "As you have done it to the least of these, My brothers,
   you have done it unto Me."
As nations rise in war
As governments oppress the poor
As passive people turn and look aside
In silence
We crucify.
Again—
We crucify.

People: As indifference forms the pattern of our lives,
As hungry children cry for food,
As widows mourn alone in empty rooms,
In apathy—
We crucify.
Again—
We crucify.

Choir *(sings)*: Were you there when they nailed Him to the tree?
O! Sometimes it causes me to tremble, tremble, tremble.

Minister: *I think of the nails that crucified my Lord.*
They were made of iron; but more—
They were made of hatred, prejudice and greed.
And I wonder—
What part of myself is found in the shadow of that mob
   that stretches down through history?
What part of myself creates nails in other forms
   that wound my brother—and my Lord?

People: You know how many times I have betrayed You, Lord.
You know the times I have chosen evil over good.
Guilt lies upon me like an iron cloak.
My soul is heavy—my burden hard.

Choir *(sings)*: Were you there when He rose up from the grave?
O! Sometimes it causes me to tremble, tremble, tremble.

Minister: *In the act of death He absorbs our sins.*
In love, He forgives our failures.
In the act of resurrection He gives the promise of acceptance,
   the assurance of forgiveness, the affirmation of eternal life.
"Your sins are forgiven you", He said, "Go and sin no more."

People: Through Your love, I am made whole,
Through Your death, I have found new life.
You are my shield, my redeemer and my hope.
My sins are forgiven—Hallelujah!

—Marilee Zdenek

THE ATONEMENT, CRUCIFIXION AND DEATH OF JESUS CHRIST

287 Were You There?

*He is . . . a man of sorrows and acquainted with grief;
and we hid as it were our faces from Him.* — Isaiah 53:3

American Folk Hymn

WERE YOU THERE
American Folk Melody

1. Were you there when they crucified my Lord? Were you there when they crucified my Lord? O! — — — Sometimes it causes me to tremble, tremble, tremble. Were you there when they crucified my Lord?
2. *Were you there when they nailed Him to the tree? Were you there when they nailed Him to the tree?* O! — — — Sometimes it causes me to tremble, tremble, tremble. *Were you there when they nailed Him to the tree?*
3. Were you there when they laid Him in the tomb? Were you there when they laid Him in the tomb? O! — — — Sometimes it causes me to tremble, tremble, tremble. Were you there when they laid Him in the tomb?
4. *Were you there when He rose up from the grave? Were you there when He rose up from the grave?* O! — — — Sometimes it causes me to tremble, tremble, tremble. *Were you there when He rose up from the grave?*

EASTER

Jesus Lives, and So Shall I

288

Now is Christ risen to become the firstfruits of them that slept.
— I Corinthians 15:20

Christian F. Gellert
Tr. by Philip Schaff

JESU, MEINE ZUVERSICHT
Johann Crüger

1. Jesus lives, and so shall I: Death, thy sting is gone forever! He for me hath deigned to die, Lives the bands of death to sever. He shall raise me from the dust: Jesus is my hope and trust.

2. *Jesus lives and reigns supreme: And, His kingdom still remaining, I shall also be with Him, Ever living, ever reigning. God has promised—be it must: Jesus is my hope and trust.*

3. Jesus lives— and by His grace, Victory o'er my passions giving, I will cleanse my heart and ways, Ever to His glory living. Me He raises from the dust: Jesus is my hope and trust.

4. *Jesus lives— I know full well Naught from Him my heart can sever, Life nor death nor powers of hell, Joy nor grief, henceforth forever. None of all His saints is lost: Jesus is my hope and trust.*

5. Jesus lives— and death is now But my entrance into glory; Courage, then, my soul, for thou Hast a crown of life before thee. Thou shalt find thy hopes were just: Jesus is my hope and trust. A-men.

EASTER

289 Christ the Lord Is Risen Today

Ye seek Jesus of Nazareth who was crucified; He is risen . . .
— Mark 16:6

Charles Wesley

EASTER HYMN
"Lyra Davidica"
Descant by Paul Sjolund

Descant

3, 4 Ah_____ Al - le - lu - ia! Ah__

1 Christ the Lord is risen to-day,
2 *Lives a-gain our glo-rious King,* Al - le - lu - ia!
3 Love's re-deem-ing work is done,
*4 Sing we to our God a-bove,

Al - le - lu - ia! Ah

1 Sons of men and an - gels say:
2 *Where, O death, is now thy sting?* Al - le - lu - ia!
3 Fought the fight, the bat - tle won,
4 Praise e - ter - nal as His love;

Al - le-lu - ia! Al-

1 Raise your joys and tri - umphs high,
2 *Dy - ing once, He all doth save,* Al - le - lu - ia!
3 Death in vain for - bids Him rise,
4 Praise Him, all ye heaven-ly host,

*Fourth verse to be sung more broadly, and in unison.
© Copyright 1976 by Paragon Associates, Inc. All rights reserved.
EASTER

1 Sing, ye heavens, and earth re-ply:
2 *Where thy vic-to-ry, O grave?*
3 Christ has o-pened par-a-dise,
4 *Fa-ther, Son, and Ho-ly Ghost.*

CHRIST THE LORD IS RISEN TODAY

Descant by Paul Sjolund

TPT. I
PART I: play on stanzas 1, 4.

TPT. II
PART II: play on stanzas 2, 4.

"Amen" after stanza 4.

EASTER

1 Corinthians 15:12-28

Now if Christ is preached as raised from the dead,
how can some of you say that there is no resurrection of the dead?
But if there is no resurrection of the dead,
then Christ has not been raised;
if Christ has not been raised,
then our preaching is in vain and your faith is in vain.

We are even found to be misrepresenting God,
because we testified of God that He raised Christ,
whom He did not raise if it is true that the dead are not raised.
For if the dead are not raised,
then Christ has not been raised.

If Christ has not been raised,
your faith is futile and you are still in your sins.

Then those also who have fallen asleep in Christ have perished.

If in this life only we have hoped in Christ,
we are of all men most to be pitied.

But, in fact, Christ has been raised from the dead,
the first fruits of those who have fallen asleep.

For as by a man came death,
by a man has come also the resurrection of the dead.
For as in Adam all die,
so also in Christ shall all be made alive.

But each in his own order:
Christ the first fruits, then at His coming those who belong to Christ.

Then comes the end,
when He delivers the kingdom to God the Father
after destroying every rule and every authority and power.

For He must reign until He has put all His enemies under His feet.

The last enemy to be destroyed is death.

"For God has put all things in subjection under His feet."

But when it says, "All things are put in subjection under Him,"
it is plain that He is excepted who put all things under Him.

When all things are subjected to Him,
then the Son Himself will also be subjected to Him who put all things under Him,
that God may be everything to everyone.

—(RSV)

EASTER

Thine Is the Glory

291

For Thine is the Kingdom, and the power, and the glory, forever.
— Matthew 6:13

Edmond L. Budry
Tr. by R. Birch Hoyle

JUDAS MACCABEUS
George Friedrich Handel

1. Thine is the glory, Risen, conquering Son; Endless is the victory Thou o'er death hast won. Angels in bright raiment Rolled the stone away, Kept the folded grave-clothes Where Thy body lay.

2. *Lo! Jesus meets us, Risen from the tomb; Lovingly He greets us, Scatters fear and gloom. Let His church with gladness Hymns of triumph sing, For her Lord now liveth: Death hath lost its sting.* Thine is the glory, Risen, conquering Son; Endless is the victory Thou o'er death hast won.

3. No more we doubt Thee, Glorious Prince of life! Life is naught without Thee: Aid us in our strife. Make us more than conquerors, Through Thy deathless love: Bring us safe through Jordan To Thy home above.

A-men.

Words from "Cantate Domino." © Copyright by World Student Christian Federation. Used by permission.

EASTER

292 Because He Lives

Because I live, ye shall live also. — John 14:19

Gloria Gaither
William J. Gaither

RESURRECTION
William J. Gaither
Final chorus arranged by Ronn Huff

1. God sent His Son, they called Him Jesus, He came to love, heal, and forgive; He lived and died to buy my pardon, An empty grave is there to prove my Savior lives.

2. *How sweet to hold a new-born baby, And feel the pride, and joy He gives; But greater still the calm assurance, This child can face uncertain days because He lives.*

3. And then one day I'll cross the river, I'll fight life's final war with pain; And then as death gives way to victory, I'll see the lights of glory and I'll know He lives.

Because He lives I can face tomorrow, Because He lives all fear is gone; Because I know He holds the

© Copyright 1971 by William J. Gaither. All rights reserved. Used by permission.
EASTER

1, 2
fu-ture. And life is worth the liv-ing just be-cause He lives.
Congregation sing melody in unison; accompaniment play as written.
3
3 lives. (Be-cause He lives I can face to-
mor - row; Be-cause He lives all fear is
tr 3
gone; Be-cause I know He holds the fu - ture,
And life is worth the liv-ing just be-cause He lives!)
3
3

293 Christ Whose Glory Fills the Skies

The sun of righteousness shall rise with healing in His wings. — Malachi 4:2

Charles Wesley

LUX PRIMA
Charles Gounod

1. Christ, whose glo-ry fills the skies, Christ, the true, the on-ly Light, Sun of Right-eous-ness, a-rise, Tri-umph o'er the shades of night; Day-spring from on high, be near; Day-star, in my heart ap-pear.
2. Dark and cheer-less is the morn Un-ac-com-pa-nied by Thee; Joy-less is the day's re-turn Till Thy mer-cy's beams I see; *Till they in-ward light im-part,* Cheer my eyes and warm my heart.
3. Vis-it, then, this soul of mine; Pierce the gloom of sin and grief; Fill me, Ra-dian-cy Di-vine; Scat-ter all my un-be-lief; More and more Thy-self dis-play, Shin-ing to the per-fect day. A-men.

294 Easter

We thank Thee for the beauty of this day, for the glorious message that all nature proclaims:
    the Easter lilies with their waxen throats eloquently singing the good news;
    the birds, so early this morning, impatient to begin their song;
    every flowering tree, shrub, and flaming bush, a living proclamation from Thee.
O pen our hearts that we may hear it too!
    Lead us, we pray Thee, to the grave that is empty, into the garden of the Resurrection where we may meet our risen Lord. May we never again live as if Thou were dead!
    In Thy presence restore our faith, our hope, our joy.
    Grant to our spirits refreshment, rest, and peace.
    Maintain within our hearts an unruffled calm, an unbroken serenity that no storms of life shall ever be able to take from us.
    From this moment, O living Christ, we ask Thee to go with us wherever we go; be our Companion in all that we do. And for this greatest of all gifts, we offer Thee our sacrifices of thanksgiving. Amen.

—Peter Marshall

EASTER

I Know That My Redeemer Lives 295

For I know that my Redeemer liveth . . . — Job 19:25

Samuel Medley

DUKE STREET
John Hatton

1. I know that my Redeemer lives: What joy the blest assurance gives! He lives, He lives, who once was dead; He lives, my everlasting Head!

2. *He lives, to bless me with His love; He lives to plead for me above; He lives, my hungry soul to feed; He lives, to help in time of need.*

3. He lives, and grants me daily breath; He lives, and I shall conquer death; He lives, my future to prepare; He lives, to bring me safely there.

4. *He lives, all glory to His Name; He lives, my Savior, still the same; What joy the blest assurance gives: I know that my Redeemer lives!* A-men.

1 Corinthians 15:51-58 296

Lo! I tell you a mystery. We shall not all sleep, but we shall all be changed, in a moment, in the twinkling of an eye, at the last trumpet. For the trumpet will sound, and the dead will be raised imperishable, and we shall be changed. For this perishable nature must put on the imperishable, and this mortal nature must put on immortality. When the perishable puts on the imperishable, and the mortal puts on immortality, then shall come to pass the saying that is written: "Death is swallowed up in victory." "O death, where is thy victory? O death, where is thy sting?" The sting of death is sin, and the power of sin is the law. But thanks be to God, who gives us the victory through our Lord Jesus Christ.

Therefore, my beloved brethren, be steadfast, immovable, always abounding in the work of the Lord, knowing that in the Lord your labor is not in vain.

—(RSV)
EASTER

297 Jesus Christ Is Risen Today

Praise ye the Lord, Sing unto the Lord a new song.
—Psalm 149:1

Latin: 14th Century
English translation, *New Version*
Charles Wesley, stanza 4

LLANFAIR
Robert Williams
Harmonized by John Roberts

1. Jesus Christ is risen today, Alleluia!
   Our triumphant holy day, Alleluia!
   Who did once upon the cross, Alleluia!
   Suffer to redeem our loss. Alleluia!

2. *Hymns of praise then let us sing,* Alleluia!
   Unto Christ, our heavenly King, Alleluia!
   Who endured the cross and grave, Alleluia!
   Sinners to redeem and save. Alleluia!

3. But the pains which He endured,
   Our salvation have procured;
   Now above the sky He's King,
   Where the angels ever sing.

4. *Sing we to our God above,*
   Praise eternal as His love;
   Praise Him, all ye heavenly host,
   Father, Son and Holy Ghost. A-men.

EASTER

Christ Arose

Thou hast led captivity captive . . .

298

Robert Lowry

CHRIST AROSE
Robert Lowry

1. Low in the grave He lay, Jesus, my Savior! Waiting the coming day, Jesus, my Lord!
2. *Vainly they watched His bed,* Jesus, my Savior! *Vainly they sealed the dead,* Jesus, my Lord!
3. Death could not keep his prey, Jesus, my Savior! He tore the bars away, Jesus, my Lord!

Up from the grave He arose, With a mighty triumph o'er His foes; He arose a victor from the dark domain, And He lives forever with His saints to reign; He arose! He arose! Hallelujah! Christ arose!

EASTER

299 He Lives

ACKLEY
Alfred H. Ackley — Alfred H. Ackley

Go quickly and tell . . . His disciples that He is risen from the dead.
— Matthew 28:7

1. I serve a ris-en Sav-ior, He's in the world to-day;
2. *In all the world a-round me I see His lov-ing care,*
3. Re-joice, re-joice, O Chris-tian, lift up your voice and sing

1. I know that He is liv-ing, what-ev-er men may say;
2. *And though my heart grows wea-ry I nev-er will de-spair;*
3. E-ter-nal hal-le-lu-jahs to Je-sus Christ the King!

1. I see His hand of mer-cy, I hear His voice of cheer,
2. *I know that He is lead-ing through all the storm-y blast,*
3. The Hope of all who seek Him, the Help of all who find,

1. And just the time I need Him He's al-ways near.
2. *The day of His ap-pear-ing will come at last.*
3. None oth-er is so lov-ing, so good and kind.

He lives, He lives, Christ Je-sus lives to-day!
         He lives,   He lives,

Copyright 1933 by Homer A. Rodeheaver, © Renewed 1961, The Rodeheaver Co., owner. All rights reserved. Used by permission.
EASTER

Easter 300

Some years ago a newspaper editor telephoned and asked me to tell in a few words what Easter means to me. My testimony was this: Easter means Christ to me. It means Christ in His kingly splendor, Christ in His serene glory, Christ in His gracious condescension. This is because Easter is the return of Christ from inflicted violence, from induced death, from imprisonment in a tomb. Easter is Christ triumphant over all that sin and death and man could do to Him. Easter means Christ.

And where Christ goes, drama goes. For it is impossible to look anywhere in the Gospels and fail to find something powerful happening. This is because Christ is Himself the Gospel and He is life, abundant life, and His life means action, pilgrimage, arrival.

Easter means life. Christ defeated death in order that life in Him might always live. And it is life that we want, life in Christ. Whether we put it in words or not, our constant thought is "Life, more life, always more and more life." We want life in ourselves, in our loved ones, in our friends, the kind of life that cannot be diminished, the kind of life that always expands. Easter is Christ's victory over all that would restrict, deny and strangle life. "For to me to live is Christ." That is Easter.

—Raymond Lindquist

301 The Easter Song

He is not here, but is risen . . .
— Luke 24:6

Anne Herring

EASTER SONG
Anne Herring

1. Hear the bells ring-ing, they're sing-ing that we can be born a-gain!
2. *Hear the bells ring-ing, they're sing-ing, "Christ is ris-en from the dead!"*

The an-gel up-on the tomb-stone said, "He is ris-en just as He said. Quick-ly now go tell His dis-ci-ples that Je-sus Christ is no long-er dead!"

© Copyright 1974 by Latter Rain Music. All rights reserved. Used by permission.

EASTER

Joy to the world, He is ris - en, Al - le - lu - ia! He's ris - en, Al - le - lu - ia! He's ris - en, Al - le - lu - ia!

He Is Risen!   302

"Why do you look
for the living
among
the
dead?

He is not here:

He has been raised!

Remember what He said to you,

while He was still in Galilee—

that the Son of Man must be betrayed into the hands of sinful men,

and must be crucified,

and must rise again on the third day."

—Luke 24:5b-7 (PHILLIPS)

EASTER

303 Christ Is Coming!

... Surely I come quickly; even so, come, Lord Jesus. — Revelation 22: 20

John R. MacDuff

BRYN CALFARIA
William Owen
Harmonized by Carlton R. Young

1. Christ is coming! let creation From her groans and travail cease;
   Let the glorious proclamation Hope restore and faith increase:
   Christ is coming, Christ is coming, Christ is coming—
   Come, Thou blessed Prince of Peace! Come, Thou blessed Prince of Peace!

2. *Earth can now but tell the story Of Thy bitter cross and pain;*
   She shall yet behold Thy glory When Thou comest back to reign:
   Christ is coming, Christ is coming, Christ is coming—
   Let each heart repeat the strain! Let each heart repeat the strain!

3. With that blessed hope before us, Let no harp remain unstrung;
   Let the mighty advent chorus Onward roll from tongue to tongue:
   Christ is coming, Christ is coming, Christ is coming—
   Come, Lord Jesus, quickly come! Come, Lord Jesus, quickly come! A-men.

Harmonization © Copyright 1964 by Abingdon Press. Used by permission.

THE SECOND COMING OF JESUS CHRIST

Christ Returneth! 304

... be ye also ready; for in such an hour as ye think not the Son of man cometh.
— Matthew 24:44

H. L. Turner

CHRIST RETURNETH
James McGranahan

1. It may be at morn, when the day is a-wak-ing, When sun-light through dark-ness and shad-ow is break-ing, That Je-sus will come in the full-ness of glo-ry, To re-ceive from the world His own.
2. *It may be at mid-day, it may be at twi-light, It may be, per-chance, that the black-ness of mid-night Will burst in-to light in the blaze of His glo-ry, When Je-sus re-ceives His own.*
3. While hosts cry "Ho-san-na," from heav-en de-scend-ing, With glo-ri-fied saints and the an-gels at-tend-ing, With grace on His brow, like a ha-lo of glo-ry, Will Je-sus re-ceive His own.
4. *O joy! O de-light! Should we go with-out dy-ing, No sick-ness, no sad-ness, no dread and no cry-ing, Caught up through the clouds with our Lord in-to glo-ry, When Je-sus re-ceives His own.*

O, Lord Je-sus, how long, how long 'Til we shout the glad song Christ re-turn-eth! Hal-le-lu-jah! hal-le-lu-jah! A-men, Hal-le-lu-jah! A-men.

THE SECOND COMING OF JESUS CHRIST

305 Jesus Is Coming Again

Watch, therefore, for ye know neither the day nor the hour . . . . — Matthew 25:13

John W. Peterson

COMING AGAIN
John W. Peterson

wonderful day it will be— Jesus is coming again!

Lo! He Comes with Clouds Descending 306

Charles Wesley
Martin Madan
Based on John Cennick
Jeff Redd, alt.

This same Jesus, . . . shall come in like manner as ye have seen Him go into Heaven.
— Acts 1:11

REGENT SQUARE
Henry T. Smart

1 Lo, He comes with clouds descending, Once for favored sinners slain;
2 *Every eye shall now behold Him, Robed in awesome majesty;*
3 Now redemption, long expected, See in solemn pomp appear;
4 *Yes, Amen! let all adore Thee, High on the eternal throne;*

1 All the many saints attending, Swell the triumph of His train:
2 *Those who once denied and killed Him, Pierced and nailed Him to the tree,*
3 All His saints, by man rejected, Now shall meet Him in the air:
4 *Savior, take the power and glory, Claim the kingdom for Your own:*

1 Alleluia! Alleluia! God appears on earth to reign.
2 *Deeply wailing, deeply wailing, Shall the true Messiah see.*
3 Alleluia! Alleluia! See the day of God appear.
4 *Alleluia! Alleluia! Christ shall reign and Christ alone!* Amen.

Text alteration © Copyright 1976 by Fred Bock Music Co. All rights reserved. Used by permission.

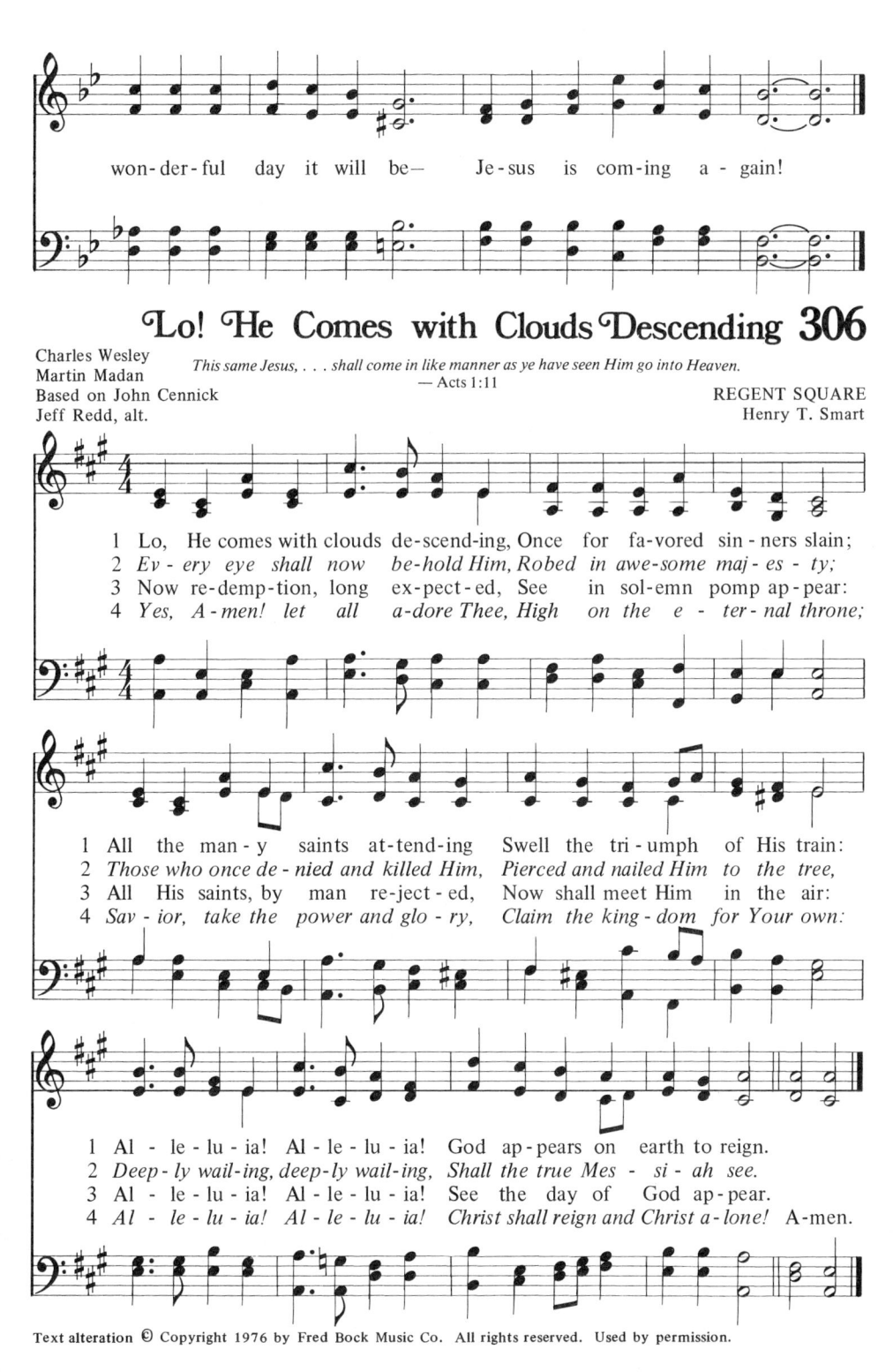

THE SECOND COMING OF JESUS CHRIST

307 This Could Be the Dawning of that Day

... Ye do well that ye take heed as unto a light, ... in a dark place, until the day dawn ....
— II Peter 1:19

Gloria Gaither
William Gaither

DAWNING
William J. Gaither

1. A parade began at Calvary, And the saints of all the ages fill its ranks; O'er the sands of time they're marching to their King's great coronation, And this could be the dawning of that day!

2. Nothing here holds their allegiance, They're not bound by shackles forged of earthly gold; Since that day they knelt at Calvary, they've been pilgrims ever wandering, Just looking for a place to rest their souls.

3. All the saints are getting restless, O what glorious expectation fills each face! Dreams and hopes of all the ages are awaiting His returning, And this could be the dawning of that day!

© Copyright 1971 by William J. Gaither. All rights reserved. Used by permission.
THE SECOND COMING OF JESUS CHRIST

THE SECOND COMING OF JESUS CHRIST

O this could be the dawn-ing of that grand and glo-rious day, When the face of Je-sus we be-hold! Dreams and hopes of all the a-ges Are a-wait-ing His re-turn-ing, And this could be the dawn-ing of that day!

308   The Son of Man in His Glory

"When the Son of man comes in His glory, and all the angels with Him, then He will sit on His glorious throne. Before Him will be gathered all the nations, and He will separate them one from another as a shepherd separates the sheep from the goats, and He will place the sheep at His right hand, but the goats at the left.

"Then the King will say to those at His right hand, 'Come, O blessed of My Father, inherit the kingdom prepared for you from the foundation of the world; for I was hungry and you gave Me food, I was thirsty and you gave Me drink, I was a stranger and you welcomed Me, I was naked and you clothed Me, I was sick and you visited Me, I was in prison and you came to Me.' Then the righteous will answer Him, 'Lord, when did we see Thee hungry and feed Thee, or thirsty and give Thee drink? And when did we see Thee a stranger and welcome Thee, or naked and clothe Thee? And when did we see Thee sick or in prison and visit Thee?' And the King will answer them, 'Truly, I say to you, as you did it to one of the least of these My brethren, you did it to Me.'

"Then He will say to those at His left hand, 'Depart from Me, you cursed, into the eternal fire prepared for the devil and his angels; for I was hungry and you gave Me no food, I was thirsty and you gave Me no drink, I was a stranger and you did not welcome Me, naked and you did not clothe Me, sick and in prison and you did not visit Me.' Then they also will answer, 'Lord, when did we see Thee hungry or thirsty or a stranger or naked or sick or in prison, and did not minister to Thee?' Then He will answer them, 'Truly, I say to you, as you did it not to one of the least of these, you did it not to Me.' And they will go away into eternal punishment, but the righteous into eternal life."

—Matthew 25:31-46 (RSV)

309   When He Shall Come

PEARCE
Almeda J. Pearce

And if I go to prepare a place for you, I will come again, . . . that where I am there ye may be also. John 14:3

1 When He shall come, re-splen-dent in His glo-ry, To take His own from out this vale of night, O may I know the joy at His ap-pear-ing— On - ly at morn to walk with Him in white!

2 *When I shall stand with-in the court of heav-en Where white-robed pil-grims pass be-fore my sight— Earth's mar-tyred saints and blood-washed o-ver-com-ers— These then are they who walk with Him in white!*

3 When He shall call, from earth's re-mot-est cor-ners, All who have stood tri-um-phant in His might, O to be wor-thy then to stand be-side them, And in that morn to walk with Him in white!

© Copyright 1934. Renewal 1962 by Almeda J. Pearce. Used by permission.
THE SECOND COMING OF JESUS CHRIST

Is It the Crowning Day? 310

Looking for and hasting unto the coming of the Day of God.
— I John 3:12

George Walker Whitcomb

GLAD DAY
Charles H. Marsh

1. Je-sus may come to-day, Glad day! Glad day! And I would see my Friend; Dan-gers and trou-bles would end If Je-sus should come to-day.
2. *I may go home to-day, Glad day! Glad day! Seems like I hear their song; Hail to the ra-di-ant throng! If I should go home to-day.*
3. Faith-ful I'll be to-day, Glad day! Glad day! And I will free-ly tell Why I should love Him so well, For He is my all to-day.

Glad day! Glad day! Is it the crown-ing day? I'll live for to-day, nor anx-ious be, Je-sus, my Lord, I soon shall see; Glad day! Glad day! Is it the crown-ing day?

Copyright 1910 by Praise Publishing Co. © Renewed 1938 (extended), The Rodeheaver Co., owner. Used by permission.

THE SECOND COMING OF JESUS CHRIST

311. What If It Were Today?

"Jesus has gone away to Heaven, and some day, just as He went, He will return." — Acts 1:11b

WHAT IF IT WERE TODAY?

Lelia N. Morris
Lelia N. Morris

1. Je-sus is com-ing to earth a-gain, What if it were to-day?
2. *Sa-tan's do-min-ion will then be o'er, O that it were to-day!*
3. Faith-ful and true would He find us here If He should come to-day?

1. Com-ing in pow-er and love to reign, What if it were to-day?
2. *Sor-row and sigh-ing shall be no more, O that it were to-day!*
3. Watch-ing in glad-ness and not in fear, If He should come to-day?

1. Com-ing to claim His cho-sen Bride, All the re-deemed and pu-ri-fied,
2. *Then shall the dead in Christ a-rise, Caught up to meet Him in the skies,*
3. Signs of His com-ing mul-ti-ply, Morning light breaks in east-ern sky,

1. O-ver this whole earth scat-tered wide, What if it were to-day?
2. *When shall these glo-ries meet our eyes? What if it were to-day?*
3. Watch, for the time is draw-ing nigh, What if it were to-day?

Glo-ry, glo-ry! Joy to my heart 'twill bring; Glo-ry,

Copyright 1912. Renewal 1940 extended, Hope Publishing Co. All rights reserved. Used by permission.

THE SECOND COMING OF JESUS CHRIST

glo - ry! When we shall crown Him King; Glo - ry, glo - ry!
Haste to pre-pare the way; Glo-ry, glo - ry! Je-sus will come some-day.

Some Golden Daybreak 312

Ye shall see the Son of man . . . coming in the clouds of Heaven – Mark 14:62

Carl Blackmore

DAYBREAK
Carl Blackmore

Some gold - en day-break, Je - sus will come;
Some gold - en day-break, bat - tles all won, He'll shout the vic - tory,
break through the blue— Some gold - en day-break, for me, for you.

Copyright 1934 by Blackmore & Son. Assigned to The Rodeheaver Co. © Renewal 1962, The Rodeheaver Co. Used by permission.

THE SECOND COMING OF JESUS CHRIST

313 The King Is Coming

Gloria Gaither, stanzas 1, 2, 3
William J. Gaither, stanzas 1, 2, 3
Charles Millhuff, stanza 3

Behold, the Lord cometh with ten thousands of His saints.
— Jude 1:14

KING IS COMING
William J. Gaither
Final chorus arranged by Ronn Huff

1. The mar-ket place is emp-ty, No more traf-fic in the streets, All the build-ers' tools are si-lent, No more time to har-vest wheat; Bus-y house-wives cease their la-bors, In the court room no de-bate, Work on earth is all sus-pend-ed As the King comes thru the gate.

2. *Hap-py fac-es line the hall-ways, Those whose lives have been redeemed, Broken homes that He has mend-ed, Those from pris-on He has freed; Lit-tle chil-dren and the a-ged Hand in hand stand all a-glow, Who were crippled, broken, ru-ined, Clad in gar-ments white as snow.*

3. I can hear the char-iots rum-ble, I can see the march-ing throng, The flur-ry of God's trum-pets Spells the end of sin and wrong; Re-gal robes are now un-fold-ing, Heav-en's grandstands all in place, Heav-en's choir is now as-sem-bled, Start to sing "A-maz-ing Grace!"

O the King is com-ing, the King is com-ing! I just heard the trumpets sounding, And now His face I see;

© Copyright 1970 by William J. Gaither. All rights reserved. Used by permission.

THE SECOND COMING OF JESUS CHRIST

O the King is com-ing, the King is com-ing! Praise God, He's com-ing for me! me! O the King is coming, the King is com-ing! I just heard the trumpet sounding, And now His face I see; O the King is coming, the King is com-ing! Praise God! He's com-ing for me!

Congregation sing melody in unison; accompanist play as written.

Final chorus arrangement © 1976 by William J. Gaither. All rights reserved. Used by permission.

THE SECOND COMING OF JESUS CHRIST

314 What a Day That Will Be

*And the Lord will wipe all tears from their eyes;
... for the former things are passed away.* — Revelation 21:4

Jim Hill

WHAT A DAY
Jim Hill

1. There is coming a day when no heart-aches shall come,
2. *There'll be no sorrow there, no more burdens to bear,*

1. No more clouds in the sky, no more tears to dim the eye; All is
2. *No more sickness, no pain, no more parting over there; And for-*

1. peace for ev-er-more on that hap-py gold-en shore— What a day,
2. *ever I will be with the One who died for me— What a day,*

1. glo-ri-ous day, that will be.
2. *glo-ri-ous day, that will be.*

What a day that will be when my Je-sus I shall see, And I look up-on His face— the One who

© Copyright 1955 by Ben. L. Speer. All rights reserved. Used by permission.
THE SECOND COMING OF JESUS CHRIST

saved me by His grace; When He takes me by the hand, and leads me through the Prom-ised Land, What a day, glo-ri-ous day, that will be.

For God So Loved the World 315

Based on John 3:16
Frances Townsend

While we were yet sinners, Christ died for us.
— Romans 5:8

GOD LOVED THE WORLD
Alfred B. Smith

Unison

For God so loved the world He gave His on-ly Son To die on Cal-vary's tree, From sin to set me free; Some day He's com-ing back, What glo-ry that will be! Won-der-ful His love to me.

© Copyright 1938. Renewal 1966 by Alfred B. Smith. Assigned to Singspiration, Inc.

THE SECOND COMING OF JESUS CHRIST

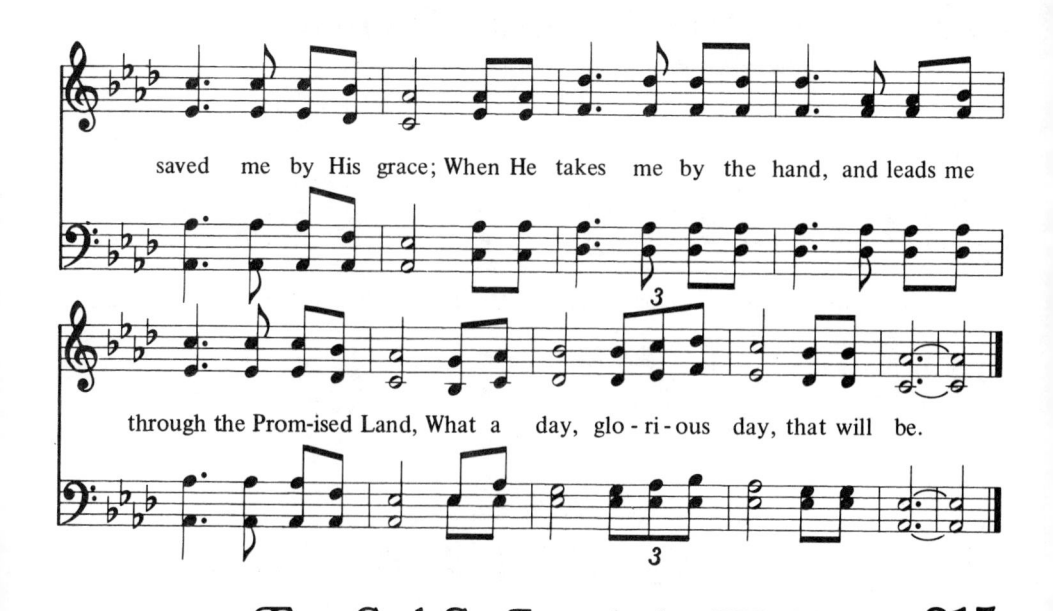

316 My Lord, What a Morning!

They shall see the Son of man coming in the clouds of heaven....
— Matthew 24:30

Traditional

STARS FALL
Traditional Spiritual

My Lord, what a morn-ing! My Lord, what a morn-ing! O my Lord, what a morn-ing, When the stars be-gin to fall.

Fine

1 You'll hear a sin-ner mourn, To wake the na-tions un-der-ground!
2 *You'll hear a sin-ner pray, To wake the na-tions un-der-ground!*
3 You'll hear a Chris-tian shout, To wake the na-tions un-der-ground!
4 *You'll hear a Chris-tian sing, To wake the na-tions un-der-ground!*

Look-ing to my God's right hand, When the stars be-gin to fall!

D.C.

THE SECOND COMING OF JESUS CHRIST

Our Love for God

317 Let's Just Praise the Lord

The Lord Jehovah is my strength and my song . . .
— Isaiah 12:2

Gloria Gaither
William J. Gaither

LET'S JUST PRAISE THE LORD
William J. Gaither

Let's just praise the Lord! Praise the Lord! Let's just lift our hearts* to heav-en and praise the Lord; Let's just praise the Lord! Praise the Lord! Let's just lift our hearts* to heav-en and praise the Lord!

Fine

*Alternate lyrics, "voices", "hands".
© Copyright 1972 by William J. Gaither. All rights reserved. Used by permission.
WORSHIP AND ADORATION

1. O we thank You for Your kindness, we thank You for Your love, We have been in heavenly places, felt blessings from above; We've been sharing all the good things, the family can afford, Let's just turn our praise toward heaven and praise the Lord.

2. Just the precious name of Jesus is worthy of our praise, Let us bow our knees before Him, our hands to heaven raise; When He comes in clouds of glory, with Him to ever reign, Let's just lift our happy voices, and praise His name.

WORSHIP AND ADORATION

318 Come, Thou Fount of Every Blessing

In that day shall a fountain be opened . . . for sin and uncleaness.
— Zechariah 13:1

Robert Robinson
Jeff Redd, 2nd stanza, alt.

NETTLETON
John Wyeth

1. Come, Thou Fount of ev-ery bless-ing, Tune my heart to sing Thy grace; Streams of mer-cy, nev-er ceas-ing, Call for songs of loud-est praise. Teach me some me-lo-dious son-net, Sung by flaming tongues a-bove; Praise the mount! I'm fixed up-on it, Mount of Thy redeeming love.

2. This my glad com-mem-o-ra-tion That 'til now I've safe-ly come; And I hope, by Thy good pleas-ure, Safe-ly to ar-rive at home. Je-sus sought me when a strang-er, Wan-dering from the fold of God; He, to res-cue me from dan-ger, Interposed His pre-cious blood.

3. O to grace how great a debt-or Dai-ly I'm con-strained to be! Let Thy good-ness, like a fet-ter, Bind my wan-dering heart to Thee: Prone to wan-der, Lord, I feel it, Prone to leave the God I love: Here's my heart, O take and seal it, Seal it for Thy courts a-bove. A-men.

Alternate ending for 2nd stanza into harmonization.

Second stanza © Copyright 1976 by Fred Bock Music Co. All rights reserved.
WORSHIP AND ADORATION

Alternate Last Verse Harmonization   Arranged by Richard Bolks

3. O to grace how great a debt-or Daily I'm con-strained to be! Let Thy good-ness like a fet-ter, Bind my wan-dering heart to Thee. Prone to wan-der, Lord, I feel it, Prone to leave the God I love: Here's my heart, O take and seal it, Seal it for Thy courts a-bove. A-men.

© Copyright 1976 by Paragon Associates, Inc. All rights reserved.

WORSHIP AND ADORATION

319 Immortal, Invisible, God Only Wise

He that keepeth thee shall not slumber . . . or sleep.
— Psalm 121: 3,4

Walter Chalmers Smith

ST. DENIO
Welsh Melody

1. Immortal, invisible, God only wise,
In light inaccessible hid from our eyes,
Most blessed, most glorious, the Ancient of Days,
Almighty, victorious, Thy great name we praise.

2. *Unresting, unhasting, and silent as light,*
Nor wanting, nor wasting, Thou rulest in might;
Thy justice like mountains high soaring above
Thy clouds, which are fountains of goodness and love.

3. To all, life Thou givest, to both great and small;
In all life Thou livest, the true life of all;
We blossom and flourish as leaves on the tree,
And wither and perish—but naught changeth Thee.

4. *Great Father of glory, pure Father of light,*
Thine angels adore Thee, all veiling their sight;
All praise we would render: O help us to see
'Tis only the splendor of light hideth Thee.

A-men.

WORSHIP AND ADORATION

Alternate Last Verse Harmonization   Arranged by Mary E. Caldwell

4 Great Father of glory, pure Father of light, Thine angels adore Thee, all veiling their sight; All praise we would render: O help us to see 'Tis only the splendor of light hideth Thee. A-men.

© Copyright 1976 by Paragon Associates, Inc. All rights reserved.

WORSHIP AND ADORATION

320 Let Us Celebrate the Glories of Our God

Now unto God and our Father be glory forever and ever. — Philippians 4:20

Bryan Jeffery Leech

BELLAMY
Jean Joseph Mouret
Arranged by Fred Bock

1. Let us cel-e-brate the glo-ries of our Lord, And let us look for His swift re-turning; What a glo-rious hope we have in the dark-est hour To know He's com-ing soon with power. 1. As we look for His ap-pear-ing, We must share the good news with ev-ery man on earth. As we see this mo-ment near-ing, We must live to serve Him for all that we are worth! 2. Let us

2. (Let us) cel-e-brate the glo-ries of our Lord, And let us tell Him how good and great He is; Let's re-hearse the songs we'll sing when He comes to reign, And take His right-ful place a-gain. 2. Je-sus Christ is now the vic-tor, Know-ing that He's with us, what cause is there to fear? There's a sound of dis-tant drum-ming, For His prom-ised com-ing is ver-y, ver-y near! 3. Let us

3. (Let us) cel-e-brate the glo-ries of our Lord, And let us men-tion His great a-chieve-ments; For we can-not tell too much how He went to die And how our God has raised Him high.

© Copyright 1976 by Fred Bock Music Co. All rights reserved. Used by permission.

WORSHIP AND ADORATION

Brethren, We Have Met to Worship 321

Jesus sayeth . . ., No man cometh unto the Father but by Me. — John 14:6

George Atkins
Alt. Bryan Jeffery Leech

HOLY MANNA
William Moore
in *Columbian Harmony*

1 Breth-ren, we have met to wor-ship To a-dore the Lord and God;
2 *Let us love our God su-preme-ly, Let us love our broth-ers too;*

1 Will you pray with ex-pec-ta-tion As we preach the liv-ing Word?
2 *Let us pray and care for peo-ple 'Til God makes their lives a-new.*

1 All is vain un-less the Spir-it Of the Ho-ly One comes down;
2 *When at last we're called to heav-en, In His pre-sence we'll sit down;*

1 Breth-ren, pray, and God's great bless-ing Will be show-ered all a-round.
2 *And the Lord will then re-ward us Giv-ing us a heaven-ly crown.*

© 1976 Fred Bock Music Company. All rights reserved. Used by permission.

WORSHIP AND ADORATION

322 When Morning Gilds the Skies

Unto Him be glory in the church by Jesus Christ throughout all ages world without end.
— Ephesians 3:21

From the German
Tr. by Edward Caswall

LAUDES DOMINI
Joseph Barnby

1. When morn-ing gilds the skies, My heart a-wak-ing cries, May Jesus Christ be praised! A-like at work and prayer To Jesus I repair, May Jesus Christ be praised!
2. Does sad-ness fill my mind? A sol-ace here I find, May Jesus Christ be praised! Or fades my earth-ly bliss? My com-fort still is this, May Jesus Christ be praised!
3. The night be-comes as day When from the heart we say, May Jesus Christ be praised! The powers of dark-ness fear When this sweet chant they hear, May Jesus Christ be praised!
4. Ye na-tions of man-kind In this your one-ness find, May Jesus Christ be praised! Let all the earth a-round Ring joy-ous with the sound, May Jesus Christ be praised!
5. Be this, while life is mine, My can-ti-cle di-vine, May Jesus Christ be praised! Be this th'e-ter-nal song Through all the a-ges long, May Jesus Christ be praised! A-men.

WORSHIP AND ADORATION

Alternate Last Verse Harmonization

Arranged by Fred Bock

5 Be this, while life is mine, My canticle divine, May Jesus Christ be praised: Be this th' eternal song, Through all the ages long, May Jesus Christ be praised! Amen.

© Copyright 1968 by Fred Bock Music Company. All rights reserved. Used by permission.

WORSHIP AND ADORATION

323 Holy! Holy! Holy! Lord God Almighty

Holy, holy, holy, Lord God Almighty; who was, and is, and is to come. — Revelation 4:8

Reginald Heber

NICAEA
John B. Dykes
Descant by David McK. Williams

Descant

Ho - - - - - - - - - ly,

1 Ho-ly, ho-ly, ho - ly! Lord God Al-might-y!
2 Ho-ly, ho-ly, ho - ly! all the saints a-dore Thee,
3 Ho-ly, ho-ly, ho - ly! though the dark-ness hide Thee,
4 Ho-ly, ho-ly, ho - ly! Lord God Al-might-y!

Ho - - - - - - - - - ly,

1 Ear - ly in the morn - ing our song shall rise to Thee;
2 Cast - ing down their gold - en crowns a - round the glass - y sea;
3 Though the eye of sin - ful man Thy glo - ry may not see;
4 All Thy works shall praise Thy name in earth and sky and sea;

Ho - - - - - - - - - ly,

1 Ho-ly, ho-ly, ho - ly! mer - ci - ful and might - y!
2 Cher - u - bim and ser - a - phim fall - ing down be - fore Thee,
3 On - ly Thou art ho - ly— there is none be - side Thee
4 Ho-ly, ho-ly, ho - ly! mer - ci - ful and might - y!

© Copyright 1948, renewed 1976 by the H. W. Gray Company, Inc. All rights reserved. Used by permission.
WORSHIP AND ADORATION

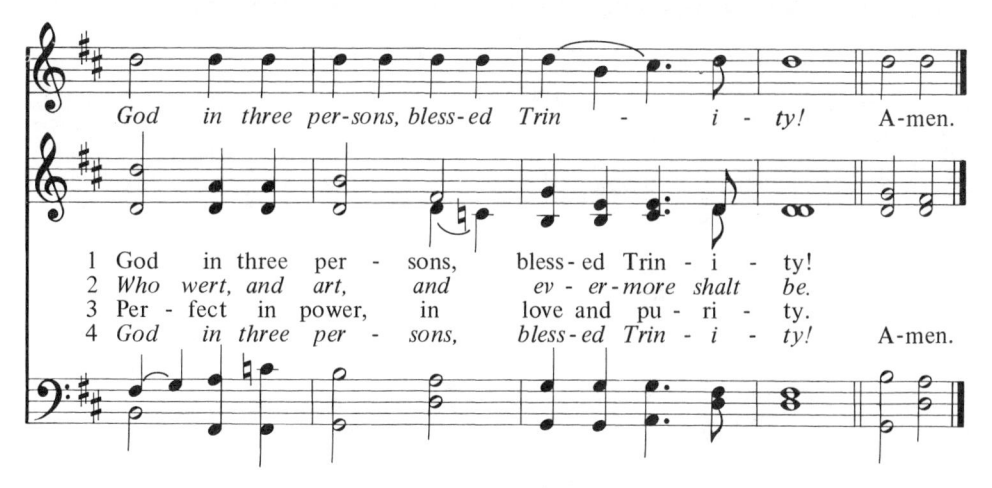

1 God in three per - sons, bless-ed Trin - i - ty!
2 Who wert, and art, and ev - er-more shalt be.
3 Per - fect in power, in love and pu - ri - ty.
4 God in three per - sons, bless-ed Trin - i - ty! A-men.

Te Deum 324

We praise Thee, O God:
We acknowledge Thee to be the Lord.
All the earth doth worship Thee, the Father everlasting.
To Thee all angels cry aloud; the heavens and all the powers therein.
To Thee cherubim and seraphim continually do cry:
Holy, Holy, Holy, Lord God of Sabaoth.
Heaven and earth are full of the majesty of Thy glory.
The glorious company of the apostles praise Thee.
The goodly fellowship of the prophets praise Thee.
The noble army of martyrs praise Thee.
The holy Church, throughout all the world, doth acknowledge Thee,
The Father of an infinite majesty;
Thine adorable, true, and only Son;
Also the Holy Spirit, the Comforter.
Thou art the King of glory, O Christ.
Thou art the everlasting Son of the Father.
When Thou tookest upon Thee to deliver man,
Thou didst humble Thyself to be born of a virgin.
When Thou hadst overcome the sharpness of death,
Thou didst open the kingdom of heaven to all believers.
Thou sittest at the right hand of God, in the glory of the Father.
We believe that Thou shalt come to be our Judge.
We therefore pray Thee, help Thy servants,
Whom Thou hast redeemed with Thy precious blood.
Make them to be numbered with Thy saints in glory everlasting.
O Lord, save Thy people, and bless Thy heritage.
Govern them, and lift them up forever.
Day by day we magnify Thee;
And we worship Thy name ever, world without end.
Vouchsafe, O Lord, to keep us this day without sin.
O Lord, have mercy upon us, have mercy upon us.
O Lord, let Thy mercy be upon us, as our trust is in Thee.
O Lord, in Thee have I trusted;
Let me never be confounded.
Amen.

WORSHIP AND ADORATION

325 All Hail the Power of Jesus' Name

Great is the Lord and greatly to be praised. — Psalm 145:3

(FIRST TUNE)

Edward Perronet
John Rippon, alt.

CORONATION
Oliver Holden

1. All hail the power of Jesus' name! Let angels prostrate fall; Bring forth the royal diadem, And crown Him Lord of all; Bring forth the royal diadem, And crown Him Lord of all!

2. Ye chosen seed of Israel's race, Ye ransomed from the fall, Hail Him who saves you by His grace, And crown Him Lord of all; Hail Him who saves you by His grace, And crown Him Lord of all!

3. Let every kindred, every tribe, On this terrestrial ball, To Him all majesty ascribe, And crown Him Lord of all; To Him all majesty ascribe, And crown Him Lord of all!

4. O that with yonder sacred throng We at His feet may fall! We'll join the everlasting song, And crown Him Lord of all; We'll join the everlasting song, And crown Him Lord of all! A-men.

WORSHIP AND ADORATION

Alternate Last Verse Harmonization
Arranged by Fred Bock

4 O that with yon-der sa-cred throng We at His feet may fall! We'll join the ev-er-last-ing song, And crown Him Lord of all. We'll join the ev-er-last-ing song, And crown Him Lord of all! A-men.

© Copyright 1968 by Fred Bock Music Company. All rights reserved. Used by permission.

WORSHIP AND ADORATION

326 All Hail the Power of Jesus' Name

Thou art worthy, O Lord, to receive glory, and honor, and power: — Revelation 4:11

(SECOND TUNE)

Edward Perronet
John Rippon, alt.

DIADEM
James Ellor

1. All hail the power of Jesus' name! Let angels prostrate fall, Let angels prostrate fall; Bring forth the royal diadem, And crown Him, crown Him, crown Him, crown Him, crown Him, crown Him, crown Him, and crown Him Lord of all.

2. Ye chosen seed of Israel's race, Ye ransomed from the fall, Ye ransomed from the fall; Hail Him who saves you by His grace, And crown Him, crown Him, crown Him, crown Him, crown Him, crown Him, crown Him, and crown Him Lord of all.

3. Let every kindred, every tribe, On this terrestrial ball, On this terrestrial ball, To Him all majesty ascribe, And crown Him, crown Him, crown Him, crown Him, crown Him, crown Him, crown Him, and crown Him Lord of all.

4. O that with yonder sacred throng We at His feet may fall, We at His feet may fall! We'll join the everlasting song, And crown Him, crown Him, crown Him, crown Him, crown Him, crown Him, crown Him, and crown Him Lord of all.

WORSHIP AND ADORATION

crown Him, And crown Him Lord of all. A-men.

Him,

All Hail the Power of Jesus' Name 327

We made known unto you the power, and coming of our Lord Jesus Christ; . . . were eyewitness of His majesty. — II Peter 1:16

Edward Perronet
John Rippon, alt.

(THIRD TUNE)

MILES LANE
William Shrubsole

1 All hail the power of Je-sus' name! Let an-gels pros-trate fall;
2 *Ye cho-sen seed of Is-rael's race, Ye ran-somed from the fall,*
3 Let ev-ery kin-dred, ev-ery tribe, On this ter-res-trial ball,
4 *O that with yon-der sa-cred throng We at His feet may fall!*

1 Bring forth the roy-al di-a-dem,
2 *Hail Him who saves you by His grace,* And crown Him, crown Him,
3 To Him all maj-es-ty as-cribe,
4 *We'll join the ev-er-last-ing song,*

crown Him, Crown Him Lord of all! A-men.

WORSHIP AND ADORATION

328 Begin, My Tongue, Some Heavenly Theme

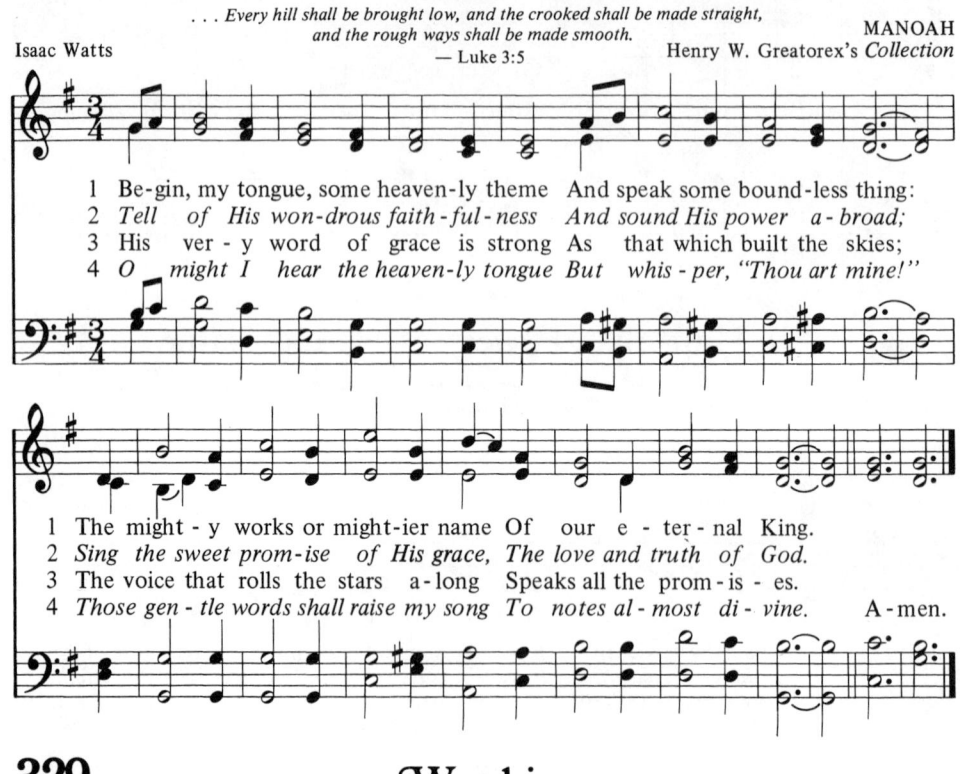

... Every hill shall be brought low, and the crooked shall be made straight, and the rough ways shall be made smooth.
— Luke 3:5

Isaac Watts

MANOAH
Henry W. Greatorex's *Collection*

1. Be-gin, my tongue, some heaven-ly theme And speak some bound-less thing: The might-y works or might-ier name Of our e-ter-nal King.
2. Tell of His won-drous faith-ful-ness And sound His power a-broad; Sing the sweet prom-ise of His grace, The love and truth of God.
3. His ver-y word of grace is strong As that which built the skies; The voice that rolls the stars a-long Speaks all the prom-is-es.
4. O might I hear the heaven-ly tongue But whis-per, "Thou art mine!" Those gen-tle words shall raise my song To notes al-most di-vine. A-men.

329   Worship

Minister: It would make a tremendous difference if this congregation would do certain things.

People: *When we come to church, we ought to come prepared.*

Minister: There are so very few people who make any preparation for worship at all. They have to hurry to get ready; they have to hurry down the road; they take their places almost at the last moment; and there is no preparation at all.

If every person who comes to church would, before he comes, or even on the road there, think of God for just a moment or two, and say a prayer for himself and for the preacher and the people who will meet in worship, it would make a whole world of difference.

People: *We should come seeking.*

Minister: To come to the services of the church should never be simply a matter of habit, a burden of duty, a hallmark of respectability, the satisfying of a convention. It should be a deliberate attempt to come out of the world and to find contact with God.

One of the great secrets of success in any of the business of life is to know what we want, when we are doing a thing; and when we come to church we should want God.

People: *We should come determined to give all of ourselves.*

Minister: He who comes to church only to get will, in the end, get nothing. We should come determined to give our interest, our prayer, our devotion, our sympathy. The success of any gathering, the happiness of any party, is always dependent on the people who are prepared to give themselves to the fellowship of the occasion.

—William Barclay

WORSHIP AND ADORATION

It Is Good to Sing Thy Praises 330

Rejoice in the Lord, O Ye righteous, for praise is comely for the upright.

— Psalm 33:1

From Psalm 92
The Psalter

ELLESDIE
Wolfgang A. Mozart

1. It is good to sing Thy prais-es And to thank Thee, O Most High,
2. *Thou hast filled my heart with gladness Thro the works Thy hands have wrought;*
3. But the good shall live be-fore Thee, Plant-ed in Thy dwell-ing place,

1. Show-ing forth Thy lov-ing-kind-ness When the morn-ing lights the sky.
2. *Thou hast made my life vic-to-rious, Great Thy works and deep Thy thought.*
3. Fruit-ful trees and ev-er ver-dant, Nour-ished by Thy bound-less grace.

1. It is good when night is fall-ing Of Thy faith-ful-ness to tell,
2. *Thou, O Lord, on high ex-alt-ed, Reign-est ev-er-more in might;*
3. In His good-ness to the right-eous God His right-eous-ness dis-plays;

1. While with sweet, me-lo-dious prais-es Songs of ad-o-ra-tion swell.
2. *All Thy en-e-mies shall per-ish, Sin be ban-ished from Thy sight.*
3. God my rock, my strength, my ref-uge, Just and true are all His ways. A-men.

WORSHIP AND ADORATION

331 Sometimes "Alleluia"

Blessed is His glorious name forever; let the whole earth be filled with His glory.
— Psalm 72:19

Chuck Girard

SOMETIMES ALLELUIA
Chuck Girard

Some-times "Al - le - lu - ia," Some-times "Praise the Lord;" Some-times gent - ly sing - ing, Our hearts in one ac- cord.

1 O let us lift our voic - es, Look toward the sky and start to sing;
2 O let our joy be un - con - fined, Let us sing with free-dom un - re - strained;
3 O let us feel His pres - ence, Let the sound of prais - es fill the air;
4 O let the Spir - it o - ver-flow, As we are filled from head to toe;

© Copyright 1974 by Dunamis Music. International copyright secured. All rights reserved. Used by permission.

WORSHIP AND ADORATION

1. O, let us now return His love—
Just let our voices ring.
2. Let's take this feeling that we're feeling now
Outside these walls and let it rain.
3. O, let us sing the song of Jesus' love
To people everywhere.
4. We love You Father, Son and Holy Ghost,
And we want this world to know.

Sometimes "Alleluia," Sometimes "Praise the Lord;"
Sometimes gently singing, Our hearts in one accord.

WORSHIP AND ADORATION

332 The God of Abraham Praise!

The eternal God is thy refuge, and underneath are the everlasting arms.
— Deuteronomy 33:27

Revised version of the *Yigdal*
Daniel ben Judah
Tr. by Newton Mann
and Max Landsberg

LEONI
Hebrew Melody
Adapted by Meyer Lyon

1. The God of A-braham praise, All prais-ed be His name, Who was, and is, and is to be, Al-ways the same! The one e-ter-nal God, Whose time-less-ness is clear; The First, the Last: be-yond all thought, Through-out the years!

2. *His spir-it flow-eth free, High surg-ing where it will; In proph-et's word He spoke of old, He speak-eth still. Es-tab-lished is His law, And change-less it shall stand, Now writ-ten deep up-on the heart, On sea or land.*

3. He hath e-ter-nal life Im-plant-ed in the soul; His love shall be our strength-en-ing While a-ges roll. Praise to the liv-ing God! All prais-ed be His name, Who was, and is, and is to be, Al-ways the same! A-men.

WORSHIP AND ADORATION

Worship 333

Worship is the highest and noblest act that any person can do. When men worship, God is satisfied! "The Father seeketh such to worship Him." Amazing, isn't it? And when you worship, you are fulfilled! Think about this: why did Jesus Christ come? He came to make worshipers out of rebels. We who were once self-centered have to be completely changed so that we can shift our attention outside of ourselves and become able to worship Him.

—Raymond C. Ortlund

We Praise Thee, O God, Our Redeemer 334

As for our Redeemer, the Lord of hosts is His name. — Isaiah 47:4

KREMSER
Netherlands Folk Song
Arranged by Edward Kremser

Julia C. Cory

1. We praise Thee, O God, our Redeemer, Creator,
In grateful devotion our tribute we bring.
We lay it before Thee, we kneel and adore Thee,
We bless Thy holy name, glad praises we sing.

2. *We worship Thee, God of our fathers, we bless Thee;*
Through life's storm and tempest our guide hast Thou been.
When perils o'ertake us, Thou wilt not forsake us,
And with Thy help, O Lord, life's battles we win.

3. With voices united our praises we offer,
And gladly our songs of true worship we raise.
Thy strong arm will guide us, our God is beside us,
To Thee, our great Redeemer, forever be praise. A-men.

WORSHIP AND ADORATION

335 Praise the Lord! Ye Heavens Adore Him

Praise ye Him sun and moon; praise Him all ye stars. — Psalm 148:3

From Psalm 148
Foundling Hospital Collection, Stanzas 1, 2
Edward Osler, Stanza 3

FABEN
John H. Willcox

1. Praise the Lord! ye heavens, adore Him, Praise Him, angels in the height;
Sun and moon, rejoice before Him, Praise Him, all ye stars of light.
Praise the Lord! for He hath spoken, Worlds His mighty voice obeyed:
Laws which never shall be broken For their guidance He hath made.

2. *Praise the Lord! for He is glorious, Never shall His promise fail;*
God hath made His saints victorious, Sin and death shall not prevail.
Praise the God of our salvation, Hosts on high, His power proclaim;
Heaven and earth and all creation Laud and magnify His name.

3. Worship, honor, glory, blessing, Lord, we offer unto Thee;
Young and old, Thy praise expressing, In glad homage bend the knee.
All the saints in heaven adore Thee, We would bow before Thy throne:
As Thine angels serve before Thee, So on earth Thy will be done. A-men.

WORSHIP AND ADORATION

Alternate Last Verse Harmonization Arranged by Ovid Young

3 Wor-ship, hon-or, glo-ry, bless-ing, Lord, we of-fer un-to Thee; Young and old, Thy praise ex-press-ing, In glad hom-age bend the knee. All the saints in heav'n a-dore Thee; We would bow be-fore Thy throne: As Thine an-gels serve be-fore Thee, So on earth Thy will be done. A-men.

© Copyright 1976 by Paragon Associates, Inc. All rights reserved.

WORSHIP AND ADORATION

336 O Worship the King

The true worshipper shall worship the Father in spirit and in truth. — John 4:23

Robert Grant

LYONS
Adapted from Johann Michael Haydn

1. O worship the King all glorious above, And gratefully sing His wonderful love; Our Shield and Defender, the Ancient of Days, Pavilioned in splendor and girded with praise.
2. *O tell of His might and sing of His grace, Whose robe is the light, whose canopy space; His chariots of wrath the deep thunder-clouds form, And dark is His path on the wings of the storm.*
3. Thy bountiful care what tongue can recite? It breathes in the air, it shines in the light, It streams from the hills, it descends to the plain, And sweetly distills in the dew and the rain.
4. *Frail children of dust, and feeble as frail, In Thee do we trust, nor find Thee to fail; Thy mercies how tender, how firm to the end, Our Maker, Defender, Redeemer and Friend.* A - men.

Alternate ending for 3rd stanza into harmonization

WORSHIP AND ADORATION

Alternate Last Verse Harmonization

Arranged by Fred Bock

Frail chil-dren of dust, and fee-ble as frail, In Thee do we trust, nor find Thee to fail; Thy mer-cies how ten-der; how firm to the end! Our Mak-er, De-fend-er, Re-deem-er and Friend! A-men.

© Copyright 1968 by Fred Bock Music Company. All rights reserved. Used by permission.

WORSHIP AND ADORATION

337 Praise to the Lord, the Almighty

For then shalt thou have delight in the Almighty.
— Job 22:26

Joachim Neander
Tr. by Catherine Winkworth

LOBE DEN HERREN
"Stralsund Gesangbuch"

1. Praise to the Lord, the Almighty, the King of creation!
   O my soul, praise Him, for He is thy health and salvation!
   All ye who hear, Now to His temple draw near;
   Join me in glad adoration!

2. Praise to the Lord, who o'er all things so wondrously reigneth,
   Shelters thee under His wings, yes, so gently sustaineth!
   Hast thou not seen How all thy longings have been
   Granted in what He ordaineth?

3. Praise to the Lord, who doth prosper thy work and defend thee;
   Surely His goodness and mercy here daily attend thee.
   Ponder anew What the Almighty can do,
   If with His love He befriend thee.

4. Praise to the Lord! O let all that is in me adore Him!
   All that hath life and breath, come now with praises before Him.
   Let the Amen Sound from His people again:
   Gladly for aye we adore Him. A-men.

WORSHIP AND ADORATION

We Sing the Greatness of Our God

Great is our Lord, and of great power; His understanding is infinite.
— Psalm 147:5

338

Isaac Watts
Jeff Redd, alt.

ELLACOMBE
"Gesangbuch der Herzogl," Wirtemberg

1. We sing the great-ness of our God That made the moun-tains rise,
   That spread the flow-ing seas a-broad And built the loft-y skies.
   We sing the wis-dom that or-dained The sun to rule the day;
   The moon shines full at His com-mand, And all the stars o-bey.

2. *We sing the good-ness of the Lord That filled the earth with food;*
   He formed the crea-tures with His word And then pro-nounced them good.
   Lord, how Thy won-ders are dis-played Wher-e'er we turn our eyes:
   In ev-ery sea-son of the year, And through the changing skies.

3. There's not a plant or flower be-low But makes Thy glo-ries known;
   And clouds a-rise and tem-pests blow By or-der from Thy throne,
   While all that bor-rows life from Thee Is ev-er in Thy care,
   And ev-ery-where that man can be, Thou, God, art pres-ent there. A-men.

© Copyright 1970 by Fred Bock Music Company. All rights reserved. Used by permission.

WORSHIP AND ADORATION

339 Praise My Soul, the King of Heaven

'Til we all come to the unity and knowledge of the Son of God. — Ephesians 4:13

Henry F. Lyte

LAUDA ANIMA
Mark Andrews
Handbell descant by Bob Burroughs

Two-octave handbells descant, 4th stanza

Unison

1. Praise, my soul, the King of heav-en, To His feet thy trib-ute bring; Ran-somed, healed, re-stored, for-giv-en, Ev-er-more His prais-es sing; Al-le-lu-ia!
2. *Praise Him for His grace and fa-vor To our fa-thers in dis-tress; Praise Him, still the same as ev-er, Slow to chide and swift to bless; Al-le-lu-ia!*
3. Frail as sum-mer's flower we flour-ish, Blows the wind and it is gone; But, while mor-tals rise and per-ish, God en-dures un-chang-ing on: Al-le-lu-ia!
4. *An-gels in the height, a-dore Him; Ye be-hold Him face to face; Saints tri-um-phant, bow be-fore Him, Gath-ered in from ev-ery race; Al-le-lu-ia!*

© Copyright 1930 G. Schirmer Inc. All rights reserved. Used by permission.
Handbell descant © Copyright 1976 by G. Schirmer Inc. All rights reserved.

WORSHIP AND ADORATION

1 Al - le - lu - ia! Praise the ev - er - last - ing King.
2 Al - le - lu - ia! Glo - rious in His faith - ful - ness.
3 Al - le - lu - ia! Praise the high e - ter - nal one.
4 Al - le - lu - ia! Praise with us the God of grace. A - men.

A Call to Worship 340

Minister: Let all who love Him come rejoicing.
People: *God is in His heaven.*
Minister: To the Almighty praises voicing!
People: *God is in His heaven!*
Minister: All nature does to Him belong,
Yet we, His children, own the song
That age to age has made us strong.
People: *God is in His heaven.*

Minister: There dawns no day but by His blessing.
People: *God is in His heaven!*
Minister: No night without the stars confessing.
People: *God is in His heaven!*
Minister: Within His hand He does contain
All pow'r of sun, moon, wind and rain,
And watchful to His vast domain:
People: *God is in His heaven.*

Minister: Through all the years that are before us:
People: *God is in His heaven!*
Minister: His love forever reigning o'er us:
People: *God is in His heaven!*
Minister: Each season in its turn shall be
A glimpse of His eternity,
As God has been, so God shall be!
People: *God is in His heaven!*

—Jacqueline Hanna McNair

WORSHIP AND ADORATION

341 Come, Thou Almighty King

Until the Ancient of Days came . . . and . . . the saints possessed the Kingdom.
— Daniel 7:22

Anonymous
ITALIAN HYMN
Felice de Giardini

1. Come, Thou Almighty King, Help us Thy name to sing, Help us to praise: Father, all-glorious, O'er all victorious, Come, and reign over us, Ancient of Days.
2. Come, Thou Incarnate Word, Gird on Thy mighty sword, Our prayer attend: Come, and Thy people bless, And give Thy word success; Spirit of holiness, On us descend.
3. Come, Holy Comforter, Thy sacred witness bear In this glad hour: Thou who almighty art, Now rule in every heart, Never from us depart, Spirit of power.
4. To Thee, great One in Three, The highest praises be, Hence evermore! Thy sovereign majesty May we in glory see, And to eternity Love and adore. A-men.

WORSHIP AND ADORATION

Alternate Last Verse Harmonization Arranged by Van Denman Thompson and Fred Bock

4 To Thee, great One in Three, The highest praises be, Hence-ev-er more! Thy sov-ereign majesty May we in glory see, And to eternity Love and adore. A - men.

© Copyright 1942, 1976 by Lorenz Publishing Company. Renewal secured. Used by permission. Published as "Hymn to the Trinity".

WORSHIP AND ADORATION

342 Come, Christians, Join to Sing

For . . . we have a building of God, a house not made with hands, eternal in the heavens.
— II Corinthians 5:1

Christian Henry Bateman

MADRID
Traditional

1. Come, Christians, join to sing Alleluia! Amen!
2. *Come, lift your hearts on high;* Alleluia! Amen!
3. Praise yet our Christ again; Alleluia! Amen!

1. Loud praise to Christ our King; Alleluia! Amen!
2. *Let praises fill the sky;* Alleluia! Amen!
3. Life shall not end the strain; Alleluia! Amen!

1. Let all, with heart and voice, Before His throne rejoice; Praise is His
2. *He is our Guide and Friend; To us He'll condescend; His love shall*
3. On heaven's blissful shore His goodness we'll adore, Singing for-

Alternate ending for 2nd stanza into harmonization

1. gracious choice: Alleluia! Amen!
2. *never end: Alleluia! Amen! Amen!*
3. evermore, "Alleluia! Amen!" Amen.

WORSHIP AND ADORATION

Alternate Last Verse Harmonization

Arranged by Fred Bock

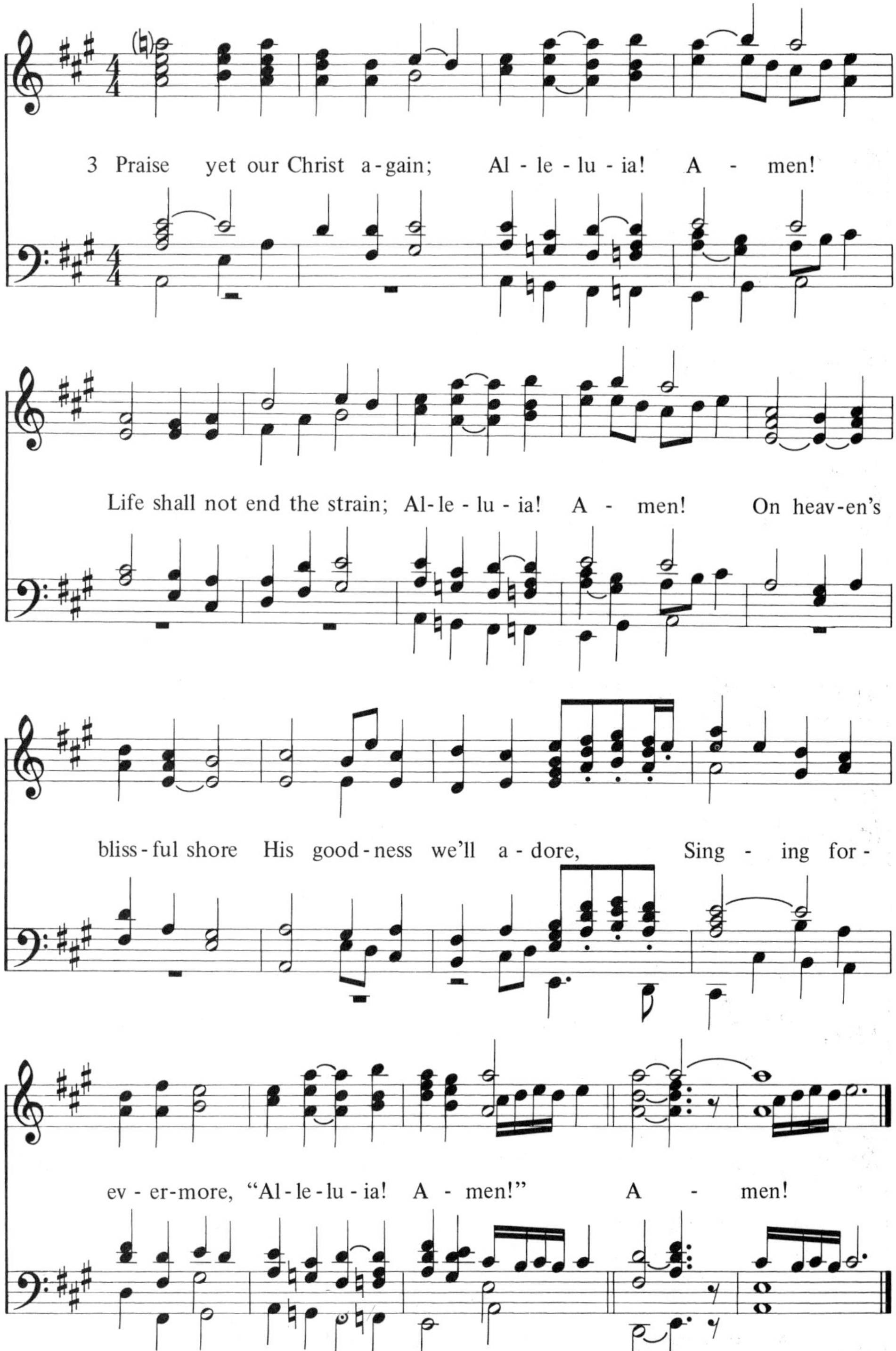

343 Sing Praise to God Who Reigns Above

The Lord reigneth; let the earth rejoice.
—Psalm 97:1

Johann J. Schütz
Tr. by Frances E. Cox

MIT FREUDEN ZART
Bohemian Brethren's "Kirchengesänge"

1. Sing praise to God who reigns above, The God of all cre-a-tion, The God of pow'r, the God of love, The God of our sal-va-tion; With heal-ing balm my soul He fills, And ev-ery faith-less mur-mer stills: To God all praise and glo-ry.

2. *What God's al-might-y power hath made His gra-cious mer-cy keep-eth; By morn-ing glow or eve-ning shade His watch-ful eye ne'er sleep-eth; With-in the king-dom of His might, Lo! all is just and all is right: To God all praise and glo-ry.*

3. The Lord is nev-er far a-way, But, through all grief dis-tress-ing, An ev-er-pres-ent help and stay, Our peace, and joy, and bless-ing; As with a moth-er's ten-der hand, He leads His own, His cho-sen band: To God all praise and glo-ry.

4. *Thus, all my glad-some way a-long, I sing a-loud His prais-es, That men may hear the grate-ful song My voice un-wea-ried rais-es, Be joy-ful in the Lord, my heart, Both soul and bod-y bear your part: To God all praise and glo-ry.* A-men.

WORSHIP AND ADORATION

O Could I Speak the Matchless Worth   **344**

This is the Lord's doing, and it is marvelous in our eyes.
— Psalm 118:23

Samuel Medley

ARIEL
Wolfgang A. Mozart
Adapted by Lowell Mason

1. O could I speak the matchless worth, O could I sound the glories forth Which in my Savior shine! I'd sing His perfect righteousness, And magnify the wondrous grace Which made salvation mine, Which made salvation mine.

2. *I'd sing the precious blood He spilt, My ransom from the dreadful guilt Of sin, and wrath divine; I'd sing His glorious holiness, In which all-perfect, heavenly dress My soul shall ever shine, My soul shall ever shine.*

3. I'd sing the character He bears, And all the forms of love He wears, Exalted on His throne; In loftiest songs of sweetest praise, I would to everlasting days Make all His glories known, Make all His glories known.

4. *Soon the delightful day will come When my dear Lord will bring me home, And I shall see His face; Then with my Savior, brother, friend, A blest eternity I'll spend, Triumphant in His grace, Triumphant in His grace.*

WORSHIP AND ADORATION

345 Crown Him with Many Crowns

And on His head were many crowns.
— Revelation 19:12

Matthew Bridges
Godfrey Thring

DIADEMATA
George J. Elvey
Descant by Paul Sjolund

1. Crown Him with man-y crowns, The Lamb up-on His throne: Hark! how the heaven-ly an-them drowns All mu-sic but its own! A-wake, my soul, and sing Of
2. *Crown Him the Lord of love: Be-hold His hands and side, Rich wounds, yet vis-i-ble a-bove, In beau-ty glo-ri-fied; No an-gel in the sky Can*
3. Crown Him the Lord of life: Who tri-umphed o'er the grave, Who rose vic-to-rious to the strife For those He came to save; His glo-ries now we sing, Who
4. *Crown Him the Lord of heaven: One with the Fa-ther known, One with the Spir-it through Him given From yon-der glo-rious throne. To Thee be end-less praise, For*
5. Crown Him the Lord of years: The po-ten-tate of time, Cre-a-tor of the roll-ing spheres, In-ef-fa-bly sub-lime. All hail, Re-deem-er, hail! For

Descant: 5 Crown Him, crown Him the Lord of years: The Lord of time, Cre-a-tor of the roll-ing spheres, In-ef-fa-bly sub-lime. All hail, Re-deem-er

© Copyright 1976 by Paragon Associates, Inc. All rights reserved.
WORSHIP AND ADORATION

hail! For Thou all praise, glo - ry

1. Him who died for thee; And hail Him as thy
2. *ful - ly bear that sight,* But *down - ward bends His*
3. died and rose on high, Who died e - ter - nal
4. *Thou for us hast died;* Be *Thou, O Lord, through*
5. Thou hast died for me; Thy praise and glo - ry

shall not fail Through - out e - ter - ni - ty. A - men.

1. match - less King Through all e - ter - ni - ty.
2. *won - dering eye At mys - ter - ies so bright.*
3. life to bring, And lives that death may die.
4. *end - less days A - dored and mag - ni - fied.*
5. shall not fail Through - out e - ter - ni - ty. A - men.

Who Shall Ascend? 346

Who shall ascend the hill of the Lord? who shall stand in the holy place? He who has clean hands and a pure heart.

—from Psalm 24
styled by Bruce Leafblad

WORSHIP AND ADORATION

347 All Creatures of Our God and King

Francis of Assisi
Tr. by William H. Draper
Bryan Jeffery Leech, stanza 5

Sing unto the Lord a new song, and praise Him in the congregation.
— Psalm 149:1

LASST UNS ERFREUEN
Geistliche Kirchengesäng

1. All crea-tures of our God and King, Lift up your voice and with us sing, Al-le-lu-ia! Al-le-lu-ia! Thou burn-ing sun with gold-en beam, Thou sil-ver moon with soft-er gleam, O praise Him! O praise Him! Al-le-lu-ia! Al-le-lu-ia! Al-le-lu-ia!

2. *Thou rush-ing wind that art so strong, Ye clouds that sail in heaven a-long, O praise Him! Al-le-lu-ia! Thou ris-ing morn, in praise re-joice, Ye lights of eve-ning, find a voice! O praise Him!*

3. Thou flow-ing wa-ter, pure and clear, Make mu-sic for thy Lord to hear, Al-le-lu-ia! Al-le-lu-ia! Thou fire so mas-ter-ful and bright, That giv-est man both warmth and light, O praise Him!

4. *Let all things their Cre-a-tor bless, And wor-ship Him in hum-ble-ness, O praise Him! Al-le-lu-ia! Praise, praise the Fa-ther, praise the Son, And praise the Spir-it, Three in One! O praise Him!*

(optional) 5. Lift up your voic-es once a-gain, And then be-fore the last "A-men!" Lis-ten to the or-gan play-ing: [— — — — — — — — — — — — — — —] O praise Him!

Words Copyright by J. Curwen & Sons. Used by permission of G. Schirmer, Inc. Stanza 5 © Copyright 1976 by Fred Bock Music Co. All rights reserved. Used by permission.

WORSHIP AND ADORATION

Bryan Jeffery Leech, stanza 5 — **Alternate Last Verse Harmonization** — Arranged by Fred Bock

5 Lift up your voic-es once a-gain, And then be-fore the last "A-men!" Lis-ten to the or-gan play-ing: [- - - - - - - - - -]

Full organ

Choir: Sing Al-le-lu-ia! Al-le-lu-ia! Sing Al-le-lu-ia! Al-le-lu - - ia!

Congregation: O praise Him! O praise Him! Al-le-lu - ia! Al-le-lu - ia! A-men.

© Copyright 1976 by Fred Bock Music Co. All rights reserved. Used by permission.

WORSHIP AND ADORATION

348 Praise to God

Leader: We lift up our hearts,
and bring You our worship and praise!

People: We lift up our voices
and sing You our worship and praise!

Leader and People: Praise and honor, glory and might,
to Him who sits on the throne,
and to the Lamb for ever and ever! Amen!!

349 O for a Thousand Tongues to Sing

My tongue shall speak . . . praise all the day long. — Psalm 35:28

Charles Wesley

AZMON
Carl G. Gläser
Descant by Eugene Butler

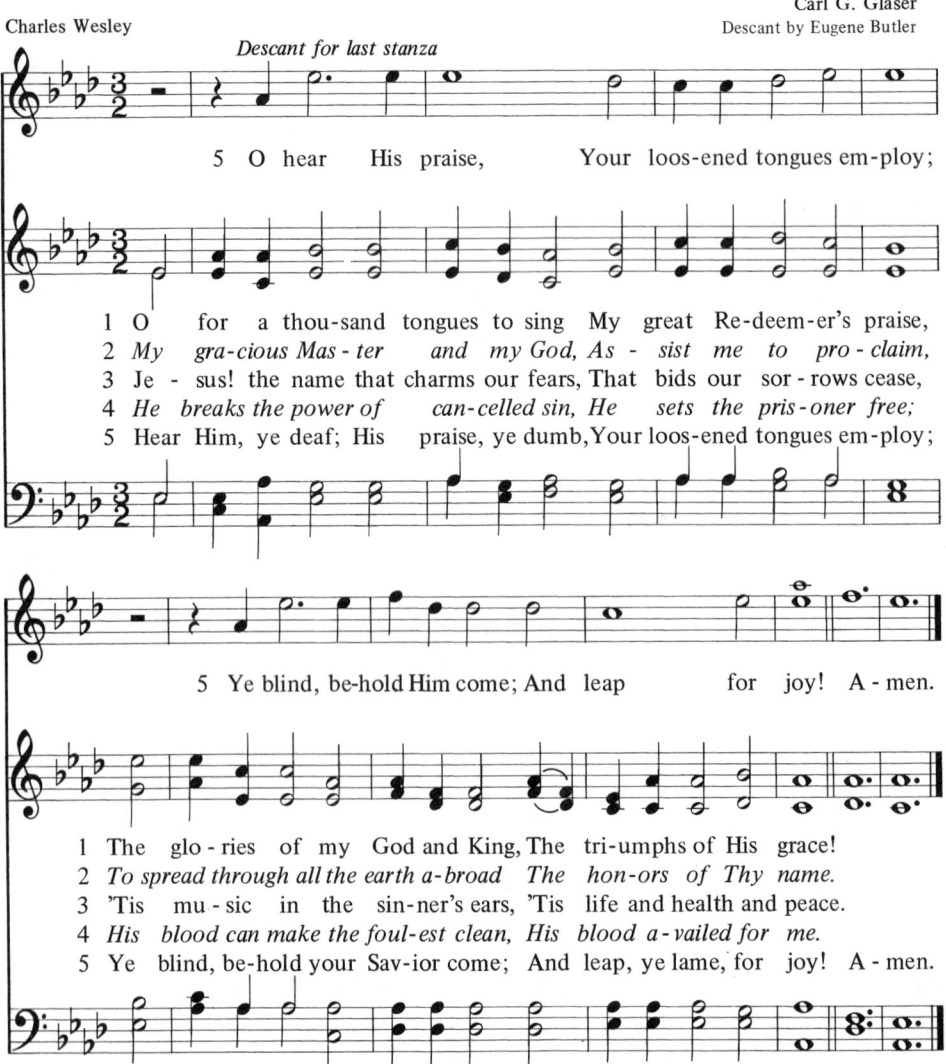

Descant for last stanza

5 O hear His praise, Your loos-ened tongues em-ploy;

1 O for a thou-sand tongues to sing My great Re-deem-er's praise,
2 My gra-cious Mas-ter and my God, As-sist me to pro-claim,
3 Je-sus! the name that charms our fears, That bids our sor-rows cease,
4 He breaks the power of can-celled sin, He sets the pris-oner free;
5 Hear Him, ye deaf; His praise, ye dumb, Your loos-ened tongues em-ploy;

5 Ye blind, be-hold Him come; And leap for joy! A-men.

1 The glo-ries of my God and King, The tri-umphs of His grace!
2 *To spread through all the earth a-broad The hon-ors of Thy name.*
3 'Tis mu-sic in the sin-ner's ears, 'Tis life and health and peace.
4 *His blood can make the foul-est clean, His blood a-vailed for me.*
5 Ye blind, be-hold your Sav-ior come; And leap, ye lame, for joy! A-men.

© Copyright 1976 by Paragon Associates, Inc. All rights reserved.

WORSHIP AND ADORATION

The Joy of His Presence   350

(A CALL TO WORSHIP)

Minister: *I was glad when they said unto me, let us go into the house of the Lord.*

Women: Calm my spirit, Lord. Stop the churning inside of me caused by the rush of getting everyone fed and here on time. Quiet my confusion, Lord. In all the tension of getting here, I know I made the effort because I really do need You. Lord, speak to me in the quietness.

Minister: *Enter His gates with thanksgiving and into His courts with praise; be thankful unto Him and bless His name. For the Lord is good.*

Men: I am thankful, Lord for what we have. But this week has been so hectic, and it seems that no matter how hard I work and how well I plan, there is always something I didn't plan on, and there isn't enough time to go around. Forgive me, Lord, for letting worry get in the way of my gratitude. You are good to us, Lord. We do have so much to praise You for.

Minister: *Make a joyful noise unto the Lord, all lands. Serve the Lord with gladness; come before His presence with singing.*

Youth (12-18): It's hard to sing so early in the morning. And it's hard to come here with gladness too sometimes. It was not so easy serving You this week at school—and especially hard to keep the joy. This world is not very fair and it seems like I can't do much to change things. But I know that it's just because the problems are so close to me that I can't seem to see the answers. But I do know that You're the answer—and for that I will sing to You with my whole heart.

Minister: *The Lord is my shepherd, I shall not want. He makes me to lie down in green pastures. He restores my soul.*

All: Restore my soul, O Lord, and renew a right spirit within me. Make me to hear joy and gladness; that the bones which You have broken may rejoice. Cast me not away from Your presence; and take not Your Holy Spirit from me. Restore to me the joy of Your salvation and uphold me with Your free spirit.

— Compiled by Gloria Gaither

WORSHIP AND ADORATION

351 At the Name of Jesus

Blessed be His glorious name forever; let the whole earth be filled with His glory.
— Psalm 72:19

Based on Philippians 2:5-11
Caroline M. Noel

KING'S WESTON
Ralph Vaughan Williams

1. At the name of Jesus Ev-ery knee shall bow,
   Ev-ery tongue con-fess Him King of glo-ry now;
   'Tis the Fa-ther's pleas-ure We should call Him Lord,
   Who from the be-gin-ning Was the might-y Word.

2. *At His voice cre-a-tion Sprang at once to sight,*
   All the an-gel fac-es, All the hosts of light,
   Thrones and dom-i-na-tions, Stars up-on their way,
   All the heaven-ly or-ders In their great ar-ray.

3. Hum-bled for a sea-son, To re-ceive a name
   From the lips of sin-ners, Un-to whom He came;
   He is God the Sav-ior, He is Christ the Lord,
   Ev-er to be wor-shipped, Trust-ed and a-dored.

4. *In your hearts en-throne Him: There let Him sub-due*
   All that is not ho-ly, All that is not true;
   Crown Him as your cap-tain In temp-ta-tion's hour,
   Let His will en-fold you In its light and power.

5. Broth-ers, this Lord Je-sus Shall re-turn a-gain,
   With His Fa-ther's glo-ry, With His an-gel train;
   For all wreaths of em-pire Meet up-on His brow,
   And our hearts con-fess Him King of glo-ry now. A-men.

Music from "Enlarged Songs of Praise" by permission of Oxford University Press.

WORSHIP AND ADORATION

Blessed Be the Name

352

For He must reign until He hath put all enemies under His feet.
— I Corinthians 15: 25

W. H. Clark
Refrain added by Ralph E. Hudson

BLESSED BE THE NAME
Ralph E. Hudson
Harmonized by William J. Kirkpatrick

1. All praise to Him who reigns a-bove In maj-es-ty su-preme,
2. *His name a-bove all names shall stand, Ex-alt-ed more and more,*
3. Re-deem-er, Sav-ior, friend of man Once ru-ined by the fall,
4. *His name shall be the Coun-sel-or, The might-y Prince of Peace,*

1. Who gave His Son for man to die, That He might man re-deem!
2. *At God the Fa-ther's own right hand, Where an-gel-hosts a-dore.*
3. Thou hast de-vised sal-va-tion's plan, For Thou hast died for all.
4. *Of all earth's king-doms con-quer-or, Whose reign shall nev-er cease.*

(in a slower tempo)

Bless-ed be the name! Bless-ed be the name! Bless-ed be the name of the Lord!

Bless-ed be the name! Bless-ed be the name! Bless-ed be the name of the Lord!

WORSHIP AND ADORATION

353 God the Omnipotent

All power is given unto me in heaven and in earth.
— Matthew 28:18

Henry F. Chorley, stanzas 1, 2, alt.
John Ellerton, stanzas 3, 4, alt.

RUSSIAN HYMN
Alexis F. Lvov
Descant by Paul Sjolund

Descant: 4 God: all the earth by Thy chas-tening

1. God the Om-nip-o-tent, King who or-dain-est
2. *God the All-mer-ci-ful, earth hath for-sak-en*
3. God the All-right-eous One, man hath de-fied Thee,
4. *God the All-prov-i-dent, earth by Thy chas-tening*

Yet shall to free-dom and truth be re-stored. O

1. Thun-der Thy clar-ion, the light-ning Thy sword,
2. *Thy ways all ho-ly, and slight-ed Thy word;*
3. Yet to e-ter-ni-ty stand-eth Thy word;
4. *Yet shall to free-dom and truth be re-stored;*

God, through the dark-ness, O bring now Thy king-dom, Lord

1. Show forth Thy pit-y on high where Thou reign-est:
2. *Bid not Thy wrath in its ter-rors a-wak-en:*
3. False-hood and wrong shall not tar-ry be-side Thee:
4. *Through the thick dark-ness Thy king-dom is has-tening:*

© Copyright 1976 by Paragon Associates, Inc. All rights reserved.
WORSHIP AND ADORATION

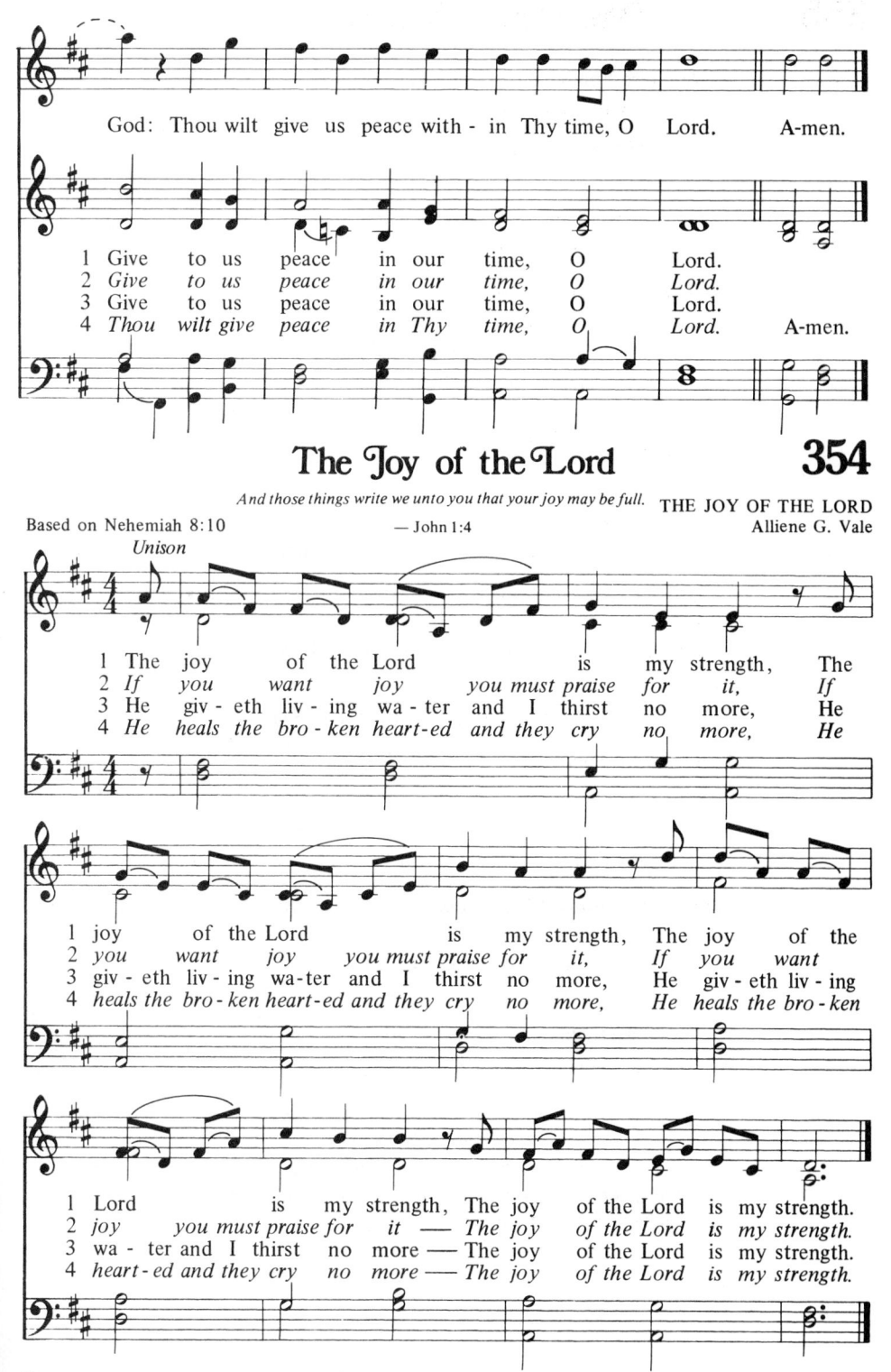

God: Thou wilt give us peace with-in Thy time, O Lord. A-men.

1 Give to us peace in our time, O Lord.
2 *Give to us peace in our time, O Lord.*
3 Give to us peace in our time, O Lord.
4 *Thou wilt give peace in Thy time, O Lord.* A-men.

The Joy of the Lord 354

And those things write we unto you that your joy may be full.

THE JOY OF THE LORD

Based on Nehemiah 8:10 — John 1:4 Alliene G. Vale

Unison

1 The joy of the Lord is my strength, The
2 *If you want joy you must praise for it, If*
3 He giv-eth liv-ing wa-ter and I thirst no more, He
4 *He heals the bro-ken heart-ed and they cry no more, He*

1 joy of the Lord is my strength, The joy of the
2 *you want joy you must praise for it, If you want*
3 giv-eth liv-ing wa-ter and I thirst no more, He giv-eth liv-ing
4 *heals the bro-ken heart-ed and they cry no more, He heals the bro-ken*

1 Lord is my strength, The joy of the Lord is my strength.
2 *joy you must praise for it — The joy of the Lord is my strength.*
3 wa-ter and I thirst no more — The joy of the Lord is my strength.
4 *heart-ed and they cry no more — The joy of the Lord is my strength.*

© Copyright 1971 by Alliene G. Vale. All rights reserved. Used by permission.

WORSHIP AND ADORATION

355 We Praise You, Father

We praise You, Father, that You have met us along the way
with mercy and love and new life in Christ.

With praise and dedication we offer ourselves.

We thank You for our responsible calling,
to be stewards of life in Your kingdom.

Help us to be good stewards of all You have placed in our care.

We thank You, Lord, for the ability to learn
and to do countless creative tasks.

*Motivate us to develop our skills
and to use them in accord with the teaching of Jesus.*

We thank You for all the rich resources
with which the world has been supplied.

*Make us determined so to use the soil, the air, the water—
all of nature's bounty—
that future generations are not robbed by our irresponsibility.*

We thank You, Father, for the family we have.

Teach us to live mindful of each other's need and each other's worth.

We thank You, Father, for the human family,
for the rich gift of each nationality and every culture.

*Grant us the spirit of Christ, to be brothers and sisters of all persons,
to be ever mindful of the needs of others,
and to be instruments of peace.*

We thank You for our wealth, great or small,
and for opportunities money brings.

*May all our earning and spending,
our saving and giving,
be acceptable in Your sight, Lord;
and grant us the resolve to fulfil our pledge of giving,
to the glory of Your name, in the ministry of Christ.
Amen.*

—James E. Dahlgren

WORSHIP AND ADORATION

The Love of Christ 356

Here is love,
    that God sent His Son,
        His Son that never offended,
        His Son that was always His delight.
    Herein is love, that He sent Him to save sinners;
        to save them by bearing their sins,
by bearing their curse, by dying their death, and by carrying their sorrows.
    Here is love, in that while we were yet enemies, Christ died for us;
    yes, here is love,
        in that while we were yet without strength, Christ died for the ungodly.

—John Bunyan

O for a Heart to Praise My God 357

God forbid that I glory, save in the cross of our Lord Jesus Christ....
— Galatians 6:14

Charles Wesley

RICHMOND
Thomas Haweis

1. O for a heart to praise my God, A heart from sin set free, A heart that always feels Thy blood So freely shed for me!
2. A humble, lowly, contrite heart, Believing, true and clean, Which neither life nor death can part From Him that dwells within.
3. A heart in ev'ry thought renewed, And full of love divine; Perfect and right and pure and good, A copy, Lord, of Thine!
4. Thy nature, gracious Lord, impart— Come quickly from above; Write Thy new name upon my heart, Thy new best name of Love. A-men.

WORSHIP AND ADORATION

358 Christ, We Do All Adore Thee

Thou art worthy, O Lord, to receive glory and honor, and power....
— Revelation 4:11

Adoramus Te
English version by Theodore Baker

ADORE THEE
From "The Seven Last Words of Christ"
Theodore Dubois

Christ, we do all a-dore Thee, and we do praise Thee for-ev-er;

Christ, we do all a-dore Thee, and we do praise Thee for-ev-er,

For on the ho-ly cross hast Thou the world from sin re-deem-ed.

Christ, we do all a-dore Thee, and we do praise Thee for-ev-er.

*Organ

Christ, we do all a-dore Thee!

*May be omitted
WORSHIP AND ADORATION

I Will Praise Him!

And they overcame Him by the blood of the Lamb.
— Revelation 12:11

359

Margaret J. Harris

I WILL PRAISE HIM
Margaret J. Harris

1. When I saw the cleans-ing foun-tain, O-pen wide for all my sin,
2. *Tho the way seems straight and nar-row, All I claimed was swept a-way;*
3. Bless-ed be the name of Je-sus! I'm so glad He took me in;
4. Glo-ry, glo-ry to the Fa-ther! Glo-ry, glo-ry to the Son!

1. I o-beyed the Spir-it's call-ing When He said, "Wilt thou be clean?"
2. *My am-bi-tions, plans and wish-es At my feet in dis-ar-ray.*
3. He's for-giv-en my trans-gres-sions, He has cleansed by heart from sin.
4. Glo-ry, glo-ry to the Spir-it! Glo-ry to the Three in One!

I will praise Him! I will praise Him! Praise the Lamb for sin-ners slain;
Give Him glo-ry, all ye peo-ple, For His blood can wash a-way each stain.

WORSHIP AND ADORATION

360 You Servants of God, Your Master Proclaim

God hath fulfilled the same unto us . . . in that He hath raised up Jesus again.
— Acts 13: 33

Charles Wesley

HANOVER
William Croft

1. You servants of God, your Master proclaim,
And publish abroad His wonderful name;
The name, all victorious, of Jesus extol:
His kingdom is glorious, He rules over all.

2. God ruleth on high, almighty to save,
And still He is nigh, His presence we have;
The great congregation His triumph shall sing,
Ascribing salvation to Jesus, our King.

3. "Salvation to God, who sits on the throne!"
Let all cry aloud and honor the Son;
The praises of Jesus the angels proclaim,
Fall down on their faces and worship the Lamb.

4. Then let us adore and give Him His right—
All glory and power, all wisdom and might,
All honor and blessing, with angels above,
And thanks never-ceasing, and infinite love.

WORSHIP AND ADORATION

Alleluia 361

*And I heard as it were the voices of a great multitude...
saying Alleluia for the Lord God omnipotent reigneth.* — Revelation 19:6

Traditional text

ALLELUIA
Traditional melody

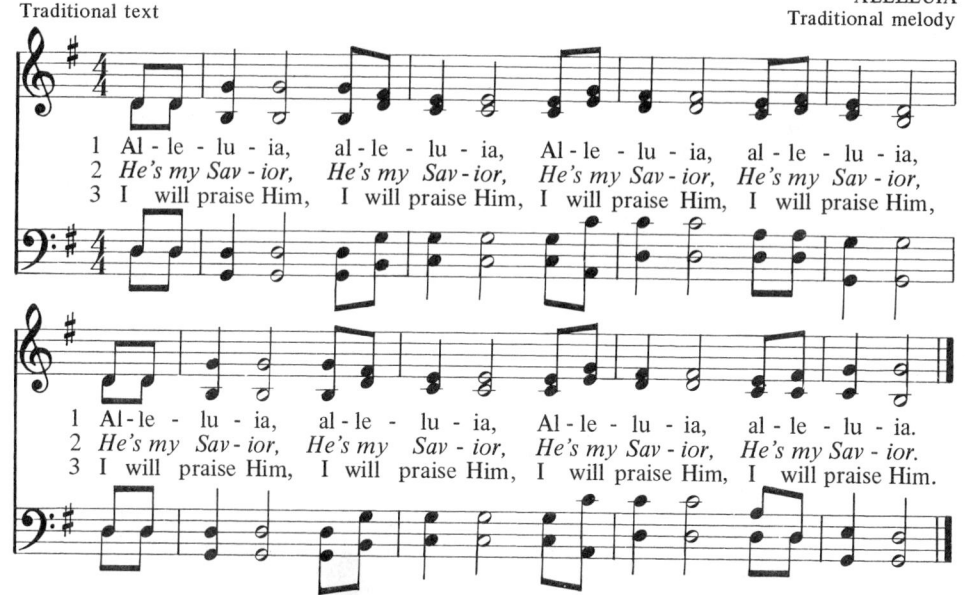

1. Al - le - lu - ia, al - le - lu - ia, Al - le - lu - ia, al - le - lu - ia,
2. *He's my Sav - ior, He's my Sav - ior, He's my Sav - ior, He's my Sav - ior,*
3. I will praise Him, I will praise Him, I will praise Him, I will praise Him,

1. Al - le - lu - ia, al - le - lu - ia, Al - le - lu - ia, al - le - lu - ia.
2. *He's my Sav - ior, He's my Sav - ior, He's my Sav - ior, He's my Sav - ior.*
3. I will praise Him, I will praise Him, I will praise Him, I will praise Him.

Praise the Savior, Ye Who Know Him 362

Blessing, and honor, and glory, and power be unto Him,
— Revelation 5:13

Thomas Kelly
Byran Jeffery Leech, alt. stanza 4

ACCLAIM
German Melody

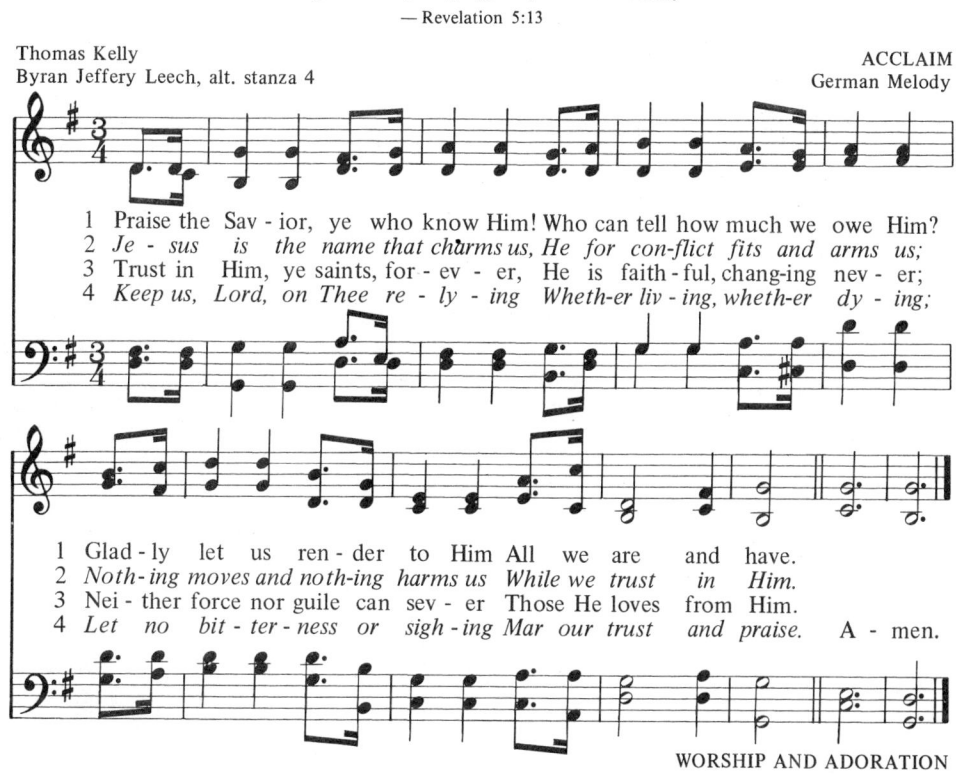

1. Praise the Sav - ior, ye who know Him! Who can tell how much we owe Him?
2. *Je - sus is the name that charms us, He for con - flict fits and arms us;*
3. Trust in Him, ye saints, for - ev - er, He is faith - ful, chang - ing nev - er;
4. *Keep us, Lord, on Thee re - ly - ing Wheth - er liv - ing, wheth - er dy - ing;*

1. Glad - ly let us ren - der to Him All we are and have.
2. *Noth - ing moves and noth - ing harms us While we trust in Him.*
3. Nei - ther force nor guile can sev - er Those He loves from Him.
4. *Let no bit - ter - ness or sigh - ing Mar our trust and praise.* A - men.

WORSHIP AND ADORATION

363 To God Be the Glory

That ye may with one mind and one mouth glorify God....
— Romans 15:6

Fanny J. Crosby

TO GOD BE THE GLORY
William H. Doane

1. To God be the glo-ry—great things He hath done! So loved He the world that He gave us His Son, Who yield-ed His life an a-tone-ment for sin, And o-pened the life-gate that all may go in.

2. O per-fect re-demp-tion, the pur-chase of blood, To ev-ery be-liev-er the prom-ise of God; The vil-est of-fen-der who tru-ly be-lieves, That mo-ment from Je-sus a par-don re-ceives.

3. Great things He hath taught us, great things He hath done, And great our re-joic-ing through Je-sus the Son; But pur-er, and high-er, and great-er will be Our won-der, our trans-port, when Je-sus we see.

Praise the Lord, praise the Lord, Let the earth hear His voice! Praise the Lord, praise the Lord, Let the peo-ple re-joice! O come to the Fa-ther thru

WORSHIP AND ADORATION

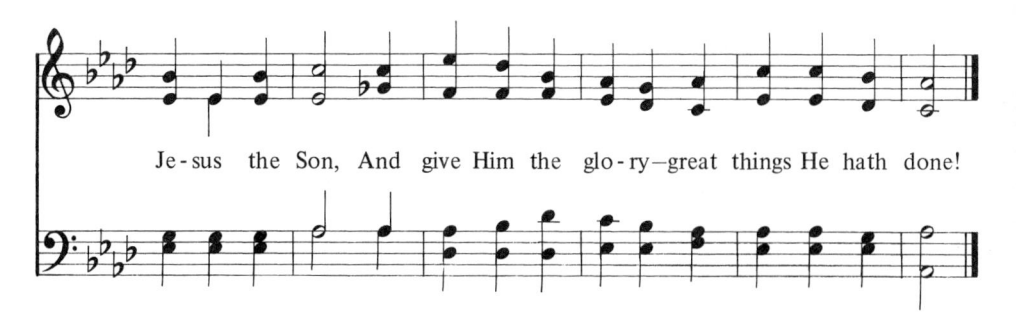

Je-sus the Son, And give Him the glo-ry—great things He hath done!

The Chief End of Man — 364

"The chief end of man
is to glorify God
and to enjoy Him forever."

It would be scripturally false to leave out the second phrase—
"and to enjoy Him forever."

The men who formulated this showed
great wisdom and insight in saying,
"and to enjoy Him forever."

Nevertheless, the first phrase is the first phrase:
"The chief end of man
is to glorify God."
And in Christianity we have a non-determined God
who did not need to create
because there was love and communication within the Trinity,
and yet having been created, we as men can glorify God.

But we must feel the force of both sides of the issue.
If we fail to emphasize that we can glorify God,
we raise the whole question of whether men are significant at all.
We begin to lose our humanity as soon as we begin to lose the emphasis
that what we do makes a difference.
We can glorify God, and both the Old and New Testament say
that we can even make God sad.

That is tremendous.

—Francis A. Schaeffer

WORSHIP AND ADORATION

365 My Tribute

Not unto us, O Lord, but unto Thy name give glory. — Psalm 115:1

Andraé Crouch

MY TRIBUTE
Andraé Crouch

How can I say thanks for the things You have done for me?
Things so un-de-served, Yet You gave to prove Your love for me; The voic-es of a mil-lion an-gels could not ex-press my gra-ti-tude.
All that I am, and ev-er hope to be; I owe it all to Thee.
To God be the glo-ry, To God be the glo-ry,

© Copyright 1971 by Lexicon Music, Inc. All rights reserved. Used by permission.

WORSHIP AND ADORATION

To God be the glory For the things He has done.

With His blood He has saved me; With His power He has raised me;

Fine

To God be the glory for the times He has done.

Just let me live my life — Let it be pleas-ing, Lord, to Thee;

D.S. al Fine

And if I gain an-y praise, Let it go to Cal - va - ry. With His

WORSHIP AND ADORATION

366 Praise Be to Jesus

Ho, everyone that thirsteth, come ye to the waters . . . . — Isaiah 55:1

Gloria Gaither

PRAISE TO JESUS
William J. Gaither

1. Let him who is thirst-y come to clear wa-ter,
   Let him who is hun-gry come by and eat;
   For mon-ey can't buy this cool liv-ing wa-ter,
   Or this milk and hon-ey so sweet.

2. The hills and the moun-tains break forth in-to sing-ing,
   The tall state-ly trees and fields clap their hands;
   In place of the thorn there shall grow a tall fir tree,
   A ten-der plant sprouts from the sand.

3. Then shall the light break forth in-to morn-ing,
   Bring-ing beau-ty for ash-es, strength for the days;
   And hearts that were heav-y shall stand in His pres-ence,
   Wrapped in the gar-ment of praise.

© Copyright 1975 by William J. Gaither. All rights reserved. Used by permission.

WORSHIP AND ADORATION

Praise be to Jesus, the sweet Rose of Sharon, Praise to the Christ, the Redeemer of men; Praise to the King who is reigning forever, The Hope of the ages, my Master and Friend.

Lord, We Praise You 367

Sing unto Him, sing unto him; talk ye of all His wondrous works.... — Psalm 105:2

LORD, WE PRAISE YOU
Otis Skillings

1. Lord, we praise You, Lord, we praise You, Lord, we praise You, We praise You, Lord!
2. Lord, we thank You, Lord, we thank You, Lord, we thank You, We thank You, Lord!
3. Lord, we love You, Lord, we love You, Lord, we love You, We love You, Lord!

© 1972 by Lillenas Publishing Co. All rights reserved. Used by permission.

368 My Wonderful Lord

His name shall be called wonderful... — Isaiah 9:6

WONDERFUL LORD
Haldor Lillenas
Haldor Lillenas

1. I have found a deep peace that I nev-er had known, And a joy this world I could not af-ford; Since I yield-ed con-trol of my bod-y and soul To my won-der-ful, won-der-ful Lord.
2. I de-sire that my life shall be or-dered by Thee, That my will be in per-fect ac-cord With Thine own sov-ereign will, Thy de-sires to ful-fill, My won-der-ful, won-der-ful Lord.
3. All the tal-ents I have I have laid at Thy feet, Thy ap-prov-al shall be my re-ward; Be my store great or small, I sur-ren-der it all To my won-der-ful, won-der-ful Lord.
4. Thou art fair-er to me than the fair-est of earth, Thou om-nip-o-tent, life-giv-ing Word; O Thou An-cient of Days, Thou art wor-thy all praise, My won-der-ful, won-der-ful Lord.

My won-der-ful Lord, my won-der-ful Lord, By an-gels and ser-aphs in heav-en a-dored! I bow at Thy shrine, my Sav-ior di-vine, My won-der-ful, won-der-ful Lord.

© Copyright 1938. Renewed 1966 by Lillenas Publishing Co. Used by permission.

WORSHIP AND ADORATION

Psalm 90 — 369

Lord, Thou hast been our dwelling place in all generations.

> Before the mountains were brought forth, or ever Thou hadst formed the earth and the world, from everlasting to everlasting Thou art God.

Thou turnest man back to the dust, and sayest, "Turn back, O children of men!"

> For a thousand years in Thy sight are but as yesterday when it is past, or as a watch in the night.

Thou dost sweep men away; they are like a dream, like grass which is renewed in the morning:

> In the morning it flourishes and is renewed; in the evening it fades and withers.

For we are consumed by Thy anger; by Thy wrath we are overwhelmed.

> Thou hast set our iniquities before Thee, our secret sins in the light of Thy countenance.

For all our days pass away under Thy wrath, our years come to an end like a sigh.

> The years of our life are threescore and ten, or even by reason of strength fourscore; yet their span is but toil and trouble; they are soon gone, and we fly away.

Who considers the power of Thy anger, and Thy wrath according to the fear of Thee?

> So teach us to number our days that we may get a heart of wisdom.

—Psalm 90:1-12 (RSV)

O God, Our Help in Ages Past — 370

Our soul waiteth for the Lord; He is our help . . . . — Psalm 33:20

Psalm 90
Isaac Watts

ST. ANNE
William Croft

1. O God, our help in ages past, Our hope for years to come,
   Our shelter from the storm-y blast, And our e-ter-nal home!
2. Un-der the shad-ow of Thy throne Still may we dwell se-cure;
   Suf-fi-cient is Thine arm a-lone, And our de-fense is sure.
3. Be-fore the hills in or-der stood, Or earth re-ceived her frame,
   From ev-er-last-ing Thou art God, To end-less years the same.
4. A thou-sand a-ges in Thy sight Are like an eve-ning gone;
   Short as the watch that ends the night, Be-fore the ris-ing sun.
5. O God, our help in ages past, Our hope for years to come,
   Be Thou our guide while life shall last, And our e-ter-nal home! A-men.

WORSHIP AND ADORATION

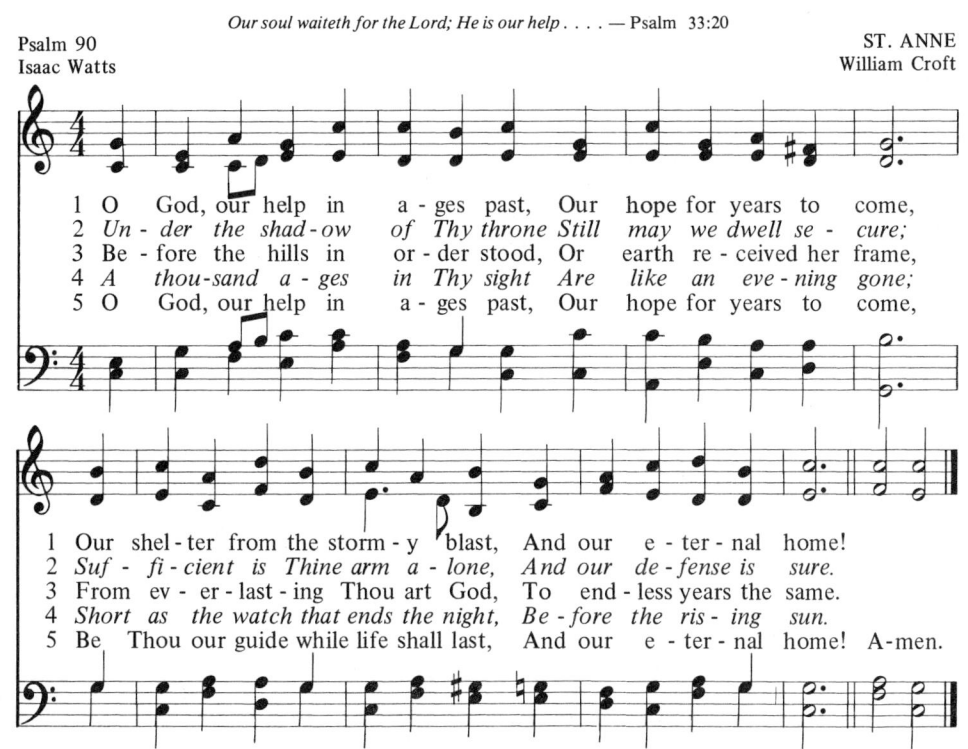

371 Free from the Guilted Cage

Lord Jesus Christ, today I want to live my life as an expression of your love rather than as an effort to earn or deserve your love. Like Paul, I have tried about everything to prove my worth. Nothing satisfies. I am weary of doing the right thing because of guilt and not grace. Thank you for the limitless power of your love which sets me free from a guilted cage to fly and soar to new heights of joyous praise today. Amen.

—Lloyd John Ogilvie

372 What a Wonderful Savior

... by the righteousness of One the free Gift came upon all men unto justification of life.
— Romans 5:18

Elisha A. Hoffman

BENTON HARBOR
Elisha A. Hoffman

1. Christ has for sin atonement made— What a wonderful Savior!
2. I praise Him for the cleansing blood— What a wonderful Savior!
3. He cleansed my heart from all its sin— What a wonderful Savior!
4. He gives me overcoming power— What a wonderful Savior!

1. We are redeemed, the price is paid— What a wonderful Savior!
2. That reconciled my soul to God— What a wonderful Savior!
3. And now He reigns and rules therein— What a wonderful Savior!
4. And triumph in each trying hour— What a wonderful Savior!

What a wonderful Savior is Jesus, my Jesus!
What a wonderful Savior is Jesus, my Lord!

WORSHIP AND ADORATION

Praise the Lord, His Glories Show 373

Great is the Lord and greatly to be praised.
— Psalm 145:3

Based on Psalm 150
Henry Francis Lyte

LLANFAIR
Robert Williams
Harmonized by John Roberts

1. Praise the Lord, His glo-ries show, Al - le - lu - ia!
2. *Earth to heaven and heaven to earth,* Al - le - lu - ia!
3. Praise the Lord, His mer-cies trace, Al - le - lu - ia!

1. Saints with-in His courts be-low, Al - le - lu - ia!
2. *Tell His won-ders, sing His worth,* Al - le - lu - ia!
3. Praise His prov-i-dence and grace, Al - le - lu - ia!

1. An-gels 'round His throne a-bove, A - le - lu - ia!
2. *Age to age and shore to shore,* A - le - lu - ia!
3. All that He for man hath done, A - le - lu - ia!

1. All that see and share His love. A - le - lu - ia!
2. *Praise Him, praise Him ev - er - more!* A - le - lu - ia!
3. All He sends us through His Son. A - le - lu - ia!

WORSHIP AND ADORATION

374 Rejoice, the Lord Is King!

Rejoice in the Lord always; and again I say, Rejoice.
— Philippians 4:4

Based on Philippians 4:4
Charles Wesley

DARWALL'S 148th
John Darwall
Handbell descant by Bob Burroughs

Two-octave handbell descant for stanza 4

1. Re-joice, the Lord is King! Your Lord and King a-dore!
2. *The Lord, our Sav-ior, reigns, The God of truth and love;*
3. His king-dom can-not fail, He rules o'er earth and heaven;
4. *Re-joice in glo-rious hope! Our Lord the judge shall come*

1. Re-joice, give thanks, and sing, And tri-umph ev-er-
2. *When He had purged our stains, He took His seat a-*
3. The keys of death and hell Are to our Je-sus
4. *And take His serv-ants up To their e-ter-nal*

1. more:
2. *bove:*
3. given:
4. *home:*

Lift up your heart, lift up your voice! Re-

© Copyright 1976 by Paragon Associates. All rights reserved.

WORSHIP AND ADORATION

joice, a-gain I say, re-joice! A - men.

Praises to the Lord 375

Praise the Lord! Praise God in His sanctuary;

> *praise Him in His mighty firmament!*

Praise Him for His mighty deeds;

> *praise Him according to His exceeding greatness!*

Praise Him with trumpet sound;

> *praise Him with lute and harp!*

Praise Him with timbrel and dance;

> *praise Him with strings and pipe!*

Praise Him with sounding cymbals;

> *praise Him with loud clashing cymbals!*

Let everything that breathes praise the Lord!

> *Praise the Lord!* *

Make a joyful noise to the Lord, all the lands!

> *Serve the Lord with gladness! Come into His presence with singing!*

Know that the Lord is God!

> *It is He that made us, and we are His; we are His people, and the sheep of His pasture.*

Enter His gates with thanksgiving, and His courts with praise!

> *Give thanks to Him, bless His name!*

For the Lord is good;

> *His steadfast love endures for ever, and His faithfulness to all generations.* †

—*Psalm 150 (RSV)
—†Psalm 100 (RSV)

WORSHIP AND ADORATION

376 Glorious Things of Thee Are Spoken

Glorious things of Thee are spoken, O City of God. — Psalm 87:3

Based on Psalm 87:3; Isaiah 33:20, 21
John Newton

AUSTRIAN HYMN
Franz Joseph Haydn

1. Glo-rious things of thee are spo-ken, Zi-on, cit-y of our God;
   He whose word can-not be bro-ken Formed thee for His own a-bode.
   On the Rock of A-ges found-ed, What can shake thy sure re-pose?
   With sal-va-tion's walls sur-round-ed, Thou mayest smile at all thy foes.

2. *See, the streams of liv-ing wa-ters, Spring-ing from e-ter-nal Love,*
   Well sup-ply thy sons and daugh-ters, And all fear of want re-move.
   Who can faint while such a riv-er Ev-er flows their thirst to assuage?
   Grace which, like the Lord, the Giv-er, Nev-er fails from age to age!

3. Round each hab-i-ta-tion hov-ering, See the cloud and fire ap-pear
   For a glo-ry and a cov-ering, Show-ing that the Lord is near!
   Thus de-riv-ing from their ban-ner Light by night and shade by day,
   Safe they feed up-on the man-na Which He gives them when they pray. A-men.

WORSHIP AND ADORATION

Alternate Last Verse Harmonization Arranged by Gordon Young

3 Round each hab-i-ta-tion hov-ering, See the cloud and fire ap-pear
For a glo-ry and a cov-ering, Show-ing that the Lord is near:
Thus de-riv-ing from their ban-ner Light by night and shade by day,
Safe they feed up-on the man-na Which He gives them when they pray. A-men.

© Copyright 1976 by Paragon Associates, Inc. All rights reserved.

WORSHIP AND ADORATION

377 Joyful, Joyful, We Adore Thee

But unto you . . . the sun of righteousness shall arise with healing in His wings. — Malachi 4:2

HYMN TO JOY
Ludwig van Beethoven
Adapted by Edward Hodges

Henry van Dyke

1. Joy-ful, joy-ful, we a-dore Thee, God of glo-ry, Lord of love;
2. *All Thy works with joy sur-round Thee, Earth and heaven re-flect Thy rays,*
3. Thou art giv-ing and for-giv-ing, Ev-er bless-ing, ev-er blest,
4. *Mor-tals, join the hap-py cho-rus With the morn-ing stars be-gan;*

1. Hearts un-fold like flowers be-fore Thee, Open-ing to the sun a-bove.
2. *Stars and an-gels sing a-round Thee, Cen-ter of un-bro-ken praise.*
3. Well-spring of the joy of liv-ing, O-cean depth of hap-py rest!
4. *Fa-ther love is reign-ing o'er us, Broth-er love binds man to man.*

1. Melt the clouds of sin and sad-ness, Drive the dark of doubt a-way;
2. *Field and for-est, vale and moun-tain, Flow-ery mead-ow, flash-ing sea,*
3. Thou our Fa-ther, Christ our Broth-er— All who live in love are Thine;
4. *Ev-er sing-ing, march we on-ward, Vic-tors in the midst of strife,*

1. Giv-er of im-mor-tal glad-ness, Fill us with the light of day.
2. *Chant-ing bird and flow-ing foun-tain, Call us to re-joice in Thee.*
3. Teach us how to love each oth-er, Lift us to the joy di-vine.
4. *Joy-ful mu-sic leads us sun-ward In the tri-umph song of life.* A-men.

Words reprinted with the permission of Charles Scribner's Sons.

WORSHIP AND ADORATION

Bless the Lord 378

Bless the Lord, O my soul;
    and all that is within me, bless His holy name!
Bless the Lord, O my soul, and forget not all His benefits,
    Who forgives all your iniquity,
Who heals all your diseases,
    Who redeems your life from the Pit,
Who crowns you with steadfast love and mercy,
    Who satisfies you with good as long as you live so that your youth is renewed like the eagle's.

The Lord has established His throne in the heavens,
    and His kingdom rules over all.
Bless the Lord, O you His angels,
    You mighty ones who do His word, hearkening to the voice of His word!
Bless the Lord, all His hosts,
    His ministers that do His will!
Bless the Lord, all His works, in all places of His dominion.
    Bless the Lord, O my soul!

—Psalm 103:1-5, 19-22 (RSV)

Bless His Holy Name 379

O Bless our God, ye people, and make the voice of His praise to be heard. — Psalm 66:8

Psalm 103
Andraé Crouch

BLESS THE LORD
Andraé Crouch

Bless the Lord, O my soul, and all that is with-in me, Bless His ho-ly Name. He has done great things, He has done great things, He has done great things, Bless His ho-ly Name.

Fine

D.C. al Fine

© Copyright 1973 by Lexicon Music, Inc. All rights reserved. Used by permission. International copyright secured.

WORSHIP AND ADORATION

380 God Is Light

Minister: God is light, and in Him there is no darkness.
PEOPLE: GREAT IS THE LORD, AND GREATLY TO BE PRAISED.
Minister: God is love, and in Him we can all be fulfilled.
PEOPLE: GREAT IS THE LORD, AND GREATLY TO BE PRAISED.
Minister: God is truth, and in His Son we see something of what He is like and something of what we can become.
PEOPLE: GREAT IS THE LORD, AND GREATLY TO BE PRAISED.
Minister: God is holy, and through His generosity we can please Him with a borrowed goodness.
PEOPLE: GREAT IS THE LORD, AND GREATLY TO BE PRAISED.
Minister: Here is the wonder, that we are recipients of grace, and grace is God giving us for free that which none of us can afford.
PEOPLE: GREAT IS THE LORD, AND GREATLY TO BE PRAISED.

—Bryan Jeffery Leech
based on I John 1:5-7

381 All People That on Earth Do Dwell

Let all the people praise thee, O God... — Psalm 67:3

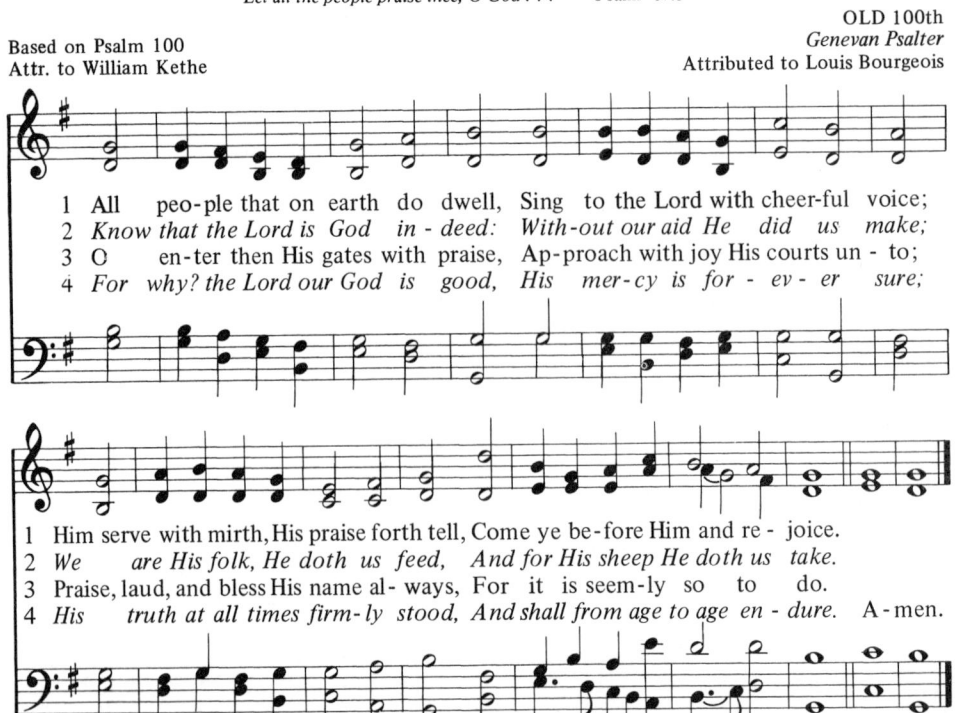

Based on Psalm 100
Attr. to William Kethe

OLD 100th
Genevan Psalter
Attributed to Louis Bourgeois

1. All people that on earth do dwell, Sing to the Lord with cheerful voice;
   Him serve with mirth, His praise forth tell, Come ye before Him and rejoice.
2. *Know that the Lord is God indeed: Without our aid He did us make;*
   We are His folk, He doth us feed, And for His sheep He doth us take.
3. O enter then His gates with praise, Approach with joy His courts unto;
   Praise, laud, and bless His name always, For it is seemly so to do.
4. *For why? the Lord our God is good, His mercy is for ever sure;*
   His truth at all times firmly stood, And shall from age to age endure. A-men.

WORSHIP AND ADORATION

Praise God, from Whom All Blessings Flow   382

... Who hath blessed us with all spiritual blessings. — Ephesians 1:3

Thomas Ken
FIRST VERSION
OLD 100th
Attributed to Louis Bourgeois
Genevan Psalter

Praise God, from whom all bless-ings flow; Praise Him, all crea-tures here be - low;

Praise Him a-bove, ye heaven-ly host; Praise Fa-ther, Son, and Ho-ly Ghost. A-men.

Prayer   383

To be there before You, Lord, that's all.
To shut the eyes of my body,
To shut the eyes of my soul,
And be still and silent,
To expose myself to You who are there, exposed to me.
To be there before You, the eternal Presence.

—Michel Quoist

Doxology   384

I will greatly praise the Lord with my mouth; yea, I will praise Him among the multitudes. — Psalm 109:30

Thomas Ken
SECOND VERSION
OLD 100th (original)
Attributed to Louis Bourgeois
Genevan Psalter

Praise God, from whom all bless-ings flow; Praise Him, all crea-tures here be - low;

Praise Him a-bove, ye heaven-ly host; Praise Fa-ther, Son, and Ho-ly Ghost. A-men.

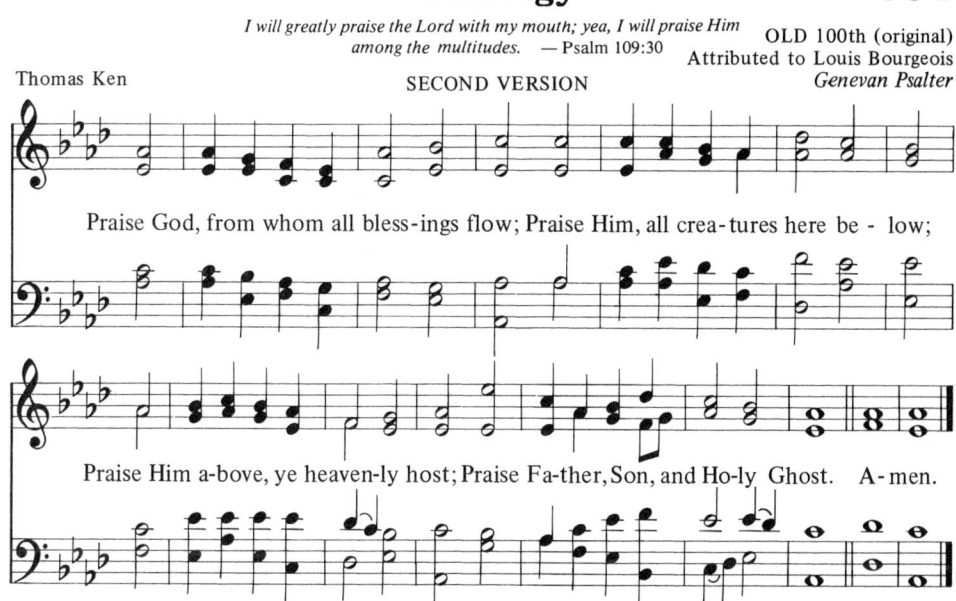

WORSHIP AND ADORATION

385 Holy God, We Praise Thy Name

I dwell in the high and holy place with him that is of a humble spirit. —Isaiah 57:15

Attr. to Ignaz Franz
Tr. by Clarence A. Walworth

GROSSER GOTT
"Allgemeines Katholisches Gesangbuch"

1. Holy God, we praise Thy name; Lord of all, we bow before Thee; All on earth Thy scepter claim, All in heaven above adore Thee: Infinite Thy vast domain, Everlasting is Thy reign.

2. *Hark, the glad celestial hymn Angel choirs above are raising; Cherubim and seraphim, In unceasing chorus praising; Fill the heavens with sweet accord:* Holy, holy, holy Lord.

3. Holy Father, holy Son, Holy Spirit: three we name Thee, Though in essence only one; Undivided God we claim Thee, And adoring, bend the knee, While we own the mystery. A-men.

WORSHIP AND ADORATION

Thanks to God for My Redeemer 386

Thanks be to God for His unspeakable gift. — II Corinthians 9:15

August Ludwig Storm
Tr. by Carl E. Backstrom

TACK O GUD
J. A. Hultman

1. Thanks to God for my Re-deem-er, Thanks for all Thou dost pro-vide!
2. *Thanks for prayers that Thou hast answered, Thanks for what Thou dost de-ny!*
3. Thanks for ros-es by the way-side, Thanks for thorns their stems contain!

1. Thanks for times now but a mem-ory, Thanks for Je-sus by my side!
2. *Thanks for storms that I have weath-ered, Thanks for all Thou dost sup-ply!*
3. Thanks for home and thanks for fire-side, Thanks for hope, that sweet re-frain!

1. Thanks for pleas-ant, balm-y spring-time, Thanks for dark and drear-y fall!
2. *Thanks for pain and thanks for pleas-ure, Thanks for com-fort in de-spair!*
3. Thanks for joy and thanks for sor-row, Thanks for heav'n-ly peace with Thee!

1. Thanks for tears by now for-got-ten, Thanks for peace within my soul!
2. *Thanks for grace that none can measure, Thanks for love beyond compare!*
3. Thanks for hope in the to-mor-row, Thanks thru all e-ter-ni-ty! A-men.

THANKSGIVING

387 We Gather Together

If God be for us who can be against us? — Romans 8:31

KREMSER
Netherlands Folk Song
Harmonized by Edward Kremser
Descant by Tom Fettke

Netherlands Folk Song
Tr. by Theodore Baker

Descant
3 We all do ex-tol Thee, Thou lead-er tri-um-phant, And

1 We gath-er to-geth-er to ask the Lord's bless-ing— He
2 *Be - side us to guide us, our God with us join - ing, Or-*
3 We all do ex - tol Thee, Thou lead - er tri - um - phant, And

pray that Thou still our de - fend - er wilt be;

1 chas - tens and has - tens His will to make known; The
2 *dain - ing, main - tain - ing His king - dom di - vine; So*
3 pray that Thou still our de - fend - er wilt be; Let

Let Thy con-gre - ga - tion es - cape trib-u - la - tion.

1 wick - ed op - press - ing now cease from dis - tress - ing: Sing
2 *from the be - gin - ning the fight we were win - ning: Thou,*
3 Thy con - gre - ga - tion es - cape trib-u - la - tion: Thy

© Copyright 1976 by Paragon Associates, Inc. All rights reserved.
THANKSGIVING

Thy name be ev-er praised! O Lord, make us free! A - men.

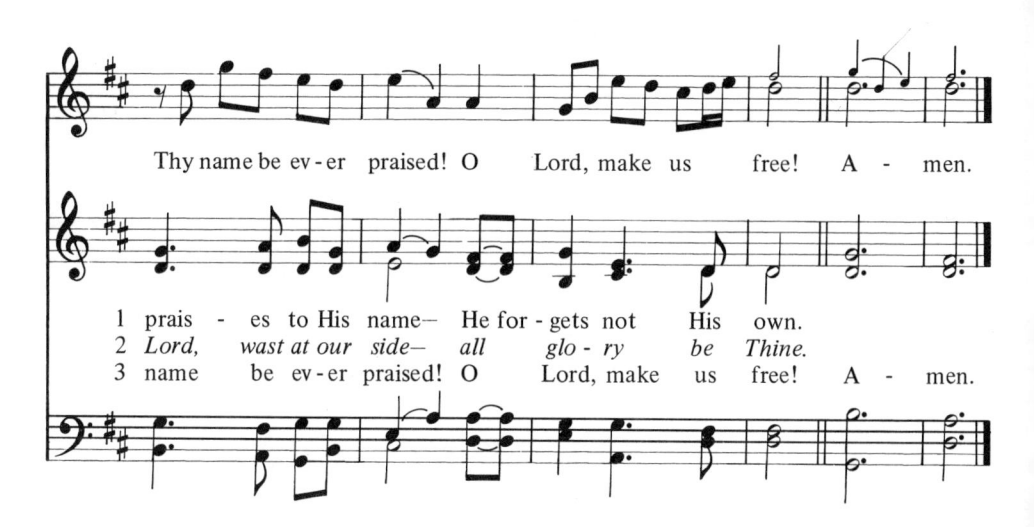

1 prais - es to His name— He for - gets not His own.
2 Lord, wast at our side— all glo - ry be Thine.
3 name be ev - er praised! O Lord, make us free! A - men.

His Love Is Everlasting 388

Leader: Give thanks to the Lord, for He is good,
People: HIS LOVE IS EVERLASTING!
Leader: Give thanks to the God of gods,
People: HIS LOVE IS EVERLASTING!
Leader: Give thanks to the Lord of lords,
People: HIS LOVE IS EVERLASTING!

Leader: He alone performs great marvels,
People: HIS LOVE IS EVERLASTING!
Leader: His wisdom made the heavens,
People: HIS LOVE IS EVERLASTING!
Leader: He set the earth on the waters,
People: HIS LOVE IS EVERLASTING!

Leader: He made the great lights,
People: HIS LOVE IS EVERLASTING!
Leader: The sun to govern the day,
People: HIS LOVE IS EVERLASTING!
Leader: Moon and stars to govern the night,
People: HIS LOVE IS EVERLASTING!

Leader: He led His people through the wilderness,
People: HIS LOVE IS EVERLASTING!
Leader: He remembered us when we were down,
People: HIS LOVE IS EVERLASTING!
Leader: And snatched us from our oppressors,
People: HIS LOVE IS EVERLASTING!

Leader: He provides for all living creatures,
People: HIS LOVE IS EVERLASTING!
Leader: Give thanks to the God of Heaven,
People: HIS LOVE IS EVERLASTING!

—Psalm 126:1-9; 16-18 (JB)

THANKSGIVING

389 Let All Things Now Living

Sing unto the Lord, all the earth, show forth from day to day His salvation.
—I Chronicles 16:23

Katherine K. Davis
Previously attributed to
John Cowley

ASH GROVE
Traditional Welsh Melody
Descant by Katherine K. Davis

Descant: 2 Ah_____ O sun, in Thy orbit, o-be-dient-ly shine. Ah_____ _____ The deeps of the o-cean pro-claim Him di-

1. Let all things now liv-ing A song of thanks-giv-ing To God the Cre-a-tor tri-um-phant-ly raise, Who fash-ioned and made us, pro-tect-ed and stayed us, Who guid-eth us on to the end of our

2. His law He en-forc-es: the stars in their cours-es, The sun in His or-bit, o-be-dient-ly shine; The hills and the moun-tains, The riv-ers and foun-tains, The deeps of the o-cean pro-claim Him di-

© Copyright 1939, renewed 1966 by E. C. Schirmer Music Co. All rights reserved. Used by permission
THANKSGIVING

THANKSGIVING

390. O Let Your Soul Now Be Filled with Gladness

Therefore God hath anointed thee with the oil of gladness....
— Hebrews 1:9

Peter Jönsson Aschan
Tr. by Karl A. Olsson

RANSOMED SOUL
Swedish Folk Melody
Harmonized by A. Royce Eckhardt

1. O let your soul now be filled with glad-ness, Your heart re-deemed, re-joice in-deed! O may the thought ban-ish all your sad-ness That in His blood you have been freed, That God's un-fail-ing love is yours, That you the on-ly Son were giv-en, That by His

2. *If you seem emp-ty of an-y feel-ing, Re-joice— you are His ran-somed bride! If those you cher-ish seem not to love you, And dark as-sails from ev-ery side, Still yours the prom-ise, come what may, In loss and tri-umph, in laugh-ter, cry-ing, In want and*

3. It is a good, ev-ery good tran-scend-ing, That Christ has died for you and me! It is a glad-ness that has no end-ing There-in God's won-drous love to see! Praise be to Him, the spot-less Lamb, Who through the des-ert my soul is lead-ing To that fair

© Copyright 1972 by Covenant Press. All rights reserved. Used by permission.
THANKSGIVING

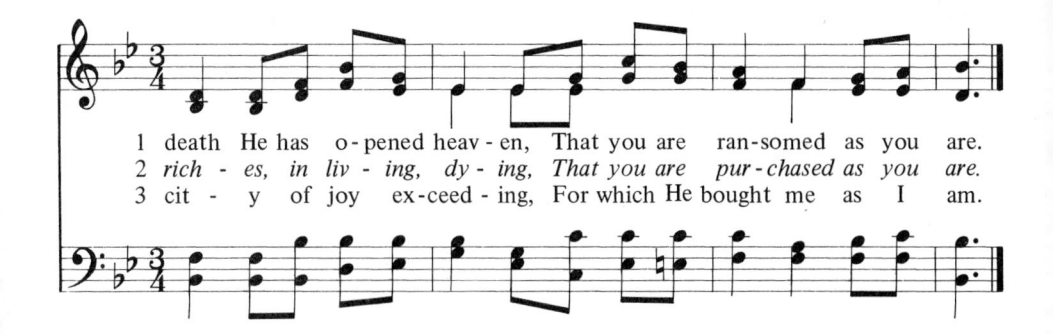

1 death He has o-pened heav-en, That you are ran-somed as you are.
2 *rich - es, in liv - ing, dy - ing, That you are pur - chased as you are.*
3 cit - y of joy ex-ceed-ing, For which He bought me as I am.

Thanksgiving Day 391

Father, we around this table thank Thee:
    for Thy great gift of life,
    that Thy love for us is not dependent upon any unworthiness of ours,
    for good health,
    that we know neither hunger nor want,
    for warm clothes to wear,
    for those who love us best,
    for friends whose words of encouragement have often chased away dark clouds,
    for the zest of living,
    for many an answered prayer,
    for kindly providences that have preserved us from danger and harm.

We thank Thee that still we live in a land bountifully able to supply all our needs, a land which still by Thy Providence knows peace, whose skies are not darkened by the machines of the enemy, whose fields and woodlands are still unblasted by the flames of war, a land with peaceful valleys and smiling meadows still serene.

O help us to appreciate all that we have, to be content with it, to be grateful for it, to be proud of it—not in an arrogant pride that boasts, but in a grateful pride that strives to be more worthy.

In Thy name, to whose bounty we owe these blessings spread before us, to Thee we give our gratitude. Amen.

—Peter Marshall

392 Come, Ye Thankful People, Come

Then shall the righteous shine forth as the sun in the Kingdom...
— Matthew 13:43

Henry Alford
ST. GEORGE'S WINDSOR
George J. Elvey

1. Come, ye thankful people, come, Raise the song of harvest-home;
   All is safely gathered in, Ere the winter storms begin:
   God, our Maker, doth provide For our wants to be supplied;
   Come to God's own temple, come, Raise the song of harvest-home.

2. *All the world is God's own field, Fruit unto His praise to yield;*
   Wheat and tares together sown, Unto joy or sorrows grown:
   First the blade, and then the ear, Then the full corn shall appear;
   Lord of harvest, grant that we Wholesome grain and pure may be.

3. For the Lord our God shall come And shall take His harvest-home;
   From His field shall in that day All offenses purge away,
   Give His angels charge at last In the fire the tares to cast,
   But the fruitful ears to store In His garner evermore.

4. *Even so, Lord, quickly come To Thy final harvest-home;*
   Gather Thou Thy people in, Free from sorrow, free from sin:
   There forever purified, In Thy presence to abide;
   Come, with all Thine angels, come, Raise the glorious harvest-home. A-men.

THANKSGIVING

Alternate Last Verse Harmonization Arranged by John Ness Beck

4 E-ven so, Lord, quick-ly come To Thy fi-nal har-vest-home; Gath-er Thou Thy peo-ple in, Free from sor-row, free from sin: There for-ev-er pu-ri-fied, In Thy pres-ence to a-bide: Come, with all Thine an-gels, come, Raise the glo-rious har-vest-home.

© Copyright 1976 by Paragon Associates, Inc. All rights reserved.

THANKSGIVING

393   Thanksgiving and Praise

Thanksgiving and praise are to be the major elements in our singing. It is possible to give thanks and praise God individually but if any congregation took time to let everyone do that, it would take all day.... Singing is something we can do together. So through the ages the believers in God both of the Old and New Testament have sung their praises and thanksgiving.... It is the reason we should be careful not to sing in a desultory manner. There is nothing more conducive to dullness in a service than half-hearted singing. So the exhortation here is most appropriate. "O, come, let us sing to the Lord: let us make a joyful noise to the rock of our salvation."

—Ray Stedman

394   Rejoice, Ye Pure in Heart

We will rejoice in Thy salvation and in the name of our God.... — Psalm 20:5

MARION
Edward H. Plumptre   Arthur H. Messiter

1. Rejoice, ye pure in heart, Rejoice, give thanks and sing;
Your festive banner wave on high, The cross of Christ your King:
Rejoice, rejoice, Rejoice, give thanks and sing. A-men.

2. *Go on through life's long path, Still chanting as ye go;*
From youth to age, by night and day, In gladness and in woe:
Rejoice, rejoice,

3. Then on, ye pure in heart, Rejoice, give thanks and sing;
Your glorious banner wave on high, The cross of Christ your King:

THANKSGIVING

Alternate Last Verse Harmonization Arranged by Fred Bock

3. Then on, ye pure in heart, Rejoice, give thanks and sing; Your glorious banner wave on high, The cross of Christ your King: Rejoice, rejoice, Rejoice, give thanks and sing! A-men.

© Copyright 1968 by Fred Bock Music Company. All rights reserved. Used by permission.

THANKSGIVING

395 We Plow the Fields and Scatter the Good Seed

The field is the world; the good seed are the children of the Kingdom.
— Matthew 13:38

Mathias Claudius
Tr. by Jane M. Campbell

WIR PFLÜGEN
Johann A. P. Schulz

1. We plow the fields and scat-ter The good seed on the land,
2. *He on-ly is the mak-er Of all things near and far,*
3. We thank Thee, then, O Fa-ther, For all things bright and good—

1. But it is fed and wa-tered By God's al-might-y hand;
2. *He paints the way-side flow-er, He lights the eve-ning star;*
3. The seed-time and the har-vest, Our life, our health, our food;

1. He sends the snow in win-ter, The warmth to swell the grain,
2. *The winds and waves o-bey Him, By Him the birds are fed:*
3. Ac-cept the gifts we of-fer For all Thy love im-parts,

1. The breez-es and the sun-shine, And soft, re-fresh-ing rain.
2. *Much more, to us His chil-dren, He gives our dai-ly bread.*
3. And, what Thou most de-sir-est, Our hum-ble, thank-ful hearts.

THANKSGIVING

All good gifts a-round us Are sent from heaven a-bove:
Then thank the Lord, O thank the Lord For all His love. A-men.

A General Thanksgiving   396

Almighty God, Father of all mercies,
we your unworthy servants give you humble thanks
for all Your goodness and loving-kindness to us
and to all men.

We bless You for our creation, preservation,
and all the blessings of this life;
but above all for Your incomparable love
in the redemption of the world by our Lord Jesus Christ;
for the means of grace, and for the hope of glory.

And, we pray, give us such an awareness of Your mercies,
that with truly thankful hearts
we may make known Your praise,
not only with our lips, but in our lives,
by giving up ourselves to Your service,
and by walking before You in holiness and righteousness all our days;
through Jesus Christ our Lord,
to whom, with You and the Holy Spirit,
be all honor and glory throughout all ages.

Amen.

—Standard Book of Common Prayer

397 I Will Serve Thee

If any man serve Me let him follow Me....
— John 12:26

Gloria Gaither
William J. Gaither

SERVING
William J. Gaither

I will serve Thee be-cause I love Thee, You have giv-en life to me; I was noth-ing be-fore You found me, You have giv-en life to me. Heart-aches, bro-ken piec-es, Ru-ined lives are why You died on Cal-vary; Your touch was what I longed for, You have giv-en life to me.

© Copyright 1969 by William J. Gaither. All rights reserved. Used by permission.

COMMITMENT AND SUBMISSION

Rise Up, O Men of God 398

. . . love the Lord, your God and serve Him . . .
— Deuteronomy 11:13

William P. Merrill

FESTAL SONG
William H. Walter

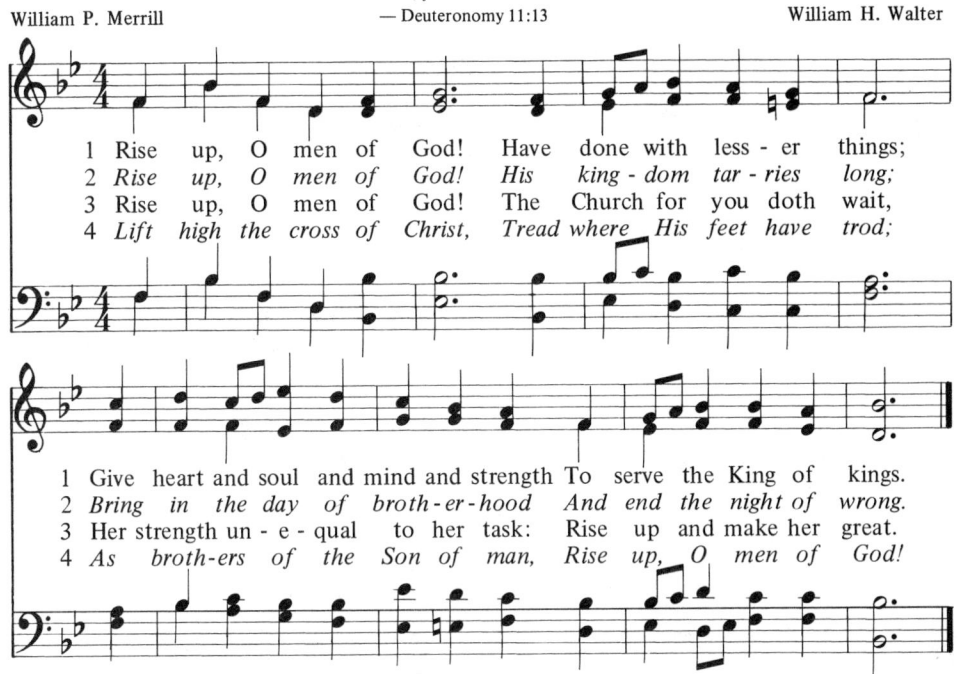

1. Rise up, O men of God! Have done with less-er things;
2. Rise up, O men of God! His king-dom tar-ries long;
3. Rise up, O men of God! The Church for you doth wait,
4. Lift high the cross of Christ, Tread where His feet have trod;

1. Give heart and soul and mind and strength To serve the King of kings.
2. Bring in the day of broth-er-hood And end the night of wrong.
3. Her strength un-e-qual to her task: Rise up and make her great.
4. As broth-ers of the Son of man, Rise up, O men of God!

Jesus Calls Us o'er the Tumult 399

Lord, if it be Thou, bid me come . . And He said, Come.
— Matthew 14:28,29

Cecil Frances Alexander
Jeff Redd, alt.

GALILEE
William H. Jude

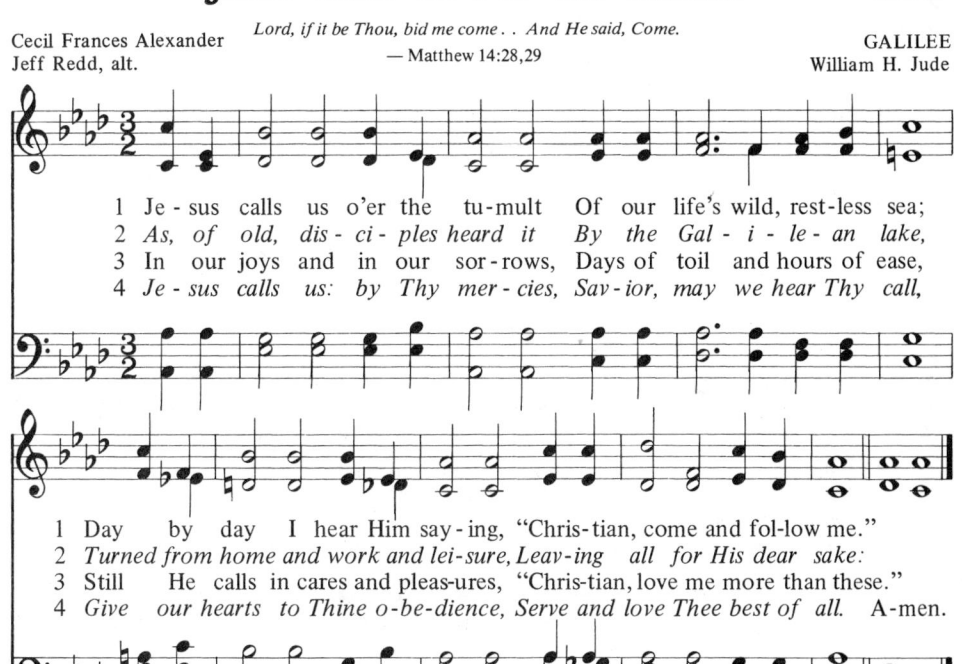

1. Je-sus calls us o'er the tu-mult Of our life's wild, rest-less sea;
2. As, of old, dis-ci-ples heard it By the Gal-i-le-an lake,
3. In our joys and in our sor-rows, Days of toil and hours of ease,
4. Je-sus calls us: by Thy mer-cies, Sav-ior, may we hear Thy call,

1. Day by day I hear Him say-ing, "Chris-tian, come and fol-low me."
2. Turned from home and work and lei-sure, Leav-ing all for His dear sake:
3. Still He calls in cares and pleas-ures, "Chris-tian, love me more than these."
4. Give our hearts to Thine o-be-dience, Serve and love Thee best of all. A-men.

COMMITMENT AND SUBMISSION

400 Have Thine Own Way, Lord!

Give me understanding and I shall keep thy Law . . . I shall observe it with all my heart.
—Psalm 119:34

Adelaide A. Pollard

ADELAIDE
George C. Stebbins

1. Have Thine own way, Lord! Have Thine own way!
Thou art the potter, I am the clay!
Mold me and make me After Thy will,
While I am waiting, Yielded and still.

2. *Have Thine own way, Lord! Have Thine own way!*
Search me and try me, Master, today!
Whiter than snow, Lord, Wash me just now,
As in Thy presence Humbly I bow.

3. Have Thine own way, Lord! Have Thine own way!
Wounded and weary, Help me, I pray!
Power—all power— Surely is Thine!
Touch me and heal me, Savior divine!

4. *Have Thine own way, Lord! Have Thine own way!*
Hold o'er my being Absolute sway!
Fill with Thy Spirit 'Til all shall see
Christ only, always, Living in me!

A-men.

© Copyright 1907. Renewal 1935 extended. Hope Publishing Co. All rights reserved. Used by permission.

COMMITMENT AND SUBMISSION

Jesus, I Come

401

The Lord . . . hath sent me to bind the broken hearted . . . .
— Isaiah 61:1

William T. Sleeper
Jeff Redd, alt.

JESUS, I COME
George C. Stebbins

1. Out of my bond-age, sor-row and night, Je-sus, I come, Je-sus, I come;
2. *Out of my shame-ful fail-ure and loss, Je-sus, I come, Je-sus, I come;*
3. Out of un-rest and ar-ro-gant pride, Je-sus, I come, Je-sus, I come;
4. *Out of the fear and dread of the tomb, Je-sus, I come, Je-sus, I come;*

1. In-to Thy free-dom, glad-ness and light, Je-sus, I come to Thee.
2. *In-to the glo-rious gain of Thy cross, Je-sus, I come to Thee.*
3. In-to Thy bless-ed will to a-bide, Je-sus, I come to Thee.
4. *In-to the joy and light of Thy home, Je-sus, I come to Thee.*

1. Out of my sick-ness in-to Thy health, Out of my need and in-to Thy wealth,
2. *Out of earth's sor-rows in-to Thy balm, Out of life's storms and in-to Thy calm,*
3. Out of my-self to dwell in Thy love, Out of de-spair to rap-tures a-bove,
4. *Out of the depths of ru-in un-told, In-to Thy peace-ful, shel-ter-ing fold,*

1. Out of my sin and in-to Thy-self, Je-sus, I come to Thee.
2. *Out of dis-tress to ju-bi-lant psalm, Je-sus, I come to Thee.*
3. Up-ward I rise on wings like a dove, Je-sus, I come to Thee.
4. *Ev-er Thy glo-rious face to be-hold, Je-sus, I come to Thee.*

COMMITMENT AND SUBMISSION

402 O Jesus, I Have Promised

He died for all that they . . . should not henceforth live unto themselves.
— II Corinthians 5:15

John E. Bode

ANGEL'S STORY
Arthur H. Mann

1. O Jesus, I have promised To serve Thee to the end; Be Thou forever near me, My Master and my Friend; I shall not fear the battle If Thou art by my side, Nor wander from the pathway If Thou wilt be my Guide.

2. O let me feel Thee near me, The world is ever near; I see the sights that dazzle, The tempting sounds I hear; My foes are ever near me, Around me and within; But, Jesus, draw Thou nearer, And shield my soul from sin.

3. O Jesus, Thou hast promised To all who follow Thee That where Thou art in glory There shall Thy servant be; And, Jesus, I have promised To serve Thee to the end; O give me grace to follow My Master and my Friend.

403 A Confession of Faith

I believe in God, who is for me spirit, love, the principle of all things.

I believe that God is in me, as I am in Him.

I believe that the true welfare of man consists in fulfilling the will of God.

I believe that from the fulfillment of the will of God there can follow nothing but that which is good for me and for all men.   *(more on next page)*

COMMITMENT AND SUBMISSION

I believe that the will of God is that every man should love his fellow men, and should act toward others as he desires that they should act toward him.

I believe that the reason of life is for each of us simply to grow in love.

I believe that this growth in love will contribute more than any other force to establish the Kingdom of God on earth.

—Leo Tolstoy

O Love That Will Not Let Me Go 404

The Lord shall be unto thee an everlasting light....
— Isaiah 60:19

George Matheson

ST. MARGARET
Albert L. Peace

1. O Love that will not let me go, I rest my weary soul in Thee; I give Thee back the life I owe, That in Thine ocean depths its flow May richer, fuller be.
2. O Light that followest all my way, I yield my flickering torch to Thee; My heart restores its borrowed ray, That in Thy sunshine's blaze its day May brighter, fairer be.
3. O Joy that seekest me through pain, I cannot close my heart to Thee; I trace the rainbow through the rain, And feel the promise is not vain That morn shall tearless be.
4. O Cross that liftest up my head, I dare not ask to fly from Thee; I lay in dust life's glory dead, And from the ground there blossoms red, Life that shall endless be. A-men.

COMMITMENT AND SUBMISSION

405 Close to Thee

He that sayeth he abideth in Him ought himself also to walk even as He walked. — I John 2:6

Fanny J. Crosby

CLOSE TO THEE
Silas J. Vail

1. Thou, my ev-er-last-ing por-tion, More than friend or life to me,
2. *Not for ease or world-ly pleas-ure Nor for fame my prayer shall be;*
3. Lead me through the vale of shad-ows, Bear me o'er life's fit-ful sea;

1. All a-long my pil-grim jour-ney, Sav-ior, let me walk with Thee.
2. *Glad-ly will I toil and suf-fer, On-ly let me walk with Thee.*
3. Then the gate of life e-ter-nal May I en-ter, Lord, with Thee.

1. Close to Thee, close to Thee, Close to Thee, close to Thee; All a-
2. *Close to Thee, close to Thee, Close to Thee, close to Thee;* Glad-ly
3. Close to Thee, close to Thee, Close to Thee, close to Thee; Then the

1. long my pil-grim jour-ney, Sav-ior, let me walk with Thee.
2. *will I toil and suf-fer, On-ly let me walk with Thee.*
3. gate of life e-ter-nal May I en-ter, Lord, with Thee. A-men.

COMMITMENT AND SUBMISSION

Lord, I'm Coming Home

406

None of his sins which he hath committed shall be mentioned unto him.
— Ezekiel 33:16

William J. Kirkpatrick

COMING HOME
William J. Kirkpatrick

1. I've wan-dered far a - way from God, Now I'm com-ing home;
2. *I've wast - ed man - y pre - cious years, Now I'm com-ing home;*
3. I've tired of sin and stray - ing, Lord, Now I'm com-ing home;
4. *My soul is sick, my heart is sore, Now I'm com-ing home;*

1. The paths of sin too long I've trod, Lord, I'm com-ing home.
2. *I now re-pent with bit - ter tears, Lord, I'm com-ing home.*
3. I'll trust Thy love, be - lieve Thy word, Lord, I'm com-ing home.
4. *My strength re-new, my hope re - store, Lord, I'm com-ing home.*

Com-ing home, com - ing home, Nev - er - more to roam,

O - pen wide Thine arms of love, Lord, I'm com-ing home.

COMMITMENT AND SUBMISSION

407 Lead Me to Calvary

And they came to a place which was called Gethsemane....
— Mark 14:32

Jennie Evelyn Hussey
LEAD ME TO CALVARY
William J. Kirkpatrick

1. King of my life I crown Thee now— Thine shall the glo-ry be;
   Lest I for-get Thy thorn-crowned brow, Lead me to Cal-va-ry.
2. Show me the tomb where Thou wast laid, Ten-der-ly mourned and wept;
   An-gels in robes of light ar-rayed Guard-ed Thee whilst Thou slept.
3. Let me like Ma-ry, through the gloom, Come with a gift to Thee;
   Show to me now the emp-ty tomb— Lead me to Cal-va-ry.
4. May I be will-ing, Lord, to bear Dai-ly my cross for Thee;
   E-ven Thy cup of grief to share— Thou hast borne all for me.

Refrain:
Lest I for-get Geth-sem-a-ne, Lest I for-get Thine ag-o-ny,
Lest I for-get Thy love for me, Lead me to Cal-va-ry. A-men.

Copyright 1921. Renewal 1949. Hope Publishing Co. All rights reserved. Used by permission.

COMMITMENT AND SUBMISSION

I Surrender All

408

He that loveth his life shall lose it; He that hateth his life in this world shall keep it unto life eternal.
— John 12:25

Judson W. Van de Venter

SURRENDER
Winfield S. Weeden

1. All to Jesus I surrender, All to Him I freely give;
   I will ever love and trust Him, In His presence daily live.
2. *All to Jesus I surrender, Humbly at His feet I bow,*
   Worldly pleasures all forsaken; Take me, Jesus, take me now.
3. All to Jesus I surrender, Make me, Savior, wholly Thine.
   Let me feel the Holy Spirit, Truly know that Thou art mine.
4. *All to Jesus I surrender, Lord, I give myself to Thee;*
   Fill me with Thy love and power, Let Thy blessing fall on me.

Refrain:
I surrender all, I surrender all,
I surrender all, I surrender all,
All to Thee, my blessed Savior, I surrender all.

COMMITMENT AND SUBMISSION

409 Who Is on the Lord's Side?

Who is on the Lord's side?
— Exodus 32:26

Frances R. Havergal

ARMAGEDDON
C. Luise Reichardt

1. Who is on the Lord's side? Who will serve the King? Who will be His helpers, Other lives to bring? Who will leave the world's side? Who will face the foe? Who is on the Lord's side? Who for Him will go? By Thy call of mercy, By Thy grace divine, We are on the Lord's side— Savior, we are Thine!

2. *Not for weight of glory, Nor for crown and palm, Enter we the army, Raise the warrior-psalm; But for Love that claimeth Lives for whom He died: He whom Jesus nameth Must be on His side. By Thy love constraining, By Thy grace divine, We are on the Lord's side— Savior, we are Thine!*

3. Jesus, Thou hast bought us, Not with gold or gem, But with Thine own life-blood, For Thy diadem; With Thy blessing filling Each who comes to Thee, Thou hast made us willing, Thou hast made us free. By Thy grand redemption, By Thy grace divine, We are on the Lord's side— Savior, we are Thine!

4. *Fierce may be the conflict, Strong may be the foe, But the King's own army None can overthrow; 'Round His standard ranging, Victory is secure, For His truth unchanging Makes the triumph sure. Joyfully enlisting, By Thy grace divine, We are on the Lord's side— Savior, we are Thine!*

COMMITMENT AND SUBMISSION

Prayer and Action 410

God is not a personage who orders us to a prostrate ourselves before Him
— a radically false position—
but one who says:
"Stand up,
here is my task for you;
take it and get on with it."

God does not require incense from us;
what He does require
is that we should *listen* and *take action*—
the true response of love.

God did not stop speaking two thousand years ago.
He speaks to you personally today
every time an inward voice asks you to do a kind or generous deed
or to suffer for the sake of someone else.

It is to you personally that God speaks at this moment,
and it is *through you* that He speaks when He inspires you to do some service.
Be brave enough to listen at first hand to what God says to you.

—John W. Harvey and Christina Yates

Am I a Soldier of the Cross? 411

No soldier that wareth entangleth himself with the affairs of this life.... — II Timothy 2:4

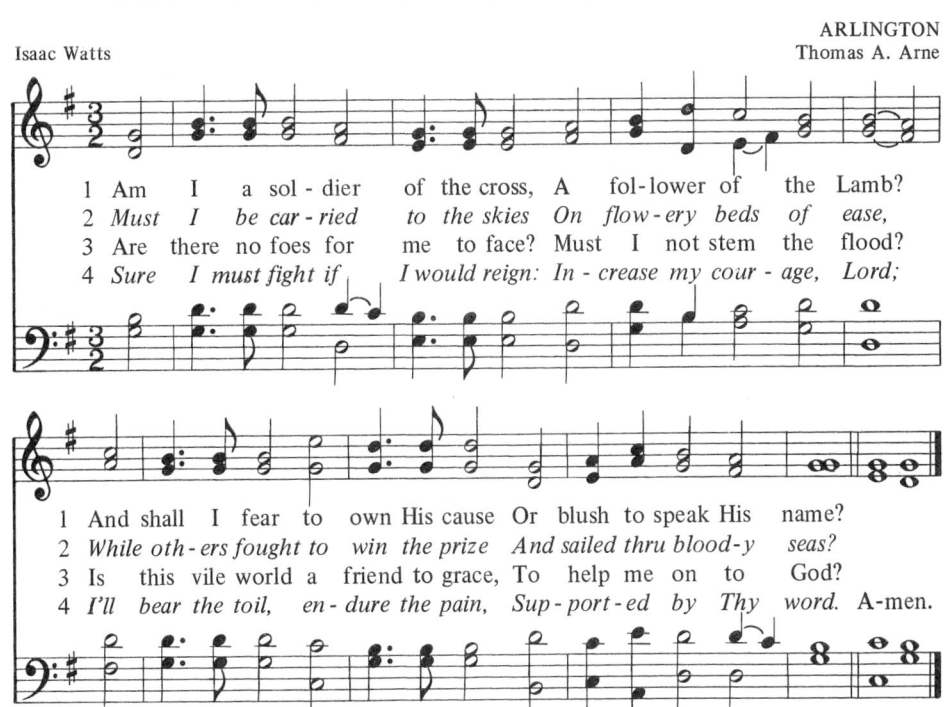

Isaac Watts

ARLINGTON
Thomas A. Arne

1. Am I a sol-dier of the cross, A fol-lower of the Lamb?
And shall I fear to own His cause Or blush to speak His name?

2. Must I be car-ried to the skies On flow-ery beds of ease,
While oth-ers fought to win the prize And sailed thru blood-y seas?

3. Are there no foes for me to face? Must I not stem the flood?
Is this vile world a friend to grace, To help me on to God?

4. Sure I must fight if I would reign: In-crease my cour-age, Lord;
I'll bear the toil, en-dure the pain, Sup-port-ed by Thy word. A-men.

COMMITMENT AND SUBMISSION

412 Under His Wings

Hide me under the shadow of Thy Wing.
—Psalm 17:8

William O. Cushing

HINGHAM
Ira D. Sankey

1. Under His wings I am safely abiding, Though the night deepens and tempests are wild; Still I can trust Him—I know He will keep me, He has redeemed me and I am His child.
2. *Under His wings, what a refuge in sorrow! How the heart yearningly turns to His rest! Often when earth has no balm for my healing, There I find comfort and there I am blest.*
3. Under His wings, O what precious enjoyment! There will I hide 'til life's trials are o'er; Sheltered, protected, no evil can harm me, Resting in Jesus I'm safe evermore.

Under His wings, under His wings, Who from His love can sever? Under His wings my soul shall abide, Safely abide forever.

COMMITMENT AND SUBMISSION

The Good News of God's Forgiveness

413

Left Side:
Those who let go of self
and hold on to Christ are forgiven.

Do you believe it?

Right Side:
With all our hearts!
Forgiveness is God's free gift
to be accepted by faith alone in Christ.

Do you believe it?

Left Side:
We do! With all our hearts!

Right Side:
Then your new name is "Set Free."

Left Side:
And yours is "Forgiven."

All:
If God no longer accuses us,
we will stop accusing ourselves.
We will celebrate His love and sing His praises!
Amen.

—Howard Childers

Father, I Adore You

414

God is a Spirit; and they that worship Him must worship him in spirit and in truth. — John 4:24

MARANATHA
Terrye Coelho   Terrye Coelho

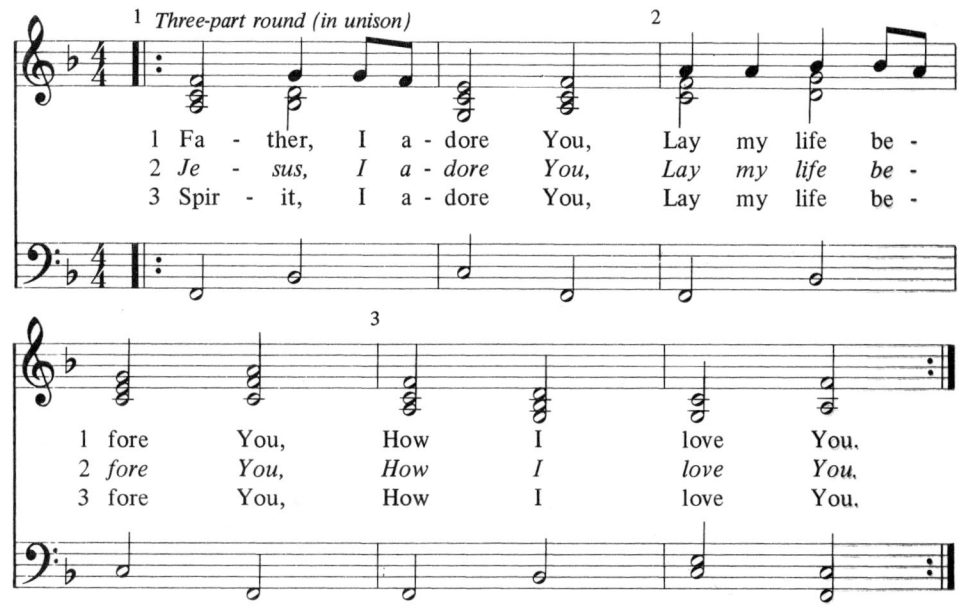

Three-part round (in unison)

1 Father, I adore You, Lay my life before You, How I love You.
2 Jesus, I adore You, Lay my life before You, How I love You.
3 Spirit, I adore You, Lay my life before You, How I love You.

Copyright 1973 Terrye Coelho. Administered by Maranatha! Music. All rights reserved. Used by permission.

COMMITMENT AND SUBMISSION

415 At Calvary

And when they were come to . . . Calvary they crucified Him . . .
— Luke 23:33

William R. Newell

CALVARY
Daniel B. Towner

1. Years I spent in vanity and pride, Caring not my Lord was crucified, Knowing not it was for me He died On Calvary.
2. By God's Word at last my sin I learned; Then I trembled at the law I'd spurned, 'Til my guilty soul imploring turned To Calvary.
3. Now I've given to Jesus everything; Now I gladly own Him as my King; Now my raptured soul can only sing Of Calvary.
4. O the love that drew salvation's plan! O the grace that brought it down to man! O the mighty gulf that God did span At Calvary.

Mercy there was great and grace was free, Pardon there was multiplied to me, There my burdened soul found liberty — At Calvary.

CONFESSION AND REPENTANCE

Pass Me Not, O Gentle Savior

And he sought to see Jesus . . . for He was to pass that way.

— Luke 19: 3-4

Fanny J. Crosby

PASS ME NOT
William H. Doane

1. Pass me not, O gen-tle Sav-ior— Hear my hum-ble cry!
2. *Let me at a throne of mer-cy Find a sweet re-lief;*
3. Trust-ing on-ly in Thy mer-it, Would I seek Thy face;
4. *Thou the spring of all my com-fort, More than life to me!*

1. While on oth-ers Thou art call-ing, Do not pass me by.
2. *Kneel-ing there in deep con-tri-tion, Help my un-be-lief.*
3. Heal my wound-ed, bro-ken spir-it, Save me by Thy grace.
4. *Whom have I on earth be-side Thee? Whom in heaven but Thee?*

Sav-ior, Sav-ior, Hear my hum-ble cry!

While on oth-ers Thou art call-ing, Do not pass me by. A-men.

CONFESSION AND REPENTANCE

417 Just As I Am, Without One Plea

Ho, everyone who is athirst, come . . . without money . . . and without price.
— Isaiah 55:1

Charlotte Elliott

WOODWORTH
William B. Bradbury

1. Just as I am, without one plea, But that Thy blood was shed for me, And that Thou biddest me come to Thee— O Lamb of God, I come, I come!
2. *Just as I am, and waiting not To rid my soul of one dark blot; To Thee, whose blood can cleanse each spot, O Lamb of God, I come, I come!*
3. *Just as I am, Thou wilt receive, Wilt welcome, pardon, cleanse, relieve; Because Thy promise I believe, O Lamb of God, I come, I come!*
4. *Just as I am, Thy love unknown Hath broken every barrier down; Now, to be Thine, yes, Thine alone, O Lamb of God, I come, I come!* A-men.

418 The General Confession

(All in unison)

Almighty and most merciful Father, we have erred, and strayed from Thy ways like lost sheep. We have offended against Thy holy laws. We have left undone those things which we ought to have done, and we have done those things which we ought not to have done; and there is no health in us.

O Lord, have mercy upon us, miserable offenders. Spare them, O Lord, which confess their faults. Restore them that are penitent, according to Thy promises declared unto mankind in Christ Jesus our Lord. And grant, O most merciful Father, for His sake, that we may hereafter live a godly, righteous, and sober life—to the glory of Thy holy name. Amen.

Kind and Merciful God   419

That . . . He might show the exceeding riches of His grace in His kindness . . .
— Ephesians 2:7

Bryan Jeffery Leech

ELFÅKER
Swedish Melody
Adapted by Bryan Jeffery Leech

1. Kind and merciful God, we have sinned in Your sight,
   We have all wandered far from Your way;
   We have followed desire, We have failed to aspire
   To the virtue we ought to display.

2. *Kind and merciful God, we've neglected Your Word*
   And the truth that would guide us aright;
   We have lived in the shade Of the dark we have made,
   When you willed us to walk in the light.

3. Kind and merciful God, we have broken Your laws
   And in conduct have veered from the norm;
   We have dreamed of the good, But the good that we could
   We have frequently failed to perform.

4. *Kind and merciful God, in Christ's death on the cross*
   You provided a cleansing from sin;
   Speak the words that forgive That henceforth we may live
   By the might of Your Spirit within.

5. Kind and merciful God, bid us lift up our heads
   And command us to rise from our knees;
   May our hearts now be changed And no longer estranged,
   Through the power of Your pardon and peace. A-men.

© Copyright 1973 by Fred Bock Music Company. All rights reserved. Used by permission.

CONFESSION AND REPENTANCE

420 The Ten Commandments

Then God spoke all these words.
He said, "I am Jehovah your God
who brought you out of the land of Egypt, out of the house of slavery.

"You shall have no gods except Me.

"You shall not make yourself a carved image of any likeness of anything
in heaven or on earth beneath or in the waters under the earth;
you shall not bow down to them or serve them.
For I, Jehovah your God, am a jealous God
and I punish the father's fault in the sons,
the grandsons, and the great-grandsons of those who hate Me;
but I show kindness to thousands of those who love Me and keep My commandments.

"You shall not utter the name of Jehovah your God to misuse it,
for Jehovah will not leave unpunished the man who utters His name to misuse it.

"Remember the sabbath day and keep it holy.
For six days you shall labor and do all your work,
but the seventh day is a sabbath for Jehovah your God.
You shall do no work that day,
neither you nor your son nor your daughter nor your servants,
men or women,
nor your animals nor the stranger who lives with you.
For in six days Jehovah made the heavens and the earth and the sea and all that these hold,
but on the seventh day He rested;
that is why Jehovah has blessed the sabbath day and made it sacred.

"Honor your father and your mother
so that you may have a long life in the land that Jehovah your God has given to you.

"You shall not kill.

"You shall not commit adultery.

"You shall not steal.

"You shall not bear false witness against your neighbor.

"You shall not covet your neighbor's house.
You shall not covet your neighbor's wife,
or his servant, man or woman, or his ox, or his donkey, or anything that is his."

—Exodus 20:1-17 (JB)

CONFESSION AND REPENTANCE

Lord, I Want to Be a Christian

421

And be renewed in the spirit of your mind. — Ephesians 4:23

American Folk Hymn

I WANT TO BE A CHRISTIAN
American Folk Melody

1. Lord, I want to be a Christian in my heart, in my heart; Lord, I want to be a Christian in my heart. In my heart, in my heart, Lord, I want to be a Christian in my heart.

2. *Lord, I want to be more loving in my heart, in my heart; Lord, I want to be more loving in my heart. In my heart, in my heart, Lord, I want to be more loving in my heart.*

3. Lord, I want to be more holy in my heart, in my heart; Lord, I want to be more holy in my heart. In my heart, in my heart, Lord, I want to be more holy in my heart.

4. *Lord, I want to be like Jesus in my heart, in my heart; Lord, I want to be like Jesus in my heart. In my heart, in my heart, Lord, I want to be like Jesus in my heart.*

CONFESSION AND REPENTANCE

422 Dear Lord and Father of Mankind

And after the earthquake, a fire; . . . And after the fire a still small voice.
— I Kings 19:12

John Greenleaf Whittier
Frederick C. Maker

REST

1. Dear Lord and Father of mankind, Forgive our foolish ways! Reclothe us in our rightful mind; In purer lives Thy service find, In deeper reverence, praise.
2. In simple trust like theirs who heard, Beside the Syrian sea, The gracious calling of the Lord, Let us, like them, without a word, Rise up and follow Thee.
3. O sabbath rest by Galilee! O calm of hills above! Where Jesus knelt to share with Thee The silence of eternity, Interpreted by love.
4. Drop Thy still dews of quietness 'Til all our strivings cease; Take from our souls the strain and stress, And let our ordered lives confess The beauty of Thy peace.
5. Breathe through the heat of our desire Thy coolness and Thy balm; Let sense be dumb, let flesh retire; Speak through the earthquake, wind, and fire, O still, small voice of calm. A-men.

Music copyright by "The Psalms and Hymns Trust." Used by permission.

423 Prayers of Confession

(All in unison)

O Lord, that we dare confess anything at all to You before our brothers and sisters here in this church today is proof that we believe that You already know us as we are; that we believe that You are able to do something about it; and that we are willing to step from our worlds of pretense, fantasy and illusion into a kind of "facing-up-to-things-as-they-are" where You can touch us, and forgive us, and love us, and accept us and make us new. This is hard, Lord, but here we are. Amen.

(Silent, personal confession)

"And now, Lord, I confess specifically to . . ." *(Pray individually and silently)*

Minister only: Amen.

— Howard Childers,

CONFESSION AND REPENTANCE

Assurance of Pardon 424

Minister: This statement is completely reliable and should be universally accepted: Christ Jesus entered the world to rescue sinners.

He personally bore our sins in His body on the cross, so that we might be dead to sin and be alive to all that is good.

God's mercy never ends. I tell you, in the name of Jesus Christ, we are forgiven.

People: Amen.

—Kenneth Working

Cleanse Me 425

He is faithful and just . . . to cleanse us from all unrighteousness. — I John 1:9

Edwin Orr

MAORI
Maori Melody

1. Search me, O God, and know my heart to-day; Try me, O Savior, know my thoughts, I pray. See if there be some wicked way in me; Cleanse me from ev-ery sin, and set me free.

2. I praise Thee, Lord, for cleansing me from sin; Ful-fill Thy Word and make me pure with-in. Fill me with fire, where once I burned with shame; Grant my de-sire to mag-ni-fy Thy name.

3. Lord, take my life, and make it whol-ly Thine; Fill my poor heart with Thy great love di-vine. Take all my will, my pas-sion, self and pride; I now sur-ren-der, Lord—in me a-bide.

4. O Ho-ly Ghost, re-viv-al comes from Thee; Send a re-viv-al, start the work in me. Thy Word de-clares Thou wilt sup-ply our need; For bless-ing now, O Lord, I hum-bly plead.

CONFESSION AND REPENTANCE

426 Psalm 51

O God, may the measure of Your eternal love
      be the measure of Your mercy.
And may the measure of Your mercy
      be sufficient to blot out my great sins
    and cancel out the guilt of my wrongdoing.

I have failed, O Lord, and my failures weigh
      heavily upon my heart.
I cannot share them all with my brother lest
      they weigh too heavily upon him
    and may even threaten my relationship with him.
But You know what they are, O God,
    and how far I have fallen short of Your
      standards and expectations.

I am only human, Lord.
It was not by my choice that I was propelled
      into this fractured world.
The weaknesses that plague me are not all
      of my doing,
    nor can I handle them by my strength alone.

I know that nothing can be hidden from You.
I can only acknowledge my indictment
      and accept Your loving forgiveness.
Purge me of my guilt, O Lord;
    heal the hurts of those
      who have been afflicted by my failures.

Revive my flagging spirit, O God.
Restore to me the joy and assurance of a right
      relationship with You.
Reinstate me in Your purposes, and help me to
      avoid the snares and pitfalls along the way.

It is only then that my tongue will be set free
      to sing Your praises
    and my hands to perform the tasks You have
      set before me.
It is only then that I can relate deeply
      and meaningfully to my brother
    and communicate to him the message
      of reconciling love.

I bring You no oblation or sacrifice, my God,
    only a foolish and self-centered heart.
I do come to You with a sincere desire to be
      Your servant,
    to walk in Your course for my life,
      to receive Your love, and to channel such love
        to my fellowmen about me.

I thank You, God, that this is acceptable to You
      and that I will remain Your child forever.

—Leslie Brandt

CONFESSION AND REPENTANCE

I Lay My Sins on Jesus

Behold the Lamb of God that taketh away the sins of the world.
— John 1:29

Horatius Bonar

CRUCIFIX
Greek Melody

427

1. I lay my sins on Jesus, The spotless Lamb of God;
   He bears them all, and frees us From every guilty load.
   I bring my guilt to Jesus, To wash my crimson stains
   White in His blood most precious, 'Til not a spot remains.

2. I lay my wants on Jesus— All fullness dwells in Him;
   He heals all my diseases, He doth my soul redeem.
   I lay my griefs on Jesus, My burdens and my cares;
   He from them all releases, He all my sorrow shares.

3. I long to be like Jesus— Pure, loving, lowly, mild;
   I long to be like Jesus— The Father's holy child.
   I long to be with Jesus, Amid the heavenly throng,
   To sing with saints His praises, To learn the angels' song.

CONFESSION AND REPENTANCE

428 Come, Ye Sinners, Poor and Needy

He that cometh unto Me I will in no wise cast out. — John 6:37

Joseph Hart

BEACH SPRING
"The Sacred Harp"
Harmonized by A. Royce Eckhardt

1 Come, ye sin-ners, poor and need-y, Bruised and bro-ken by the fall;
2 *Let not con-science make you lin-ger, Nor of fit-ness fond-ly dream;*
3 Lo! th'in-car-nate God, as-cend-ed, Pleads the mer-it of His blood;

1 Je-sus read-y stands to save you, Full of par-doning love for all.
2 *All that He re-quires of sin-ners Is to turn and trust in Him.*
3 Ven-ture on Him, ven-ture whol-ly Let no oth-er trust in-trude;

1 He is a-ble, He is a-ble, He is will-ing, doubt no more;
2 *He will save you, He will save you, 'Tis the gos-pel's con-stant theme.*
3 None but Je-sus, none but Je-sus Can do help-less sin-ners good.

1 He is a-ble, He is a-ble, He is will-ing, doubt no more.
2 *He will save you, He will save you, 'Tis the gos-pel's con-stant theme.*
3 None but Je-sus, none but Je-sus Can do help-less sin-ners good.

Harmonization © Copyright 1972 by Covenant Press. All rights reserved. Used by permission.

INVITATION

Even So, Lord Jesus, Come

He which testifieth these things saith, Surely, I come quickly...
— Revelation 22:20

Gloria Gaither
William J. Gaither

LORD JESUS, COME
William J. Gaither

429

1. In a world of fear and tur-moil, In a race that seems so hard to run; Lord, I need Thy rich in-fill-ing, E-ven so, Lord Je-sus, come. E-ven so, Lord Je-sus, come— My heart doth long for Thee; Though I've failed and be-trayed Thy trust, E-ven so, Lord Je-sus, come.

2. *When my eyes shall span the riv-er, When I gaze in-to the vast un-known; May I say with calm as-sur-ance, "E-ven now, Lord Je-sus, come."*

© Copyright 1963 by William J. Gaither. All rights reserved. Used by permission.

INVITATION

430 Reach Out to Jesus

When she had heard of Jesus, came . . . and touched his garment.
— Mark 5:27

Ralph Carmichael

REACH OUT TO JESUS
Ralph Carmichael

1. Is your burden heavy as you bear it all alone?
2. *Is the life you're living filled with sorrow and despair?*

1. Does the road you travel harbor danger yet unknown?
2. *Does the future press you with its worry and its care?*

1. Are you growing weary in the struggle of it all? Jesus will
2. *Are you tired and friendless, have you almost lost your way?* Jesus will

1. help you when on His name you call.
2. *help you, just come to Him today.*

He is always there, hearing every prayer, faithful and true; Walking by our side,

© Copyright 1968 by Lexicon Music, Inc. All rights reserved. Used by permission.
INVITATION

in His love we hide all the day through. When you get dis-cour-aged just re-mem-ber what to do— Reach out to Je-sus, He's reach-ing out to you.

Prayer of Acceptance 431

Minister:

*Here is a simple prayer
for those who have decided to receive Jesus:—*

People:

*Dear Father,
I believe that Jesus Christ is Your only begotten Son,
and that He became a human being,
shed His blood and died on the Cross
to clean away my sin that was separating me from You.
I believe that He rose from the dead,
physically,
to give me new life.
Lord Jesus, I invite You to come into my heart.
I accept You as my Savior and Lord.
I confess my sins, and ask You to wash them away.
I believe that You have come and are living in me right now.
Thank you, Jesus!
Amen.*

—Dennis and Rita Bennett

INVITATION

432 Softly and Tenderly

Come unto Me, all ye who labor and are heavy laden....
— Matthew 11:28

Will L. Thompson

THOMPSON
Will L. Thompson

1. Softly and tenderly Jesus is calling, Calling for you and for me;
Patient and loving, He's waiting and watching, Watching for you and for me.

2. *Why should we linger when Jesus is pleading, Pleading for you and for me?*
Why should we wait, then, and heed not His mercies, Mercies for you and for me?

3. O for the wonderful love He has promised, Promised for you and for me;
Tho' we have sinned He has mercy and pardon, Pardon for you and for me.

Come home, come home, Ye who are weary, come home;
Earnestly, tenderly, Jesus is calling— Calling, "O sinner, come home!"

INVITATION

Let Jesus Come Into Your Heart

433

Behold, now is the accepted time . . . now is the day of salvation.
—II Corinthians 6:2

Lelia N. Morris

McCONNELSVILLE
Lelia N. Morris

1. If you are tired of the load of your sin, Let Jesus come
2. If 'tis for pu - ri - ty now that you sigh, Let Jesus come
3. If there's a tem - pest your voice can - not still, Let Jesus come
4. If you would join the glad songs of the blest, Let Jesus come

1. in - to your heart; If you de - sire a new life to be - gin,
2. in - to your heart; Foun-tains for cleans-ing are flow-ing near by,
3. in - to your heart; If there's a void this world nev - er can fill,
4. in - to your heart; If you would en - ter the man-sions of rest,

Let Je - sus come in - to your heart. Just now, your

doubt-ings give o'er; Just now, re - ject Him no more; Just now, throw

o - pen the door; Let Je - sus come in - to your heart.

INVITATION

434 Jesus Is Calling

Be of good comfort; He calleth thee.
—Matthew 10:49

John 11:28
Fanny J. Crosby

CALLING TODAY
George C. Stebbins

1. Jesus is tenderly calling you home—
   Calling today, calling today;
   Why from the sunshine of love will you roam
   Farther and farther away?

2. *Jesus is calling the weary to rest—*
   Calling today, calling today;
   Bring Him your burden and you shall be blest—
   He will not turn you away.

3. Jesus is waiting, O come to Him now—
   Waiting today, waiting today;
   Come with your sins, at His feet lowly bow—
   Come, and no longer delay.

4. *Jesus is pleading, O hear now His voice—*
   Hear Him today, hear Him today;
   They who believe on His name shall rejoice—
   Quickly arise and away.

Calling today, Calling today, Jesus is calling, Is tenderly calling today.

INVITATION

The Savior Is Waiting

435

Today if ye hear His voice harden not your heart.
— Hebrews 3:7,8

Ralph Carmichael

CARMICHAEL
Ralph Carmichael

1. The Sav-ior is wait-ing to en-ter your heart, Why don't you let Him come in? There's noth-ing in this world to keep you a-part, What is your an-swer to Him?

2. *If you'll take one step toward the Sav-ior, my friend, You'll find His arms o-pen wide; Re-ceive Him, and all of your dark-ness will end, With-in your heart He'll a-bide.*

Time af-ter time He has wait-ed be-fore, And now He is wait-ing a-gain To see if you're will-ing to o-pen the door: O how He wants to come in.

© Copyright 1958 by Sacred Songs, Waco, Texas, 76703. International copyright secured. Arr. © Copyright 1966 by Sacred Songs. All rights reserved. Used by permission.

INVITATION

436 For Those Tears I Died

But whosoever drinketh of the water that I shall give him shall never thirst.
— John 4:14

Marsha Stevens

CHILDREN OF THE DAY
Marsha Stevens

1. You said You'd come and share all my sorrows, You said You'd be there for all my tomorrows; I came so close to sending You away, But just like You promised You came there to stay — I just had to pray.

2. Your goodness so great I can't understand, And dear Lord, I know that all this was planned; I know You're here now, and always will be, Your love loosed my chains and in You I'm free — But Jesus, why me?

3. Jesus, I give you my heart and my soul, I know that without God I'd never be whole; Savior, You opened all the right doors, And I thank You, and praise You from earth's humble shores — Take me, I'm Yours.

© Copyright 1969 Children of the Day. This arr. © Copyright 1976 by Children of the Day. Used by permission. All rights reserved.

INVITATION

And Jesus said, "Come to the water, stand by my side; I know you are thirsty, you won't be denied. I felt every teardrop when in darkness you cried, And I strove to remind you that for those tears I died."

INVITATION

437 Almost Persuaded

I would to God that not only thou, ... but all ...
were both almost and altogether such as I am ... — Acts 26:29

Philip P. Bliss

ALMOST
Philip P. Bliss

1. "Almost persuaded" now to believe; "Almost persuaded" Christ to receive: Seems now some soul will say, "Go, Spirit, go Thy way; Some more convenient day On Thee I'll call."
2. "Almost persuaded," come, come today; "Almost persuaded," turn not away: Jesus invites you here, Angels are lingering near, Prayers rise from hearts so dear, O wanderer, come.
3. "Almost persuaded," harvest is past! "Almost persuaded," doom comes at last! "Almost" cannot avail, "Almost" is but to fail! Sad, sad, that bitter wail, "Almost," but lost!

438 Psalm 144

O God, it is difficult to understand how You can regard man with such high regard and show him so much concern.
His years upon this earth are so few.
He is little more than a wisp of wind in the time and space of Your great universe.
You created him as the object of Your love—only to see him turn from You to play with his foolish toys.
You tried to teach him to love his fellowman—only to see him express his fear and suspicion and hate through cruel acts of violence and war.
You showered upon him Your abundant gifts—only to see him make them his ultimate concern.
Still You continue to love him and seek incessantly to save him from destroying himself and the world You have placed in his hands.
Even while he rejects You, You reach out to draw him back to Yourself.
Even while he suffers the painful consequences of his rank rebelliousness, You offer to him Your healing and demonstrate Your desire to restore him to love and joy.
And when he finally turns to You, he finds You waiting for him, ready to forgive his sins and to reunite him to Your life and purposes once more.
That man who returns to his God is happy indeed!
He will forever be the object of God's love and blessings.

—Leslie Brandt

INVITATION

Sweet Hour of Prayer

Now Peter and John went up together . . . at the hour of prayer.
— Acts 3:1

William W. Walford

SWEET HOUR
William B. Bradbury

1. Sweet hour of prayer, sweet hour of prayer, That calls me from a world of care,
And bids me at my Father's throne Make all my wants and wishes known:
In seasons of distress and grief My soul has often found relief,
And oft escaped the tempter's snare By thy return, sweet hour of prayer.

2. Sweet hour of prayer, sweet hour of prayer, Thy wings shall my petition bear
To Him whose truth and faithfulness Engage the waiting soul to bless:
And since He bids me seek His face, Believe His Word, and trust His grace,
I'll cast on Him my every care, And wait for thee, sweet hour of prayer.

PRAYER AND INTERCESSION

440 The Lord's Prayer

And when thou hast shut thy door, pray to the Father... — Matthew 6:6

MALOTTE
Albert Hay Malotte
Arranged by Fred Bock

Matthew 6:9-13

Our Father, which art in heaven, hallowed be Thy name. Thy kingdom come, Thy will be done on earth as it is in heaven. Give us this day our daily

© Copyright 1935 by G. Schirmer, Inc. This arrangement © Copyright 1976 by G. Schirmer, Inc.. All rights reserved. Used by permission.

PRAYER AND INTERCESSION

PRAYER AND INTERCESSION

441 Prayer

More things are wrought by prayer
Than this world dreams of. Wherefore, let thy voice
Rise like a fountain for me night and day.
For what are men better than sheep or goats
That nourish a blind life within the brain,
If, knowing God, they lift not hands of prayer
Both for themselves and those who call them friends,
For so the whole round earth is every way
Bound by gold chains about the feet of God.

—*Alfred Lord Tennyson*

442 O Master, Let Me Walk with Thee

Washington Gladden
He that loseth his life for My sake shall find it. — Matthew 10:39

MARYTON
H. Percy Smith

1. O Master, let me walk with Thee In lowly paths of service free; Tell me Thy secret—help me bear The strain of toil, the fret of care.
2. Help me the slow of heart to move By some clear, winning word of love; Teach me the wayward feet to stay, And guide them in the homeward way.
3. Teach me Thy patience: still with Thee In closer, dearer company, In work that keeps faith sweet and strong, In trust that triumphs over wrong.
4. In hope that sends a shining ray Far down the future's broadening way, In peace that only Thou canst give, With Thee, O Master, let me live. A-men.

PRAYER AND INTERCESSION

I Need Thee Every Hour 443

Your Father knoweth what things ye have need of before ye ask.
— Matthew 6:8

Annie S. Hawks
Robert Lowry

NEED
Robert Lowry

1. I need Thee ev-ery hour, Most gra-cious Lord;
   No ten-der voice like Thine Can peace af-ford.
2. I need Thee ev-ery hour, Stay Thou near by;
   Temp-ta-tions lose their power When Thou art nigh.
3. I need Thee ev-ery hour, In joy or pain;
   Come quick-ly, and a-bide, Or life is vain.
4. I need Thee ev-ery hour, Teach me Thy will,
   And Thy rich prom-is-es In me ful-fill.

I need Thee, O I need Thee; Ev-ery hour I need Thee!
O bless me now, my Sav-ior— I come to Thee. A-men.

PRAYER AND INTERCESSION

444 Speak, Lord, in the Stillness

And the Lord came, and stood, and called.... Then Samuel answered, Speak Lord, for thy servant heareth. — I Samuel 3:10

E. May Grimes

QUIETUDE
Harold Green

1. Speak, Lord, in the still-ness, While I wait on Thee; Hushed my heart to lis-ten In ex-pec-tan-cy.
2. *Speak, O bless-ed Mas-ter, In this qui-et hour,* Let me see Thy face, Lord, Feel Thy touch of power.
3. For the words Thou speak-est, "They are life" in-deed; Liv-ing Bread from heav-en, Now my spir-it feed!
4. All to Thee is yield-ed, I am not my own; *Bliss-ful, glad sur-ren-der, I am Thine a-lone.*
5. Fill me with the know-ledge Of Thy glo-rious will; All Thine own good pleas-ure In my life ful-fill. A-men.

445 Colossians 1:11-20

We are praying, too, that you will be filled with His mighty, glorious strength so that you can keep going no matter what happens—always full of the joy of the Lord, and always thankful to the Father who has made us fit to share all the wonderful things that belong to those who live in the kingdom of light. For He has rescued us out of the darkness and gloom of Satan's kingdom and brought us into the kingdom of His dear Son, who bought our freedom with His blood and forgave us all our sins.

Christ is the exact likeness of the unseen God. He existed before God made anything at all, and, in fact, Christ Himself is the Creator who made everything in heaven and earth, the things we can see and the things we can't; the spirit world with its kings and kingdoms, its rulers and authorities; all were made by Christ for His own use and glory. He was before all else began and it is His power that holds everything together. He is the Head of the body made up of His people—that is, His church—which He began; and

PRAYER AND INTERCESSION

He is the Leader of all those who arise from the dead, so that He is first in everything; for God wanted all of Himself to be in His Son.

It was through what His Son did that God cleared a path for everything to come to Him—all things in heaven and on earth—for Christ's death on the cross has made peace with God for all by His blood.

—(LB)

Prayer Is the Soul's Sincere Desire 446

... One of His disciples said unto Him, Lord, teach us to pray .... — Luke 11:1

James Montgomery

SINCERE DESIRE
William A. Schulthes

1. Prayer is the soul's sincere desire, Uttered or unexpressed; The motion of a hidden fire That trembles in the breast.
2. *Prayer is the Christian's vital breath, The Christian's native air, His watch-word at the gates of death: He enters heaven with prayer.*
3. No prayer is made on earth alone, The Holy Spirit pleads; And Jesus on th' eternal throne For sinners intercedes.
4. O Thou by whom we come to God, The Life, the Truth, the Way, The path of prayer Thyself hast trod: Lord, teach us how to pray. A-men.

PRAYER AND INTERCESSION

447 We Are Living, We Are Dwelling

Thou therefore endure hardness, as a good soldier of Jesus Christ. — II Timothy 2:3

Arthur C. Coxe

BLAENHAFREN
Welsh Melody

1. We are living, we are dwelling In a grand and awesome time,
In an age on ages telling— To be living is sublime.
Hark! the waking up of nations, Hosts advancing to the fray;
Hark! what soundeth is creation's Groaning for the latter day.

2. Will ye play then? will ye dally Far behind the battle line?
Up! it is Jehovah's rally— God's own arm hath need of thine.
Worlds are charging, heaven beholding—Thou hast but an hour to fight;
Now, the blazoned cross unfolding, On, right onward for the right!

3. Sworn to yield, to waver, never, Consecrated, born again,
Sworn to be Christ's soldiers ever, O for Christ at least be men!
O let all the soul within you For the truth's sake go abroad!
Strike! let every nerve and sinew Tell on ages, tell for God!

DEDICATION AND DEVOTION

In the Year that King Uzziah Died   448

In the year that King Uzziah died I saw the Lord sitting upon a throne, high and lifted up; and His train filled the temple. Above Him stood the seraphim; each had six wings: with two he covered his face, and with two he covered his feet, and with two he flew. And one called to another and said: "Holy, holy, holy is the Lord of hosts; the whole earth is full of His glory."

And the foundations of the thresholds shook at the voice of Him who called, and the house was filled with smoke. And I said: "Woe is me! For I am lost; for I am a man of unclean lips, and I dwell in the midst of a people of unclean lips; for my eyes have seen the King, the Lord of hosts!"

Then flew one of the seraphim to me, having in his hand a burning coal which he had taken with tongs from the altar. And he touched my mouth and said: "Behold, this has touched your lips; your guilt is taken away, and your sin is forgiven." And I heard the voice of the Lord saying, "Whom shall I send, and who will go for us?" Then I said, "Here am I! Send me."

—Isaiah 6:1-8 (RSV)

Psalms 122 & 123   449

How good it is to enter the sanctuary of the Lord!
    I know that God is not confined within man's four-walled creations,
      nor is He attached to altars and brass symbols.
            And yet, in the beauty and quietness of God's house
              I find His presence very real and fulfilling.

        God is with me and about me
    even as I make my way through the concrete and steel jungles
                    of the cold and unfriendly city.
            He is present
    even behind the anonymous faces of the rushing crowds
        elbowing their way to their respective destinations.
    I find Him in the hearts and lives of His children
who infiltrate the urban masses and who are running His errands
            and fulfilling His purposes in the course of their daily duties.

I cannot outrun or evade my God.
        He goes before me and follows closely behind me.
    He will keep me and sustain me wherever I am.

                And yet I rejoice as I enter His sanctuary
  and mingle with those who honor His name and seek His grace.
There, shielded from the screaming tensions and ear-splitting sounds of the city,
        in the company of those who love one another,
    I happily open my heart to the loving mercy of God.

—Leslie Brandt

DEDICATION AND DEVOTION

450 I Need Jesus

Bow down Thine ear, O Lord, and hear me; for I am poor and needy . . . — Psalm 86:1

George O. Webster

I NEED JESUS
Charles H. Gabriel

1. I need Jesus: my need I now confess, No Friend like Him in times of deep distress; I need Jesus; the need I gladly own, Though some may bear their load alone, Yet I need Jesus.

2. *I need Jesus: I need a Friend like Him, A Friend to guide when paths of life are dim;* I need Jesus; when foes my soul assail, Alone, I know I can but fail, So I need Jesus.

3. I need Jesus: I need Him to the end, No one like Him— He is the sinners' Friend; I need Jesus; no other Friend will do, So constant, kind, so strong and true— Yes, I need Jesus.

I need Jesus; I need Jesus. I need Jesus every day. Need Him in the sunshine hour, need Him when the

© Copyright 1924 by Homer A. Rodeheaver. © Renewed 1952, The Rodeheaver Co., owner. All rights reserved. Used by permission.

DEDICATION AND DEVOTION

storm clouds lower, Ev-ery day a-long my way, Yes, I need Je-sus.

Jesus, Thou Joy of Loving Hearts 451

... Ye rejoice with joy unspeakable and full of glory. — I Peter 1:8

Attr. to Bernard of Clairvaux
Tr. by Ray Palmer

QUEBEC
Henry Baker

1. Je-sus, Thou joy of lov-ing hearts, Thou fount of life, Thou light of men, From the best bliss that earth im-parts We turn un-filled to Thee a-gain.
2. *Thy truth un-changed hath ev-er stood, Thou sav-est those that on Thee call; To them that seek Thee Thou art good, To them that find Thee all in all.*
3. We taste Thee, O Thou liv-ing bread, And long to feast up-on Thee still; We drink of Thee, the foun-tain-head, And thirst our souls from Thee to fill.
4. *Our rest-less spir-its yearn for Thee, Wher-e'er our change-ful lot is cast: Glad when Thy gra-cious smile we see, Blest when our faith can hold Thee fast.*
5. O Je-sus, ev-er with us stay, Make all our mo-ments calm and bright; Chase the dark night of sin a-way, Shed o'er the world Thy ho-ly light. A-men.

DEDICATION AND DEVOTION

452 I Could Never Outlove the Lord

Give and it shall be given unto you; good measure, . . . and running over . . .
— Luke 6:38

Gloria Gaither
William J. Gaither

NEVER OUTLOVE
William J. Gaither

1. There've been times when giv-ing and lov-ing brought pain,
And I prom-ised I would nev-er let it hap-pen a-gain;
But I found out that lov-ing was well worth the risk,
And that e-ven in los-ing you win.

2. He showed us that on-ly through dy-ing we live,
And He gave when it seemed there was noth-ing to give;
He loved when lov-ing brought heart-ache and loss,
He for-gave from an old rug-ged cross.

I'm going to live the way He wants me to live, I'm going to give un-til there's just

© Copyright 1972 by William J. Gaither. All rights reserved. Used by permission.
DEDICATION AND DEVOTION

no more to give; I'm going to love, love 'til there's just no more love— I could nev-er, nev-er out-love the Lord.

I'll Live for Him 453

That they might live . . . unto Him who died for them.   II Corinthians 5:15

Ralph E. Hudson

DUNBAR
C. R. Dunbar

1 My life, my love I give to Thee, Thou Lamb of God who died for me;
2 *I now be-lieve Thou dost re-ceive, For Thou hast died that I might live;*
3 O Thou who died on Cal-va-ry, To save my soul and make me free,
Ref. *I'll live for Him who died for me, How hap-py then my life shall be!*

D.C. Refrain

1 O may I ev-er faith-ful be, My Sav-ior and my God!
2 *And now hence-forth I'll trust in Thee, My Sav-ior and my God!*
3 I'll con-se-crate my life to Thee, My Sav-ior and my God!
Ref. *I'll live for Him who died for me, My Sav-ior and my God!*

DEDICATION AND DEVOTION

454 Trust and Obey

To obey is better than sacrifice...
— I Samuel 15:22

James H. Sammis

TRUST AND OBEY
Daniel B. Towner

1. When we walk with the Lord In the light of His Word,
2. *Not a shad-ow can rise, Not a cloud in the skies,*
3. Not a bur-den we bear, Not a sor-row we share,
4. *Then in fel-low-ship sweet We will sit at His feet,*

1. What a glo-ry He sheds on our way! While we do His good will,
2. *But His smile quick-ly drives it a-way; Not a doubt or a fear,*
3. But our toil He doth rich-ly re-pay; Not a grief or a loss,
4. *Or we'll walk by His side in the way; What He says we will do,*

1. He a-bides with us still, And with all who will trust and o-bey.
2. *Not a sigh or a tear, Can re-main when we trust and o-bey.*
3. Not a frown or a cross, But is blest if we trust and o-bey.
4. *Where He sends we will go, Nev-er fear, on-ly trust and o-bey.*

Trust and o-bey, for there's no oth-er way
To be hap-py in Je-sus, but to trust and o-bey.

DEDICATION AND DEVOTION

I Am Thine, O Lord

455

... What would Thou have me to do?
— Acts 9:6

Fanny J. Crosby

I AM THINE
William H. Doane

1. I am Thine, O Lord— I have heard Thy voice, And it told Thy love to me; But I long to rise in the arms of faith And be clos-er drawn to Thee.
2. Con-se-crate me now to Thy serv-ice, Lord, By the power of grace di-vine; Let my soul look up with a stead-fast hope And my will be lost in Thine.
3. O the pure de-light of a sin-gle hour That be-fore Thy throne I spend, When I kneel in prayer and with Thee, my God, I com-mune as friend with friend.
4. There are depths of love that I can-not know 'Til I cross the nar-row sea; There are heights of joy that I may not reach 'Til I rest in peace with Thee.

Draw me near-er, nearer, blessed Lord, To the cross where Thou hast died; Draw me near-er, near-er, near-er, bless-ed Lord, To Thy pre-cious, bleed-ing side. A-men.

DEDICATION AND DEVOTION

456 My Jesus, I Love Thee

William R. Featherston
We love Him because He first loved us.
— I John 4:19
GORDON
Adoniram J. Gordon

1. My Jesus, I love Thee, I know Thou art mine; For Thee all the follies of sin I resign; My gracious Redeemer, my Savior art Thou: If ever I loved Thee, my Jesus, 'tis now.

2. *I love Thee because Thou hast first loved me, And purchased my pardon on Calvary's tree; I love Thee for wearing the thorns on Thy brow: If ever I loved Thee, my Jesus, 'tis now.*

3. I'll love Thee in life, I will love Thee in death, And praise Thee as long as Thou lendest me breath; And say when the death-dew lies cold on my brow: If ever I loved Thee, my Jesus, 'tis now.

4. *In mansions of glory and endless delight, I'll ever adore Thee in heaven so bright; I'll sing with the glittering crown on my brow: If ever I loved Thee, my Jesus, 'tis now.* A-men.

457 Take Time to Be Holy

William D. Longstaff
Because it is written: Be ye holy for I am holy. — I Peter 1:16
LONGSTAFF
George C. Stebbins

1. Take time to be holy, Speak often with God; Find rest in Him

2. *Take time to be holy, The world rushes on; Much time spend in*

3. Take time to be holy, Let Him be Thy guide, And run not be-

DEDICATION AND DEVOTION

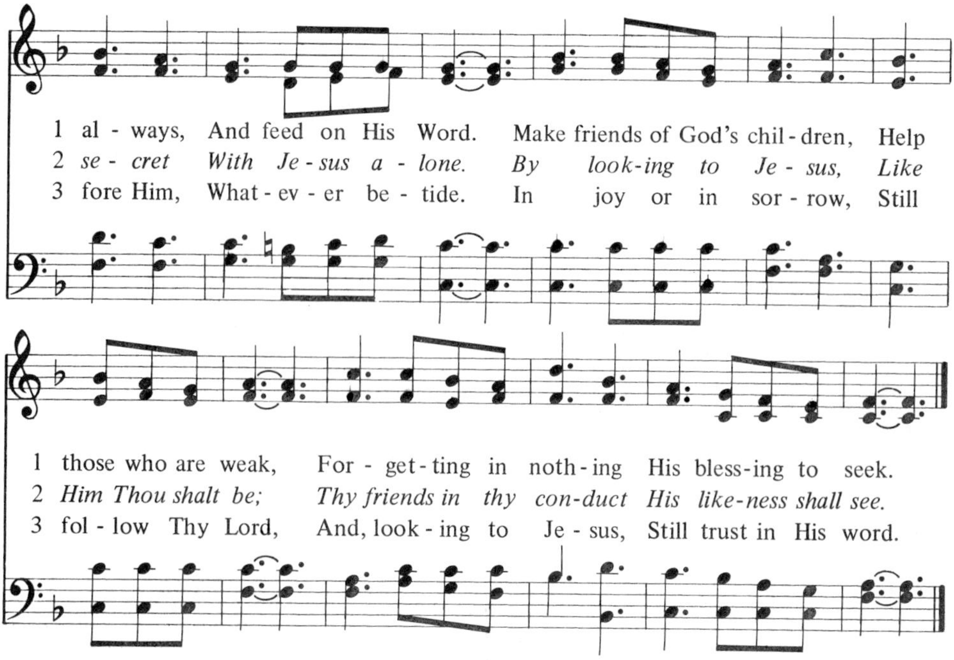
1 al - ways, And feed on His Word. Make friends of God's chil - dren, Help
2 se - cret With Je - sus a - lone. By look-ing to Je - sus, Like
3 fore Him, What - ev - er be - tide. In joy or in sor - row, Still
1 those who are weak, For - get - ting in noth - ing His bless-ing to seek.
2 Him Thou shalt be; Thy friends in thy con-duct His like-ness shall see.
3 fol - low Thy Lord, And, look - ing to Je - sus, Still trust in His word.

Take My Life, and Let It Be Consecrated

458

Present your bodies a living sacrifice.
— Romans 12:1

Frances R. Havergal

HENDON
Henri A. César Malan

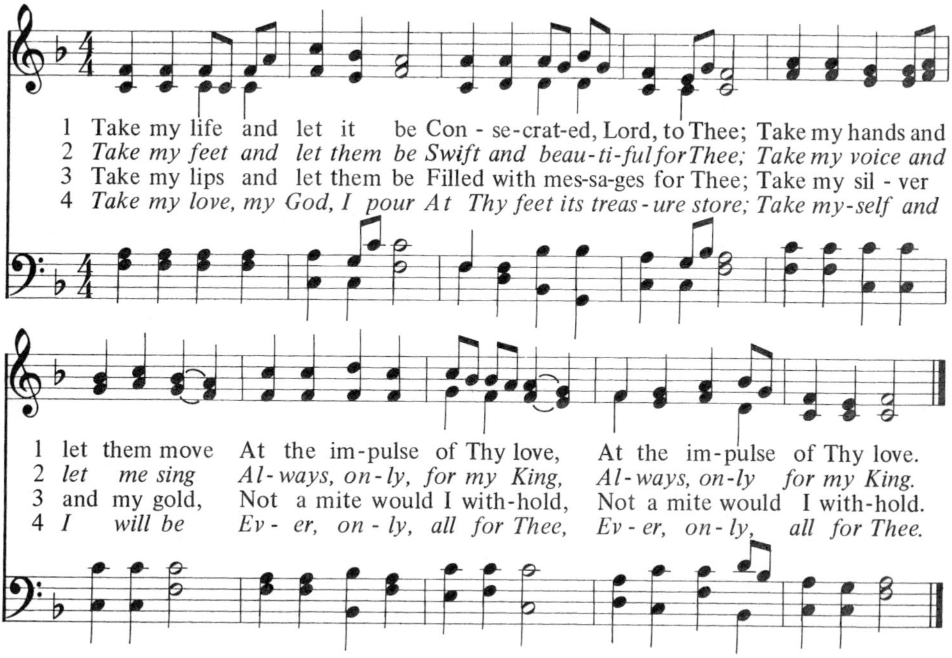
1 Take my life and let it be Con - se-crat-ed, Lord, to Thee; Take my hands and
2 Take my feet and let them be Swift and beau-ti-ful for Thee; Take my voice and
3 Take my lips and let them be Filled with mes-sa-ges for Thee; Take my sil - ver
4 Take my love, my God, I pour At Thy feet its treas - ure store; Take my-self and
1 let them move At the im-pulse of Thy love, At the im-pulse of Thy love.
2 let me sing Al-ways, on-ly, for my King, Al-ways, on-ly for my King.
3 and my gold, Not a mite would I with-hold, Not a mite would I with-hold.
4 I will be Ev - er, on - ly, all for Thee, Ev - er, on - ly, all for Thee.

459 All for Jesus

Ye are bought with a price; therefore glorify God in your body...
— I Corinthians 6:20

Mary D. James

CONSTANCY
Unknown

1. All for Je-sus, all for Je-sus! All my be-ing's ran-somed powers:
2. Let my hands per-form His bid-ding, Let my feet run in His ways;
3. Since my eyes were fixed on Je-sus, I've lost sight of all be-side,
4. O what won-der! how a-maz-ing! Je-sus, glo-rious King of kings,

1. All my thoughts and words and do-ings, All my days and all my hours:
2. Let my eyes see Je-sus on-ly, Let my lips speak forth His praise:
3. So en-rapt my spir-it's vi-sion, Look-ing at the Cru-ci-fied:
4. Deigns to call me His be-lov-ed, Lets me rest be-neath His wings:

1. All for Je-sus! all for Je-sus! All my days and all my hours;
2. All for Je-sus! all for Je-sus! Let my lips speak forth His praise;
3. All for Je-sus! all for Je-sus! Look-ing at the Cru-ci-fied;
4. All for Je-sus! all for Je-sus! Rest-ing now be-neath His wings;

1. All for Je-sus! all for Je-sus! All my days and all my hours.
2. All for Je-sus! all for Je-sus! Let my lips speak forth His praise.
3. All for Je-sus! all for Je-sus! Look-ing at the Cru-ci-fied.
4. All for Je-sus! all for Je-sus! Rest-ing now be-neath His wings.

DEDICATION AND DEVOTION

Prayer — 460

Eternal Heavenly Father, we know that You are more eager to hear our prayers than we are to pray them, and more concerned to respond to them than we expect You to be. Forgive us now with that complete pardon that eases the troubled conscience and replaces its sharp torment with a permanent peace. This we ask that Your risen Son may be more alive among us. Amen.

—Bryan Jeffery Leech

Jesus, We Just Want to Thank You — 461

Gloria Gaither
William J. Gaither

Enter into His gates with thanksgiving and into His courts with praise.
—Psalm 100:4

THANK YOU
William J. Gaither

1. Je-sus, we just want to thank You, Je-sus, we just want to thank You, Je-sus, we just want to thank You, Thank You for be-ing so good.
2. Je-sus, we just want to praise You, Je-sus, we just want to praise You, Je-sus, we just want to praise You, Praise You for be-ing so good.
3. Je-sus, we just want to tell You, Je-sus, we just want to tell You, Je-sus, we just want to tell You, We love You for be-ing so good.
4. Sav-ior, we just want to serve You, Sav-ior, we just want to serve You, Sav-ior, we just want to serve You, Serve You for be-ing so good.
5. Je-sus, we know You are com-ing, Je-sus, we know You are com-ing, Je-sus, we know You are com-ing, Take us to live in Your home.

© Copyright 1974 by William J. Gaither. All rights reserved. Used by permission.

DEDICATION AND DEVOTION

462 Living for Jesus

Present your bodies a living sacrifice, holy, ... acceptable ...
— Romans 12:1

Thomas O. Chisholm
C. Harold Lowden

LIVING

1. Living for Jesus a life that is true, Striving to please Him in all that I do; Yielding allegiance, glad-hearted and free, This is the pathway of blessing for me.
2. *Living for Jesus who died in my place, Bearing on Calvary my sin and disgrace; Such love constrains me to answer His call, Follow His leading and give Him my all.*
3. Living for Jesus wherever I am, Doing each duty in His holy name; Willing to suffer affliction and loss, Taking each trial as a part of my cross.
4. *Living for Jesus through earth's little while, My dearest treasure, the light of His smile; Seeking the lost ones He died to redeem, Bringing the weary to find rest in Him.*

O Jesus, Lord and Savior, I give myself to Thee, For Thou, in Thy atonement, Didst give Thyself for me; I own no other Master, My heart shall be Thy

Copyright 1917 by Heidelberg Press. © Renewed 1945 (extended) by C. Harold Lowden. Assigned to The Rodeheaver Co. Used by permission.

DEDICATION AND DEVOTION

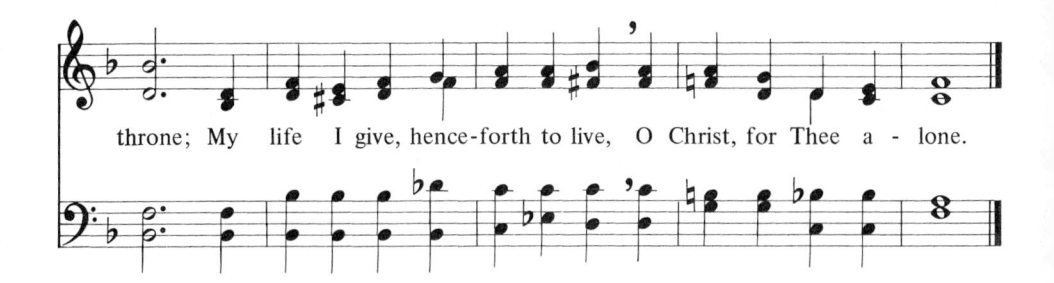

throne; My life I give, hence-forth to live, O Christ, for Thee a - lone.

The Example of Jesus Christ 463

With so many witnesses in a great cloud on every side of us, we too, then, should throw off everything that hinders us, especially the sin that clings so easily, and keep running steadily in the race we have started. Let us not lose sight of Jesus, who leads us in our faith and brings it to perfection: for the sake of the joy which was still in the future, He endured the cross, disregarding the shamefulness of it, and *from now on has taken His place at the right* of God's throne. Think of the way He stood such opposition from sinners and then you will not give up for want of courage. In the fight against sin, you have not yet had to keep fighting to the point of death.

Have you forgotten that encouraging text in which you are addressed as sons? *My son, when the Lord corrects you, do not treat it lightly; but do not get discouraged when He reprimands you. For the Lord trains the ones that He loves and He punishes all those that He acknowledges as His sons.* Suffering is part of your *training;* God is treating you as His *sons.* Has there ever been any *son* whose father did not *train* him? If you were not getting this training, as all of you are, then you would not be *sons* but bastards. Besides, we have all had our human fathers who punished us, and we respected them for it; we ought to be even more willing to submit ourselves to our spiritual Father, to be given life. Our human fathers were thinking of this short life when they punished us, and could only do what they thought best; but He does it all for our own good, so that we may share His own holiness. Of course, any punishment is most painful at the time, and far from pleasant; but later, in those on whom it has been used, it bears fruit in peace and goodness. So *hold up your limp arms and steady your trembling knees* and *smooth out the path you tread;* then the injured limb will not be wrenched, it will grow strong again.

—Hebrews 12:1-13 (JB)

DEDICATION AND DEVOTION

464   Liberation from Materialism

Forbid it, Lord, that our roots become too firmly attached to this earth, that we should fall in love with things.

Help us to understand that the pilgrimage of this life is but an introduction, a preface, a training school for what is to come.

Then shall we see all of life in its true perspective. Then shall we not fall in love with the things of time, but come to love the things that endure. Then shall we be saved from the tyranny of possessions which we have no leisure to enjoy, of property whose care becomes a burden. Give us, we pray, the courage to simplify our lives.

So may we be mature in our faith, childlike but never childish, humble but never cringing, understanding but never conceited.

So help us, O God, to live and not merely to exist, that we may have joy in our work. In Thy name, who alone can give us moderation and balance and zest for living, we pray.

Amen.

—Peter Marshall

465   Jesus, the Very Thought of Thee

For me to live is Christ, and to die is gain. — Philippians 1:21

Latin: 12th Century
Tr. by Edward Caswall

ST. AGNES
John B. Dykes

1. Jesus, the very thought of Thee With sweetness fills my breast; But sweeter far Thy face to see And in Thy presence rest.
2. *No voice can sing, no heart can frame, Nor can the memory find A sweeter sound than Thy blest name, O Savior of mankind.*
3. O hope of every contrite heart, O joy of all the meek, To those who fall, how kind Thou art! How good to those who seek!
4. *But what to those who find? Ah, this No tongue or pen can show; The love of Jesus, what it is None but His loved ones know.*
5. Jesus, our only joy be Thou, As Thou our prize wilt be; Jesus, be Thou our glory now And through eternity. A-men.

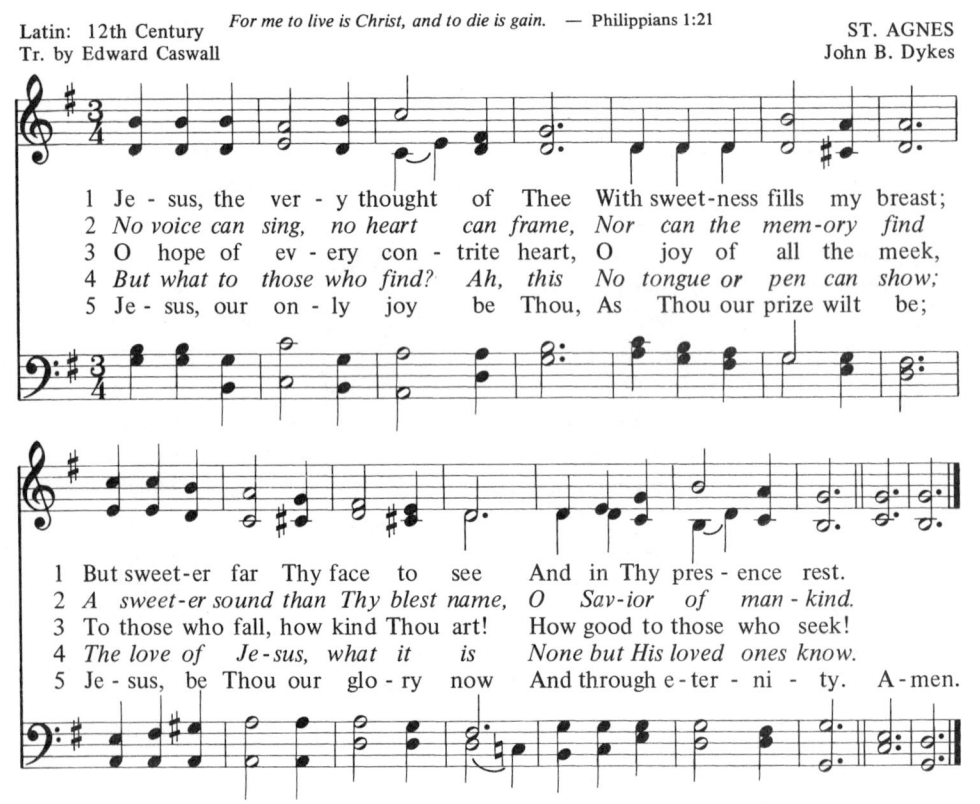

DEDICATION AND DEVOTION

What a Friend We Have in Jesus

... In whom we have boldness and access with confidence by faith in Him.
— Ephesians 3:12

Joseph M. Scriven

ERIE
Charles C. Converse

1. What a friend we have in Jesus, All our sins and griefs to bear!
2. *Have we tri-als and temp-ta-tions? Is there trou-ble an-y-where?*
3. Are we weak and heav-y-lad-en, Cum-bered with a load of care?

1. What a priv-i-lege to car-ry Ev-ery-thing to God in prayer!
2. *We should nev-er be dis-cour-aged— Take it to the Lord in prayer!*
3. Pre-cious Sav-ior, still our ref-uge— Take it to the Lord in prayer!

1. O what peace we oft-en for-feit, O what need-less pain we bear,
2. *Can we find a friend so faith-ful, Who will all our sor-rows share?*
3. Do thy friends de-spise, for-sake thee? Take it to the Lord in prayer!

1. All be-cause we do not car-ry Ev-ery-thing to God in prayer.
2. *Je-sus knows our ev-ery weak-ness— Take it to the Lord in prayer!*
3. In His arms He'll take and shield thee— Thou wilt find a sol-ace there.

DEDICATION AND DEVOTION

467 Take Thou Our Minds, Dear Lord

Let this mind be in you which is also in Christ Jesus.
— Philippians 2:5

William Hiram Foulkes

HALL
Calvin W. Laufer

1 Take Thou our minds, dear Lord, we humbly pray;
2 Take Thou our hearts, O Christ — they are Thine own;
3 Take Thou our wills, dear God! hold Thou full sway;
4 Take Thou ourselves, O Lord, heart, mind, and will;

1 Give us the mind of Christ throughout each day,
2 Come Thou within our souls and claim Thy throne,
3 Have in our inmost souls Thy perfect way,
4 Through our surrendered souls Thy plans fulfill.

1 Teach us to know the truth that sets us free;
2 Help us to shed abroad Thy generous love;
3 Guard Thou each sacred hour from selfish ease;
4 We yield ourselves to Thee— time, talents, all;

1 Grant us in all our thoughts to honor Thee.
2 Use us to make the earth like heaven above.
3 Guide Thou our ordered lives as Thou dost please.
4 We hear, and henceforth heed, Thy sovereign call. A-men.

DEDICATION AND DEVOTION

Be Thou My Vision

468

Ancient Irish
Tr. by Mary Byrne
Versified by Eleanor Hull

Leave us not I pray thee . . . . and thou mayest be to us instead of eyes.
— Numbers 10:31

SLANE
Traditional Irish Melody
Harmonization by David Evans

1. Be Thou my Vision, O Lord of my heart;
   Nought be all else to me, save that Thou art—
   Thou my best thought, by day or by night,
   Waking or sleeping, Thy presence my light.

2. Be Thou my Wisdom, and Thou my true Word;
   I ever with Thee and Thou with me, Lord;
   Thou my great Father, I Thy true son;
   Thou in me dwelling, and I with Thee one.

3. Riches I heed not, nor man's empty praise,
   Thou mine inheritance, now and always:
   Thou and Thou only, first in my heart,
   High King of heaven, my Treasure Thou art.

4. High King of heaven, my victory won,
   May I reach heaven's joys, O bright heaven's Sun!
   Heart of my own heart, whatever befall,
   Still be my Vision, O Ruler of all. A-men.

Words used by permission of the Editor's Literary Estate, and Chatto & Windus, Ltd. Harmony copyright; from "The Church Hymnary," Revised Edition; used by permission of Oxford University Press.

ASPIRATION

469 Higher Ground

Lead me to the Rock that is higher than I. . . .
— Psalm 61:2

Johnson Oatman, Jr.

HIGHER GROUND
Charles H. Gabriel

1. I'm pressing on the upward way, New heights I'm gaining every day; Still praying as I'm onward bound, "Lord, plant my feet on higher ground."
2. *My heart has no desire to stay Where doubts arise and fears dismay; Though some may dwell where these abound, My prayer, my aim is higher ground.*
3. I want to live above the world, Though Satan's darts at me are hurled; For faith has caught the joyful sound, The song of saints on higher ground.
4. *I want to scale the utmost height And catch a gleam of glory bright; But still I'll pray, 'til heaven I've found, "Lord, lead me on to higher ground."*

Lord, lift me up and let me stand By faith on heaven's tableland, A higher plane than I have found: Lord, plant my feet on higher ground.

ASPIRATION

"Are Ye Able", Said the Master 470

Are ye able to drink of the cup that I shall drink of....
— Matthew 20:20

Earl Marlatt

BEACON HILL
Harry S. Mason

1. "Are ye a - ble," said the Mas - ter, "To be cru - ci - fied with Me?"
2. *"Are ye a - ble" to re - mem - ber, When a thief lifts up his eyes,*
3. "Are ye a - ble?" still the Mas - ter Whis - pers down e - ter - ni - ty,

1. "Yea," the stur - dy dream - ers an - swered, "To the death we fol - low Thee:"
2. *That his par - doned soul is wor - thy Of a place in par - a - dise?*
3. And he - ro - ic spir - its an - swer, Now, as then in Gal - i - lee:

"Lord, we are a - ble"— our spir - its are Thine; Re - mold them—

make us like Thee, di - vine. Thy guid - ing ra - diance a -

bove us shall be A bea - con to God, to love and loy - al - ty.

ASPIRATION

471   The Teacher

Lord, who am I to teach the way
To little children day by day,
So prone myself to go astray?

I teach them *knowledge,* but I know
How faint they flicker, and how low
The candles of my knowledge glow.

I teach them *power* to will and do,
But only now to learn anew
My own great weakness through and through.

I teach them *love* for all mankind
And all God's creatures, but I find
My love comes lagging far behind.

Lord, if their guide I still must be,
O let the little children see
The teacher leaning hard on Thee.

—Leslie Pinckney Hill

472   Teach Me Your Way, O Lord

Show me Thy way O Lord; teach me Thy way.
—Psalm 25:4, 5

B. Mansell Ramsey   CAMACHA   B. Mansell Ramsey

1. Teach me Your way, O Lord, Teach me Your way! Your guiding grace afford—Teach me Your way! Help me to walk aright, More by faith, less by sight; Lead me with heavenly light— Teach me Your way!

2. *When I am sad at heart, Teach me Your way! When earthly joys depart, Teach me Your way! In hours of loneliness, In times of dire distress, In failure or success, Teach me Your way!*

3. When doubts and fears arise, Teach me Your way! When storm-clouds fill the skies, Teach me Your way! Shine thru the wind and rain, Thru sorrow, grief and pain; Make now my pathway plain—Teach me Your way!

4. *Long as my life shall last, Teach me Your way! Wher-e'er my lot be cast, Teach me Your way! Until the race is run, Until the journey's done, Until the crown is won, Teach me Your way!* A-men.

Used by permission of George Taylor, The Cross Printing Works, Stainland, Halifax.
ASPIRATION

Make Me a Blessing

473

And I will make them and the places round about my hill a blessing....
— Ezekiel 34:26

Ira B. Wilson

SCHULER
George S. Schuler

1. Out in the high-ways and by-ways of life, Man-y are wea-ry and sad;
2. *Tell the sweet sto-ry of Christ and His love, Tell of His power to for - give;*
3. Give as 'twas giv-en to you in your need, Love as the Mas-ter loved you;

1. Car - ry the sun-shine where dark-ness is rife, Mak - ing the sor - row-ing glad.
2. *Oth-ers will trust Him if on - ly you prove True, ev - ery mo-ment you live.*
3. Be to the help-less a help - er in-deed, Un - to your mis-sion be true.

Make me a bless - ing, Make me a bless - ing — Out of my life May Je - sus shine; Make me a bless - ing, O Sav - ior, I pray, Make me a bless - ing to some - one to - day.

Copyright 1924 by George S. Schuler. © Renewed 1952, The Rodeheaver Co., owner. Used by permission.

ASPIRATION

474 Eternal Life

The things which are not seen are eternal.
— II Corinthians 4:18

St. Francis of Assisi

ETERNAL LIFE
Olive Dungan
Arranged by Fred Bock

Lord, make me an in-stru-ment of Thy peace:
Where there is ha-tred, let me sow love; Where there is in-ju-ry, par-don;
Where there is doubt, faith; Where there is de-spair, hope;
Where there is dark-ness, light; Where there is sad-ness, joy.

© Copyright 1949 by The John Church Company. This arrangement © Copyright 1976 by The John Church Company. All rights reserved. Used by permission.

DISCIPLESHIP

O Divine Master, grant that I may not so much seek
To be consoled as to console, To be understood as to understand,
To be loved as to love; For it is in giving that we receive;
It is in pardoning that we are pardoned;
It is in dying that we are born to eternal life!

DISCIPLESHIP

475 — A Prayer

Lord Jesus Christ,
because You looked ahead to a future joy,
You were able to stand the agony of Your disgraceful death,
and as a result of this You now stand in the position of supreme and exalted rank.
Help me to follow You in this.
To look beyond my hardships as You did Yours.
To see in them a way through to maturity and ultimately to eternal reward.
Give me a determination like Yours to battle temptation and to give sin a wide berth.
Keep me from losing heart when the tension and pull away from You are the greatest.
Teach me how to learn from my sufferings
lest they make me embittered.
Lord, it really comforts me to know that in praying to You
I'm talking to the only one who can completely identify with me
where I am right now. Amen.

—Bryan Jeffery Leech

476 — More Love to Thee, O Christ

And this I pray, that your love may abound more and more. . . . — Philippians 1:9

MORE LOVE TO THEE
Elizabeth P. Prentiss
William H. Doane

1. More love to Thee, O Christ, More love to Thee! Hear Thou the prayer I make On bended knee; This is my earnest plea: More love, O Christ, to Thee, More love to Thee, More love to Thee! A-men.

2. *Once earthly joy I craved, Sought peace and rest; Now Thee alone I seek, Give what is best; This all my prayer shall be:* More love, O Christ, to Thee, More love to Thee, More love to Thee! A-men.

3. Then shall my every breath Sing out Your praise; This be the only song My heart shall raise; This still my prayer shall be: More love, O Christ, to Thee, More love to Thee, More love to Thee! A-men.

ASPIRATION

More About Jesus Would I Know

477

But grow in grace in the knowledge of our Lord Jesus Christ
— II Peter 3:18

Eliza E Hewitt

SWENEY
John R. Sweney

1. More a-bout Je-sus would I know, More of His grace to oth-ers show;
2. *More a-bout Je-sus let me learn, More of His ho-ly will dis-cern;*
3. More a-bout Je-sus; in His word, Hold-ing com-mun-ion with my Lord;
4. *More a-bout Je-sus on His throne, Rich-es in glo-ry all His own;*

1. More of His sav-ing full-ness see, More of His love who died for me.
2. *Spir-it of God, my teach-er be, Show-ing the things of Christ to me.*
3. Hear-ing His voice in ev-ery line, Mak-ing each faith-ful say-ing mine.
4. *More of His king-dom's sure in-crease; More of His com-ing, Prince of Peace.*

More, more, a-bout Je-sus, More, more, a-bout Je-sus;

More of His sav-ing full-ness see, More of His love who died for me.

ASPIRATION

478 Psalm 1

Blessed is the man who walks not in the counsel of the wicked,
    nor stands in the way of sinners, nor sits in the seat of scoffers;
but his delight is in the law of the Lord,
    and on His law he meditates day and night.
He is like a tree planted by streams of water,
    that yields its fruit in its season,
and its leaf does not wither.
    In all that he does, he prospers.

The wicked are not so,
    but are like chaff which the wind drives away.
Therefore the wicked will not stand in the judgment,
    nor sinners in the congregation of the righteous;
for the Lord knows the way of the righteous,
    but the way of the wicked will perish.

—(RSV)

479 Fill Thou My Life, O Lord My God

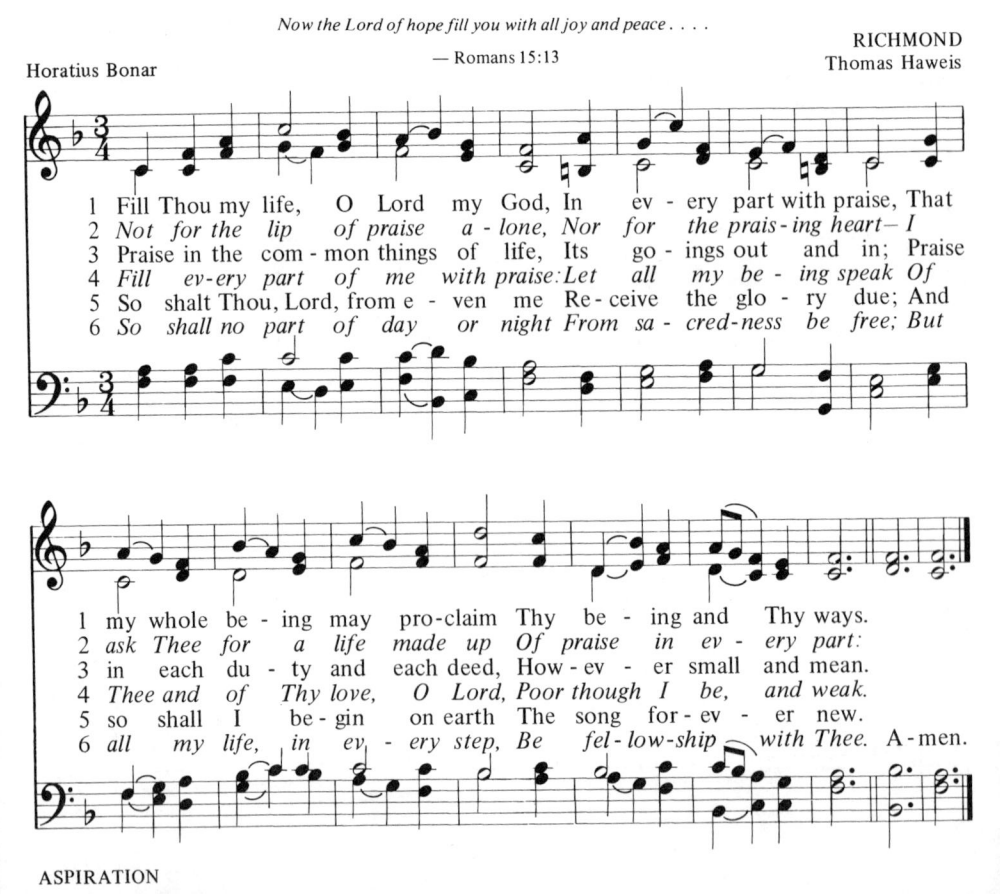

Now the Lord of hope fill you with all joy and peace....
— Romans 15:13

Horatius Bonar
RICHMOND
Thomas Haweis

1. Fill Thou my life, O Lord my God, In ev-ery part with praise, That my whole be-ing may pro-claim Thy be-ing and Thy ways.
2. *Not for the lip of praise a-lone, Nor for the prais-ing heart— I ask Thee for a life made up Of praise in ev-ery part:*
3. Praise in the com-mon things of life, Its go-ings out and in; Praise in each du-ty and each deed, How-ev-er small and mean.
4. *Fill ev-ery part of me with praise: Let all my be-ing speak Of Thee and of Thy love, O Lord, Poor though I be, and weak.*
5. So shalt Thou, Lord, from e-ven me Re-ceive the glo-ry due; And so shall I be-gin on earth The song for-ev-er new.
6. *So shall no part of day or night From sa-cred-ness be free; But all my life, in ev-ery step, Be fel-low-ship with Thee.* A-men.

ASPIRATION

O To Be Like Thee

480

And every man that hath this hope in him purifieth himself, even as He is pure. —1 John 3:3

Thomas O. Chisholm

CHRISTLIKE
William J. Kirkpatrick

1. O to be like Thee! Bless-ed Re-deem-er, This is my con-stant long-ing and prayer; Glad-ly I'll for-feit all of earth's treas-ures, Je-sus, Thy per-fect like-ness to wear.
2. *O to be like Thee! Full of com-pas-sion, Lov-ing, for-giv-ing, ten-der and kind, Help-ing the help-less, cheer-ing the faint-ing, Seek-ing the wan-dering sin-ner to find!*
3. O to be like Thee! Low-ly in spir-it, Ho-ly and harm-less, pa-tient and brave; Meek-ly en-dur-ing cru-el re-proach-es, Will-ing to suf-fer oth-ers to save.
4. *O to be like Thee! Lord, I am com-ing, Now to re-ceive th'a-noint-ing di-vine; All that I am and have I am bring-ing. Lord, from this mo-ment all shall be Thine.*
5. O to be like Thee! While I am plead-ing, Pour out Thy Spir-it, fill with Thy love; Make me a tem-ple deemed to re-ceive You: Fit me for life and heav-en a-bove.

O to be like Thee! O to be like Thee, Bless-ed Re-deem-er, pure as Thou art! Come in Thy sweet-ness, come in Thy full-ness; Stamp Thine own im-age deep on my heart.

ASPIRATION

481 Fill My Cup, Lord

I will take the cup of my salvation. . . . —Psalm 116:13

Richard Blanchard

FILL MY CUP
Richard Blanchard

1. Like the wom-an at the well I was seek-ing For things that I could not sat-is-fy; And then I heard my Sav-ior speak-ing: "Draw from My well that nev-er shall run dry."

2. *There are mil-lions in this world who are crav-ing The pleas-ure earth-ly things af-ford; But none can match the won-drous treas-ure That I find in Je-sus Christ my Lord.*

3. So, my broth-er, if the things this world gave you Leave hun-gers that won't pass a-way, My bless-ed Lord will come and save you, If you kneel to Him and hum-bly pray:

Fill my cup, Lord, I lift it up, Lord! Come and quench this thirst-ing of my soul; Bread of heav-en, feed me 'til I want no more—Fill my cup, fill it up and make me whole!

© Copyright 1959 by Richard Blanchard. © Copyright 1964 by Sacred Songs. All rights reserved. Used by permission.
ASPIRATION

Psalm 59 — 482

Deliver me, O God, from the enemies of my soul.
I am no longer afraid of men who stand in my way, even of those who obstruct Your purposes and who deceive their fellowmen with their arrogant and clever cliches.
They anger me, but they do not frighten me.
My pain and confusion come by way of my own weaknesses and faithlessness.

I strive for success and am fractured by failure.
I reach for ecstacy and am clobbered with depression.
I wait for guidance and Your heavens are gray with silence.
I ask for infilling and am confronted with emptiness.
I seek opportunities and run into stone walls.

I overcome these pernicious demons in the morning—only to face them again when day turns into night.
They refuse to die, these persistent devils.
They plague my days and haunt my nights and rob me of the peace and joy of God-motivated living.

And yet, O Lord, You have surrounded my life like a great fortress.
There is nothing that can touch me save by Your loving permission.

—Leslie Brandt

May the Mind of Christ, My Savior — 483

Let this mind be in you which is also in Christ Jesus.... — Philippians 2:5

Kate B. Wilkinson

ST. LEONARDS
Cyril Barham-Gould

1. May the mind of Christ, my Savior, Live in me from day to day,
By His love and power controlling All I do and say.

2. May the word of God dwell richly In my heart from hour to hour,
So that all may see I triumph Only through His power.

3. May the peace of God, my Father, Rule my life in everything,
That I may be calm to comfort Sick and sorrowing.

4. May the love of Jesus fill me, As the waters fill the sea;
Him exalting, self abasing— This is victory.

5. May I run the race before me, Strong and brave to face the foe,
Looking only unto Jesus As I onward go.

6. May His beauty rest upon me As I seek the lost to win,
And may they forget the channel, Seeing only Him.

Music used by permission of the Executors of the estate of C. Barham-Gould.
Words used by permission of Gordon Hitchcock.

ASPIRATION

484 Real Prayer

The prayer preceding all prayers is,
"May it be the real I who speaks.
May it be the real Thou
that I speak to."

—C. S. Lewis

485 Nearer, Still Nearer

Order my steps in Thy word and let not any iniquity have dominion over me. — Psalm 119:133

Lelia N. Morris

MORRIS
Lelia N. Morris

1. Nearer, still nearer, close to Thy heart,
Draw me, my Savior, so precious Thou art;
Fold me, O fold me close to Thy breast,
Shelter me safe in that "Haven of Rest,"
Shelter me safe in that "Haven of Rest."

2. *Nearer, still nearer, nothing I bring,*
Naught as an offering to Jesus my King;
Only my sinful, now contrite heart,
Grant me the cleansing Thy blood doth impart,
Grant me the cleansing Thy blood doth impart.

3. Nearer, still nearer, while life shall last,
'Til safe in glory my anchor is cast;
Through endless ages, ever to be,
Nearer, my Savior, still nearer to Thee,
Nearer, my Savior, still nearer to Thee. A-men.

ASPIRATION

Open My Eyes That I May See

486

Many prophets and kings have desired to see those things which ye see. — Luke 10:23-24

Clara H. Scott
Jeff Redd, alt.

OPEN MY EYES
Clara H. Scott

1. O-pen my eyes, that I may see Glimp-ses of truth You have for me;
2. *O-pen my ears, that I may hear Voic-es of truth so sharp and clear;*
3. O-pen my mouth, let me de-clare Words of as-sur-ance ev-ery-where;

1. Place in my hands the won-der-ful key That shall un-lock and set me free.
2. *And while the mes-sage sounds in my ear, Ev-ery-thing else will dis-ap-pear.*
3. O-pen my heart, and let me pre-pare Your lov-ing kind-ness-es to share.

Si-lent-ly now I wait for You, Read-y, my God, Your will to do;

1. O-pen my eyes, il-lu-mine me, Spir-it di-vine!
2. *O-pen my ears, il-lu-mine me, Spir-it di-vine!*
3. O-pen my heart, il-lu-mine me, Spir-it di-vine! A-men.

ASPIRATION

487 Prayer of Dedication

Lord, call us into the church.
Call us in often,
    and teach us the old words and old songs
      with their new meanings.
Lord, give us new words
    for the words we wear out.
Give us new songs
    for those that have lost their spirit.
Give us new reasons for coming in
    and for going out,
      into our streets and to our homes.
As the house of the Lord once moved
    like a tent through the wilderness,
      so keep our churches from being rigid.
Make our congregation alive and free.
Give us ideas we never had before,
    so that alleluia and gloria and amen
      are like the experiences we know in daily living.
Alleluia! O Lord, be praised!
In worship and in work, be praised! Amen.

—Herbert Brokering

488 We Are Climbing Jacob's Ladder

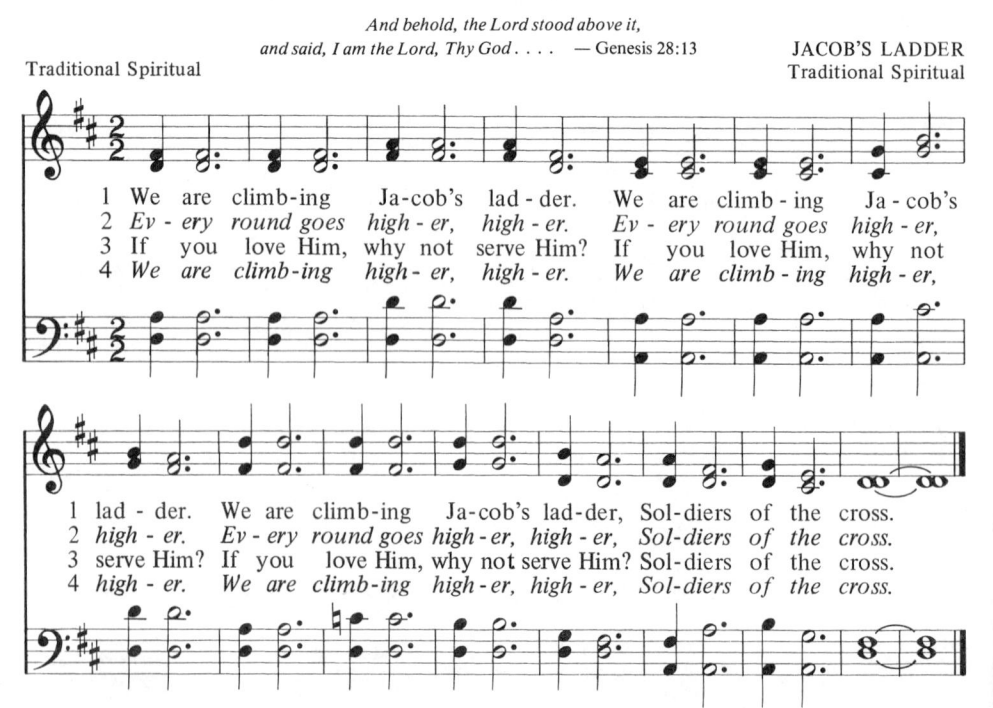

*And behold, the Lord stood above it,
and said, I am the Lord, Thy God....* — Genesis 28:13

Traditional Spiritual

JACOB'S LADDER
Traditional Spiritual

1. We are climbing Jacob's ladder. We are climbing Jacob's ladder. We are climbing Jacob's ladder, Soldiers of the cross.
2. Every round goes higher, higher. Every round goes higher, higher. Every round goes higher, higher, Soldiers of the cross.
3. If you love Him, why not serve Him? If you love Him, why not serve Him? If you love Him, why not serve Him? Soldiers of the cross.
4. We are climbing higher, higher. We are climbing higher, higher. We are climbing higher, higher, Soldiers of the cross.

ASPIRATION

In Heavenly Love Abiding   489

Abide in Me, and I in you, as the branch cannot bear fruit unless it abide in the vine...
— John 15:4

Anna L. Waring

SEASONS
Felix Mendelssohn

1. In heavenly love abiding, No change my heart shall fear;
   And safe is such confiding, For nothing changes here.
   The storm may roar without me, My heart may low be laid,
   But God is round about me, And can I be dismayed?

2. *Wherever He may guide me, No fear shall turn me back;*
   My Shepherd is beside me, And nothing shall I lack.
   His wisdom ever waketh, His sight is never dim;
   He knows the way He taketh, And I will walk with Him.

3. Green pastures are before me, Which yet I have not seen;
   Bright skies will soon be o'er me, Where darkest clouds have been.
   My hope I cannot measure, My path to life is free;
   My Savior is my treasure, And He will walk with me.

INNER PEACE

490 Psalm 83

I am so depressed tonight, O God.
I feel as if I am the sole target of an enemy barrage—that all the demons of hell are bent
 upon damning my soul for eternity.

I remember Your precious promises, but I do not witness their fulfillment.
I talk to people about Your love, and they drown my zeal with scorn.
I step forth to carry out Your will, but I feel no sense of accomplishment.
I mouth words, wave my arms, and beat the air with fruitless endeavor.
Then I fall like a wounded warrior, bone-weary, defeated, and lonely.
And I wonder if You are truly my God, and if I am really Your child.

Consume, O God, these demons that depress, these enemies that plague my soul.
May the whirlwind of Your Spirit sweep them out of my life forever.
May I awaken in the morning with a heart full of joy, and with the strength and the courage
 to walk straight and secure in the dangerous and difficult paths before me.

—Leslie Brandt

491 Peace, Perfect Peace

My peace I give unto you: not as the world giveth . . . – John 14:27

Edward H. Bickersteth

PAX TECUM
George T. Caldbeck

1. Peace, perfect peace, in this dark world of sin?
 The blood of Jesus whispers peace within.
2. Peace, perfect peace, by thronging duties pressed?
 To do the will of Jesus— this is rest.
3. Peace, perfect peace, with sorrows surging round?
 On Jesus' bosom naught but calm is found.
4. Peace, perfect peace, with loved ones far away?
 In Jesus' keeping we are safe, and they.
5. Peace, perfect peace, our future all unknown?
 Jesus we know, and He is on the throne.
6. Peace, perfect peace, death shadowing us and ours?
 Jesus has vanquished death and all its powers.
7. It is enough: earth's struggles soon shall cease,
 And Jesus call us to heaven's perfect peace.

INNER PEACE

Lasting Peace 492

Have no anxiety about anything, but in everything by prayer and supplication with thanksgiving let your requests be made known to God. And the peace of God, which passes all understanding, will keep your hearts and your minds in Christ Jesus.

—Philippians 4:6, 7 (RSV)

Thou Wilt Keep Him in Perfect Peace 493

. . . because he trusteth in Thee.

— Isaiah 26:3

Isaiah 26:3
Vivian Kretz

PERFECT PEACE
Vivian Kretz

"Thou wilt keep him in per-fect peace whose mind is stayed on Thee."

When the sha-dows come and dark-ness falls, He giv-eth in-ward peace. O He is the on-ly per-fect rest-ing place, He giv-eth per-fect peace!

"Thou wilt keep him in per-fect peace whose mind is stayed on Thee."

INNER PEACE

494 Wonderful Peace

And the peace of God, which passeth all understanding shall keep your hearts and minds.
— Philippians 4:7

W. D. Cornell

WONDERFUL PEACE
W. G. Cooper

1. Far a-way in the depths of my spir-it to-night Rolls a mel-o-dy sweet-er than psalm; In ce-les-tial-like strains it un-ceas-ing-ly falls O'er my soul like an in-fi-nite calm.
2. *What a treas-ure I have in this won-der-ful peace, Bur-ied deep in the heart of my soul; So se-cure that no pow-er can mine it a-way While the years of e-ter-ni-ty roll;*
3. I am rest-ing to-night in this won-der-ful peace, Rest-ing sweet-ly in Je-sus' con-trol; For I'm kept from all dan-ger by night and by day, And His glo-ry is flood-ing my soul.
4. *And I think when I rise to that cit-y of peace, Where the au-thor of peace I shall see, That one strain of the song which the ran-somed will sing, In that heav-en-ly king-dom shall be:*
5. O my soul, are you here with-out com-fort or rest, March-ing down the rough path-way of time? Make the Sav-ior your friend when the shad-ows grow dark; O ac-cept this sweet peace so sub-lime.

Peace! Peace! won-der-ful peace, Coming down from the Fa-ther a-bove; Sweep

INNER PEACE

o-ver my spir-it for-ev-er, I pray, In fath-om-less bil-lows of love.

It Is Well with My Soul — 495

Horatio G. Spafford
But God will redeem my soul from the power of death, for He will receive me. —Psalm 49:15
VILLE DU HAVRE
Philip P. Bliss

1. When peace, like a riv-er, at-tend-eth my way, When sor-rows like sea bil-lows roll— What-ev-er my lot, Thou hast taught me to say, It is well, it is well with my soul. It is well with my soul, It is well, it is well with my soul.

2. *My sin— O the joy of this glo-ri-ous thought—My sin, not in part, but the whole, Is nailed to the cross, and I bear it no more: Praise the Lord, praise the Lord, O my soul!* It is well with my soul, It is well, it is well with my soul.

3. And, Lord, haste the day when my faith shall be sight, The clouds be rolled back as a scroll: The trump shall re-sound and the Lord shall de-scend, "E-ven so"— it is well with my soul. It is well with my soul, It is well, it is well with my soul.

INNER PEACE

496 Security

We need not fear if the world and the mountains crumble into the sea.
— Psalm 46:2

Based on Isaiah 54:10
Lina Sandell
Tr. by E. Lincoln Pearson, stanzas 1, 4, alt.
Bryan Jeffery Leech, stanzas 2, 3

BERGEN MÅ VIKA
Source unknown

1. Great hills may tremble and mountains may crumble,
God's loving-kindness remaineth secure;
Peace He will give to the contrite and humble:
Thus saith the Lord— His promise is sure.

2. *Though peace be shattered by war's agitation,
Though change and tension give birth to great fears,
God still remains an unshaken foundation,
Strong to support us through turbulent years;*

3. *Strong to preserve us in moments of danger,
Strong when frustration and frailty increase;
Strong to equip us for loving the stranger,
Strong where our human resources may cease.*

4. *Teach us, O Lord, Thy commandments to ponder,
Help us to heed them wherever we roam,
Waiting the day Thou shalt call us up yonder,
Trusting Thy promise to carry us home.* A-men.

Words copyright 1950, 1973 by Covenant Press. All rights reserved. Used by permission.
INNER PEACE

Like a River Glorious
497

Then had Thy peace been like a river and Thy righteousness as the waves....
— Isaiah 48:18

Frances Ridley Havergal
Jeff Redd, alt., stanza 3

WYE VALLEY
James Mountain

1. Like a river glorious Is God's perfect peace, O-ver all vic-torious In its bright in-crease; Per-fect, yet it flow-eth Full-er every day, Per-fect, yet it grow-eth Deep-er all the way.
2. *Hid-den in the hol-low Of His bless-ed hand, Nev-er foe can fol-low, Nev-er trai-tor stand; Not a surge of wor-ry, Not a shade of care, Not a blast of hur-ry Touch the spir-it there.*
3. Ev-ery joy or test-ing Comes from God a-bove, Giv-en to His chil-dren As an act of love; We may trust Him ful-ly All for us to do— Those who trust Him whol-ly Find Him whol-ly true.

Trust-ing in Je-ho-vah, Hearts are ful-ly blest—
Find-ing, as He prom-ised, Per-fect peace and rest.

INNER PEACE

498 Through the Love of God, Our Savior

... I know that it shall be well with them that fear God.
— Ecclesiastes 8:12

Mary Peters

AR HYD Y NOS
Welsh melody

1. Through the love of God, our Savior, All will be well;
   Free and changeless is His favor— All will be well.
   Precious is the blood that healed us, Perfect is the grace that sealed us,
   Strong the hand stretched out to shield us— All will be well.

2. *Though we pass through tribulation, All will be well;*
   Ours is such a full salvation— All will be well.
   Happy when in God confiding, Fruitful if in Christ abiding,
   Holy through the Spirit's guiding— All will be well.

3. We expect a bright tomorrow, All will be well;
   Faith can sing through days of sorrow, All will be well.
   On our Father's love relying, Jesus every need supplying
   In our living, in our dying, All will be well.

INNER PEACE

Peace 499

I know not what I shall become: it seems to me that peace of soul and repose of spirit descend on me, even in sleep. To be without the sense of this peace, would be affliction indeed....

I know not what God purposes with me, or keeps me for; I am in a calm so great that I fear naught. What can I fear, when I am with Him: and with Him, in His Presence, I hold myself the most I can. May all things praise Him. Amen.

—Brother Lawrence

Abide With Me 500

And now, ... abide in Him, that when He shall appear we may have confidence, and not be ashamed ... — 1 John 2:28

Henry F. Lyte

EVENTIDE
William H. Monk

1. A-bide with me—fast falls the e-ven-tide; The dark-ness deep-ens— Lord, with me a-bide; When oth-er help-ers fail and com-forts flee, Help of the help-less, O a-bide with me.

2. Swift to its close ebbs out life's lit-tle day; Earth's joys grow dim, its glo-ries pass a-way; Change and de-cay in all a-round I see; O Thou who chang-est not, a-bide with me.

3. I need Thy pres-ence ev-ery pass-ing hour; What but Thy grace can foil the temp-ter's power? Who like Thy-self my guide and stay can be? Through cloud and sun-shine, O a-bide with me.

4. I fear no foe, with Thee at hand to bless; Ills have no weight and tears no bit-ter-ness; Where is death's sting? where, grave, thy vic-to-ry? I tri-umph still if Thou a-bide with me.

5. Hold Thou Thy cross be-fore my clos-ing eyes; Shine thru the gloom and point me to the skies; Heaven's morn-ing breaks and earth's vain shad-ows flee; In life, in death, O Lord, a-bide with me. A-men.

INNER PEACE

501 'Til the Storm Passes By

A man shall be ... like the shadow of a great rock in a weary land.
— Isaiah 32:2

Mosie Lister

LISTER
Mosie Lister

1. In the dark of the midnight Have I oft hid my face,
While the storms howl above me, And there's no hiding place.
'Mid the crash of the thunder, Precious Lord, hear my cry,
"Keep me safe 'til the storm passes by."

2. Many times Satan whispered, "There is no use to try,
For there's no end of sorrow, There's no hope by and by."
But I know Thou art with me, And tomorrow I'll rise
Where the storms never darken the skies.

3. When the long night has ended, And the storms come no more,
Let me stand in Thy presence On that bright, peaceful shore.
In that land where the tempest Never comes, Lord, may I
Dwell with Thee when the storm passes by.

© 1958 by Lillenas Publishing Co. All rights reserved. Used by permission.

INNER PEACE

'Til the storm pass-es o-ver, 'Til the thun-der sounds no more,

'Til the clouds roll for-ev-er from the sky,

Hold me fast, Let me stand in the hol-low of Thy hand;

Keep me safe 'til the storm pass-es by.

INNER PEACE

502 I'll Go Where You Want Me to Go

Paul, a servant of Jesus Christ . . . separated unto the Gospel of God. — Romans 1:1

Mary Brown, stanza 1
Charles E. Prior, stanzas 2, 3

I'LL GO
Carrie E. Rounsefell

1. It may not be on the mountain's height Or over the stormy sea,
2. Perhaps today there are loving words Which Jesus would have me speak,
3. There's surely somewhere a lowly place In earth's harvest fields so wide,

1. It may not be at the battlefront My Lord will have need of me;
2. There may be now, in the paths of sin, Some wanderer whom I should seek;
3. Where I may labor thru life's short day For Jesus the Crucified;

1. But if by a still, small voice He calls To paths I do not know,
2. O Savior, if Thou wilt be my Guide, Tho dark and rugged the way,
3. So, trusting my all unto Thy care— I know Thou lovest me—

1. I'll answer, dear Lord, with my hand in Thine, I'll go where You want me to go.
2. My voice shall echo the message sweet, I'll say what You want me to say.
3. I'll do Thy will with a heart sincere, I'll be what You want me to be.

I'll go where You want me to go, dear Lord, O'er mountain or plain or sea;

DISCIPLESHIP

I'll say what You want me to say, dear Lord, I'll be what You want me to be.

Glorifying God in the Everyday — 503

The wonder of the Incarnation slips into the Life of ordinary childhood; the marvel of the Transfiguration descends to the valley and the demon-possessed boy, and the glory of the Resurrection merges into Our Lord providing breakfast for His disciples on the sea shore in the early dawn. The tendency in early Christian experience is to look for the marvellous. We are apt to mistake the sense of the heroic for being heroes. It is one thing to go through a crisis grandly, but a different thing to go through every day glorifying God when there is no witness, no limelight, and no one paying the remotest attention to you. If we don't want medieval haloes, we want something that will make people say— What a wonderful man of prayer he is! What a pious, devoted woman she is! If anyone says that of you, you have not been loyal to God.

—Oswald Chambers

Must Jesus Bear the Cross Alone — 504

If any man come after Me let him . . . take up his cross and follow . . . — Matthew 16:24

Thomas Shepherd

MAITLAND
George N. Allen

1. Must Jesus bear the cross a-lone, And all the world go free?
   No; there's a cross for ev-ery one, And there's a cross for me.
2. *The con-se-crat-ed cross I'll bear, 'Til death shall set me free,*
   And then go home my crown to wear, For there's a crown for me.
3. O pre-cious cross! O glo-rious crown! O res-ur-rec-tion day!
   Ye an-gels, from the stars come down, And take my soul a-way. A-men.

DISCIPLESHIP

505 Your Cause Be Mine

For this cause was I born . . . that I should bear witness unto the truth.
— John 18:37

Bryan Jeffery Leech

RICHMOND BEACH
A. Royce Eckhardt

1. Your cause be mine, great Lord divine, Your aim be my ambition: For wasted is my greatest strength Unless it find expression, In love that gives itself away, In life responsive to o-

2. *Your cause be mine, great Lord divine, This be my life's vocation: To seek the prize when life is done— Your loving approbation. Diminish pride, increase my love, O may Your Spirit now re-*

3. Your cause be mine, great Lord divine, The world's emancipation: To let Your light invade the dark In every situation, To prove You in a thousand ways, To serve You well with zeal a-

© Copyright 1973 by Covenant Press. All rights reserved. Used by permission.

DISCIPLESHIP

1 bey	The terms	of Your com - mis - sion.	
2 *move*	All self - ish mo - ti - va - tion.	
3 blaze	Through life's un-known du - ra - tion.	A - men.

Make Us Worthy, Lord 506

Make us worthy, Lord,
to serve our fellow men throughout the world
who live and die in poverty and hunger.

Give them, through our hands, this day
their daily bread, and by our understanding love give Peace and Joy.

Lord, make a channel of Thy peace,

that where there is hatred I may bring love;

that where there is wrong, I may bring the spirit of forgiveness;

that where there is doubt, I may bring faith;

that where there is error, I may bring truth;

that where there is discord, I may bring harmony;

that where there is despair, I may bring hope;

that where there are shadows, I may bring light;

that where there is sadness, I may bring joy.

Lord,
grant that I may seek rather to comfort than to be comforted;

to understand than to be understood;

to love than to be loved;

for it is by forgetting self that one finds;

it is by dying that one awakens to eternal life.

Amen.

—Mother Teresa

DISCIPLESHIP

507 Come, All Christians, Be Committed

No man having put his hand to the plow, and looking back is fit....
— Luke 9:62

BEACH SPRING
"The Sacred Harp"
Harmonized by James H. Wood

Eva B. Lloyd

1. Come, all Christians, be committed To the service of the Lord;
Make your lives for Him more fitted, Tune your hearts with one accord.
Come into His courts with gladness, Each His sacred vows renew,
Turn away from sin and sadness, Be transformed with life anew.

2. *Of your time and talents give ye, They are gifts from God above;
To be used by Christians freely To proclaim His wondrous love.
Come again to serve the Savior, Tithes and off'rings with you bring.
In your work, with Him find favor, And with joy His praises sing.*

3. God's command to love each other Is required of every man;
Showing mercy to a brother Mirrors His redemptive plan.
In compassion He has given Of His love that is divine;
On the cross sins were forgiven; Joy and peace are fully thine.

4. *Come in praise and adoration, All who on Christ's name believe;
Worship Him with consecration, Grace and love will you receive.
For His grace give Him the glory, For the Spirit and the Word,
And repeat the gospel story 'Til all men His name have heard.*

Words © Copyright 1966 Broadman Press. All rights reserved. Tune © Copyright 1958 Broadman Press. All rights reserved. Used by permission.

DISCIPLESHIP

Give Me a Dream 508

Father,
   once I had such big dreams, so much anticipation of the future.
Now no shimmering horizon beckons me; my days are lack-lustre
   I see so little of lasting value in the daily round.
         Where is Your plan for my life?

   You have told us that without vision, we men perish. So, Father
in heaven, knowing that I can ask in confidence for what is Your
expressed will to give me, I ask You to deposit in my mind and heart
that particular dream, the special vision You have for my life.

   And along with the dream, will You give me whatever graces,
patience, and stamina it takes to see the dream through to fruition?

      I sense this may involve adventures I have not bargained for.

            But I want to trust You
               enough to follow even if You lead along new paths.

   I admit to liking some of my ruts.

         But I know that habit patterns
            that seem like cozy nests from the inside,
                     from Your vantage point
                           may be prison cells.
         Lord,
      if You have to break down
               any prisons of mine
         before I can see the stars and catch the vision,
            then, Lord, begin the process now.
   In joyous expectation.
            Amen.   —Catherine Marshall

My Eternal King 509

My God, I love Thee;
Not because I hope for heaven thereby,
Nor yet because who love Thee not
Must die eternally.

Thou, O my Jesus, Thou didst me
Upon the cross embrace,
For me didst bear the nails and spear,
And manifold disgrace.

Then why, O blessed Jesus Christ,
Should I not love Thee well?
Not for the hope of winning heaven,
Or of escaping hell.

E'en so I love Thee, and will love
And in Thy praise will sing,
Solely because Thou art my God,
And my eternal King!

—Francis Xavier
Tr. Edward Caswall

ASPIRATION

510 Glorious Is Thy Name, Most Holy

We love Him because He first loved us . . . — I John 4:19

Ruth Elliot

HOLY MANNA
William Moore

1. Glorious is Thy name, Most Holy, God and Father of us all;
We Thy servants bow before Thee, Strive to answer every call.
Thou with life's great good hast blest us, Cared for us from earliest years;
Unto Thee our thanks we render; Thy deep love o'ercomes all fears.

2. *For our world of need and anguish We would lift to Thee our prayer.
Faithful stewards of Thy bounty, May we with our brothers share.
In the name of Christ our Savior, Who redeems and sets us free,
Gifts we bring of heart and treasure, That our lives may worthier be.*

3. In the midst of time we journey, From Thy hand comes each new day;
We would use it in Thy service, Humbly, wisely, while we may.
So to Thee, Lord and Creator, Praise and honor we accord,
Thine the earth and Thine the heavens, Through all the Eternal Word.

Words from "Ten New Stewardship Hymns." © Copyright 1961 by The Hymn Society of America; Used by permission.

STEWARDSHIP

A Stewardship Prayer   511

Lord, we gather in comfort and security today, while many of Your children huddle in fear and die of starvation. We know that merely feeling guilty for our comfort does not minister to the needs of others. Lord, we want to be involved in helping, and serving, and healing. Help us this day to gain more understanding, to feel more deeply the hurt of others, to come to new commitments of ourselves and our substance to You. Amen.

—Gary W. Demarest

Little Is Much, When God Is in It   512

There is a small boy here with five loaves and two fishes.
— John 6:9

Mrs. F. W. Suffield   Mrs. F. W. Suffield

1. In the har-vest field now rip-ened, There's a work for all to do;
2. *Does the place you're called to la-bor Seem so small and lit-tle known?*
3. When the con-flict here is end-ed And our race on earth is run;

1. Hark, the voice of God is call-ing, To the har-vest call-ing you.
2. *It is great if God is in it, And He'll not for-get His own.*
3. He will say, if we are faith-ful, "Wel-come home, my child, well done."

Lit-tle is much when God is in it, La-bor not for wealth or fame;

There's a crown and you can win it, If you go in Je-sus' name.

STEWARDSHIP

513 God, Whose Giving Knows No Ending

A man can receive nothing except it be given to him from heaven.
— John 3:27

Robert Lansing Edwards

NETTLETON
Traditional American Melody
John Wyeth

1. God, whose giv-ing knows no end-ing, All our life is from Thy store:
   Na-ture's won-der, Je-sus' wis-dom, Cost-ly cross, grave's shat-tered door.
   Gift-ed by Thee, turn we to Thee, Of-f'ring up our-selves in praise;
   Thank-ful song shall rise for-ev-er, Gra-cious Do-nor of our days.

2. *Skills and time are ours for press-ing T'ward the goals of Christ, Thy Son:*
   Men at peace in health and free-dom, Rac-es joined, the Church made one.
   Now di-rect our dai-ly la-bor, Lest we strive for self a-lone;
   Born with tal-ents, make us serv-ants Fit to an-swer at Thy throne.

3. Treas-ure too Thou hast en-trust-ed, Gain thru pow'rs Thy grace con-ferred:
   Ours to use for home and kin-dred, And to spread the gos-pel word.
   O-pen wide our hands in shar-ing, As we heed Christ's age-less call,
   Heal-ing, teach-ing, and re-claim-ing, Serv-ing Thee who lov-est all.

4. *Lend Thy joy to all our giv-ing, Let it light our pil-grim way:*
   From the dark of anx-ious keep-ing, Loose us in-to gen-'rous day.
   Then when years on earth are o-ver, Rich t'ward Thee and fel-low-man,
   Lord, ful-fill be-yond our dream-ing All our stew-ard-life be-gan. A-men.

Words from "Ten New Stewardship Hymns." © Copyright 1961 by The Hymn Society of America; Used by permission.

STEWARDSHIP

True Charity 514

C. S. Lewis didn't talk about percentage giving.
He said the only safe rule is to give more than we can spare.
Our charities should pinch and hamper us.

If we live at the same level of affluence
as other people who have our level of income,
we are probably giving away too little.

Obstacles to charity include
greed for luxurious living,
greed for money itself,
fear of financial insecurity,
and showy pride.

—Kathryn Ann Lindskoog

We Give Thee but Thine Own 515

Of thine own have we given Thee. — I Chronicles 29:14

William W. How

SCHUMANN
Mason and Webb's *Cantica Laudis*

1. We give Thee but Thine own, What-e'er the gift may be:
All that we have is Thine a-lone, A trust, O Lord, from Thee.
2. May we Thy boun-ties thus As stew-ards true re-ceive,
And glad-ly, as Thou bless-est us, To Thee our first-fruits give.
3. To com-fort and to bless, To find a balm for woe,
To tend the lone and fa-ther-less Is our great task be-low.
4. And we be-lieve Thy word, Though dim our faith may be:
What-ev-er task we do, O Lord, We do it un-to Thee. A-men.

STEWARDSHIP

516 Give of Your Best to the Master

Ye are My friends if ye do whatsoever I command you.
— John 15:14

Howard B. Grose

BARNARD
Charlotte A. Barnard

1. Give of your best to the Mas-ter, Give of the strength of your youth;
2. *Give of your best to the Mas-ter, Give Him first place in your heart;*
3. Give of your best to the Mas-ter, Naught else is wor-thy His love;

Refrain: Give of your best to the Mas-ter; Give of the strength of your youth;

1. Throw your soul's fresh, glowing ar - dor In - to the bat-tle for truth.
2. *Give Him first place in your ser - vice; Con-se-crate ev - ery part.*
3. He gave him-self for your ran - som, Gave up His glo-ry a - bove;

Clad in sal - va-tion's full ar - mor, Join in the bat-tle for truth.

1. Je - sus has set the ex - am - ple – Daunt-less was He, young and brave;
2. *Give, and to you shall be giv - en. – God His be - lov-ed Son gave;*
3. Laid down His life with-out mur - mur, You from sin's ru-in to save;

1. Give Him your loy - al de - vo - tion, Give Him the best that you have.
2. *Grate-ful-ly seek-ing to serve Him, Give Him the best that you have.*
3. Give Him your heart's ad-o - ra - tion, Give Him the best that you have.

STEWARDSHIP

Evening Prayer 517

*O Lord my God, I thank Thee that Thou
hast brought this day to a close;
I thank Thee that Thou hast given me peace
in body and in soul.
Thy hand has been over me and has protected
and preserved me,*

*Forgive my puny faith,
the ill that I this day have done,
and help me to forgive all who
have wronged me.*

*Grant me a quiet night's sleep beneath
Thy tender care.
And defend me from all the temptations
of darkness.*

*Into Thy hands I commend my loved ones,
and all who dwell in this house;
I commend my body and soul.*

—Dietrich Bonhoeffer

All Praise to Thee, My God 518

My praise shall be of Thee in the great congregation; — Psalm 22:25

Thomas Ken

TALLIS' CANON
Thomas Tallis

1. All praise to Thee, my God, this night, For all the bless-ings of the light!
2. For-give me, Lord, for Thy dear Son, The ill that I this day have done,
3. O may my soul on Thee re-pose, And with sweet sleep mine eye-lids close,
4. Praise God, from whom all bless-ings flow; Praise Him, all crea-tures here be-low;

1. Keep me, O keep me, King of kings, Be-neath Thine own al-might-y wings.
2. That with the world, my-self, and Thee, I, when I sleep, at peace may be.
3. Sleep that may me more vig-orous make To serve my God when I a-wake.
4. Praise Him a-bove, ye heaven-ly host; Praise Fa-ther, Son, and Ho-ly Ghost. A-men.

CLOSING HYMNS

519 Savior, Again to Thy Dear Name We Raise

And when they had sung a hymn they went out....
— Matthew 26:30

John Ellerton
ELLERS
Edward J. Hopkins

1. Savior, again to Thy dear name we raise
With one accord our parting hymn of praise:
Once more we pray before our worship cease;
That Thou wilt grant to us Thy word of peace.

2. *Grant us Thy peace upon our homeward way;
With Thee began, with Thee shall end the day;
Guard Thou the lips from sin, the hearts from shame,
That in this house have called upon Thy name.*

3. Grant us Thy peace, Lord, through the coming night;
Turn Thou for us its darkness into light:
From harm and danger keep Thy children free,
For dark and light are both alike to Thee.

4. *Grant us Thy peace throughout our earthly life,
Our joy in sorrow, and our strength in strife;
Then, when Thy voice shall bid our conflict cease,
Call us, O Lord, to Thine eternal peace.* A-men.

CLOSING HYMNS

Lord, Dismiss Us with Your Blessing

Salvation belongeth to the Lord; Thy blessing is upon Thy people.

— Psalm 3:8

John Fawcett

SICILIAN MARINERS
Tattersall's *Psalmody*

1. Lord, dismiss us with Your blessing, Fill our hearts with joy and peace; Let us each, Your love possessing, Triumph in redeeming grace. O refresh us, O refresh us, Traveling through this wilderness.

2. *Thanks we give and adoration For Your gospel's joyful sound; May the fruits of Your salvation In our hearts and lives abound. Ever faithful, ever faithful To the truth may we be found.* A-men.

CLOSING HYMNS

521 A Prayer

God be in my head, and in my understanding;
God be in mine eyes and in my looking;
God be in my mouth, and in my speaking;
God be in my heart, and in my thinking;
God be at mine end, and at my departing. Amen.

—Ancient Prayer

522 The Lord Bless You and Keep You

The Lord bless thee and keep thee, . . . and make His face to shine upon thee . . . .
— Numbers 6:24, 25

Numbers 6:24-26

BENEDICTION
Peter C. Lutkin

CLOSING HYMNS

God Be with You 'Til We Meet Again 523

May the Lord watch between me and thee.... — Genesis 31:49

GOD BE WITH YOU
Jeremiah E. Rankin
William G. Tomer

1 God be with you 'til we meet a-gain, By His coun-sels guide, up-hold you,
2 *God be with you 'til we meet a-gain, 'Neath His wings protecting hide you,*
3 God be with you 'til we meet a-gain, If life's tri-als should con-found you,
4 *God be with you 'til we meet a-gain, Keep love's banner floating o'er you,*

1 With His sheep se-cure-ly fold you: God be with you 'til we meet a-gain.
2 *Dai - ly man-na still pro-vide you: God be with you 'til we meet a-gain.*
3 God will put His arms a-round you: God be with you 'til we meet a-gain.
4 *Smite death's threat'ning wave before you: God be with you 'til we meet a-gain.*

Benediction 524

May the Lord take from you all resistance to His will.

May He give to you the fullness of His life

   and the sufficiency of His practical, daily help.

May the Lord send you during this week to come to those

   He can only serve through your unique experience of life

   and your very special abilities.

May the Lord bring us together even when we are apart,

   as we learn to be supportive of one another in our prayers

   and our service. Amen.

—Bryan Jeffery Leech

CLOSING HYMNS

525 Now Thank We All Our God

Our God, we thank Thee and praise Thy glorious name.
— I Chronicles 29:13

Martin Rinkart
Tr. by Catherine Winkworth

NUN DANKET
Johann Crüger
Harmonized by Felix Mendelssohn

1. Now thank we all our God With hearts and hands and voices,
2. O may this boun-teous God Through all our life be near us,
3. All praise and thanks to God The Fa-ther now be giv-en,

1. Who won-drous things hath done, In whom His world re-joic-es;
2. With ev-er joy-ful hearts And bless-ed peace to cheer us;
3. The Son, and Him who reigns With them in high-est heav-en,

1. Who, from our moth-ers' arms, Hath blessed us on our way
2. And keep us in His grace, And guide us when per-plexed,
3. The one e-ter-nal God, Whom earth and heaven a-dore;

1. With count-less gifts of love, And still is ours to-day.
2. And free us from all ills In this world and the next.
3. For thus it was, is now, And shall be ev-er more. A-men.

HERITAGE

*Our Love
for the Family of God*

526 Faith of Our Fathers

... You should earnestly contend for the faith which was once delivered unto the saints.
— Jude 1:3

Frederick W. Faber

ST. CATHERINE
Henri F. Hemy
Descant by Bob Burroughs

1 Faith of our fa - thers, liv - ing still In spite of dun - geon,
2 Faith of our fa - thers, God's great power Shall win all na - tions
3 Faith of our fa - thers, we will love Both friend and foe in

1 fire, and sword, O how our hearts beat high with joy
2 un - to thee, And through the truth that comes from God
3 all our strife, And preach thee too as love knows how,

1 When-e'er we hear that glo - rious word! Faith of our fa - thers,
2 Man - kind shall then in - deed be free. Faith of our fa - thers,
3 By kind - ly words and vir - tuous life. Faith of our fa - thers,

© Copyright 1976 by Paragon Associates, Inc. All rights reserved.
HERITAGE

fa - thers, ho - ly faith, We will be true 'til death. A - men.

1 ho - ly faith, We will be true to thee 'til death.
2 ho - ly faith, We will be true to thee 'til death.
3 ho - ly faith, We will be true to thee 'til death. A - men.

Answered Prayer 527

I asked God for strength,
    that I might achieve,
  I was made weak,
    that I might learn humbly to obey . . .
I asked for health,
    that I might do greater things,
  I was given infirmity,
    that I might do better things . . .
I asked for riches,
    that I might be happy,
  I was given poverty,
    that I might be wise . . .
I asked for power,
    that I might have the praise of men,
  I was given weakness,
    that I might feel the need of God . . .
I asked for all things,
    that I might enjoy life,
  I was given life,
    that I might enjoy all things . . .
I got nothing that I asked for—
but everything I had hoped for;
    Almost despite myself,
    my unspoken prayers were answered.
        I am among all men most richly blessed.

—Unknown Confederate Soldier

HERITAGE

528 God of Grace and God of Glory

Put on the whole armour of God that ye may be able to stand. — Ephesians 6:11

Harry Emerson Fosdick

CWM RHONDDA
John Hughes

1. God of grace and God of glory, On Thy people pour Thy power; Crown Thine an-cient church's sto-ry, Bring her bud to glo-rious flower. Grant us wis-dom, Grant us cour-age, For the fac-ing of this hour, For the fac-ing of this hour.

2. *Lo! the hosts of e-vil round us Scorn Thy Christ, as-sail His ways! From the fears that long have bound us, Free our hearts to faith and praise. Grant us wis-dom, Grant us cour-age, For the liv-ing of these days, For the liv-ing of these days.*

3. Cure Thy chil-dren's war-ring mad-ness; Bend our pride to Thy con-trol; Shame our wan-ton, self-ish glad-ness, Rich in things and poor in soul. Grant us wis-dom, Grant us cour-age, Lest we miss Thy kingdom's goal, Lest we miss Thy king-dom's goal.

4. *Set our feet on loft-y plac-es, Gird our lives that they may be Ar-mored with all Christ-like grac-es In the fight to set men free. Grant us wis-dom, Grant us cour-age, That we fail not man nor Thee, That we fail not man nor Thee.* A-men.

Words used by permission of Elinor Fosdick Downs. Music © by Mrs. Dilys Webb c/o Mechanical-Copyright Protection Society Limited, and reproduced by permission of the legal representatives of the composer, who reserve all rights therein.

HERITAGE

Alternate Last Verse Harmonization Arranged by Robert Elmore

4 Set our feet on lofty places, Gird our lives that they may be
Armored with all Christ-like graces In the fight to set men free.
Grant us wisdom, Grant us courage, That we fail not man nor Thee,
That we fail not man nor Thee. A-men.

(TPT.)

© Copyright 1976 by Paragon Associates, Inc. All rights reserved.

HERITAGE

529 Marriage

As male and female we look to the Spirit.
He makes us stewards of life
   to plan its beginning,
   to live its living,
   to care in its dying.
He makes us the stewards of marriage
   with its lifelong commitment to love;
yet He knows our frailty of heart.

            —*"Our Song of Hope"*

530 O Perfect Love

A man shall cleave unto his wife; and they shall be one flesh. — Genesis 2:24

Dorothy Gurney
O PERFECT LOVE
Joseph Barnby

1. O perfect Love, all human thought transcending, Lowly we kneel in prayer before Thy throne, That theirs may be the love which knows no ending, Whom Thou for evermore dost join in one.
2. O perfect Life, be Thou their full assurance Of tender charity and steadfast faith, Of patient hope, and quiet, brave endurance, With childlike trust that fears nor pain nor death.
3. Grant them the joy which brightens earthly sorrow, Grant them the peace which calms all earthly strife, And to life's day the glorious unknown morrow That dawns upon eternal love and life. A-men.

MARRIAGE

Womanhood 531

If you can find a truly good wife, she is worth more than precious gems.

Her husband can trust her, and she will richly satisfy his needs. She will not hinder him, but help him all his life.

She finds wool and flax and busily spins it. She buys imported foods, brought by ship from distant ports.

She gets up before dawn to prepare breakfast for her household, and plans the day's work for her servant girls.

She goes out to inspect a field, and buys it; with her own hands she plants a vineyard. She is energetic, a hard worker, and watches for bargains. She works far into the night!

She sews for the poor, and generously gives to the needy. She has no fear of winter for her household, for she has made warm clothes for all of them.

Her husband is well known, for he sits in the council chamber with the other civic leaders.

She is a woman of strength and dignity, and has no fear of old age.

When she speaks, her words are wise, and kindness is the rule for everything she says.

She watches carefully all that goes on throughout her household, and is never lazy.

Her children stand and bless her; so does her husband. He praises her with these words: "There are many fine women in the world, but you are the best of them all."

Charm can be deceptive and beauty doesn't last, but a woman who fears and reverences God shall be greatly praised.

—Proverbs 31:10-21, 23, 25-30 (LB)

Manhood 532

Men and boys:

THE WORLD NEEDS MEN

. . . who cannot be bought;

. . . whose word is their bond;

. . . who put character above wealth;

. . . who are larger than their vocations;

. . . who do not hesitate to take chances;

. . . who will not lose their identity in a crowd;

. . . who will be as honest in small things as in great things;

. . . who will make no compromise with wrong;

. . . whose ambitions are not confined to their own selfish desires;

. . . who will not say they do it "because everybody else does it;"

. . . who are true to their friends through good report and evil report, in adversity as well as in prosperity;

. . . who do not believe that shrewdness and cunning are the best qualities for winning success;

. . . who are not ashamed to stand for the truth when it is unpopular;

. . . who can say "no" with emphasis, although the rest of the world say "yes."

God, make *me* this kind of man.

—Leonard Wagner

FAMILY AND HOME

533 Prayer for the Family

Minister: *We have heard it said that the Home is the heart of our society. If this is true, our society is in trouble.*

People: *Lord, help us to build strong Christian homes. Help children to develop a sense of responsibility and personal discipline which will bring honor to Christ and happiness to the family. Help parents to love one another as You love them and outdo one another in acts of kindness, generosity and thoughtfulness.*

In Jesus' name. Amen.

—Donn Moomaw

534 The Parents' Creed

I believe that my children are a gift of God—the hope of a new tomorrow.

I believe that immeasurable possibilities lie slumbering in each son and daughter.

I believe that God has planned a perfect plan for their future, and that His love shall always surround them; and so

I believe that they shall grow up!—first creeping, then toddling, then standing, stretching skyward for a decade and a half—until they reach full stature—a man and a woman!

I believe that they can and will be molded and shaped between infancy and adulthood—as a tree is shaped by the gardener, and the clay vessel in the potter's hand, or the shoreline of the sea under the watery hand of the mighty waves; by home and church; by school and street, through sights and sounds and the touch of my hand on their hand and Christ's spirit on their heart! So,

I believe that they shall mature as only people can—through laughter and tears, through trial and error, by reward and punishment, through affection and discipline, until they stretch their wings and leave their nest to fly!

O God — I believe in my children. Help me so to live that they may always believe in me—and so in Thee.

—Robert H. Schuller

FAMILY AND HOME

In the Circle of Each Home

And all thy children shall be taught of the Lord; and great shall be the peace of thy children.

— Isaiah 54:13

BEL AIR

Bryan Jeffery Leech — Bryan Jeffery Leech

536 Children As a Trust

We don't own our children; we hold them in trust for God, who gave them to us. The eighteen or twenty years of provision and oversight and training that we normally have, represent our fulfillment of that trust.

—Joseph Bayly

537 The Wise May Bring Their Learning

Then Peter said, "Silver and gold have I none, but such as I have, I give unto you." — Acts 3:6

Anonymous, in *The Book of Praise for Children*

FOREST GREEN
Arranged by Ralph Vaughan Williams

1. The wise may bring their learning, The rich may bring their wealth, And some may bring their brilliance, And some bring strength and health; We too, would bring our treasures To offer to the King; We have no gifts deserving: What shall we children bring?

2. *We'll bring Him hearts that love Him; We'll bring Him thankful praise, And young souls humbly striving To walk in holy ways: And these shall be our treasures We offer to the King, And these are gifts that even The youngest child may bring.*

3. We'll come and show the Savior The things we do each day; We'll try our best to please Him At home, at school or play: And better are these treasures To offer to our King Than richest gifts without them: Yet these a child may bring. A-men.

FAMILY AND HOME

A Christian Home

538

Train up a child in the way he should go, and when he is old he will not depart from it.
— Proverbs 22:6

Barbara B. Hart

FINLANDIA
Jean Sibelius

1. O give us homes built firm up-on the Sav-ior, Where Christ is Head and Coun-sel-lor and Guide; Where ev-ery child is taught His love and fa-vor And gives his heart to Christ, the cru-ci-fied: How sweet to know that though his foot-steps wa-ver His faith-ful Lord is walk-ing by his side!

2. O give us homes with god-ly fa-thers, moth-ers, Who al-ways place their hope and trust in Him; Whose ten-der pa-tience tur-moil nev-er both-ers, Whose calm and cour-age trou-ble can-not dim; A home where each finds joy in serv-ing oth-ers, And love still shines, tho days be dark and grim.

3. O Lord, our God, our homes are Thine for-ev-er! We trust to Thee their prob-lems, toil, and care; Their bonds of love no en-e-my can sev-er If Thou art al-ways Lord and Mas-ter there: Be Thou the cen-ter of our least en-deav-or— Be Thou our Guest, our hearts and homes to share. A-men.

© Copyright 1965 by Singspiration, Inc. All rights reserved. Used by permission.

FAMILY AND HOME

539 Lord, I Want to Remember

"Lord, I want to remember that my children are not my children. Let me let them manage themselves at the right pace. May they have the self-respect which comes from a growing self-government. Free them from unnecessary resentment.

"From infancy up, may they know how to love because they have seen love at its best. Here in our home may they be taught that they are children of God. And may they sense the Divine in others also.

"May they know the joy of work well done. Early may they learn what they need for discipline and staying power. As they tie into the problems of society, may they be angry when they should, as they should.

"For the future of all, this is my prayer."

— Charlie W. Shedd

540 Happy the Home When God Is There

Henry Ware, Jr.
Bryan Jeffery Leech, alt.

When I call to remembrance the . . . faith that is in thee, which dwelt first in thy grandmother, . . . and thy mother. — II Timothy 1:5

ST. AGNES
John B. Dykes

1. Happy the home when God is there And love fills every one,
When with united work and prayer The Master's will is done.

2. *Happy the home where God's strong love Is starting to appear,*
Where all the children hear His fame And parents hold Him dear.

3. Happy the home where prayer is heard And praise is everywhere,
Where parents love the sacred Word And its true wisdom share.

4. *Lord, let us in our homes agree This blessed peace to gain;*
Unite our hearts in love to Thee, And love to all will reign. A-men.

Text Revision © Copyright 1976 by Fred Bock Music Co. All rights reserved. Used by permission.

FAMILY AND HOME

Ephesians 3:14-4:6 — 541

For this reason I kneel before the Father, from whom the whole family of believers in heaven and on earth derives its name. I pray that out of His glorious riches He may strengthen you with power through His Spirit in your inner being, so that Christ may dwell in your hearts through faith. And I pray that you, being rooted and established in love, may have power, together with all the saints, to grasp how wide and long and high and deep is the love of Christ, and to know this love that surpasses knowledge—that you may be filled to the measure of all the fullness of God.

Now to Him who is able to do immeasurably more than all we ask or imagine, according to His power that is at work within us, to Him be glory in the church and in Christ Jesus throughout all generations, for ever and ever!

As a prisoner for the Lord, then, I urge you to live a life worthy of the calling you have received. Be completely humble and gentle; be patient, bearing with one another in love. Make every effort to keep the unity of the Spirit through the bond of peace. There is one body and one Spirit—just as you were called to one hope when you were called—one Lord, one faith, one baptism; one God and Father of all, who is over all and through all and in all.

—(NIV)

Prayer — 542

Lord,
All around us we see brokenness, and we are aware of the fragility of life.

There is a child's delicate trust and sense of wonder which can be so easily trampled and broken.

There is a teenager's sense of self-worth which can be completely shattered by a word or simply by a disapproving look.

There is a family's unit of love, respect, and closeness which can be marred by criticism or misunderstandings, dividing family members into torn and fragmented individuals.

There is a marriage (we all thought was so whole and sturdy) which can splinter into pieces before our eyes.

There is an old man, a young boy, and a middle-aged woman who all suffer from the crushing effects of daily pressures. Their minds are emotionally disturbed and frail.

O dear Lord, be the glue that holds our fragmented hearts and minds together and never let us forget Your words:

"I am leaving you with a gift—peace of mind and heart! And the peace I give isn't fragile like the peace the world gives. So don't be troubled or afraid."

Thank You, Lord, for that because these *are* very fragile times and sometimes we *are* afraid.

—Joyce Landorf

FAMILY AND HOME

543 The Family of God

Gloria Gaither
William J. Gaither

*And God said, I will dwell in them . . . and they shall be My people;
. . . and ye shall be My sons and daughters.* — II Corinthians 6:16, 18

FAMILY OF GOD
William J. Gaither

I'm so glad I'm a part of the fam-ily of God— I've been washed in the foun-tain, cleansed by His blood! Joint heirs with Je-sus as we trav-el this sod, For I'm part of the fam-ily, the fam-ily of God.

Fine

1. You will no-tice we say "broth-er and sis-ter" 'round here— It's be-cause we're a fam-ily and these folks are so near;
2. *From the door of an or-phanage to the house of the King— No long-er an out-cast, a new song I sing;*

© Copyright 1970 by William J. Gaither. All rights reserved. Used by permission.
THE CHURCH—FAMILY OF BELIEVERS

1 When one has a heartache we all share the tears,
2 From rags unto riches, from the weak to the strong,

1 And rejoice in each victory In this family so dear.
2 I'm not worthy to be here, But, praise God, I belong!

D.C.

The Bond of Love

544

Otis Skillings
By this shall all men know that ye are My disciples — if ye love one another.
— John 13:35

BOND OF LOVE
Otis Skillings

1 We are one in the bond of love, We are one in the
2 Let us sing now, everyone, Let us feel His

1 bond of love; We have joined our spirit with the
2 love begun; Let us join our hands that the

1 Spirit of God, We are one in the bond of love.
2 world will know We are one in the bond of love.

© Copyright 1971 by Lillenas Publishing Co. All rights reserved. Used by permission.

THE CHURCH–FAMILY OF BELIEVERS

545 I Love Your Kingdom, Lord

The Kingdom of God is . . . righteousness and peace, and joy in the Holy Spirit.
— Romans 14:17

Based on Psalm 26:8
Timothy Dwight

ST. THOMAS
Williams' *New Universal Psalmodist*

1. I love Your kingdom, Lord, The house of Your abode,
   The Church our blest Redeemer saved With His own precious blood.
2. *I love Your Church, O God— Her walls before Your stand,*
   Dear as the apple of Your eye, And held within Your hand.
3. For her my tears shall fall, For her my prayers ascend,
   To her my cares and toils be given 'Til all concerns shall end.
4. *Sure as Your truth shall last, To Zion shall be given*
   The brightest glories earth can yield, And brighter joys of heaven. A-men.

Handbell descant by Darlene Lawrence

© Copyright 1976 by Paragon Associates, Inc. All rights reserved.

THE CHURCH—FAMILY OF BELIEVERS

We Are God's People

We are His people, and the sheep of His pastures.
— Psalm 100:3

546

Bryan Jeffery Leech

SYMPHONY
Johannes Brahms
Arranged by Fred Bock

1. We are God's people, the chosen of the Lord,
Born of His Spirit, established by His Word;
Our cornerstone is Christ alone, And strong in Him we stand:
O let us live transparently, And walk heart to heart and hand in hand.

2. We are God's loved ones, the Bride of Christ our Lord,
For we have known it, the love of God outpoured;
Now let us learn how to return The gift of love once given:
O let us share each joy and care, And live with a zeal that pleases Heaven.

3. We are the Body of which the Lord is Head,
Called to obey Him, now risen from the dead;
He wills us be a family Diverse yet truly one:
O let us give our gifts to God, And so shall His work on earth be done.

4. We are a Temple, the Spirit's dwelling place,
Formed in great weakness, a cup to hold God's grace;
We die alone, for on its own Each ember loses fire:
Yet joined in one the flame burns on To give warmth and light, and to inspire.

© Copyright 1976 by Fred Bock Music Co. All rights reserved. Used by permission.

THE CHURCH—FAMILY OF BELIEVERS

547 The Church's One Foundation

Other foundation can no man lay than is laid . . . Jesus Christ.
— I Corinthians 3:11

Samuel J. Stone

AURELIA
Samuel S. Wesley

1. The Church's one foun-da-tion Is Jesus Christ her Lord,
   She is His new cre-a-tion By wa-ter and the word;
   From heaven He came and sought her To be His ho-ly bride;
   With His own blood He bought her, And for her life He died.

2. E-lect from ev-ery na-tion, Yet one o'er all the earth,
   Her char-ter of sal-va-tion, One Lord, one faith, one birth;
   One ho-ly name she bless-es, Par-takes one ho-ly food,
   And to one hope she press-es, With ev-ery grace en-dued.

3. 'Mid toil and trib-u-la-tion, And tu-mult of her war,
   She waits the con-sum-ma-tion Of peace for ev-er-more;
   Till with the vi-sion glo-rious, Her long-ing eyes are blest,
   And the great Church vic-to-rious Shall be the Church at rest.

4. Yet she on earth hath un-ion With God, the Three in One,
   And mys-tic sweet com-mun-ion With those whose rest is won;
   O hap-py ones and ho-ly! Lord, give us grace that we
   Like them, the meek and low-ly, On high may dwell with Thee. A-men.

THE CHURCH—FAMILY OF BELIEVERS

Alternate Last Verse Harmonization — Arranged by Eric Thiman

4. Yet she on earth hath union With God, the Three in One, And mystic sweet communion With those whose rest is won; O happy ones and holy! Lord, give us grace that we Like them, the meek and lowly, On high may dwell with Thee. A-men.

Used by permission of Oxford University Press. From "Varied Harmonizations."

548 Getting Used to the Family of God

"But you are... a people set apart to sing the praises of God."
— I Peter 2:9

Gloria Gaither
William J. Gaither

TOGETHER
William J. Gaither

1. Climb-ing the moun-tains, cross-ing the plains, Ford-ing the rivers, shar-ing the pains; Some-times the loss-es and some-times the gain, Get-ting used to the fam-'ly of God.

2. Reach-ing our hands to a broth-er that's new, Learn-ing to say that I real-ly love you; Learn-ing to walk as the Mas-ter would do, Get-ting used to the fam-'ly of God.

Go-ing to-geth-er, en-joy-ing the trip, Get-ting used to the fam-'ly I'll spend e-ter-ni-ty with; Learn-ing to love you, how

© Copyright 1974 by William J. Gaither. All rights reserved. Used by permission.
THE CHURCH—FAMILY OF BELIEVERS

eas - y   it   is,   Get-ting   used   to   the   fam-'ly   of   God.

Prayer for Unity   549

*Our Father, we thank You for the privilege of being together
   at this time and in this place.*

*As Your people, we pray that Your love will unite us into a
   fellowship of discovery.*

*Cleanse us of everything that would sap our strength for
   togetherness.*

*Unravel the knots in our spirits.
Cleanse the error of our minds.
Free us from the bondage of our negative imaginations.
Break down the barriers that sometimes keep us apart and
   cause us to drift along without a dream.*

*As we go from here—
Explode in us new possibilities for service.
Kindle within us the fires of Your compassion so that we
   may not wait too long to learn to love.*

*May we be a people with loving purposes—
Reaching out . . .
Breaking walls . . .
Building bridges . . .
Let us be Your alleluia in a joyless, fragmented world.*

*In the name of our Lord, we pray.
Amen.*

—*Champ Traylor*

550 Come, We that Love the Lord

Ye are come unto Mount Zion, and unto the city of the living God.... — Hebrews 12:22

Isaac Watts
Robert Lowry

MARCHING TO ZION
Robert Lowry

1. Come, we that love the Lord, And let our joys be known; Join in a song with sweet ac-cord, Join in a song with sweet ac-cord And thus sur-round the throne, And thus sur-round the throne.

2. *Let those re-fuse to sing* Who nev-er knew our God; But chil-dren of the heaven-ly King, But chil-dren of the heaven-ly King May speak their joys a-broad, May speak their joys a-broad.

3. Then let our songs a-bound And ev-ery tear be dry; We're march-ing thru Em-man-uel's ground, We're march-ing thru Em-man-uel's ground To fair-er worlds on high, To fair-er worlds on high.

Refrain:
We're march-ing to Zi-on, Beau-ti-ful, beau-ti-ful Zi-on; We're march-ing up-ward to Zi-on, The beau-ti-ful cit-y of God.

THE CHURCH—FAMILY OF BELIEVERS

There's a Church Within Us, O Lord 551

Behold, the Kingdom of God is within you.
— Luke 17:21

THE CHURCH WITHIN US
Kent E. Schneider

Kent E. Schneider

1. There's a church with-in us, O Lord,
2. There's po-ten-tial with-in us, O Lord;
3. There's a fire with-in us, O Lord;
4. There's some build-ing to be done, O Lord,
5. There's the church with-in us, O Lord,

1. There's a church with-in us, O Lord.
2. Some-thing's stir-ring with-in us, O Lord.
3. A new life's a-burn-in', O Lord.
4. There's some build-ing to be done, O Lord.
5. There's the church with-in us, O Lord.

1. Not a build-ing, but a soul, Not a por-tion, but a
2. Some-thing's strain-ing to have birth, To be vis-i-ble on
3. A fire for new life, Com-bat-ing pres-ent
4. Not with steel, not with stone, But with lives which are our
5. Not a build-ing, but one soul, Not a por-tion, but one

1. whole— There's a church with-in us, O Lord.
2. earth— There's po-ten-tial with-in us, O Lord.
3. strife— There's a fire with-in us, O Lord.
4. own— There's the church to be built, O Lord.
5. whole— We are your church in the world.

© Copyright 1967 by Hope Publishing Co., owner. All rights reserved. Used by permission.

THE CHURCH - FAMILY OF BELIEVERS

552 Plenty of Room in the Family

Once you were not a people . . . now you are the people of God.
— I Peter 2:10a

Gloria Gaither
William J. Gaither

PLENTY OF ROOM
William J. Gaither

Plen-ty of room in the fam - ily, Room for the young and the old;

Plen-ty of hap - pi-ness, plen-ty of love, Plen-ty of room in the fold.

Fine

1. There's plen-ty of food at the ta - ble, No need to e-con-o-mize there; There's all you can hold and there's
2. *There's lots to be done in the fam - ily, A job that will fit ev-ery man;* There's car-ing and lift - ing and
3. If you're lone-ly and look - ing for friend - ship, If you're lost and you want to be found, There's plen-ty of room in the

© Copyright 1974 by William J. Gaither. All rights reserved. Used by permission.

THE CHURCH—FAMILY OF BELIEVERS

D.C. al Fine

1. plen-ty be-sides, The store-house will nev-er be bare.
2. lov-ing to do, So pitch in and do all you can.
3. fam-ily of God, There's plen-ty of love to go 'round.

Psalm 15 — 553

Who is the one, O Lord, that remains a part
　　of Your kingdom?
What are the prerequisites for membership
　　in Your family?

It is that one who walks circumspectly—
　　and in obedience to Your precepts and principles.
He must be open and honest before God and man.
He must speak and act in love toward his neighbor.
He cannot condone that which is evil
　　and must not participate in that
　　which promotes injustice.
He must listen to his brother's griefs
　　and complaints.
He must seek to lighten his burden
　　and to share in his sorrow and pain.
He must reach out to heal rather than to hurt,
　　to be kind and gentle to all who cross his path.

Those who lovingly relate to God and fellowman
　　will never be separated from the family of God.

　　　　　　　　　　　—Leslie Brandt

Hear Our Prayer, O Lord — 554

Hear our prayer, O Lord;
Incline Thine ear to us
And grant us Thy peace. Amen.

　　　　　　　　　　　—Traditional

THE CHURCH—FAMILY OF BELIEVERS

555 Built on the Rock

. . . they drank of the Spiritual Rock . . . and that Rock is Christ. — I Corinthians 10:4

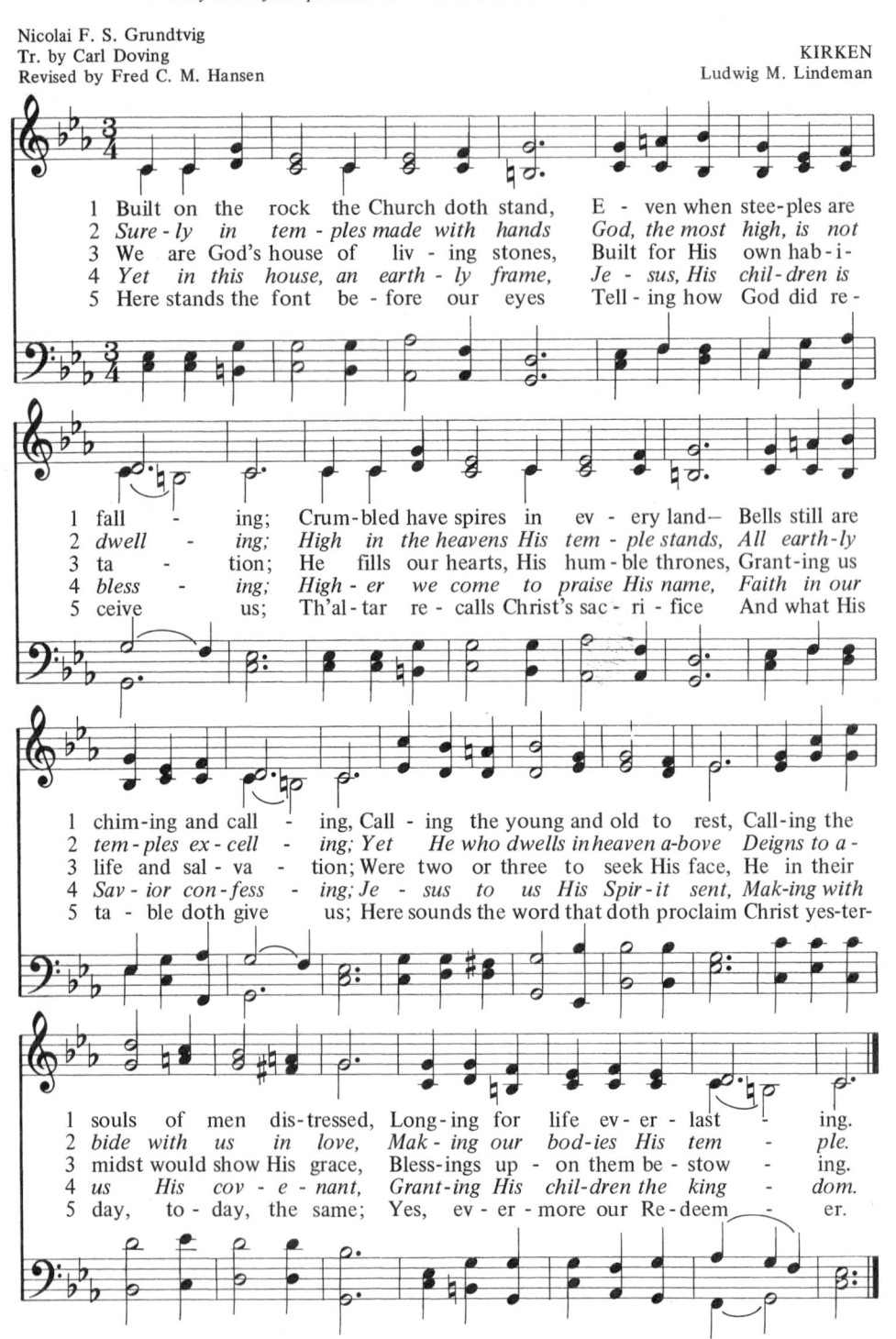

Nicolai F. S. Grundtvig
Tr. by Carl Doving
Revised by Fred C. M. Hansen

KIRKEN
Ludwig M. Lindeman

1. Built on the rock the Church doth stand, E-ven when stee-ples are fall-ing; Crum-bled have spires in ev-ery land— Bells still are chim-ing and call-ing, Call-ing the young and old to rest, Call-ing the souls of men dis-tressed, Long-ing for life ev-er-last-ing.

2. *Sure-ly in tem-ples made with hands God, the most high, is not dwell-ing; High in the heavens His tem-ple stands, All earth-ly tem-ples ex-cell-ing; Yet He who dwells in heaven a-bove Deigns to a-bide with us in love, Mak-ing our bod-ies His tem-ple.*

3. We are God's house of liv-ing stones, Built for His own hab-i-ta-tion; He fills our hearts, His hum-ble thrones, Grant-ing us life and sal-va-tion; Were two or three to seek His face, He in their midst would show His grace, Bless-ings up-on them be-stow-ing.

4. *Yet in this house, an earth-ly frame, Je-sus, His chil-dren is bless-ing; High-er we come to praise His name, Faith in our Sav-ior con-fess-ing; Je-sus to us His Spir-it sent, Mak-ing with us His cov-e-nant, Grant-ing His chil-dren the king-dom.*

5. Here stands the font be-fore our eyes Tell-ing how God did re-ceive us; Th'al-tar re-calls Christ's sac-ri-fice And what His ta-ble doth give us; Here sounds the word that doth proclaim Christ yes-ter-day, to-day, the same; Yes, ev-er-more our Re-deem-er.

THE CHURCH—FAMILY OF BELIEVERS

There's a Quiet Understanding

556

I will pray with the understanding, . . . also, I will sing with the understanding . . . . — I Corinthians 14:15

QUIET UNDERSTANDING

Tedd Smith

Tedd Smith

1 There's a qui-et un-der-stand-ing, When we're gath-ered in the Spir-it, It's a prom-ise that He gives us, When we gath-er in His name. There's a love we feel in Je-sus, There's a man-na that He feeds us, It's a prom-ise that He gives us When we gath-er in His name.

2 And we know when we're to-geth-er, shar-ing love and un-der-stand-ing, That our broth-ers and our sis-ters Feel the one-ness that He brings. Thank You, thank You, thank You, Je-sus, For the way You love and feed us, For the man-y ways You lead us, Thank You, thank You, Lord.

Copyright © 1973 by Hope Publishing Co. All rights reserved. Used by permission.

THE CHURCH—FAMILY OF BELIEVERS

557 Christ Is Made the Sure Foundation

And built upon the foundation . . . Jesus Christ himself being the chief cornerstone.
—Ephesians 2:20

Latin: 7th Century
Tr. by John M. Neale

REGENT SQUARE
Henry T. Smart

1. Christ is made the sure foun-da-tion, Christ the head and cor-ner-stone, Chos-en of the Lord and prec-ious, Bind-ing all the Church in one, Ho-ly Zi-on's help for-ev-er, And her con-fi-dence a-lone.

2. *To this tem-ple, where we call Thee, Come, O Lord of hosts, to-day; With ac-cus-tomed lov-ing-kind-ness Hear Thy peo-ple as they pray, And Thy full-est ben-e-dic-tion Shed with-in its walls al-way.*

3. Here vouch-safe to all Thy serv-ants What they ask of Thee to gain, What they gain from Thee for-ev-er With the bless-ed to re-tain, And here-aft-er in Thy glo-ry Ev-er-more with Thee to reign.

4. *Laud and hon-or to the Fa-ther, Laud and hon-or to the Son, Laud and hon-or to the Spir-it, Ev-er three and ev-er one, One in might and one in glo-ry, While un-end-ing a-ges run. A-men.*

THE CHURCH–FAMILY OF BELIEVERS

The People of God 558

My dear people, let us love one another since love comes from God and everyone who loves is begotten by God and knows God. Anyone who fails to love can never have known God, because God is love. God's love for us was revealed when God sent into the world His only Son so that we could have life through Him; this is the love I mean: not our love for God, but God's love for us when He sent His Son to be the sacrifice that takes our sins away. My dear people, since God has loved us so much, we too should love one another. No one has ever seen God; but as long as we love one another God will live in us and His love will be complete in us. We can know that we are living in Him and He is living in us because He lets us share His Spirit.

We ourselves saw and we testify that the Father sent His Son as Savior of the world. If anyone acknowledges that Jesus is the Son of God, God lives in Him, and He in God. We ourselves have known and put our faith in God's love towards ourselves. God is love and anyone who lives in love lives in God, and God lives in Him. Love will come to its perfection in us when we can face the day of judgement without fear; because even in this world we have become as He is. In love there can be no fear, but fear is driven out by perfect love: because to fear is to expect punishment, and anyone who is afraid is still imperfect in love. We are to love, then because He loved us first. Anyone who says, "I love God", and hates his brother, is a liar, since a man who does not love the brother that he can see cannot love God, whom he has never seen. So this is the commandment that He has given us, that anyone who loves God must also love his brother.

— 1 John 4:7-21 (JB)

Come, Holy Spirit, Dove Divine 559

We are buried with Him in baptism. — Romans 6:4

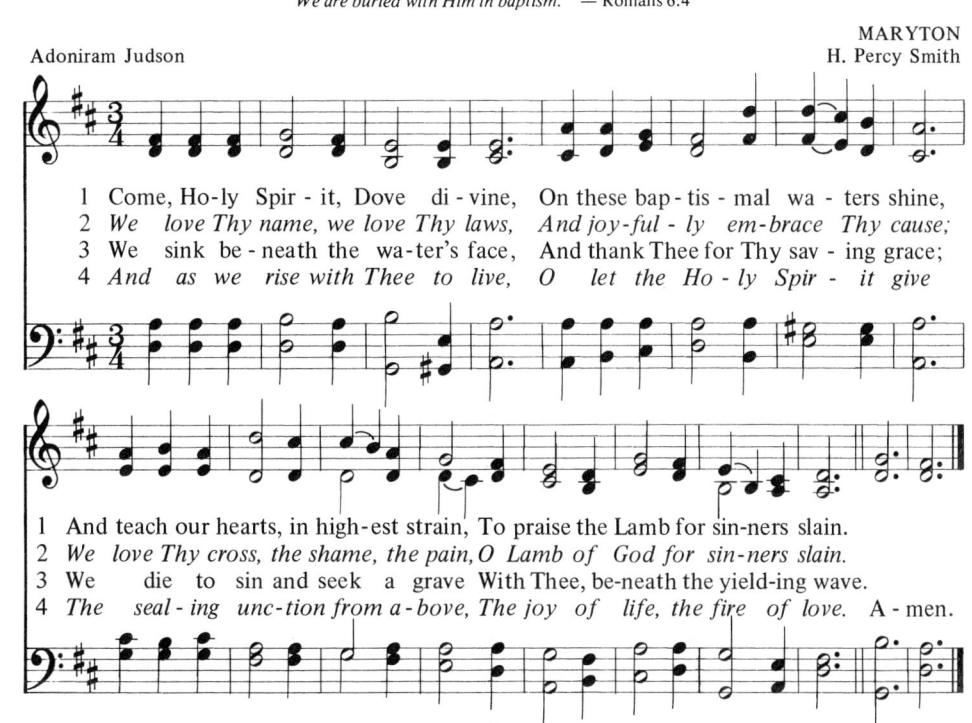

Adoniram Judson

MARYTON
H. Percy Smith

1 Come, Ho-ly Spir-it, Dove di-vine, On these bap-tis-mal wa-ters shine,
2 We love Thy name, we love Thy laws, And joy-ful-ly em-brace Thy cause;
3 We sink be-neath the wa-ter's face, And thank Thee for Thy sav-ing grace;
4 And as we rise with Thee to live, O let the Ho-ly Spir-it give

1 And teach our hearts, in high-est strain, To praise the Lamb for sin-ners slain.
2 We love Thy cross, the shame, the pain, O Lamb of God for sin-ners slain.
3 We die to sin and seek a grave With Thee, be-neath the yield-ing wave.
4 The seal-ing unc-tion from a-bove, The joy of life, the fire of love. A-men.

THE CHURCH—FAMILY OF BELIEVERS

560 Blest Be the Tie That Binds

Ye are the body of Christ and members in particular. . . . — I Corinthians 12:27

John Fawcett

DENNIS
Johann G. Naegeli
Arranged by Lowell Mason

1. Blest be the tie that binds Our hearts in Chris-tian love;
   The fel-low-ship of kin-dred minds Is like to that a-bove.
2. Be-fore our Fa-ther's throne We pour our ar-dent prayers;
   Our fears, our hopes, our aims are one, Our com-forts and our cares.
3. We share each oth-er's woes, Each oth-er's bur-dens bear;
   And oft-en for each oth-er flows The sym-pa-thiz-ing tear.
4. From sor-row, toil, and pain, And sin we shall be free;
   And per-fect love and joy shall reign Through all e-ter-ni-ty. A-men.

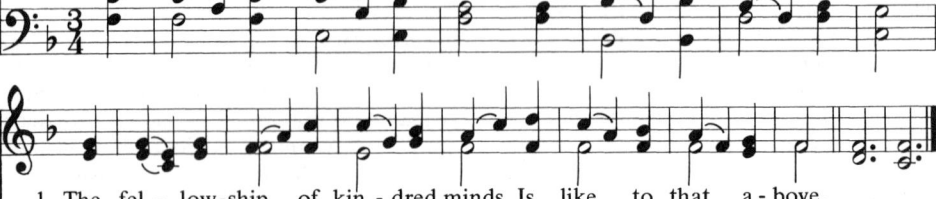

561 Thanksgiving

Thank You, Father, for Your magnificence in nature.
Thank You, Father, for the inner promptings of Your Spirit.
Thank You, Father, for fresh truth to live by.
Thank You, Father, for people whose lives illustrate Your word.
Thank You, Father, for this church to which I belong,
    for those who help me,
    intercede for me,
    support me,
    love me,
    inspire me.
Lord, I cannot live as a Christian without them, for I need that part of Yourself that You have placed within them.
And they cannot live without me, because they need the gifts that You have deposited in me.
Lord, free us of the selfishness, the self-centeredness, the ego-trips, the independence of spirit that keeps us from binding ourselves into one.
Lord, help us to think first of those things which will benefit others before we begin listing our own needs.
Give us grace to live in such a way that we *draw* attention to You. Amen.

—Bryan Jeffery Leech

THE CHURCH—FAMILY OF BELIEVERS

Two Communion Readings

I Corinthians 11:17-29 — 562

    The teaching I gave you
was given me personally by the Lord Himself,
and it was this:

        the Lord Jesus,
in the same night in which He was betrayed,
    took bread and when He had given thanks
    He broke it and said,
"This is My body — and it is for you.
Do this in remembrance of Me."

    Similarly, when supper was ended,
He took the cup saying,
"This cup is the new agreement made by My blood:
do this, whenever you drink it,
in remembrance of Me."

This can only mean that whenever you eat this bread and drink this cup,
you are proclaiming the Lord's death until He comes again.

So that, whoever eats the bread or drinks the cup of the Lord
    without proper reverence
    is sinning against the body and blood of the Lord.

No, a man should thoroughly examine himself,
    and only then
should he eat the bread or drink of the cup.
He that eats and drinks carelessly
is eating and drinking a condemnation of himself,
    for he is blind to the presence of the Body.

—(J.B. Phillips)

Revelation 22:16-17 — 563

"I, Jesus,
  have sent my angel to you with this testimony for the churches.
I am the root and the offspring of David,
    the bright morning star."

    The Spirit and the Bride say, "Come."
    And let him who hears say, "Come."
        And let him who is thirsty come,
        let him who desires
        take the water of life without price.

—(RSV)

THE CHURCH—FAMILY OF BELIEVERS

564 Let Us Break Bread Together

He took bread and blessed it, and brake, and gave to them.
— Luke 24:30

American Folk Hymn

LET US BREAK BREAD
American Folk Melody

1. Let us break bread to-geth-er on our knees;
2. *Let us drink wine to-geth-er on our knees;*
3. Let us praise God to-geth-er on our knees;

When I fall on my knees, With my face to the ris-ing sun, O Lord, have mer-cy on me.

COMMUNION

A Hymn of Joy We Sing 565

... I went with them to the house of God with ... joy and praise. — Psalm 42:4

Based on Matthew 26:30
Aaron R. Wolfe

SCHUMANN
Mason and Webb's *Cantica Laudis*

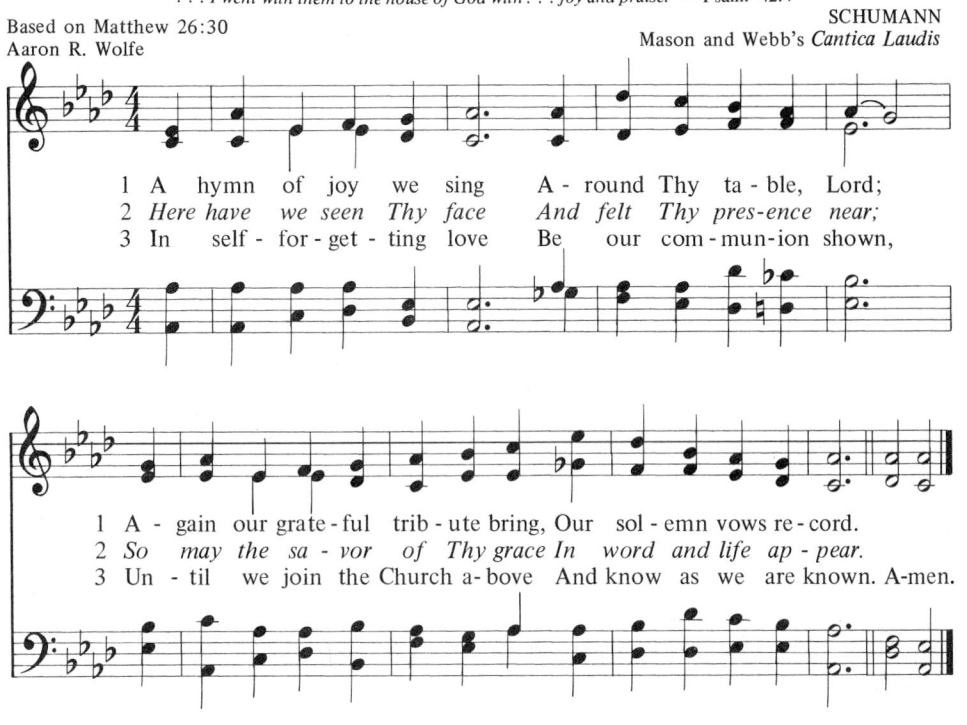

1. A hymn of joy we sing A-round Thy ta-ble, Lord;
   A-gain our grate-ful trib-ute bring, Our sol-emn vows re-cord.
2. *Here have we seen Thy face And felt Thy pres-ence near;*
   So may the sa-vor of Thy grace In word and life ap-pear.
3. In self-for-get-ting love Be our com-mun-ion shown,
   Un-til we join the Church a-bove And know as we are known. A-men.

One Solitary Life 566

Born in an obscure village, He was the child of a peasant woman. He worked in a carpenter shop until He was thirty years old, and then for three years He travelled around the country, stopping long enough to talk and to listen to people, and help where He could. He never wrote a book, He never had a hit record, He never went to college, He never ran for public office, He never had a family, or owned a house. He never did any of the things that usually accompany greatness. He had no credentials but Himself. But when He was only thirty-three years old, the tide of public opinion turned against Him, and His friends all rejected Him. When He was arrested, very few wanted anything to do with Him. After the trial, He was executed by the State along with admitted thieves. Only because a generous friend offered his own cemetery plot was there any place to bury Him. This all happened nineteen centuries ago, and yet today He is the leading figure of the human race, and the ultimate example of love. Now it is no exaggeration to say that all the armies that have ever marched, all the navies that have ever set sail, all the rulers that have ever ruled, all the kings that have ever reigned on this earth, all put together have not affected the life of man on earth like this One Solitary Life.

—Fred Bock (alt.)

COMMUNION

567 Here, O My Lord, I See Thee Face to Face

Horatius Bonar
Thy Face, Lord, will I seek. —Psalm 27:8
PENITENTIA
Edward Dearle

1. Here, O my Lord, I see Thee face to face,
   Here would I touch and handle things unseen;
   Here grasp with firmer hand eternal grace,
   And all my weariness upon Thee lean.

2. Here would I feed upon the bread of God,
   Here drink with Thee the royal wine of heaven;
   Here would I lay aside each earthly load,
   Here taste afresh the calm of sin forgiv'n.

3. I have no help but Thine, nor do I need
   Another arm save Thine to lean upon;
   It is enough, my Lord, enough indeed—
   My strength is in Thy might, Thy might alone.

4. Mine is the sin, but Thine the righteousness,
   Mine is the guilt, but Thine the cleansing blood;
   Here is my robe, my refuge, and my peace—
   Thy blood, Thy righteousness, O Lord, my God. A-men.

COMMUNION

We Dedicate This Temple

I have built a house of habitation for thee. — II Chronicles 6:2a

Ernest K. Emurian

568

AURELIA
Samuel S. Wesley

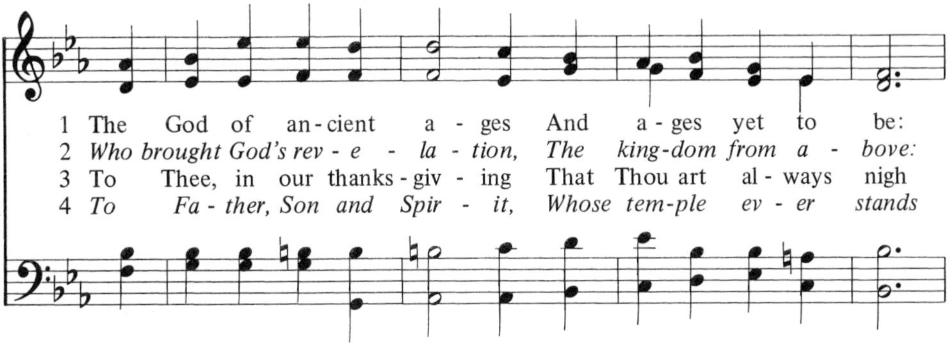

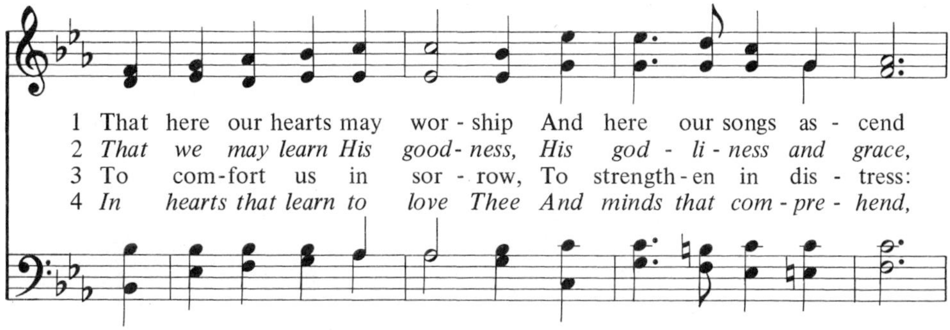

1. We dedicate this temple, O Father, unto Thee,
The God of ancient ages And ages yet to be:
That here our hearts may worship And here our songs ascend
In loving adoration And praise that knows no end.

2. We dedicate this temple To Christ, the Lord of love,
Who brought God's revelation, The kingdom from above:
That we may learn His goodness, His godliness and grace,
Who holds all men and nations Within His love's embrace.

3. We dedicate this temple, O Spirit from on high,
To Thee, in our thanksgiving That Thou art always nigh
To comfort us in sorrow, To strengthen in distress:
That we, through truth and mercy, May walk in holiness.

4. We dedicate this temple, This labor of our hands,
To Father, Son and Spirit, Whose temple ever stands
In hearts that learn to love Thee And minds that comprehend,
In wills empowered to witness Thy kingdom without end! Amen.

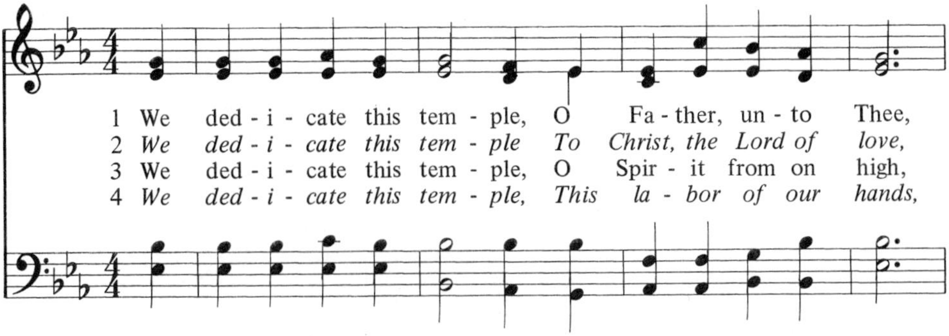

Words copyright 1952 by Ernest K. Emurian. Used by permission.

DEDICATION SERVICES

569 Welcoming a Child

The Child's Parents: Lord, You have trusted us with one of Your priceless treasures, a human child. You have allowed us to share with You in the miracle of creation and now that miracle has become flesh—and we hold it in our arms. We are excited and full of joy! But we are also fearful. O, Lord, we are imperfect parents in such an imperfect world. Speak to us. Assure us of Your nearness—now, as we wait with this child, speak to us.

Minister: *Unless you are converted and become as little children, you shall not enter into the kingdom of heaven. Whosoever shall humble himself as this little child, the same is the greatest in the kingdom of heaven. And whoever shall receive one such little child in My name receives Me.* [1]

Choir: Train up a child in the way he should go: and when he is old, he will not depart from it. [2] I am the Way, the Truth, and the Life. [3]

Minister: *And all thy children shall be taught of the Lord, and great shall be the peace of your children.* [4]

Choir: Cast all your cares upon Him for He cares for you.

People: *Trust in the Lord with all your heart; and lean not to your own understanding. In all your ways acknowledge Him, and He shall direct your paths.* [5]

Prayer by Layman: Lord, we have here in our church family a new child, a new person, a new soul. The responsibility for this little person is too much for any two parents alone. They need the loving support of the fellowship of believers as they train and guide and nurture little _(name)_ . We give ourselves today, Lord, to that task. We accept the responsibility of helping to bring _(name)_ to maturity in You. We will uphold him (her) with our love, teach him (her) the word of God, encourage him (her) when he (she) fails, and we will be careful not to bruise this tender bud by harsh words, quick judgments, and cruel criticism. For truly, Father, this is our child, and we want to protect and teach him (her) and to bring him (her) to the moment when he (she) will choose for himself (herself) to know You as Savior and Lord of his (her) life. Amen.

— Gloria Gaither

1. Matthew 18:3-5
2. Proverbs 22:6
3. John 14:6
4. Isaiah 54:13
5. Proverbs 3:5 (KJV)

DEDICATION SERVICES

Thank God for Children 570

Children possess an uncanny ability to cut to the core of the issue, to expose life to the bone, and strip away the barnacles that cling to the hull of our too sophisticated pseudo-civilization. One reason for this, I believe, is that children have not mastered our fine art of deception, that we call "finesse." Another is that they are so "lately come from God" that faith and trust are second nature to them. They have not acquired the obstructions to faith that come with education; they possess instead unrefined wisdom, a gift from God.

—Gloria Gaither

This Child We Dedicate to Thee 571

And Hannah prayed . . . and the child Samuel grew on, and was in favor with God . . . and man.
— I Samuel 2:1 & 26

From the German
Tr. by Samuel Gilman

FEDERAL STREET
Henry K. Oliver

1. This child we dedicate to Thee, O God of grace and purity! In Thy great love its life prolong, Shield it, we pray, from sin and wrong.
2. O may Thy Spirit gently draw Its willing soul to keep Thy law; May virtue, piety, and truth Dawn even with its dawning youth. A-men.

DEDICATION SERVICES

572 Renew Thy Church, Her Ministries Restore

... Thou hath lost thy first love. — Revelation 2:4

Kenneth Lorne Cober

ALL IS WELL
J. T. White's "Sacred Harp"

1. Renew Thy church, her ministries restore: Both to serve and adore.
2. *Teach us Thy Word, reveal its truth divine; On our path let it shine.*
3. Teach us to pray, for Thou art ever near; Thy still voice let us hear.
4. *Teach us to love, with strength of heart and mind, Everyone, all mankind.*

1. Make her again as salt throughout the land, And as light from a stand.
2. *Tell of Thy works, Thy mighty acts of grace; From each page show Thy face.*
3. Our souls are restless till they rest in Thee: This our glad destiny.
4. *Break down old walls of prejudice and hate; Leave us not to our fate.*

1. 'Mid somber shadows of the night Where greed and hatred spread their blight,
2. *As Thou hast loved us, sent Thy Son, And our salvation now is won,*
3. Before Thy presence keep us still, That we may find for us Thy will
4. *As Thou hast loved and given Thy life To end hostility and strife,*

1. O send us forth with power endued: Help us, Lord, be renewed!
2. *O let our hearts with love be stirred: Help us, Lord, know Thy Word!*
3. And seek Thy guidance every day: Teach us, Lord, how to pray!
4. *O share Thy grace from heaven above: Teach us, Lord, how to love!* A-men.

Words copyright 1960 by Kenneth L. Cober. Used by permission.

RENEWAL AND REVIVAL

Renewal 573

Renewal begins
when a person is exposed to the forces that will stretch him
and help him to discover the power of Christ
in the relationships where he feels least secure.
A church discovers renewal when it preaches and acts
in a way which motivates the members to move from their specialties
into other dimensions of life.

—Keith Miller & Bruce Larson

Revive Us Again 574

Wilt Thou not revive us again; that Thy people may rejoice in Thee? — Psalm 85:6

REVIVE US AGAIN
William P. Mackay / John J. Husband

1. We praise Thee, O God, for the Son of Thy love,
   For Jesus who died and is now gone above.
2. We praise Thee, O God, for Thy Spirit of light,
   Who has shown us our Savior and banished our night.
3. All glory and praise to the Lamb that was slain,
   Who has taken our sins and has cleansed every stain.
4. Revive us again— fill each heart with Thy love;
   May each soul be rekindled with fire from above.

Hallelujah, Thine the glory! Hallelujah, amen! Hallelujah, Thine the glory! Revive us again. A-men.

RENEWAL AND REVIVAL

575 If My People Will Pray

If My people . . . pray and seek My face . . . I will forgive . . . — II Chronicles 7:14

Based on II Chronicles 7:14

CHRONICLES
Jimmy Owens

Then will I hear and will forgive, forgive their sin.
If my people which are called by My name, Shall humble themselves, shall humble themselves and pray;
I will forgive their sin, I will forgive their sin,
I will forgive their sin, And heal their land.

RENEWAL AND REVIVAL

576 Thou, Whose Purpose Is to Kindle

But who may abide the day of His coming? . . . for He is a refiner's fire.
— Malachi 3:2, 3

Based on Luke 12:49
David Elton Trueblood

HYFRYDOL
Rowland H. Prichard

1. Thou, whose purpose is to kindle: Now ignite us with Thy fire; While the earth awaits Thy burning calmness, Rouse us with redemptive shame; Baptize with Thy fiery Spirit, Crown our lives with tongues of flame.

2. *Thou, who in Thy holy gospel Will that man should truly live: Make us sense our share of failure, Our tranquility forgive. Teach us courage as we struggle In all liberating strife; Lift the smallness of our vision By Thine own abundant life.*

3. Thou, who still a sword delivers Rather than a placid peace: With Thy sharpened word disturb us, From complacency release! Save us now from satisfaction When we privately are free, Yet are undisturbed in spirit By our brother's misery.

"Baptism by Fire" in "The Incendiary Fellowship" by Elton Trueblood. Copyright © 1967 by Elton Trueblood. By permission of Harper & Row, Publishers, Inc.

RENEWAL AND REVIVAL

Comparison 577

Jesus Christ is unique, and one cannot be in His presence and not reveal the man he really is. Jesus pulls each person from behind his mask. In the exposure of that bleeding love on the cross, men become what they really are.

You may think you are wonderful until you stand in the presence of the One who is purity itself. It is the pure light of God that pierces a man. You can keep up your pretense of being holy until you stand in that light. Then immediately there is nowhere to hide, all your masks are torn away, all your hollow smiles fade.

Revival means to be exposed for what we are. The presence of the Lord is revealing.

—Festo Kivengere

II Chronicles 7:8-18 578

For the next seven days, they celebrated the Tabernacle Festival, with large crowds coming in from all over Israel; they arrived from as far away as Hamath at one end of the country to the brook of Egypt at the other. A final religious service was held on the eighth day. Then, on October 7, he sent the people home, joyful and happy because the Lord had been so good to David and Solomon and to His people Israel.

So Solomon finished building the Temple as well as his own palace. He completed what he had planned to do.

One night the Lord appeared to Solomon and told him, "I have heard your prayer and have chosen this Temple as the place where I want you to sacrifice to Me. If I shut up the heavens so that there is no rain, or if I command the locust swarms to eat up all of your crops, or if I send an epidemic among you, then if my people will humble themselves and pray, and search for me, and turn from their wicked ways, I will hear them from heaven and forgive their sins and heal their land. I will listen, wide awake, to every prayer made in this place. For I have chosen this Temple and sanctified it to be my home forever; my eyes and my heart shall always be here.

As for yourself, if you will follow me as your father David did, then I will see to it that you and your descendants will always be kings of Israel.

—(LB)

579 O Breath of Life

... He breathed on them and saith unto them: Receive Ye the Holy Ghost. — John 20:22

Bessie Porter Head

BLOMQVIST
Joel Blomqvist

1. O Breath of Life, come sweeping through us,
   Revive Your Church with life and power;
   O Breath of Life, come, cleanse, renew us,
   And fit Your Church to meet this hour.

2. O Wind of God, come bend us, break us,
   'Til humbly we confess our need;
   Then in Your tenderness remake us,
   Revive, restore— for this we plead.

3. O Breath of Love, come breathe within us,
   Renewing thought and will and heart;
   Come, love of Christ, afresh to win us,
   Revive Your Church in every part.

4. O Heart of Christ, once broken for us,
   In You we find our strength and rest;
   Our broken contrite hearts now solace,
   And let Your waiting Church be blest.

5. Revive us, Lord! Is zeal abating
   While harvest fields are vast and white?
   Revive us, Lord— the world is waiting!
   Equip Your Church to spread the light. A-men.

RENEWAL AND REVIVAL

There Shall Be Showers of Blessing 580

Who hath blessed us with all spiritual blessings. — Ezekiel 34:26

Daniel W. Whittle
SHOWERS OF BLESSING
James McGranahan

1. There shall be show-ers of bless-ing: This is the prom-ise of love;
2. *There shall be show-ers of bless-ing— Pre-cious re-viv-ing a-gain;*
3. There shall be show-ers of bless-ing: Send them up-on us, O Lord;
4. *There shall be show-ers of bless-ing: O, that to-day they might fall,*

1. There shall be sea-sons re-fresh-ing, Sent from the Sav-ior a-bove.
2. *O-ver the hills and the val-leys, Sound of a-bun-dance of rain.*
3. Grant to us now a re-fresh-ing, Come, and now hon-or Thy Word.
4. *Now as to God we're con-fess-ing, Now, as on Je-sus we call!*

Show-ers of bless-ing, Show-ers of bless-ing we need:

Mer-cy-drops 'round us are fall-ing, But for the show-ers we plead.

RENEWAL AND REVIVAL

581 It Is No Secret

*For I am persuaded that none of these things are hidden . . .
for this thing was not done in a corner.* — Acts 26:26

IT IS NO SECRET
Stuart Hamblen

Stuart Hamblen

1 The chimes of time ring out the news; An-oth-er day is through.
2 There is no night, for in His light You'll nev-er walk a-lone.

1 Some-one slipped and fell. Was that some-one you? You may have longed for
2 Al-ways feel at home where-ev-er you may roam. There is no power can

1 add-ed strength, your cour-age to re-new. Do not be dis-
2 con-quer you, while God is on your side. Just take Him at His

1 heart-ened, for I bring hope to you. It is no se-cret
2 prom-ise; Don't run a-way and hide.

what God can do. What He's done for oth-ers, He'll do for

© Copyright 1950 by Duchess Music Corp. International copyright secured. All rights reserved. Used by permission.
ENCOURAGEMENT

you. With arms wide o - pen, He'll par-don you,

It is no se - cret what God can do.

Jeremiah's Hope Within Hopelessness

582

Jerusalem had been devastated by Nebuchadnezzar.

He was boxed-in with gloom,—a proud city destroyed,—friends taken captive,—once-beautiful people left rotting in the streets,—infants with parched tongues cleaving to roofs of mouths,—some so hungry they turned to cannibalism. He penned his lamentation.

But then in his "Easter Eve" of the human soul, when all is lost, he senses *hope* within *hopelessness.* This soul weighed down by God's judgment springs forth with a confidence in the Lord's unconquerable mercy.

"And therefore I have hope: The steadfast love of the Lord never ceases. His mercies never come to an end!" Praise be to God for such hope!

—John A. Huffman, Jr.
Lamentations 3:21, 22

ENCOURAGEMENT

583   God's Power in Our Weakness

Worship Leader: *And He said unto me, My grace is sufficient for thee: for My strength is made perfect in weakness.*

People: He said . . . "I am with you; that is all you need. My power shows up best in weak people."

Worship Leader: *Most gladly will I glory in my infirmities that the power of Christ may rest upon me.*

People: Now I am glad to boast about how weak I am; I am glad to be a living demonstration of Christ's power, instead of showing off my own power and abilities.

Worship Leader: *For when I am weak, then am I strong.*

People: For when I am weak, then I am strong—the less I have, the more I depend on Him!

All: Yes. God's power shows up best in weak people. So I boast of my weakness, for because of it others are able to know for sure that the power and glory they see in me has got to be the *power of God*—and if that power can be present in one such as I, it surely is available to them as well!

—Gloria Gaither

584   God Is at Work Within You

For it is God who worketh in you . . . — Philippians 2:13

Philippians 2:13

TOPEKA
Fred Bock

God is at work within you, helping you want to obey Him, And then helping you do what He wants, helping you do what He wants you to do.

Text used by permission of Tyndale House Foundation.
© Copyright 1971 by Fred Bock Music Company. All rights reserved. Used by permission.

ENCOURAGEMENT

Only Believe 585

It is Thy Father's good pleasure to give you the kingdom.
— Luke 12:32

Paul Rader

ONLY BELIEVE
Paul Rader

1. Fear not, little flock, from the cross to the throne, From death into life He went for His own; All power in earth, all power above, Is given to Him for the flock of His love.
2. *Fear not, little flock, He goeth ahead, Your Shepherd selecteth the path you must tread; The waters of Marah He'll sweeten for thee— He drank all the bitter in Gethsemane.*
3. Fear not, little flock, whatever your lot; He enters all rooms, "the doors being shut." He never forsakes, He never is gone— So count on His presence in darkness and dawn.

Only believe, only believe; All things are possible, only believe;
Only believe, only believe; All things are possible, only believe.

Copyright 1921 by Paul Rader. © Renewed 1949 by Mary C. Rader. Assigned to The Rodeheaver Co. Used by permission.

ENCOURAGEMENT

You, my brothers, were called to be free. But do not use your freedom to indulge your sinful nature; rather, serve one another in love. The entire law is summed up in a single command: "Love your neighbor as yourself." If you keep on biting and devouring each other, watch out or you will be destroyed by each other.

So I say, live by the Spirit, and you will not gratify the desires of your sinful nature. For the sinful nature desires what is contrary to the Spirit, and the Spirit what is contrary to the sinful nature. They are in conflict with each other, so that you do not do what you want. But if you are led by the Spirit, you are not under law.

The acts of the sinful nature are obvious: sexual immorality, impurity and debauchery; idolatry and witchcraft; hatred, discord, jealousy, fits of rage, selfish ambition, dissensions, factions and envy; drunkenness, orgies, and the like. I warn you, as I did before, that those who live like this will not inherit the kingdom of God.

But the fruit of the Spirit is love, joy, peace, patience, kindness, goodness, faithfulness, gentleness and self-control. Against such things there is no law. Those who belong to Christ Jesus have crucified their sinful nature with its passions and desires. Since we live by the Spirit, let us keep in step with the Spirit. Let us not become conceited, provoking and envying each other.

Brothers, if a man is trapped in some sin, you who are spiritual should restore him gently. But watch yourself; you also may be tempted. Carry each other's burdens, and in this way you will fulfill the law of Christ.

—(NIV)

He Keeps Me Singing

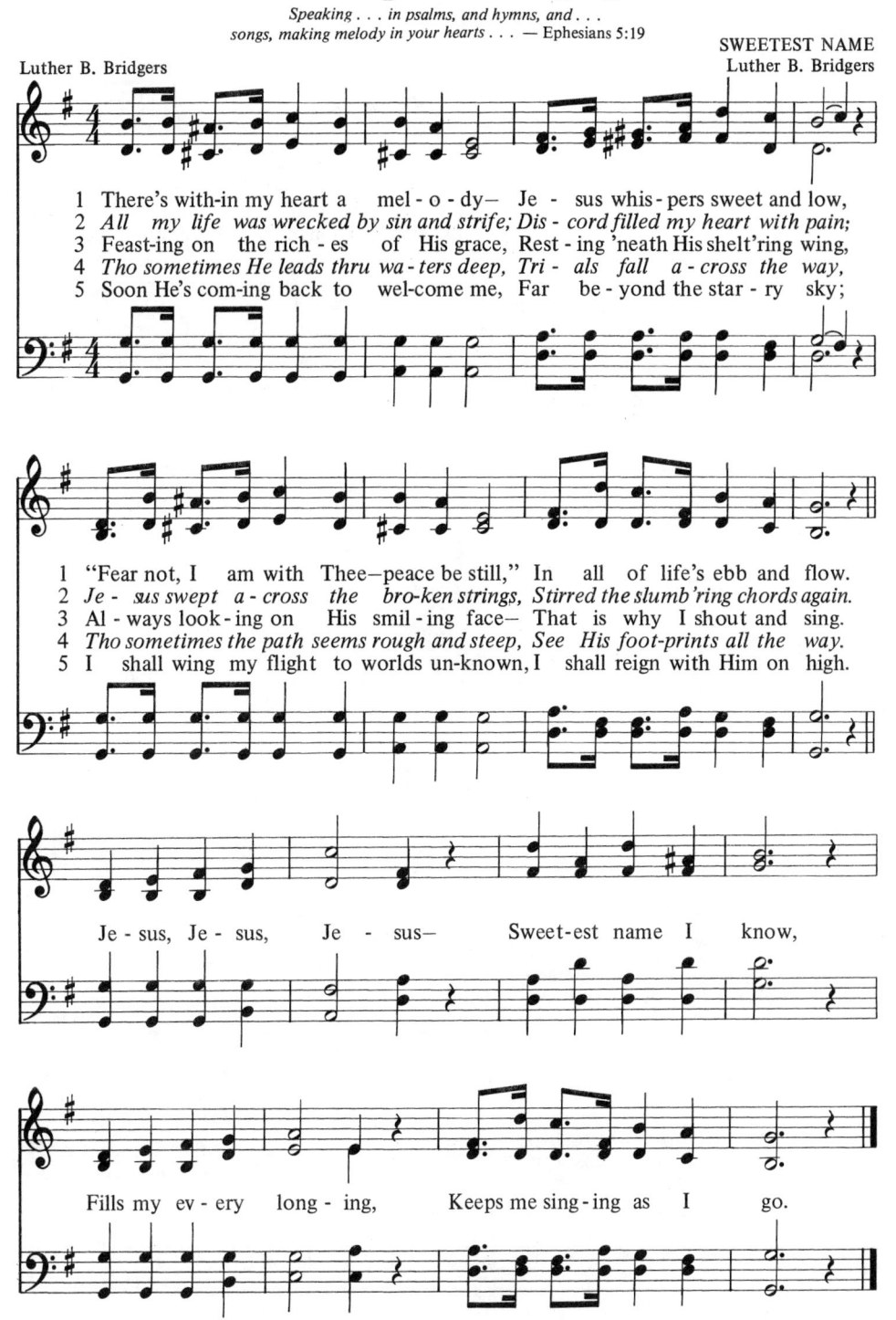

587

*Speaking . . . in psalms, and hymns, and . . .
songs, making melody in your hearts . . .* — Ephesians 5:19

SWEETEST NAME

Luther B. Bridgers

Luther B. Bridgers

1. There's with-in my heart a mel-o-dy— Je-sus whis-pers sweet and low,
2. *All my life was wrecked by sin and strife; Dis-cord filled my heart with pain;*
3. Feast-ing on the rich-es of His grace, Rest-ing 'neath His shelt'ring wing,
4. *Tho sometimes He leads thru wa-ters deep, Tri-als fall a-cross the way,*
5. Soon He's com-ing back to wel-come me, Far be-yond the star-ry sky;

1. "Fear not, I am with Thee—peace be still," In all of life's ebb and flow.
2. *Je-sus swept a-cross the bro-ken strings, Stirred the slumb'ring chords again.*
3. Al-ways look-ing on His smil-ing face— That is why I shout and sing.
4. *Tho sometimes the path seems rough and steep, See His foot-prints all the way.*
5. I shall wing my flight to worlds un-known, I shall reign with Him on high.

Je-sus, Je-sus, Je-sus— Sweet-est name I know,

Fills my ev-ery long-ing, Keeps me sing-ing as I go.

© Copyright 1910. Renewal 1937 Broadman Press. All rights reserved. Used by permission.

FELLOWSHIP WITH GOD

588 In the Garden

And they heard the voice of the Lord walking in the garden...
— Genesis 3:8

C. Austin Miles

GARDEN
C. Austin Miles

1. I come to the gar-den a-lone, While the dew is still on the ros-es; And the voice I hear, fall-ing on my ear, The Son of God dis-clos-es.
2. *He speaks, and the sound of His voice Is so sweet the birds hush their sing-ing, And the mel-o-dy that He gave to me With-in my heart is ring-ing.*
3. *I'd stay in the gar-den with Him Though the night a-round me be fall-ing, But He bids me go; through the voice of woe, His voice to me is call-ing.*

And He walks with me, and He talks with me, And He tells me I am His own; And the joy we share as we tar-ry there, None oth-er has ev-er known.

Copyright 1912 by Hall-Mack Co. © Copyright renewal 1940 (extended). The Rodeheaver Co., owner. All rights reserved. Used by permission.

FELLOWSHIP WITH GOD

The Beatitudes

$\mathcal{N}$ow when He saw the crowds,
He went up on a mountainside
and sat down.
His disciples came to Him,
and He began to teach them,
saying:

"Blessed are the poor in spirit,
for theirs is the kingdom of heaven.
Blessed are those who mourn,
for they will be comforted.
Blessed are the meek,
for they will inherit the earth.
Blessed are those who hunger
and thirst for righteousness,
for they will be filled.
Blessed are the merciful,
for they will be shown mercy.
Blessed are the pure in heart,
for they will see God.
Blessed are the peacemakers,
for they will be called sons of God.
Blessed are those who are persecuted
because of righteousness,
for theirs is
the kingdom of heaven.
Blessed are you when people insult you,
persecute you and falsely say
all kinds of evil against you
because of Me.
Rejoice and be glad,
because great is your reward in heaven,
for in the same way
they persecuted the prophets
who were before you."

—Matthew 5:1-12 (NIV)

FELLOWSHIP WITH GOD

590 I Am His and He Is Mine

*... Yea, I have loved you with an everlasting love;
with loving kindness have I drawn thee.*
— Jeremiah 31:3

George Robinson

EVERLASTING LOVE
James Mountain

1. Loved with ev-er-last-ing love, Led by grace that love to know—
Spir-it breath-ing from a-bove, Thou hast taught me it is so!
O this full and per-fect peace From His pres-ence all di-vine—
In a love which can-not cease, I am His and He is mine; mine.

2. *Heaven a-bove is soft-er blue, Earth a-round is sweet-er green;*
Some-thing lives in ev-ery hue Christ-less eyes have nev-er seen!
Birds in song His glo-ries show, Flow'rs with deep-er beau-ties shine,
Since I know, as now I know, I am His and He is mine; mine.

3. Things that once were wild a-larms Can-not now dis-turb my rest;
Closed in ev-er-last-ing arms, Pil-lowed on the lov-ing breast!
O to lie for-ev-er here, Doubt and care and self re-sign,
While He whis-pers in my ear— I am His and He is mine; mine.

4. *His for-ev-er, on-ly His— Who the Lord and me shall part?*
Ah, with what a rest of bliss Christ can fill the lov-ing heart!
Heav'n and earth may fade and flee, First-born light in gloom de-cline,
But while God and I shall be, I am His and He is mine; mine.

FELLOWSHIP WITH GOD

Just a Closer Walk with Thee 591

For we also are weak in Him, but we shall live with Him by the power of God.
— II Corinthians 13:4

Unknown

CLOSER WALK
Traditional Folk Song

1. I am weak but Thou art strong; Je-sus, keep me from all wrong;
2. *Through this world of toil and snares,* *If I fal-ter, Lord, who cares?*
3. When my fee-ble life is o'er, Time for me will be no more;

Refrain: Just a clos-er walk with Thee, Grant it, Je-sus, is my plea,

D.C. for Refrain

1. I'll be sat-is-fied as long As I walk, let me walk close to Thee.
2. *Who with me my bur-den shares?* *None but Thee, dear Lord, none but Thee.*
3. Guide me gent-ly, safe-ly o'er To Thy king-dom shore, to Thy shore.

Refrain: Dai-ly walk-ing close to Thee, Let it be, dear Lord, let it be.

John 14 : 24-30   592

If anyone loves Me he will keep My word, and My Father will love him, and we shall come to him, and make our home with him.

Those who do not love Me do not keep My words.

And My word is not My own: it is the word of the One who sent Me.

I have said these things to you while still with you; but the Advocate, the Holy Spirit, whom the Father will send in My name, will teach you everything and remind you of all I have said to you.

Peace I bequeath to you, My own peace I give you, a peace the world cannot give, this is My gift to you.

Do not let your hearts be troubled or afraid.

You heard Me say: I am going away, and shall return.

If you loved Me you would have been glad to know that I am going to the Father, for the Father is greater than I.

I have told you this now before it happens, so that when it does happen you may believe.

I shall not talk with you any longer.

—(JB)

FELLOWSHIP WITH GOD

593   Take His Peace

Congregation:	*When the whirlwinds of doubt*
	Churn their way into your soul,
Minister:	Take His peace.
Congregation:	*When your world's reduced to ashes,*
	Leaving nothing firm and whole,
Minister:	Take His peace.
Minister:	There amidst the broken wreckage
	In the midnight of your day,
	In the apex of the stormcloud,
	He's the quiet place to stay,
Congregation & Minister:	**Take His peace, take His peace.**
Congregation:	*When your mind gropes for answers*
	To the questions that you face,
Minister:	Take His peace.
Congregation:	*When your past comes back to haunt you*
	And you need amazing grace,
Minister:	Take His peace.
Minister:	There's an answer beyond question,
	It's the truth for which you yearn:
	There's forgiveness without merit,
	There's a love you needn't earn,
Congregation & Minister:	**Take His peace, take His peace.**
Congregation:	*When your're weary of the struggle*
	And you need a place to rest,
Minister:	Take His peace.
Congregation:	*When you lose more than you're winning*
	And you're failing every test,
Minister:	Take His peace.
Minister:	There's no need to win a battle
	That's been fought and won before;
	You can lay back in the Victory,
	Freely share His boundless store,
Congregation & Minister:	**Take His peace, take His peace.**
Congregation:	*When you're worried and you're fearful*
	For the children you hold dear,
Minister:	Take His peace.
Congregation:	*Let a loving Heavenly Father*
	Share each joy and dry each tear,
Minister:	Take His peace.
Minister:	God has promised if we teach them
	And we guide them from the start,
	Then the seed of truth and peace
	Shall find rich soil in their hearts,
Congregation & Minister:	**Claim His peace, claim His peace!**

–Gloria Gaither
William J. Gaither

FELLOWSHIP WITH GOD

Anywhere with Jesus

594

... He led them... by a cloudy pillar;... and by a pillar of fire...
— Nehemiah 9:12

Jessie B. Pounds
Adapted by Helen C. Dixon

SECURITY
Daniel B. Towner

1. An-y-where with Je-sus I can safe-ly go,
   An-y-where He leads me in this world be-low;
   An-y-where with-out Him dear-est joys would fade,
   An-y-where with Je-sus I am not a-fraid.

2. *An-y-where with Je-sus I am not a-lone,*
   Oth-er friends may fail me, He is still my own;
   Though His hand may lead me o-ver drear-y ways,
   An-y-where with Je-sus is a house of praise.

3. An-y-where with Je-sus o-ver land and sea,
   Tell-ing souls in dark-ness of sal-va-tion free;
   Read-y as He sum-mons me to go or stay,
   An-y-where with Je-sus when He points the way.

An-y-where! an-y-where! Fear I can-not know;
An-y-where with Je-sus I can safe-ly go.

GUIDANCE

595 Lead On, O King Eternal

If the Lord be God, follow Him.... —I Kings 18:21

Ernest W. Shurtleff

LANCASHIRE
Henry T. Smart
Descant by John Ness Beck

Descant:
3 Lead on, Lead on, O King e-ter-nal,
For glad-ness breaks like morn-ing Wher-e'er Thy face ap-pears.
Thy cross is lift-ed o'er us, We jour-ney in its light;

1. Lead on, O King e-ter-nal, The day of march has come;
Hence-forth in fields of con-quest Thy tents shall be our home.
Through days of prep-a-ra-tion Thy grace has made us strong, And

2. *Lead on, O King e-ter-nal, Till sin's fierce war shall cease,*
And ho-li-ness shall whis-per The sweet a-men of peace.
For not with swords' loud clash-ing, Nor roll of stir-ring drums—With

3. Lead on, O King e-ter-nal, We fol-low not with fears,
For glad-ness breaks like morn-ing Wher-e'er Thy face ap-pears.
Thy cross is lift-ed o'er us, We jour-ney in its light; The

GUIDANCE

The crown awaits the con-quest: Lead on, O God of might. Lead on! A-men.

1 now, O King e-ter-nal, We lift our bat-tle song.
2 deeds of love and mer-cy The heaven-ly king-dom comes.
3 crown a-waits the con-quest: Lead on, O God of might. A-men.

Alternate Last Verse Harmonization
Arranged by John Ness Beck

3 Lead on, O King e-ter-nal, we fol-low, not with fears, For glad-ness breaks like morn-ing Where-e'er Thy face ap-pears. Thy cross is lift-ed o'er us, We jour-ney in its light; The crown a-waits the con-quest: Lead on, O God of might. A-men.

© Copyright 1976 by Paragon Associates, Inc. All rights reserved.

GUIDANCE

596 Gentle Shepherd

I am the good Shepherd and know My sheep....
— John 10:14

Gloria Gaither
William J. Gaither

GENTLE SHEPHERD
William J. Gaither

Gen-tle Shep-herd, come and lead us, For we need You to help us find our way. Gen-tle Shep-herd, come and feed us, For we need Your strength from day to day. There's no oth-er we can turn to Who can help us face an-oth-er day; Gen-tle Shep-herd, come and lead us, For we need You to help us find our way.

© Copyright 1974 by William J. Gaither. All rights reserved. Used by permission.
GUIDANCE

God Leads Us Along

597

*... And the sheep hear His voice;
and He calls His own sheep by name, and He leadeth them out.* — John 10:3

G. A. Young

GOD LEADS US
G. A. Young

1. In shad-y, green pas-tures, so rich and so sweet, God leads His dear children a-long; Where the wa-ter's cool flow bathes the wea-ry one's feet,
2. *Some-times on the mount where the sun shines so bright, God leads His dear children a-long; Some-times in the val-ley, in dark-est of night,*
3. Though sor-rows be-fall us and e-vils op-pose, God leads His dear children a-long; Thru grace we can con-quer, de-feat all our foes,

God leads His dear children a-long. Some thru the wa-ters, some thru the flood, Some thru the fire, but all thru the blood; Some thru great sor-row, but God gives a song, In the night sea-son and all the day long.

GUIDANCE

598 All the Way My Savior Leads Me

I have glorified Thee; . . . I have finished the work which thou gavest me.
— John 17:4

Fanny J. Crosby

ALL THE WAY
Robert Lowry

1. All the way my Savior leads me— What have I to ask beside?
2. *All the way my Savior leads me— Cheers each winding path I tread,*
3. All the way my Savior leads me— O the fullness of His love!

1. Can I doubt His tender mercy, Who through life has been my guide?
2. *Gives me grace for every trial, Feeds me with the living bread.*
3. Perfect rest to me is promised In my Father's house above.

1. Heavenly peace, divinest comfort, Here by faith in Him to dwell!
2. *Though my weary steps may falter And my soul a-thirst may be,*
3. When my spirit, clothed immortal, Wings its flight to realms of day,

1. For I know, what-e'er befall me, Jesus doeth all things well;
2. *Gushing from the Rock before me, Lo! a spring of joy I see;*
3. This my song through endless ages: Jesus led me all the way;

GUIDANCE

1 For I know, what-e'er be-fall me, Je-sus do-eth all things well.
2 *Gush-ing from the Rock be-fore me, Lo! a spring of joy I see.*
3 This my song through end-less a-ges: Je-sus led me all the way.

Freedom of the Will 599

We remember how Jesus said, ". . . I have finished the work which Thou gavest me to do" (John 17:4). That statement reveals that God had a definite plan for Jesus' life, that He could and did know what that plan was, and that it was possible for Him to accomplish it. That was true for Christ; it is also true for each one of us. No one of us is here by accident nor by chance. God has a plan for your life—of that you can be sure.

However, God gave to each person power of choice and freedom of will. We remember how our Lord prayed, ". . . nevertheless not my will, but Thine be done" (Luke 22:42). That prayer teaches two very important truths: first, one might have a will for his own life that is contrary to God's will for him. Second, it is possible to follow your own will and turn your back on God's will for you. Were those two facts not true, then Christ's prayer would have been mockery.

—Charles L. Allen

600 Take Thou My Hand, O Father

Teach me Thy Way, O Lord; Lead me in a plain path....
— Psalm 27:11

Julie Katharina Hausmann
Tr. by Herman Brückner
Jeff Redd, alt.

SO NIMM DENN MEINE HÄNDE
Friedrich Silcher

1. Take Thou my hand, O Father, And lead Thou me,
   Until I end my journey, and heaven see.
   Alone I would not wander One single day;
   Be Thou my true companion And with me stay.

2. O cover with Thy mercy My poor, weak heart!
   Let every thought rebellious From me depart.
   Permit Thy child to linger Here at Thy feet,
   To fully trust Thy goodness With faith complete.

3. Lord, make my heart responsive, And stir my soul,
   Until through all the darkness, I reach my goal.
   Then take my hand, O Father, And lead Thou me
   Until I end my journey, and heaven see. A-men.

Text revision © Copyright 1976 by Fred Bock Music Co. All rights reserved. Used by permission.

GUIDANCE

Savior, Like a Shepherd Lead Us

601

. . . . That great shepherd of the sheep . . . make you perfect in every good work.
— Hebrews 13:20-21

Attributed to Dorothy A. Thrupp

BRADBURY
William B. Bradbury

1. Savior, like a Shepherd lead us, Much we need Thy tender care;
   In Thy pleasant pastures feed us; For our use Thy folds prepare.
   Blessed Jesus, Blessed Jesus, Thou hast bought us, Thine we are;
   Blessed Jesus, Blessed Jesus, Thou hast bought us, Thine we are.

2. *We are Thine; do Thou befriend us; Be the guardian of our way;*
   Keep Thy flock; from sin defend us; Seek us when we go astray.
   Blessed Jesus, Blessed Jesus, Hear Thy children when they pray;
   Blessed Jesus, Blessed Jesus, Hear Thy children when they pray.

3. Early let us seek Thy favor; Early let us do Thy will;
   Blessed Lord and only Savior, With Thy love our bosoms fill.
   Blessed Jesus, Blessed Jesus, Thou hast loved us, love us still;
   Blessed Jesus, Blessed Jesus, Thou hast loved us, love us still. A-men.

GUIDANCE

602 James 1:5-8

If there is any one of you who needs wisdom, he must ask God, who gives to all freely and ungrudgingly; it will be given to him. But he must ask with faith, and no trace of doubt, because a person who has doubts is like the waves thrown up in the sea when the wind drives. That sort of person, in two minds, wavering between going different ways, must not expect that the Lord will give him anything.

—(JB)

603 God Moves in a Mysterious Way

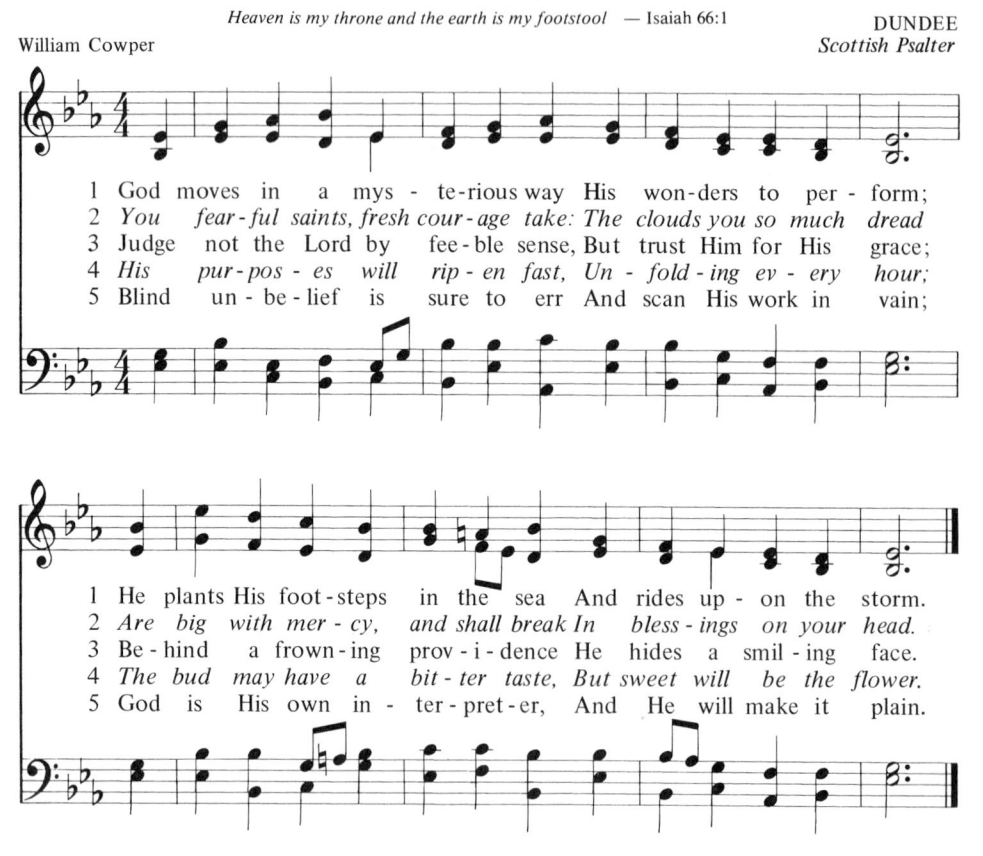

Heaven is my throne and the earth is my footstool — Isaiah 66:1

William Cowper

DUNDEE
Scottish Psalter

1. God moves in a mysterious way His wonders to perform;
   He plants His footsteps in the sea And rides upon the storm.
2. You fearful saints, fresh courage take: The clouds you so much dread
   Are big with mercy, and shall break In blessings on your head.
3. Judge not the Lord by feeble sense, But trust Him for His grace;
   Behind a frowning providence He hides a smiling face.
4. His purposes will ripen fast, Unfolding every hour;
   The bud may have a bitter taste, But sweet will be the flower.
5. Blind unbelief is sure to err And scan His work in vain;
   God is His own interpreter, And He will make it plain.

604 The Tangle of the Mind

To seek the meaning of things and God's will does not spare us either from error or from doubt; nor does it solve all the mysteries of our destiny, all the insoluble problems which are set us by any event of Nature or in our lives; nevertheless, it does give a new meaning to our lives.

—Paul Tournier

GUIDANCE

If You Will Only Let God Guide You

605

Howbeit, when He, the spirit of truth is come,
He will guide you into all truth. — John 16:13

Georg Neumark
Tr. by Catherine Winkworth
Jeff Redd, alt.

NEUMARK
Georg Neumark

1 If you will only let God guide you And hope in Him through all your ways, He'll give you strength whatever happens And take you through the evil days; Who trusts in God's unchanging love Builds on the rock that cannot move.

2 *Only be still and wait His leisure In cheerful hope, with heart content. Take all as part of God's good pleasure Which His all-caring love has sent; For all our inmost wants are known To Him who chose us for His own.*

3 Sing, pray and keep His ways unswerving— So do your own part faithfully; And trust His word, its every promise Shows forth our God's integrity; God never yet forsook the need Of one who trusted Him to lead. A-men.

Text revision © Copyright 1976 by Fred Bock Music Company. All rights reserved. Used by permission.

GUIDANCE

606 He Leadeth Me, O Blessed Thought

He leadeth me in the paths of righteousness. — Psalm 23:3

Joseph H. Gilmore

HE LEADETH ME
William B. Bradbury
Descant by Tom Fettke

Descant
3 And when my task on earth is done, When by Thy grace the vic-tory's won,

1 He lead-eth me, O blessed thought! O words with heav'nly comfort fraught!
2 Lord, *I would clasp Thy hand in mine, Nor ev-er mur-mur nor re-pine;*
3 And when my task on earth is done, When by Thy grace the vic-t'ry's won,

E'en death's cold wave I will not flee, Since God thru Jor-dan lead-eth me.

1 What-e'er I do, where-e'er I be, Still 'tis God's hand that lead-eth me.
2 *Con-tent what-ev-er lot I see, Since 'tis my God that lead-eth me.*
3 E'en death's cold wave I will not flee, Still God through Jor-dan lead-eth me.

He lead-eth, lead-eth me, By His own hand He lead-eth me;

He lead-eth me, He lead-eth me, By His own hand He lead-eth me;

© Copyright 1976 by Paragon Associates, Inc. All rights reserved.

GUIDANCE

His faithful follower I would be, For by His hand He leadeth me.

His faithful follower I would be, For by His hand He leadeth me.

Where He Leads Me — 607

Master, I will follow Thee whithersoever Thou goest.
— Matthew 8:19

E. W. Blandy

NORRIS
John S. Norris

1. I can hear my Savior calling, I can hear my Savior calling,
2. I'll go with Him thru the judgment, I'll go with Him thru the judgment,
3. He will give me grace and glory, He will give me grace and glory,

Refrain:
Where He leads me I will follow, Where He leads me I will follow,

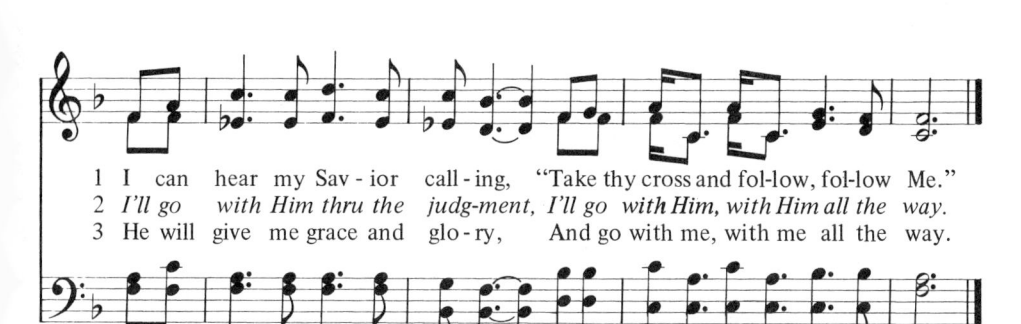

1. I can hear my Savior calling, "Take thy cross and follow, follow Me."
2. I'll go with Him thru the judgment, I'll go with Him, with Him all the way.
3. He will give me grace and glory, And go with me, with me all the way.

Refrain:
Where He leads me I will follow— I'll go with Him, with Him all the way.

GUIDANCE

608 Guide Me, O Thou Great Jehovah

He will guide us even unto death. — Psalm 48:14

William Williams
Tr. by Peter Williams

CWM RHONDDA
John Hughes

1. Guide me, O Thou great Jehovah, Pilgrim through this barren land; I am weak, but Thou art mighty— Hold me with Thy powerful hand: Bread of heaven, Bread of heaven, Feed me 'til I want no more, Feed me 'til I want no more.

2. *Open now the crystal fountain, Whence the healing stream doth flow; Let the fire and cloudy pillar Lead me all my journey through: Strong Deliverer, strong Deliverer, Be Thou still my strength and shield, Be Thou still my strength and shield.*

3. When I reach the river Jordan, Bid my anxious fears subside; Bear me through the swelling current, Land me safe on Canaan's side: Songs of praises, songs of praises I will ever give to Thee, I will ever give to Thee. A-men.

Music © by Mrs. Dilys Webb, c/o Mechanical-Copyright Protection Society Limited, and reproduced by permission of the legal representatives of the composer who reserve all rights therein.

GUIDANCE

Jesus Will Walk with Me

609

But if we walk in the light as He is in the light....

— John 1:7

JESUS WILL WALK WITH ME

Haldor Lillenas

Haldor Lillenas

1. Je-sus will walk with me down thru the val-ley, Je-sus will walk with me o-ver the plain; When in the shad-ow or when in the sun-shine, If He goes with me I shall not com-plain.
2. *Je-sus will walk with me when I am tempt-ed, Giv-ing me strength as my need may de-mand; When in af-flic-tion His pres-ence is near me, I am up-held by His al-might-y hand.*
3. Je-sus will walk with me, guarding me ev-er, Giv-ing me vic-tory thru storm and thru strife; He is my Com-fort-er, Coun-sel-or, Lead-er, O-ver the un-e-ven jour-ney of life.
4. *Je-sus will walk with me in life's fair morn-ing, And when the shadows of eve-ning must come; Liv-ing or dy-ing, He will not for-sake me, Je-sus will walk with me all the way home.*

Je-sus will walk with me, He will talk with me; He will walk with me; In joy or in sor-row, to-day and to-mor-row, I know He will walk with me.

Copyright 1922. Renewed 1950 by Lillenas Publishing Co. All rights reserved. Used by permission.

GUIDANCE

610 Prayer

Give us

   A pure heart

      That we may see Thee,

A humble heart

   That we may hear Thee,

      A heart of love

         That we may serve Thee,

   A heart of faith

      That we may live Thee.

—Dag Hammarskjöld

611 Precious Lord, Take My Hand

Thou wilt show me the path of life:
at Thy right hand there are pleasures for evermore.
— Psalm 6:11

Thomas A. Dorsey

PRECIOUS LORD
Arranged by Thomas A. Dorsey

1. Precious Lord, take my hand, Lead me on, help me stand; I am tired, I am weak, I am worn; Thru the storm, thru the night, Lead me on to the light, Take my hand, precious Lord, lead me home.

2. When my way grows drear, Precious Lord, linger near; When my life is almost gone, Hear my cry, hear my call, Hold my hand lest I fall; Take my hand, precious Lord, lead me home.

Copyright © 1938 by Hill and Range Songs, Inc. Copyright renewed, assigned to Unichappell Music, Inc., New York, N.Y. Belinda Music, Publisher. International copyright secured. All rights reserved. Used by permission.

GUIDANCE

Ephesians 6:10-20 — 612

Finally then, find your strength in the Lord, in His mighty power. Put on all the armour which God provides, so that you may be able to stand firm against the devices of the devil. For our fight is not against human foes, but against cosmic powers, against the authorities and potentates of this dark world, against the superhuman forces of evil in the heavens. Therefore, take up God's armour; then you will be able to stand your ground when things are at their worst, to complete every task and still to stand. Stand firm, I say. Fasten on the belt of truth; for coat of mail put on integrity; let the shoes on your feet be the gospel of peace, to give you firm footing; and, with all these, take up the great shield of faith, with which you will be able to quench all the flaming arrows of the evil one. Take salvation for helmet; for sword, take that which the Spirit gives you—the words that come from God. Give yourselves wholly to prayer and entreaty; pray on every occasion in the power of the Spirit. To this end keep watch and persevere, always interceding for all God's people; and pray for me, that I may be granted the right words when I open my mouth, and may boldly and freely make known His hidden purpose, for which I am an ambassador—in chains. Pray that I may speak of it boldly, as it is my duty to speak. —(NEB)

Fight the Good Fight — 613

Fight the good fight of faith. —1 Timothy 6:12

John S. B. Monsell

PENTECOST
William Boyd

1. Fight the good fight with all thy might! Christ is thy strength, and Christ thy right. Lay hold on life, and it shall be Thy joy and crown e-ter-nal-ly.
2. *Run the straight race through God's good grace; Lift up thine eyes, and seek His face. Life with its way be-fore us lies; Christ is the path, and Christ the prize.*
3. Cast care a-side, lean on thy guide; His bound-less mer-cy will pro-vide. Trust, and thy trust-ing soul shall prove Christ is its life, and Christ its love.
4. *Faint not nor fear, His arms are near; He chang-eth not, and thou art dear. On-ly be-lieve, and thou shalt see That Christ is all in all to thee.* A-men.

LOYALTY AND COURAGE

614 For All the Saints

SINE NOMINE

William W. How
Ralph Vaughan Williams

God is not ashamed to be called their God; for He hath prepared for them a city.
— Hebrews 11:16

1. For all the saints who from their la-bors rest, Who
2. *Thou wast their rock, their for-tress, and their might, Thou,*
3. O may Thy sol-diers, faith-ful, true, and bold,
4. O blest com-mu-nion, fel-low-ship di-vine!
5. But lo! there breaks a yet more glo-rious day; The
6. From earth's wide bounds, from o-cean's far-thest coast, Through

1. Thee by faith be-fore the world con-fessed, Thy
2. *Lord, their cap-tain in the well-fought fight;*
3. Fight as the saints who no-bly fought of old, And
4. *We fee-bly strug-gle, they in glo-ry shine; Yet*
5. saints tri-um-phant rise in bright ar-ray; The
6. gates of pearl streams in the count-less host,

1. name, O Je-sus, be for-ev-er blest:
2. *Thou, in the dark-ness drear, their one true light:*
3. win with them the vic-tor's crown of gold:
4. *all are one in Thee, for all are Thine:*
5. King of glo-ry pass-es on His way:
6. Sing-ing to Fa-ther, Son, and Ho-ly Ghost:

Music from "The English Hymnal" by permission of Oxford University Press.
LOYALTY AND COURAGE

Al - le - lu - ia! Al - le - lu - ia! A - men.

The Temptation to Quit **615**

    The program of God through history is like a relay race. Let one runner drop out and the whole team loses. Let one runner lose the baton and the whole team is eliminated. Let one runner break the rules and the whole team is disqualified. The work of no runner counts until every runner does his share and the anchor man has hit the tape at the finish line.

    The phrase "let us keep our eyes fixed on Jesus" is the key. The idea is clear. There are lots of distractions as we run. Bypaths beckon us; false goals attract us; competition discourages us; opposition causes us to falter. Jesus, however, a tried and trusted leader who blazed the trail of faith by His own obedience and perseverance and who finished the course in a burst of glory is both our guide and our goal. We look away from everything else to Him, if we want to run well.

—David Hubbard

LOYALTY AND COURAGE

616 Stand Up, Stand Up for Jesus

Watch ye, stand fast in the faith. — I Corinthians 16:13

George Duffield
WEBB
George J. Webb

1. Stand up, stand up for Jesus, Ye soldiers of the cross;
   Lift high His royal banner, It must not suffer loss.
   From vict'ry unto vict'ry His army shall He lead,
   'Til every foe is conquered And Christ is Lord indeed.

2. Stand up, stand up for Jesus, The trumpet call obey;
   Forth to the mighty conflict, In this His glorious day.
   Ye that are men now serve Him Against unnumbered foes;
   Let courage rise with danger And strength to strength oppose.

3. Stand up, stand up for Jesus, Stand in His strength alone;
   The arm of flesh will fail you, Ye dare not trust your own.
   Put on the gospel armor, Each piece put on with prayer;
   Where duty calls, or danger Be never wanting there.

4. Stand up, stand up for Jesus, The strife will not be long;
   This day the noise of battle, The next the victor's song.
   To him that overcometh A crown of life shall be:
   He with the King of glory Shall reign eternally.

LOYALTY AND COURAGE

Onward, Christian Soldiers

617

Thou therefore endure hardness as a good soldier . . . — II Timothy 2:3

Sabine Baring-Gould

ST. GERTRUDE
Arthur S. Sullivan

1. On-ward, Chris-tian sol-diers, march-ing as to war, With the cross of Je-sus go-ing on be-fore: Christ, the roy-al Mas-ter, leads a-gainst the foe; For-ward in-to bat-tle, see His ban-ners go.
2. *Like a might-y ar-my moves the Church of God; Broth-ers, we are tread-ing where the saints have trod, We are not di-vid-ed, all one bod-y we: One in hope and doc-trine, one in char-i-ty.*
3. Crowns and thrones may per-ish, king-doms rise and wane, But the Church of Je-sus con-stant will re-main, Gates of hell can nev-er 'gainst that Church pre-vail; We have Christ's own prom-ise, and that can-not fail.
4. *On-ward, then, ye peo-ple, join our hap-py throng; Blend with ours your voic-es in the tri-umph song, Glo-ry, laud, and hon-or un-to Christ the King: This through count-less a-ges men and an-gels sing.*

On-ward, Chris-tian sol-diers, march-ing as to war, With the cross of Je-sus go-ing on be-fore.

LOYALTY AND COURAGE

618 I Will Sing the Wondrous Story

Rejoice with me, for I have found my sheep which was lost. — Luke 15:6

Francis H. Rowley

WONDROUS STORY
Peter P. Bilhorn

1. I will sing the won-drous sto-ry Of the Christ who died for me,
2. *I was lost but Je-sus found me, Found the sheep that went a-stray,*
3. I was bruised but Je-sus healed me, Faint was I from man-y a fall;
4. *Days of dark-ness still come o'er me, Sor-row's paths I oft-en tread,*

1. How He left His home in glo-ry For the cross of Cal-va-ry.
2. *Threw His lov-ing arms a-round me, Drew me back in-to His way.*
3. Sight was gone, and fears pos-sessed me, But He freed me from them all.
4. *But the Sav-ior still is with me, By His hand I'm safe-ly led.*

Yes, I'll sing the won-drous sto-ry Of the Christ who died for me, Sing it with the saints in glo-ry Gath-ered by the crys-tal sea.

TESTIMONY, WITNESS AND EVANGELISM

Our
Love for Others

619 I Love to Tell the Story

... They that were scattered abroad went everywhere preaching the word.
— Acts 8:4

Katherine Hankey

HANKEY
William G. Fischer

1. I love to tell the story Of unseen things above,
   Of Jesus and His glory, Of Jesus and His love;
   I love to tell the story— Because I know 'tis true,
   It satisfies my longings As nothing else can do.

2. I love to tell the story— More wonderful it seems
   Than all the golden fancies Of all our golden dreams;
   I love to tell the story— It did so much for me,
   And that is just the reason I tell it now to Thee.

3. I love to tell the story— 'Tis pleasant to repeat
   What seems, each time I tell it, More wonderfully sweet;
   I love to tell the story— For some have never heard
   The message of salvation From God's own holy word.

4. I love to tell the story— For those who know it best
   Seem hungering and thirsting To hear it like the rest;
   And when in scenes of glory I sing the new, new song,
   'Twill be the old, old story That I have loved so long.

TESTIMONY, WITNESS AND EVANGELISM

I love to tell the sto-ry! 'Twill be my theme in glo-ry—
To tell the old, old sto-ry Of Je-sus and His love.

I Stand by the Door 620

I stand by the door.
I neither go too far in, nor stay too far out,
The door is the most important door in the world—
It is the door through which men walk when they find God.
There's no use my going way inside, and staying there,
When so many are still outside and they, as much as I,
Crave to know where the door is.
And all that so many ever find
Is only the wall where a door ought to be.
They creep along the wall like blind men,
With outstretched, groping hands;
Feeling for a door, knowing there must be a door,
Yet they never find it . . .
                So I stand by the door.

                      —Samuel Shoemaker

TESTIMONY, WITNESS AND EVANGELISM

621 Turn Your Eyes upon Jesus

I am come that they might have life, and that they might have it more abundantly. — John 10:10

LEMMEL

Helen H. Lemmel / Helen H. Lemmel

1. O soul, are you weary and troubled? No light in the darkness you see? There's light for a look at the Savior, And life more abundant and free!
2. *Through death into life everlasting He passed, and we follow Him there; Over us sin no more hath dominion— For more than conquerors we are!*
3. His word shall not fail you—He promised; Believe Him, and all will be well: Then go to a world that is dying, His perfect salvation to tell!

Turn your eyes upon Jesus, Look full in His wonderful face, And the things of earth will grow strangely dim In the light of His glory and grace.

Copyright 1922. Renewal 1950 by H. H. Lemmel. Assigned to Singspiration, Inc. All rights reserved. Used by permission.

TESTIMONY, WITNESS AND EVANGELISM

O How He Loves You and Me 622

As the Father hath loved Me, so I have loved you;
— John 15:9

HE LOVES YOU AND ME
Kurt Kaiser

Kurt Kaiser

1. O how He loves you and me.
2. Jesus to Calvary did go,

1. O how He loves you and me;
2. His love for mankind to show;

1. He gave His life, what more could He give:
2. What He did there brought hope from despair:

1. O how He loves you, O, how He loves me,
2. O how He loves you, O, how He loves me,

1. O how He loves you and me.
2. O how He loves you and me.

© Copyright 1975 and this arr. © 1976 by Word Music, Inc. All rights reserved. Used by permission.

TESTIMONY, WITNESS AND EVANGELISM

623 The Longer I Serve Him

... He that loseth his life for My sake shall find it.
— Matthew 10:39

William J. Gaither

THE SWEETER HE GROWS
William J. Gaither

1. Since I start-ed for the King-dom, Since my life He con-trols, Since I gave my heart to Je-sus, The long-er I serve Him, the sweet-er He grows.
2. Ev-ery need He is sup-ply-ing, Plen-teous grace He be-stows; Ev-ery day my way gets bright-er, The long-er I serve Him, the sweet-er He grows.

The long-er I serve Him the sweet-er He grows, The more that I love Him, more love He be-stows; Each day is like heav-en, my heart o-ver-flows, The long-er I serve Him the sweet-er He grows.

© Copyright 1965 by William J. Gaither. All rights reserved. Used by permission.
TESTIMONY, WITNESS AND EVANGELISM

Prayer 624

Lord, remind us that Your call is not just to the treasured time of worship or to those peaceful moments of prayer, but, because of the resurrection, it is to move with courage into the encounters and arenas of life where many have not heard the Gospel's call. Help us to speak when it is not easy, to act when it is safer to just go along with wrong. Help us to know that in the day of Jesus Christ, His kingdom will come; and let us, O God, be bound by a love amazing and divine, and then go out and embrace a weary and despairing world and lift that world to You. Amen.

—Kenneth Working

Lord, Speak to Me 625

And He that searcheth the hearts knoweth what is in the mind of the Spirit.
— Romans 8:27

Frances Ridley Havergal
CANONBURY
Robert Schumann

1. Lord, speak to me, that I may speak In living echoes of Thy tone; As Thou hast sought, so let me seek Thy erring children lost and lone.
2. O lead me, Lord, that I may lead The wandering and the wavering feet; O feed me, Lord, that I may feed Thy hungering ones with manna sweet.
3. O teach me, Lord, that I may teach The precious things Thou dost impart; And wing my words, that they may reach The hidden depths of many a heart.
4. O fill me with Thy fullness, Lord, Until my very heart o'erflow In kindling thought and glowing word, Thy love to tell, Thy praise to show.
5. O use me, Lord, use even me, Just as Thou wilt, and when, and where, Until Thy blessed face I see— Thy rest, Thy joy, Thy glory share. A-men.

TESTIMONY, WITNESS AND EVANGELISM

626 It Took a Miracle

If any man be in Christ he is a new creature... — II Corinthians 5:17

John W. Peterson

MONTROSE
John W. Peterson

1. My Father is omnipotent, And that you can't deny;
   A God of might and miracles— 'Tis written in the sky.
2. *Though here His glory has been shown, We still can't fully see*
   The wonders of His might, His throne—'Twill take eternity.
3. The Bible tells us of His power And wisdom all way through,
   And every little bird and flower Are testimonies too.

Refrain:
It took a miracle to put the stars in place, It took a miracle to hang the world in space; But when He saved my soul, Cleansed and made me whole, It took a miracle of love and grace!

© Copyright 1948. Renewal 1976 by John W. Peterson. Assigned to Singspiration. Division of the Zondervan Corp. All rights reserved. Used by permission.

TESTIMONY, WITNESS AND EVANGELISM

Jesus Is All the World to Me 627

Greater love hath no man than this . . . . — John 15:13

Will L. Thompson

ELIZABETH
Will L. Thompson

1. Jesus is all the world to me, My life, my joy, my all;
He is my strength from day to day, Without Him I would fall.
When I am sad to Him I go, No other one can cheer me so;
When I am sad He makes me glad, He's my Friend.

2. Jesus is all the world to me, My Friend in trials sore;
I go to Him for blessings, and He gives them o'er and o'er.
He sends the sunshine and the rain, He sends the harvest's golden grain;
Sunshine and rain, harvest of grain, He's my Friend.

3. Jesus is all the world to me, And true to Him I'll be;
O how could I this Friend deny, When He's so true to me?
Following Him I know I'm right, He watches o'er me day and night;
Following Him by day and night, He's my Friend.

4. Jesus is all the world to me, I want no better friend;
I trust Him now, I'll trust Him when Life's fleeting days shall end.
Beautiful life with such a Friend; Beautiful life that has no end;
Eternal life, eternal joy, He's my Friend.

TESTIMONY, WITNESS AND EVANGELISM

628 He Touched Me

And Jesus put forth His hand and touched him, saying, I will; be thou clean.
— Matthew 8:3

HE TOUCHED ME
William J. Gaither

William J. Gaither

1. Shack-led by a heav-y bur-den, 'Neath a load of guilt and shame — Then the hand of Je-sus touched me, And now I am no long-er the same.
2. Since I met this bless-ed Sav-ior, Since He cleansed and made me whole, I will nev-er cease to praise Him — I'll shout it while e-ter-ni-ty rolls.

He touched me, O He touched me, And O the joy that floods my soul; Some-thing

© Copyright 1963 by William Gaither. All rights reserved. Used by permission.

TESTIMONY, WITNESS AND EVANGELISM

hap-pened, and now I know, He touched me and made me whole.

Only Trust Him 629

Trust ye in the Lord forever; for in the Lord . . . is everlasting strength. — Isaiah 26:4

MINERVA

John H. Stockton John H. Stockton

1 Come, ev-ery soul by sin op-pressed, There's mer-cy with the Lord;
2 *For Je-sus shed His pre-cious blood, Rich bless-ings to be-stow;*
3 Yes, Je-sus is the Truth, the Way, That leads you in-to rest:

1 And He will sure-ly give you rest By trust-ing in His word.
2 *He of-fers now the crim-son flood To wash us white as snow.*
3 Be-lieve in Him with-out de-lay, And you are ful-ly blest.

On-ly trust Him, on-ly trust Him, On-ly trust Him now;
He will save you, He will save you, He will save you now.

TESTIMONY, WITNESS AND EVANGELISM

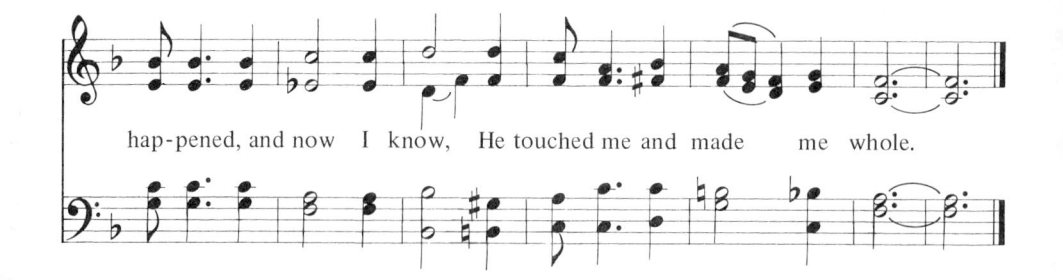

630 There Is Sunshine in My Soul Today

For God who commanded light to shine out of darkness hath shined in our hearts.
— II Corinthians 4:6

Eliza E. Hewitt

SUNSHINE
John R. Sweney

1. There is sunshine in my soul to-day, More glorious and bright
2. There is music in my soul to-day, A carol to my King,
3. There is spring-time in my soul to-day, For when the Lord is near
4. There is gladness in my soul to-day, And hope and praise and love,

1. Than glows in any earthly sky, For Jesus is my light.
2. And Jesus, listening can hear The songs I cannot sing.
3. The dove of peace sings in my heart, The flowers of grace appear.
4. For blessings which He gives me now, For joys laid up above.

O there's sun-shine, blessed sun-shine, When the peaceful, happy moments roll; When Jesus shows His smiling face, There is sunshine in my soul.

TESTIMONY, WITNESS AND EVANGELISM

I Know Whom I Have Believed

631

. . . He is able to keep that which I have committed unto Him . . .
— II Timothy 1:12

Based on II Timothy 1:12
Daniel W. Whittle

EL NATHAN
James McGranahan

1. I know not why God's won-drous grace To me He hath made known,
   Nor why, un-wor-thy, Christ in love Re-deemed me for His own.
2. I know not how this sav-ing faith To me He did im-part,
   Nor how be-liev-ing in His word Wrought peace with-in my heart.
3. I know not how the Spir-it moves, Con-vinc-ing men of sin,
   Re-veal-ing Je-sus through the word, Cre-at-ing faith in Him.
4. I know not when my Lord may come, At night or noon-day fair,
   Nor if I walk the vale with Him, Or meet Him in the air.

But "I know whom I have be-liev-ed, and am per-suad-ed that He is a-ble To keep that which I've com-mit-ted Un-to Him a-gainst that day."

TESTIMONY, WITNESS AND EVANGELISM

632 He's Everything to Me

... What is man that Thou art mindful of him? — Psalm 8:4

Ralph Carmichael

WOODLAND HILLS
Ralph Carmichael

1. In the stars His hand-i-work I see, On the wind He speaks with maj-es-ty; Though He rul-eth o-ver land and sea, What is that to me? What is that to me? 'Til by faith I met Him face to face And I felt the won-der of His grace,

2. I will cel-e-brate na-tiv-i-ty, For it has a place in his-to-ry; Sure, He came to set His peo-ple free,

© Copyright 1964 by Lexicon Music, Inc. All rights reserved. International copyright secured. Used by permission.
TESTIMONY, WITNESS AND EVANGELISM

Then I knew that He was more than just a God who did-n't care, who lived a-way out there, And now He walks be-side me day by day, Ev-er watch-ing o'er me lest I stray, Help-ing me to find that nar-row way, He's ev-ery-thing to me. He's ev-ery-thing to me.

TESTIMONY, WITNESS AND EVANGELISM

633 In My Heart There Rings A Melody

Serve the Lord with gladness: come before His presence with singing.
— Psalm 100:2

Elton M. Roth

HEART MELODY
Elton M. Roth

1. I have a song that Jesus gave me, It was sent from heaven above; There never was a sweeter melody, 'Tis a melody of love.
2. I love the Christ who died on Calvary, For He washed my sins away; He put within my heart a melody, And I know it's there to stay.
3. 'Twill be my endless theme in glory, With the angels I will sing; 'Twill be a song with glorious harmony, When the courts of heaven ring.

In my heart there rings a melody, There rings a melody with heaven's harmony; In my heart there rings a melody, There rings a melody of love.

© Copyright 1924. Renewal 1951. Hope Publishing Co. All rights reserved. Used by permission.

TESTIMONY, WITNESS AND EVANGELISM

O, How I Love Jesus

634

He that loveth not knoweth not God; for He is love. — I John 4:8

O, HOW I LOVE JESUS
American Melody
Descant by Ralph H. Good Pasteur

Frederick Whitfield

1. There is a name I love to hear, I love to sing its worth;
   It sounds like music in my ear, The sweetest name on earth.
2. *It tells me of a Savior's love, Who died to set me free;*
   It tells me of His precious blood, The sinner's perfect plea.
3. It tells of One whose loving heart Can feel my deepest woe,
   Who in each sorrow bears a part That none can bear below.

Descant: To me, it's wonderful, To me, it's wonderful! To me, it's wonderful To know that Jesus is mine!

O, how I love Jesus, O, how I love Jesus, O, how I love Jesus— Because He first loved me!

TESTIMONY, WITNESS AND EVANGELISM

635 Why Do I Sing About Jesus?

I live by the faith of the Son of God who loved me and gave Himself for me. — Galatians 2:21

Albert A. Ketchum

KETCHUM
Albert A. Ketchum

1. Deep in my heart there's a gladness — Jesus has saved me from sin! Praise to His name, what a Savior! Cleansing without and within!
2. *Only a glimpse of His goodness, That was sufficient for me; Only one look at the Savior, Then was my spirit set free.*
3. He is the fairest of fair ones, He is the Lily, the Rose; Rivers of mercy surround Him, Grace, love, and pity He shows.

Why do I sing about Jesus? Why is He precious to me? He is my Lord and my Savior: Dying, He set me free!

© Copyright 1931. Renewal 1959. Hope Publishing Co., owner. All rights reserved. Used by permission.

TESTIMONY, WITNESS AND EVANGELISM

The Light of the World Is Jesus 636

Christ shall give thee light. — Ephesians 5:14

Philip P. Bliss

LIGHT OF THE WORLD
Philip P. Bliss

1. The whole world was lost in the dark-ness of sin— The Light of the world is Je-sus; Like sun-shine at noon-day His glo-ry shone in— The Light of the world is Je-sus.
2. *No dark-ness have we who in Je-sus a-bide— The Light of the world is Je-sus; We walk in the Light when we fol-low our Guide— The Light of the world is Je-sus.*
3. No need of the sun-light in heav-en, we're told— The Light of that world is Je-sus; The Lamb is the Light in the Cit-y of Gold— The Light of that world is Je-sus.

Come to the Light, 'tis shin-ing for thee! Sweet-ly the Light has dawned up-on me; Once I was blind, but now I can see— The Light of the world is Je-sus.

TESTIMONY, WITNESS AND EVANGELISM

637 Now I Belong to Jesus

Abide in Me, and I in you. — John 15:4

Norman J. Clayton

ELLSWORTH
Norman J. Clayton

1. Jesus my Lord will love me forever, From Him no power of evil can sever, He gave His life to ransom my soul; Now I belong to Him.
2. Once I was lost in sin's degradation, Jesus came down to bring me salvation, Lifted me up from sorrow and shame, Now I belong to Him.
3. Joy floods my soul for Jesus has saved me, Freed me from sin that long had enslaved me; His precious blood He gave to redeem, Now I belong to Him.

Refrain: Now I belong to Jesus, Jesus belongs to me, Not for the years of time alone, But for eternity.

Copyright 1938 and 1943 by Norman J. Clayton. © Renewed 1966 by Norman Clayton Publishing Co., owner. All rights reserved. Used by permission.

TESTIMONY, WITNESS AND EVANGELISM

Something Worth Living For

638

*He hath sent me to heal the brokenhearted;
to preach deliverance to the captives....* — Isaiah 61:1

Dale Oldham

SOMETHING MORE
William J. Gaither

1. Life was shattered and hope was gone— Crushing the load that I bore; Then out of the depths I cried, "O God, Give me something worth living for."
2. *There, with life at its lowest ebb, Who could heal and restore? Then He came and mended my broken heart— He gave me something worth living for.*
3. O the joy of sins forgiven— Nothing's the same as before; My life overflows since Jesus came And gave me something worth living for.

Something more than my yesterdays, More than I had before, Something more than wealth or fame— He gave me something worth living for.

© Copyright 1967 by William J. Gaither. All rights reserved. Used by permission.

TESTIMONY, WITNESS AND EVANGELISM

639 Since Jesus Came Into My Heart

But the fruit of the spirit is love, joy, peace, ... — Galatians 5:22

Rufus H. McDaniel

McDANIEL
Charles H. Gabriel

1. What a won-der-ful change in my life has been wrought Since Je-sus came in-to my heart! I have light in my soul for which long I have sought,
2. *I have ceased from my wan-dering and go-ing a-stray, Since Je-sus came in-to my heart! And my sins, which were man-y, are all washed a-way,*
3. I shall go there to dwell in that Cit-y, I know, Since Je-sus came in-to my heart! And I'm hap-py, so hap-py, as on-ward I go,

Since Je-sus came in-to my heart! Since Je-sus came in-to my heart, Since Je-sus came in-to my heart, Floods of joy o'er my soul like the sea bil-lows roll, Since Je-sus came in-to my heart.

Copyright 1914 by Charles H. Gabriel. © Copyright renewed 1942 (extended), The Rodeheaver Co., owner. Used by permission.

TESTIMONY, WITNESS AND EVANGELISM

Forgiveness 640

I went very unwillingly to a society in Aldersgate Street, where one was reading Luther's preface to the *Epistle to the Romans*. While he was describing the change which God makes in the heart through faith in Christ, I felt my heart strangely warmed. I felt I did trust in Christ, Christ alone for salvation; and an assurance was given me that He had taken away *my* sins, even *mine*, and saved *me* from the law of sin and death.

—John Wesley

Pass It On 641

PASS IT ON
Kurt Kaiser

If God so loved us we ought also to love one another. — I John 4:11

Kurt Kaiser

1 It on-ly takes a spark to get a fire go-ing,
2 What a won-drous time is spring—when all the trees are bud-ding,
3 I wish for you, my friend, this hap-pi-ness that I've found—

1 And soon all those a-round can warm up in its glow-ing;
2 The birds be-gin to sing, the flow-ers start their bloom-ing;
3 You can de-pend on Him, it mat-ters not where you're bound;

1 That's how it is with God's love, once you've ex-per-i-enced it:
2 That's how it is with God's love, once you've ex-per-i-enced it:
3 I'll shout it from the moun-tain top, I want my world to know:

1 You spread His love to ev-ery-one, you want to pass it on.
2 You want to sing, it's fresh like spring, you want to pass it on.
3 The Lord of love has come to me, I want to pass it on.

© Copyright 1969 by Lexicon Music, Inc. International copyright secured. All rights reserved. Used by permission.

TESTIMONY, WITNESS AND EVANGELISM

642 If I Gained the World

For what is a man profited if he gain the whole world and lose his own soul? — Matthew 16:26

Anna Ölander
Tr. composite

TRUE RICHES
Swedish Melody

1. If I gained the world but lost the Savior, Were my life worth living for a day? Could my yearning heart find rest and comfort In the things that soon must pass away? If I gained the world, but lost the Savior, Would my gain be

2. Had I wealth and love in fullest measure, And a name revered both far and near, Yet no hope beyond, no harbor waiting Where my storm-tossed vessel I could steer— If I gained the world, but lost the Savior, Who endured the

3. O what emptiness without the Savior Mid the sins and sorrows here below! And eternity, how dark without Him— Only night and tears and endless woe! What though I might live without the Savior, When I come to

4. O the joy of having all in Jesus! What a balm the broken heart to heal! Ne'er a sin so great but He'll forgive it, Nor a sorrow that He does not feel! If I have but Jesus, only Jesus, Nothing else in

TESTIMONY, WITNESS AND EVANGELISM

1 worth the life-long strife? Are all earthly pleasures worth com-
2 cross and died for me, Could then all the world afford a
3 die, how would it be? O to face the valley's gloom with-
4 all the world beside, O then everything is mine in

1 paring For a moment with a Christ-filled life?
2 refuge, Whither in my anguish I might flee?
3 out Him! And without Him all eternity!
4 Jesus— For my needs and more He will provide.

Christ Be with Me 643

I arise today
Through God's strength to pilot me:
God's might to uphold me,
God's wisdom to guide me,
God's eye to look before me,
God's ear to hear me,
God's word to speak for me,
God's hand to guard me,
God's way to lie before me,
God's shield to protect me.

Christ be with me, Christ before me, Christ behind me,
Christ in me, Christ beneath me, Christ above me,
Christ on my right, Christ on my left,
Christ when I lie down, Christ when I sit down, Christ when I arise,
Christ in the heart of every man who thinks of me,
Christ in the mouth of every one who speaks of me,
Christ in every eye that sees me,
Christ in every ear that hears me.

—St. Patrick

644 Since I Have Been Redeemed

I know that my redeemer liveth.... — Job 19:25

Edwin O. Excell

OTHELLO
Edwin O. Excell

1. I have a song I love to sing, Since I have been redeemed,
   Of my Redeemer, Savior, King— Since I have been redeemed.

2. *I have a Christ that satisfies, Since I have been redeemed,
   To do His will my highest prize— Since I have been redeemed.*

3. I have a witness bright and clear, Since I have been redeemed,
   Dispelling every doubt and fear— Since I have been redeemed.

4. *I have a home prepared for me, Since I have been redeemed,
   Where I shall dwell eternally— Since I have been redeemed.*

Since I have been redeemed, Since I have been redeemed, I will glory in His name:
Since I have been redeemed, I will glory in my Savior's name.

TESTIMONY, WITNESS AND EVANGELISM

There's Room at the Cross

645

... While we were yet sinners, Christ died for us. — Romans 5:8

Ira F. Stanphill

STANPHILL
Ira F. Stanphill

1. The cross up-on which Je-sus died Is a shel-ter in which we can hide; And its grace so free is suf-fi-cient for me, And deep is its foun-tain— as wide as the sea.
2. *Though mil-lions have found Him a friend And have turned from the sins they have sinned, The Sav-ior still waits to o-pen the gates And wel-come a sin-ner be-fore it's too late.*
3. The hand of my Sav-ior is strong, And the love of my Sav-ior is long; Through sun-shine or rain, through loss or in gain, The blood flows from Cal-vary to cleanse ev-ery stain.

There's room at the cross for you, There's room at the cross for you; Though millions have come, There's still room for one— Yes, there's room at the cross for you.

Copyright 1946. Renewal 1974 by Ira Stanphill. Assigned to Singspiration, Division of The Zondervan Corporation. All rights reserved. Used by permission.

TESTIMONY, WITNESS AND EVANGELISM

646 Redeemed

Let the redeemed of the Lord say so.... — Psalm 107:2

Fanny J. Crosby

REDEEMED
William J. Kirkpatrick

1. Redeemed—how I love to proclaim it! Redeemed by the blood of the Lamb;
2. Redeemed and so happy in Jesus, No language my rapture can tell;
3. I think of my blessed Redeemer, I think of Him all the day long;
4. I know I shall see in His beauty The King in whose law I delight;

1. Redeemed through His infinite mercy, His child, and forever, I am.
2. I know that the light of His presence With me shall continually dwell.
3. I sing, for I cannot be silent; His love is the theme of my song.
4. Who lovingly guards every footstep, And gives me a song in the night.

Refrain:
Redeemed, redeemed, Redeemed by the blood of the Lamb.
Redeemed, redeemed, His child, and forever, I am.

TESTIMONY, WITNESS AND EVANGELISM

O Happy Day! 647

Let the wicked forsake his way for He will abundantly pardon. — Isaiah 55:7

Philip Doddridge
Gloria Gaither, stanza 4, alt.

HAPPY DAY
Edward F. Rimbault

1. O hap-py day that fixed my choice On Thee, my Sav-ior and my God!
2. *O hap-py bond that seals my vows To Him who mer-its all my love!*
3. It's done, the great trans-ac-tion's done—I am my Lord's and He is mine;
4. *At peace, my long-di-vid-ed heart, Can in this calm as-sur-ance rest;*

1. Well may this glow-ing heart re-joice And tell its rap-tures all a-broad.
2. *Let cheer-ful an-thems fill His house, While to that sa-cred shrine I move.*
3. He drew me, and I fol-lowed on, Thrilled to con-fess the voice di-vine.
4. *There is no power can make me part From Love by which I've been pos-sessed.*

Hap-py day, hap-py day, When Je-sus washed my sins a-way!

He taught me how to watch and pray And live re-joic-ing ev-ery day;

Hap-py day, hap-py day, When Je-sus washed my sins a-way!

Stanza 4 © Copyright 1976 by Paragon Associates, Inc. All rights reserved.

TESTIMONY, WITNESS AND EVANGELISM

648 I'll Tell the World That I'm A Christian

For I am not ashamed of the gospel of Christ . . . — Romans 1:16

Baynard L. Fox

TUCKER
Baynard L. Fox

1. I'll tell the world that I'm a Christian— I'm not ashamed His name to bear; I'll tell the world that I'm a Christian— I'll take Him with me anywhere. I'll tell the world how Jesus saved me, And how He gave me a life brand-new; And I know that if you trust Him That all He gave me He'll give to you. I'll tell the world

2. I'll tell the world that He is coming— It may be near or far away; But we must live as if His coming Would be tomorrow or today. For when He comes and life is over, For those who love Him there's more to be; Eyes have never seen the wonders That He's preparing for you and me. O tell the world

© Copyright 1958, 1963 by Fox Music Publications. All rights reserved. Used by permission.

TESTIMONY, WITNESS AND EVANGELISM

1 that He's my Sav-ior, No oth-er one could love me so; My life, my
2 *that you're a Chris-tian, Be not a-shamed His name to bear; O tell the*

1 all is His for - ev - er, And where He leads me I will go.
2 *world that you're a Chris-tian, And take Him with you ev - ery - where.*

Where Has All the Witness Gone? 649

Lord, we admit to ourselves and to You that we have often enjoyed our faith and the privilege of being Your people, while avoiding the responsibility for making our spiritual discoveries known to others.

Our lives should be living illustration of the truth, but they are frequently hard to read and even sometimes misleading.

We are frequently too busy to think through our faith and to be prepared to give a defense of our position and an introduction to the Savior.

We are fearful of rejection and even of being thought different.

We consign to professional people in the church the task that belongs to us all, of recommending the Master to the man in the street.

We are unwilling to suffer even slight inconvenience that someone else may turn from a meaningless existence to purposeful living. And sometimes with lop-sided concern we pray too much for our loved ones and insufficiently for Your loved ones—the poor, the defenseless, the neglected little people of the world. Too often, Lord, we try to predict who will respond and who will not, and we recommend with presumptive rashness when and how You are to fulfill our prayers for the salvation of others. Father, forgive these wrong and unhealthy attitudes.

Help us to love You so ardently and so courageously that, with tact and a sense of humor and great graciousness, we may begin to find all sorts of opportunities to recommend You to those who desperately need You. Amen.

—Bryan Jeffery Leech

650 I'd Rather Have Jesus

... but as for me and my house, we will serve the Lord. — Joshua 24:15b

Rhea F. Miller

I'D RATHER HAVE JESUS
George Beverly Shea

1. I'd rather have Jesus than silver or gold, I'd rather be His than have riches untold; I'd rather have Jesus than houses or lands, I'd rather be led by His nail-pierced hand.

2. *I'd rather have Jesus than men's applause, I'd rather be faithful to His dear cause; I'd rather have Jesus than world-wide fame, I'd rather be true to His holy name.*

3. He's fairer than lilies of rarest bloom, He's sweeter than honey from out the comb; He's all that my hungering spirit needs, I'd rather have Jesus and let Him lead.

Than to be the king of a vast domain Or be held in sin's dread sway; I'd rather have Jesus than anything This world affords today.

Words copyright 1922. Renewal 1950. Music copyright 1939. Renewal 1966. Assigned to Chancel Music, Inc. International copyright secured. All rights reserved. Used by permission.

TESTIMONY, WITNESS AND EVANGELISM

Jesus Never Fails

651

*Heaven and earth will pass away
but My words shall not....* — Matthew 24:35

Arthur A. Luther

JESUS NEVER FAILS
Arthur A. Luther

1. Earth-ly friends may prove un-true, Doubts and fears as-sail;
2. *Though the sky be dark and drear, Fierce and strong the gale,*
3. In life's dark and bit-ter hour Love will still pre-vail;

1. One still loves and cares for you, One who will not fail.
2. *Just re-mem-ber He is near, And He will not fail.*
3. Trust His ev-er-last-ing power— Je-sus will not fail.

Je-sus nev-er fails, Je-sus nev-er fails;
Heaven and earth may pass a-way, But Je-sus nev-er fails.

© Copyright 1927. Renewal 1955 by A. A. Luther. Assigned to Singspiration, Inc. All rights reserved. Used by permission.

TESTIMONY, WITNESS AND EVANGELISM

652 Get All Excited

And He hath on His vesture and on His thigh a name written: KING OF KINGS, and LORD OF LORDS. — Revelation 19:16

William J. Gaither

GET ALL EXCITED
William J. Gaither

Get all excited, go tell everybody that Jesus Christ is King! Get all excited, go tell everybody that Jesus Christ is King! Get all excited, go tell everybody that Jesus Christ is King, Jesus Christ is still the King of kings, King of kings!

Fine

© Copyright 1972 by William J. Gaither. All rights reserved. Used by permission.

TESTIMONY, WITNESS AND EVANGELISM

You talk a-bout peo-ple, you talk a-bout things that real-ly aren't im-port-ant at all, You talk a-bout weath-er, you talk a-bout prob-lems we have here at home and a-broad; But, friend, I'm ex-cit-ed a-bout a so-lu-tion for the world—I'm going to shout and sing,

D.C. al Fine

"Je-sus Christ is still the King of kings, King of kings!

TESTIMONY, WITNESS AND EVANGELISM

653 He Lifted Me

He brought me up out of a horrible pit . . . — Psalm 40:2

Charles H. Gabriel

HE LIFTED ME
Charles H. Gabriel

1. In loving-kindness Jesus came My soul in mercy to reclaim,
2. He called me long before I heard, Before my sinful heart was stirred,
3. His brow was pierced with many a thorn, His hands by cruel nails were torn,
4. Now on a higher plane I dwell, And with my soul I know 'tis well;

1. And from the depths of sin and shame Through grace He lifted me.
2. But when I took Him at His word, Forgiven He lifted me.
3. When from my guilt and grief, forlorn, In love He lifted me.
4. Yet how or why, I cannot tell, He should have lifted me.

From sinking sand He lifted me, With tender hand He lifted me;

From shades of night to plains of light, O praise His name, He lifted me!

TESTIMONY, WITNESS AND EVANGELISM

Have You Any Room For Jesus? 654

Behold, I stand at the door and knock . . . — Revelation 3:20

Unknown

ANY ROOM
C. C. Williams

1. Have you an-y room for Jesus, He who bore your load of sin?
2. *Room for pleas-ure, room for busi-ness—But, for Christ the cru-ci-fied,*
3. Have you an-y room for Jesus, As in grace He calls a-gain?
4. *Room and time now give to Jesus, Soon will pass God's day of grace;*

1. As He knocks and asks ad-mis-sion, Will you ev-er let Him in?
2. *Not a place that He can en-ter, In the heart for which He died?*
3. Here to-day is time ac-cept-ed, To-mor-row you may call in vain.
4. *Soon thy heart left cold and si-lent, And thy Sav-ior's plead-ing cease.*

Room for Je-sus, King of glo-ry! Has-ten now, His word o-bey;

Swing your heart's door wide-ly o-pen, Bid Him en-ter while you may.

TESTIMONY, WITNESS AND EVANGELISM

655 Reach Out and Touch

... And as many as touched became perfectly whole. — Matthew 14:36

Charles F. Brown

REACH OUT
Charles F. Brown

1. Reach out and touch a soul that is hungry, Reach out and touch a spirit in despair, Reach out and touch a life torn and dirty, A man who is lonely— If you care! Reach out and touch that neighbor who hates you, Reach out and touch that stranger who meets you, Reach out and touch the brother who needs you, Reach out

2. Reach out and touch a friend who is weary, Reach out and touch a seeker unaware, Reach out and touch, though touching means losing A part of your own self— If you dare! Reach out and give your love to the loveless, Reach out and make a home for the homeless, Reach out and shed God's light in the darkness, Reach out

© Copyright 1971 by Word, Inc. Arr. © 1975 by Word Music, Inc. All rights reserved. Used by permission.

TESTIMONY, WITNESS AND EVANGELISM

1 and let the smile of God touch thru you.
2 and let the smile of God touch thru you.

Something Beautiful   656

There is therefore now no condemnation to them that are in Christ Jesus.... — Romans 8:1

Gloria Gaither

SOMETHING BEAUTIFUL
William J. Gaither

Some-thing beau-ti-ful, some-thing good;
All my con-fu-sion He un-der-stood;
All I had to of-fer Him was bro-ken-ness and strife, But He made some-thing beau-ti-ful of my life.

© Copyright 1971 by William J. Gaither. All rights reserved. Used by permission.

TESTIMONY, WITNESS AND EVANGELISM

657 Heaven Came Down and Glory Filled My Soul

And suddenly there shone round about Him a light from Heaven; — Acts 9:3

John W. Peterson

HEAVEN CAME DOWN
John W. Peterson

1. O what a won-der-ful, won-der-ful day— Day I will nev-er for-get; Aft-er I'd wan-dered in dark-ness a-way, Je-sus my Sav-ior I met. O what a ten-der, com-pas-sion-ate friend— He met the need of my heart; Shad-ows dis-pel-ling, With

2. Born of the Spir-it with life from a-bove In-to God's fam-ily di-vine, Jus-ti-fied ful-ly through Cal-va-ry's love, O what a stand-ing is mine! And the trans-ac-tion so quick-ly was made When as a sin-ner I came, Took of the of-fer Of

3. Now I've a hope that will sure-ly en-dure Aft-er the pass-ing of time; I have a fu-ture in heav-en for sure, There in those man-sions sub-lime. And it's be-cause of that won-der-ful day When at the cross I be-lieved; Rich-es e-ter-nal And

© Copyright 1961 by Singspiration, Inc. Arr. © 1966 by Singspiration, Inc. All rights reserved. Used by permission.

TESTIMONY, WITNESS AND EVANGELISM

1 joy I am tell-ing, He made all the dark-ness de-part!
2 *grace He did prof-fer— He saved me, O praise His dear name!*
3 bless-ings su-per-nal From His pre-cious hand I re-ceived.

Heav-en came down and glo-ry filled my soul,

When at the cross the Sav-ior made me whole; My

sins were washed a-way And my night was turned to day—

Heav-en came down and glo-ry filled my soul!

TESTIMONY, WITNESS AND EVANGELISM

658 O Zion, Haste, Thy Mission High Fulfilling

Go ye therefore, and teach all nations.... — Matthew 28:19

Mary A. Thomson

TIDINGS
James Walch

1. O Zion, haste, thy mission high fulfilling, To tell to all the world that God is light; That He who made all nations is not willing One soul should perish, lost in shades of night.

2. *Proclaim to every people, tongue, and nation That God in whom they live and move is love; Tell how He stooped to save His lost creation, And died on earth that man might live above.*

3. Give of thy sons to bear the message glorious, Give of thy wealth to speed them on their way; Pour out thy soul for them in prayer victorious, And haste the coming of the glorious day.

Publish glad tidings, tidings of peace, Tidings of Jesus, redemption, and release. A-men.

MISSIONS

Alternate Last Verse Harmonization Arranged by Eugene Butler

3. Give of thy sons to bear the message glorious, Give of thy wealth to speed them on their way; Pour out thy soul for them in prayer victorious, And haste the coming of the glorious day. Publish glad tidings, tidings of peace, Tidings of Jesus, redemption, and release. A-men.

© Copyright 1976 by Paragon Associates, Inc. All rights reserved.

MISSIONS

659 We've a Story to Tell to the Nations

Go ye, therefore, and teach all nations.... — Matthew 28:19

H. Ernest Nichol

MESSAGE
H. Ernest Nichol

1. We've a story to tell to the nations That shall turn their hearts to the right, A story of truth and mercy, A story of peace and light, A story of peace and light.
2. We've a song to be sung to the nations That shall lift their hearts to the Lord, A song that shall conquer evil And shatter the spear and sword, And shatter the spear and sword.
3. We've a message to give to the nations—That the Lord who reigneth above Hath sent us His Son to save us And show us that God is love, And show us that God is love.
4. We've a Savior to show to the nations Who the path of sorrow hath trod, That all of the world's great peoples Might come to the truth of God, Might come to the truth of God.

For the darkness shall turn to dawning, And the dawning to noonday bright,

MISSIONS

And Christ's great king-dom shall come on earth, The king-dom of love and light.

Acts 17:22-31   660

"Men of Athens! I see that in every way you are very religious. For as I walked around and observed your objects of worship, I found even an altar with this inscription: TO AN UNKNOWN GOD. Now what you worship as something unknown I am going to proclaim to you.

"The God who made the world and everything in it is the Lord of heaven and earth and does not live in temples built by hands. And He is not served by human hands, as if He needed anything, because He Himself gives all men life and breath and everything else. From one man He made every nation of men, that they should inhabit the whole earth; and He determined the times set for them and the exact places where they should live. God did this so that men would seek Him and perhaps reach out for Him and find Him, though He is not far from each one of us. For in Him we live and move and have our being. As some of your own poets have said, 'We are His children.'

"Therefore since we are God's children, we should not think that the Divine Being is like gold or silver or stone—an image made by man's design and skill. In the past God overlooked such ignorance, but now He commands all people everywhere to repent. For He has set a day when He will judge the world with justice by the man He has appointed. He has given proof of this to all men by raising Him from the dead."

—(NIV)

MISSIONS

661 Rescue the Perishing

And His disciples came to Him. . . , saying, Lord, save us, we perish. — Matthew 8:25

Fanny J. Crosby

RESCUE
William H. Doane

1. Res-cue the per-ish-ing, Care for the dy-ing, Snatch them in pit-y from sin and the grave; Weep o'er the err-ing one, Lift up the fall-en, Tell them of Je-sus, the might-y to save.
2. Tho they are slight-ing Him, Still He is wait-ing, Wait-ing the pen-i-tent child to re-ceive; Plead with them ear-nest-ly, Plead with them gen-tly, He will for-give if they on-ly be-lieve.
3. Down in the hu-man heart, Crushed by the tempt-er, Feel-ings lie bur-ied that grace can re-store; Touched by a lov-ing heart, Wak-ened by kind-ness, Chords that are bro-ken will vi-brate once more.
4. Res-cue the per-ish-ing— Du-ty de-mands it! Strength for thy la-bor the Lord will pro-vide; Back to the nar-row way Pa-tient-ly win them, Tell the poor wan-derer a Sav-ior has died.

Res-cue the per-ish-ing, Care for the dy-ing; Je-sus is mer-ci-ful, Je-sus will save.

MISSIONS

Let Your Heart Be Broken

A vessel unto honor . . . for the Master's use. — II Timothy 2:21

662

Bryan Jeffery Leech

BJORKLUND MAJOR
Bryan Jeffery Leech
Arranged by Fred Bock

Unison

1. Let your heart be broken For a world in need:
2. *Here on earth applying Principles of love,*
3. Blest to be a blessing, Privileged to care,
4. *Add to your believing Deeds that prove it true,*
5. Let your heart be tender And your vision clear;

1. Feed the mouths that hunger, Soothe the wounds that bleed,
2. *Visible expression— God still rules above—*
3. Challenged by the need— Apparent everywhere.
4. *Knowing Christ as Savior, Make Him Master, too.*
5. See mankind as God sees, Serve Him far and near.

1. Give the cup of water And the loaf of bread—
2. *Living illustration Of the Living Word*
3. Where mankind is wanting, Fill the vacant place.
4. *Follow in His footsteps, Go where He has trod;*
5. Let your heart be broken By a brother's pain;

1. Be the hands of Jesus, Serving in His stead.
2. *To the minds of all who've Never seen or heard.*
3. Be the means through which the Lord reveals His grace.
4. *In the world's great trouble Risk yourself for God.*
5. Share your rich resources, Give and give again.

© Copyright 1975 by The Evangelical Covenant Church of America. This arr. © Copyright 1976 by Fred Bock Music Company. Used by permission.

MISSIONS

663 Send the Light

*For God who commanded the light to shine out of darkness,
hath shined in our hearts....* — II Corinthians 4:6

Charles H. Gabriel

McCABE
Charles H. Gabriel

1. There's a call comes ring-ing o'er the rest-less wave, "Send the light!
2. *We have heard the Mac-e-do-nian call to-day, "Send the light!*
3. Let us pray that grace may ev-ery-where a-bound, Send the light!
4. *Let us not grow wea-ry in the work of love, Send the light!*

1. Send the light!" There are souls to res-cue, there are souls to save,
2. *Send the light!" And a gold-en of-fering at the cross we lay,*
3. Send the light! And a Christ-like spir-it ev-ery-where be found,
4. *Send the light! Let us gath-er jew-els for a crown a-bove,*

Send the light! Send the light! Send the light, the bless-ed gos-pel light;

Let it shine from shore to shore! Send the shine from shore to shore!

MISSIONS

So Send I You 664

Peace be unto you; as My Father hath sent me, even also send I you. — John 20:21

Based on John 20:21
E. Margaret Clarkson

SO SEND I YOU
John W. Peterson

1. So send I you— by grace made strong to triumph O'er hosts of hell, o'er darkness, death and sin, My name to bear, and in that name to conquer—So send I you, my victory to win.

2. *So send I you— to take to souls in bondage The word of truth that sets the captive free, To break the bonds of sin, to loose death's fetters—So send I you, to bring the lost to me.*

3. So send I you— My strength to know in weakness, My joy in grief, My perfect peace in pain, To prove My power, My grace, My promised presence—So send I you, eternal fruit to gain.

4. *So send I you— to bear My cross with patience, And then one day with joy to lay it down, To hear My voice, "Well done, My faithful servant— Come, share My throne, my kingdom and My crown!" "As the Father hath sent Me, So send I you."*

Copyright 1954, 1963 by Singspiration, Inc. All rights reserved. Used by permission.

MISSIONS

665 Where Cross the Crowded Ways of Life

And unto you which believe He is precious.... — I Peter 2:7

Frank M. North

GERMANY
William Gardiner's *Sacred Melodies*

1. Where cross the crowd-ed ways of life, Where sound the cries of race and clan,
2. *In haunts of wretch-ed-ness and need, On shad-owed thresh-olds dark with fears,*
3. The cup of wa-ter given for Thee Still holds the fresh-ness of Thy grace;
4. *O Mas-ter, from the moun-tain side, Make haste to heal these hearts of pain,*
5. 'Til sons of men shall learn Thy love And fol-low where Thy feet have trod:

1. A-bove the noise of self-ish strife, We hear Thy voice, O Son of man!
2. *From paths where hide the lures of greed, We catch the vi-sion of Thy tears.*
3. Yet long these mul-ti-tudes to see The sweet com-pas-sion of Thy face.
4. *A-mong these rest-less throngs a-bide, O tread the cit-y's streets a-gain;*
5. 'Til glo-rious from Thy heaven a-bove Shall come the cit-y of our God. A-men.

666 Vision

1st Reader: After this I looked, and behold, a great multitude which no man could number, from every nation, from all tribes and peoples and tongues, standing before the throne and before the Lamb, clothed in white robes, with palm branches in their hands, and crying out with a loud voice,

People: *"Salvation belongs to our God who sits upon the throne and to the Lamb!"*

1st Reader: And all the angels stood round the throne and round the elders and the four living creatures, and they fell on their faces before the throne and wor-shipped God, saying,

PEOPLE: *"Amen! Blessing and glory and wisdom and thanksgiving and honor and power and might be to our God for ever and ever! Amen."*

1st Reader: Then one of the elders addressed me, saying,

2nd Reader: "Who are these, clothed in white robes, and whence have they come?"

1st Reader: I said to him, "Sir, you know." And he said to me,

2nd Reader: "These are they who have come out of the great tribulation; they have washed their robes and made them white in the blood of the Lamb. There-fore are they before the throne of God, and serve Him day and night within His temple; and He who sits upon the throne will shelter them with His presence . . . and God will wipe every tear from their eyes.

—**Revelation 7:9-17 (RSV)**

MISSIONS

Jesus Saves!

667

...Joy shall be in heaven over one sinner that repenteth.... — Luke 15:7

Priscilla J. Owens

JESUS SAVES
William J. Kirkpatrick

1. We have heard the joy-ful sound: Je-sus saves! Je-sus saves!
2. *Waft it on the roll-ing tide: Je-sus saves! Je-sus saves!*
3. Sing a-bove the bat-tle strife: Je-sus saves! Je-sus saves!
4. *Give the winds a might-y voice: Je-sus saves! Je-sus saves!*

1. Spread the ti-dings all a-round: Je-sus saves! Je-sus saves!
2. *Tell to sin-ners far and wide: Je-sus saves! Je-sus saves!*
3. By His death and end-less life: Je-sus saves! Je-sus saves!
4. *Let the na-tions now re-joice: Je-sus saves! Je-sus saves!*

1. Bear the news to ev-ery land, Climb the steeps and cross the waves;
2. *Sing, ye is-lands of the sea; Ech-o back, ye o-cean caves;*
3. Sing it soft-ly through the gloom, When the heart for mer-cy craves;
4. *Shout sal-va-tion full and free, High-est hills and deep-est caves;*

1. On-ward! 'tis our Lord's com-mand; Je-sus saves! Je-sus saves!
2. *Earth shall keep her ju-bi-lee: Je-sus saves! Je-sus saves!*
3. Sing in tri-umph o'er the tomb: Je-sus saves! Je-sus saves!
4. *This our song of vic-to-ry: Je-sus saves! Je-sus saves!*

MISSIONS

668 Macedonia

And the word of the Lord was published throughout all the region. — Acts 13:49

Anne Ortlund

ALL SAINTS, NEW
Henry S. Cutler

1. The vi-sion of a dy-ing world Is vast be-fore our eyes;
   We feel the heart-beat of its need, We hear its fee-ble cries:
   Lord Je-sus Christ, re-vive Thy church In this, her cru-cial hour!
   Lord Je-sus Christ, a-wake Thy church With Spir-it-giv-en power.

2. The sav-age hugs his god of stone And fears de-scent of night;
   The cit-y dwell-er cring-es lone A-mid the gar-ish light:
   Lord Je-sus Christ, a-rouse Thy church To see their mute dis-tress!
   Lord Je-sus Christ, e-quip Thy church With love and ten-der-ness.

3. To-day, as un-der-stand-ing's bounds Are stretched on ev-ery hand,
   O clothe Thy Word in bright, new sounds, And speed it o'er the land;
   Lord Je-sus Christ, em-pow-er us To preach by ev-ery means!
   Lord Je-sus Christ, em-bold-en us In near and dis-tant scenes.

4. The warn-ing bell of judg-ment tolls, A-bove us looms the cross;
   A-round are ev-er dy-ing souls— How great, how great the loss!
   O Lord, con-strain and move Thy church, The glad news to im-part!
   And Lord, as Thou dost stir Thy church, Be-gin with-in my heart. A-men.

Words copyright © 1966 Anne Ortlund. International copyright secured. All rights reserved. Used by permission.

MISSIONS

Hear the Voice of Jesus Calling 669

They will not believe in Him unless they have heard of Him. — Romans 10:14b

Daniel March
Bryan Jeffery Leech, alt.

RIPLEY
Gregorian Chant
Adapted by Lowell Mason

1. Hear the voice of Jesus calling, "Who will go and work to-day?"
   Fields are white and harvests ready, Who will bear the sheaves away?
   Loud and long the Master calls you, Rich reward He offers free;
   Who will answer, gladly saying, "Here am I, send me, send me."

2. *If you do not cross the ocean And a distant land explore,*
   You can give a loving witness, healing those whose hearts are sore.
   Though your talents may be meager, Offer up the things you can,
   All that you can do for Jesus Will be useful in His hand.

3. If you cannot be a watchman Standing high on Zion's wall,
   Pointing men to find the Savior, Who is life and peace to all,
   With your gifts and intercessions You can do as He commands,
   Joining with all faithful spokesmen Serving Him in distant lands.

4. *Never find yourself repeating, "There is nothing I can do;"*
   While a world of men is dying, There's a work God calls you to.
   Gladly take the task He gives you, Let His will your pleasure be;
   Answer quickly, when He calls you, "Here am I, send me, send me."

Text revision © Copyright 1976 by Fred Bock Music Co. All rights reserved. Used by permission.

MISSIONS

670 Once to Every Man and Nation

Choose you this day whom ye will serve. — Joshua 24:15

James Russell Lowell

EBENEZER
Thomas J. Williams

1. Once to ev-ery man and na-tion Comes the mo-ment to de-cide, In the strife of truth with false-hood, For the good or e-vil side; Some great cause, God's new Mes-si-ah, Of-fering
2. *Then to side with truth is no-ble, When we share her wretch-ed crust, Ere her cause bring fame and prof-it And 'tis pros-perous to be just; Then it is the brave man choos-es, While the*
3. *By the light of burn-ing mar-tyrs, Christ, Thy bleed-ing feet we track, Toil-ing up new Cal-varies ev-er With the cross that turns not back; New oc-ca-sions teach new du-ites, Time makes*
4. *Though the cause of e-vil pros-per, Yet 'tis truth a-lone is strong; Though her por-tion be the scaf-fold And up-on the throne be wrong; Yet that scaf-fold sways the fu-ture, And, be-*

Music copyright by Gwenlyn Evans, Ltd. Used by permission.

MISSIONS

	1	2	3	4	5	6	7	8
1	each	the	bloom	or	blight,	And the	choice	goes
2	cow-ard	stands	a-side,	Till the	mul-ti-
3	an-cient	good	un-couth;	They must	up-ward
4	hind	the	dim	un-known,	Stand-eth	God	with-

1 by for - ev - er 'Twixt that dark - ness and that light.
2 tude make vir - tue Of the faith they had de - nied.
3 still, and on - ward, Who would keep a - breast of truth.
4 in the shad - ow, Keep - ing watch a - bove His own.

Indifference 671

When Jesus came to Golgotha they hanged Him on a tree,
They drove great nails through hands and feet, and made a Calvary;
They crowned Him with a crown of thorns, red were His wounds and deep,
For those were crude and cruel days, and human flesh was cheap.

When Jesus came to our town, they simply passed Him by,
They never hurt a hair of Him, they only let Him die;
For men had grown more tender, and they would not give Him pain,
They only just passed down the street, and left Him in the rain.

Still Jesus cried, "Forgive them, for they know not what they do,"
And still it rained the winter rain that drenched Him through and through;
The crowds went home and left the streets without a soul to see,
And Jesus crouched against a wall and cried for Calvary.

—G. A. Studdert-Kennedy

MISSIONS

672 Through All the World

And it shall be to Me a name of joy, a praise and honor before all the nations. — Jeremiah 33:9

Bryan Jeffery Leech

CONRAD
Paul F. Liljestrand

1. Through all the world let ev-ery na-tion sing To God, the King! As Lord may Christ pre-side Where now He is de-fied, And sov-ereign place His throne In hearts not yet His own.
2. Through all the world let ev-ery man ex-press True righ-teous-ness! May Christ be now the norm To which all men con-form, His pas-sion cure the sin That fes-ters from with-in.
3. Through all the world let ev-ery man em-brace The gift of grace! May Christ's great light con-sume Our cit-ies' dark-est gloom, May Christ's great love ef-face Hos-til-i-ties of race.
4. If all the world in ev-ery part shall hear And God re-vere, We must be moved to care And in His name to share The lib-er-at-ing Word Which must be told a-broad.

From "The Hymn," Copyright 1970 by the Hymn Society of America. Used by permission.
MISSIONS

1. Through all the world let ev-ery na-tion sing To God, the King!
2. *Through all the world let ev-ery man ex - press True righ - teous - ness!*
3. Through all the world let ev-ery man em - brace The gift of grace!
4. *Then all the world in ev-ery part shall hear And God re - vere!*

Precious in God's Sight 673

In God's sight a person is the most precious of all values. This truth possessed Jesus and never let Him go. He thought it, taught it, and lived it with full devotion. He illustrated it with stories of the lost sheep, the lost coin, and the lost son.

Every individual is inherently worthful to the Father—every child everywhere, of every race, of every condition. Love requires response, and parenthood craves companionship and cooperation. Therefore every human being on this globe is indispensable to God, indispensable in the sense that God can never be fully Himself without loving comradeship, and He can never complete His work without faithful cooperation from every individual everywhere.

Jesus taught and lived the twin truths that man needs God and God needs man, which is to say, parents and child are so bound together that cleavage is disastrous. No idea could be further from the mind of our Lord than the persistent doctrine that God is so transcendent, so holy, so sovereign that He is unknowable, inaccessible, and unresponsive. In the prayer which He taught His disciples, Jesus makes it clear that men should carry all their needs to the Father, even a petition for the satisfaction of daily bodily requirements. Jesus knew men to be frail, sinful, easily corrupted, sometimes monstrously depraved, capable of cruel and atrocious behavior—but always, always, always a child of God, and, even when a prodigal, indispensable to the lonely and yearning heart of the Father.

—Kirby Page

MISSIONS

674 Far, Far Away in Sin and Darkness Dwelling

Then said I, Here am I; send me. — Isaiah 6:8

Based on Matthew 28:18-20
James McGranahan

GO YE
James McGranahan

1. Far, far a-way, in sin and dark-ness dwell-ing, Mil-lions of souls for-ev-er may be lost; Who then will go, sal-va-tion's sto-ry tell-ing, Look-ing to Je-sus, mind-ing not the cost?

2. *See o'er the world wide o-pen doors in-vit-ing, Sol-diers of Christ, a-rise and en-ter in! Chris-tians, a-wake! your forc-es all u-nit-ing, Send forth the gos-pel, break the chains of sin.*

3. "Why will ye die?" the voice of God is call-ing, "Why will ye die?" re-ech-o in His name; Je-sus hath died to save from death ap-pall-ing, Life and sal-va-tion there-fore go pro-claim.

4. God speed the day, when those of ev-ery na-tion "Glo-ry to God!" tri-um-phant-ly shall ring; Ran-somed, re-deemed, re-joic-ing in sal-va-tion, Shout Hal-le-lu-jah, for the Lord is King.

Refrain: "All power is giv-en un-to Me, All power is giv-en un-to Me, Go ye in-to all the world and preach the gos-pel, And lo, I am with you al-way,"

MISSIONS

Prayer of Concern for Others

*F*ather, help me to talk like a Christian:
> to speak in such a way that I build up another person's confidence in himself, instead of tearing down his reputation.

Father, help me to drive like a Christian:
> to be watchful and careful lest I cause harm to someone else on the highways.

Father, help me to give like a Christian:
> without thought of return, without anyone knowing what I do, and with Your approval as sufficient reward.

Father, help me to dress like a Christian:
> by not attracting attention to myself for being too fashionable or too casual; and help me to show by my appearance that I want people to know me for what I am inside myself.

Father, help me to sleep like a Christian:
> at peace with myself because sin is forgiven; and at peace with others because I do not allow my anger to last through a day.

Father, help me to eat like a Christian:
> to eat healthily, to eat moderately, to eat gratefully, giving thanks to You who provide my food, and for the one who prepares my food.

Father, keep me from being so pious that I keep You out of the practical areas of life. Be with me when I am alone, and when I shed my inhibitions, lest in those moments I cancel out all that I seem to be when I'm on my best behavior.

Father, I ask this because I follow a Master who was never guilty of the slightest wrong-doing, and who always showed His love in the small details of living. Amen.

—Bryan Jeffery Leech

676 I Am Praying for You

We give thanks . . . praying always for you. — Colossians 1:3

S. O'Maley Cluff

INTERCESSION
Ira D. Sankey

1. I have a Savior—He's pleading in glory, A dear, loving Savior, though earth-friends be few; And now He is watching in tenderness o'er me, But O that my Savior were your Savior, too.

2. I have a Father—to me He has given A hope for eternity, blessed and true; And soon He will call me to meet Him in heaven, But O that He'd let me bring you with me, too!

3. I have a robe; 'tis resplendent in whiteness, Awaiting in glory my wondering view; O, when I receive it all shining in brightness, Dear friend, could I see you receiving one, too!

4. When He has found you—tell others the story, That my loving Savior is your Savior, too; Then pray that your Savior will bring them to glory, And prayer will be answered—'twas answered for you!

Refrain: For you I am praying, For you I am praying, For you I am praying, I'm praying for you.

CONCERN FOR OTHERS

They'll Know We Are Christians by Our Love

677

Based on John 13:35
Peter Scholtes

...that they may be one, even as We are one.... — John 17:22

ST. BRENDAN'S
Peter Scholtes

1. We are one in the Spir-it, we are one in the Lord,
2. *We will walk with each oth-er, we will walk hand in hand,*
3. We will work with each oth-er, we will work side by side,
4. *All praise to the Fa-ther, from whom all things come,*

1. We are one in the Spir-it, we are one in the Lord,
2. *We will walk with each oth-er, we will walk hand in hand,*
3. We will work with each oth-er, we will work side by side,
4. *And all praise to Christ Je-sus, His on-ly Son,*

1. And we pray that all u-ni-ty may one day be re-stored:
2. *And to-geth-er we'll spread the news that God is in our land:*
3. And we'll guard each man's dig-ni-ty and save each man's pride:
4. *And all praise to the Spir-it, who makes us one:*

And they'll know we are Christ-ians by our love, by our love,

Yes, they'll know we are Christ-ians by our love.

© Copyright 1966 by F.E.L. Publications, Ltd., 1925 Pontius Avenue, Los Angeles, CA 90025. Performance rights licensed through ASCAP. Further reproduction, even words only, not permitted without F.E.L.'s written permission.

CONCERN FOR OTHERS

678 The Hungry Man & I

To allow the hungry man to remain hungry would be blasphemy against God and one's neighbor, for what is nearest to God is precisely the need of one's neighbor. It is for the love of Christ, which belongs as much to the hungry man as to myself, that I share my bread with him and that I share my dwelling with the homeless. If the hungry man does not attain to faith, then the fault falls on those who refused him bread. To provide the hungry man with bread is to prepare the way for the coming of grace.

Dietrich Bonhoeffer

679 Eternal Father, Strong to Save

For the Lord knoweth how to deliver... — II Peter 2:9

William Whiting, stanzas 1, 4
Robert Nelson Spencer, stanzas 2, 3

MELITA
John Bacchus Dykes

1. E-ter-nal Fa-ther, strong to save, Whose arm hath bound the rest-less wave, Who bids the might-y o-cean deep Its own ap-point-ed lim-its keep: O hear us when we

2. O Christ, the Lord of hill and plain O'er which our traf-fic runs a-main By moun-tain pass or val-ley low: Wher-ev-er, Lord, our breth-ren go, Pro-tect them by Thy

3. O Spir-it, whom the Fa-ther sent To spread a-broad the fir-ma-ment: O wind of heav-en, by Thy might Save all who dare the ea-gle's flight, And keep them by Thy

4. O Trin-i-ty of love and power, Our breth-ren shield in dan-ger's hour; From rock and tem-pest, fire and foe, Pro-tect them where-so-e'er they go; Thus ev-er-more shall

The words to St. 2 & 3 used by permission of Parish Press.

CONCERN FOR OTHERS

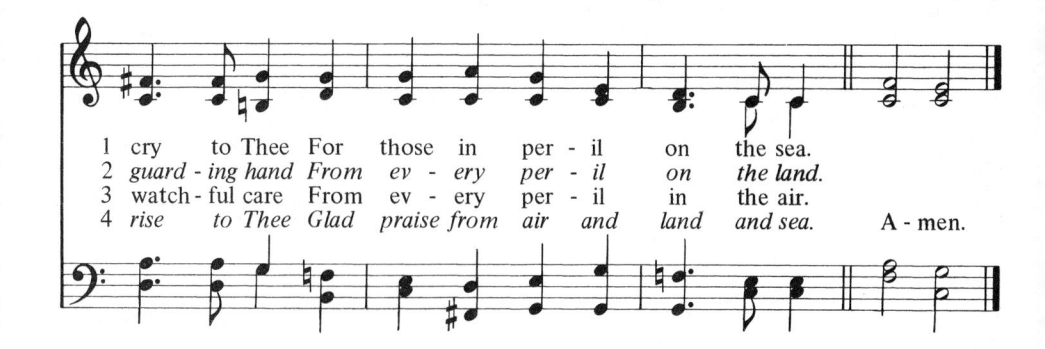

1 cry	to Thee For	those in	per - il	on	the sea.		
2 guard - ing hand	From	ev - ery	per - il	on	the land.		
3 watch - ful care	From	ev - ery	per - il	in	the air.		
4 rise	to Thee Glad	praise from	air and	land	and sea.	A - men.	

Can This World Be Fed? 680

Everything I know and understand causes me to come down on the optimistic side of this question. It can be done.

> Not easily.
> Not inexpensively.
> Certainly not without some changes.
> But it can be done.

It is not the way that is lacking. It is the will. The more you understand about basic causes of hunger in the world today, the more you cannot avoid the conclusion that God has given man and the earth the capacity to conquer and control it.

If we treated all humanity with the dignity and love they are due as the offspring of God, if we acted toward our environment as its caretakers and not its ravishers, if we viewed the mandate to "tend and dress" the earth as the Creator's orders to us, men could live together in peace and the earth would bring forth its abundance.

> THAT WAS GOD'S PLAN.

Anything short of that is the result of man's sin—his sin against God, against his fellow man, against his environment.

> It is history.
> And it is prophecy.

. . . If we have the capacity to relieve suffering and save life—and we do—and refuse to do it, that will undoubtedly be a part of our judgment.

—W. Stanley Mooneyham

CONCERN FOR OTHERS

681 Let There Be Peace on Earth

Peace, I leave with you, My peace I give unto you.... — John 14:27

Sy Miller
Jill Jackson

WORLD PEACE
Sy Miller
Jill Jackson

Unison

Let there be peace on earth, and let it be - gin with me. Let there be peace on earth, the peace that was meant to be. With God as our Fa - ther, bro - thers all are we. Let me walk with my bro - ther in per - fect har - mon - y.

© Copyright 1955 by Jan-Lee Music. All rights reserved. Used by permission.
BROTHERHOOD and WORLD PEACE

Let peace be-gin with me; let this be the mo-ment now. With ev-ery step I take, let this be my sol-emn vow: To take each mo-ment, and live each mo-ment in peace e-ter-nal-ly! Let there be peace on earth, and let it be-gin with me.

BROTHERHOOD and WORLD PEACE

682 A Song of Peace

... My peace I give unto you; not as the world giveth .... — John 14:27

Lloyd Stone, stanzas 1, 2
Georgia Harkness, stanza 3
Bryan Jeffery Leech, stanza 4

FINLANDIA
Jean Sibelius

1. This is my song, O God of all the nations, A song of peace for lands afar and mine; This is my home, the country where my heart is; Here are my hopes, my dreams, my holy shrine: But other hearts in other lands are beating With hopes and dreams as true and high as mine.

2. *My country's skies are bluer than the ocean, And sunlight beams on cloverleaf and pine; But other lands have sunlight too, and clover, And skies are everywhere as blue as mine:* O, hear my song, Thou God of all the nations, A song of peace for their land and for mine.

3. This is my prayer, O Lord of all earth's kingdoms, Thy kingdom come on earth Thy will be done; Let Christ be lifted up 'til all men serve Him, And hearts united learn to live as one: O, hear my prayer, Thou God of all the nations, Myself I give Thee, let Thy will be done.

4. *This is my song, O God of all the nations, A song of peace for men in every place; And yet I pray for my beloved country The reassurance of continued grace: Lord, help us find our oneness in the* Savior, In spite of differences of age and race.

Copyright 1930 by Breitkopf and Haertel. Used by permission of Associated Music Publishers, Inc., agent.
Stanzas 1, 2, Copyright 1934, renewed 1962 by Lorenz Publishing Company. Stanza 3 Copyright 1964 by Lorenz Publishing Company; Used by permission. Stanza 4 Copyright 1976 by Fred Bock Music Company. All rights reserved. Used by permission.

BROTHERHOOD AND WORLD PEACE

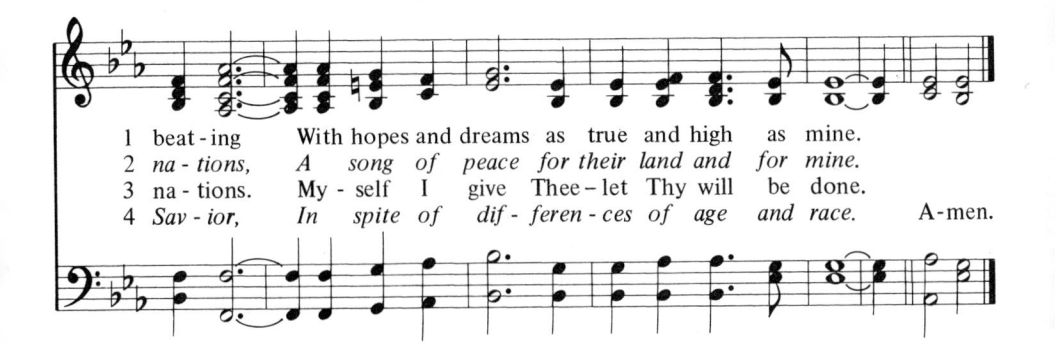

1 beat-ing	With hopes and dreams as true and high as mine.
2 na-tions,	A song of peace for their land and for mine.
3 na-tions.	My-self I give Thee – let Thy will be done.
4 Sav-ior,	In spite of dif-feren-ces of age and race. A-men.

1 Corinthians 13:1-13   683

If I speak in the tongues of men and of angels, but have not love, I am only a resounding gong or a clanging cymbal. If I have the gift of prophecy, and can fathom all mysteries and all knowledge, and if I have a faith that can move mountains, but have not love, I am nothing. If I give all I possess to the poor and surrender my body to the flames, but have not love, I gain nothing.

Love is patient, love is kind. It does not envy, it does not boast, it is not proud. It is not rude, it is not self-seeking, it is not easily angered, it keeps no record of wrongs. Love does not delight in evil but rejoices in the truth. It always protects, always trusts, always hopes, always perseveres.

Love never fails. But where there are prophecies, they will cease; where there are tongues, they will be stilled; where there is knowledge, it will pass away. For we know in part and we prophesy in part, but when perfection comes, the imperfect disappears. When I was a child, I talked like a child, I thought like a child, I reasoned like a child. When I became a man, I put childish ways behind me. Now we see but a poor reflection; then we shall see face to face. Now I know in part; then I shall know fully, even as I am fully known.

And now these three remain: faith, hope and love. But the greatest of these is love.

— (NIV)

684 Within the Church

There is no color barrier with God.
He is color-blind.
There are many practical problems
which still have to be wisely and understandingly worked out.

But one thing is certain,
that the color barrier
and the Christian Church
cannot go together.

It was the world which God so loved,
and within the Church
it is the world which is
the family of God.

—William Barclay

685 In Christ There Is No East or West

... In every nation he that feareth Him, and worketh righteousness, is accepted with Him. — Acts 10:35

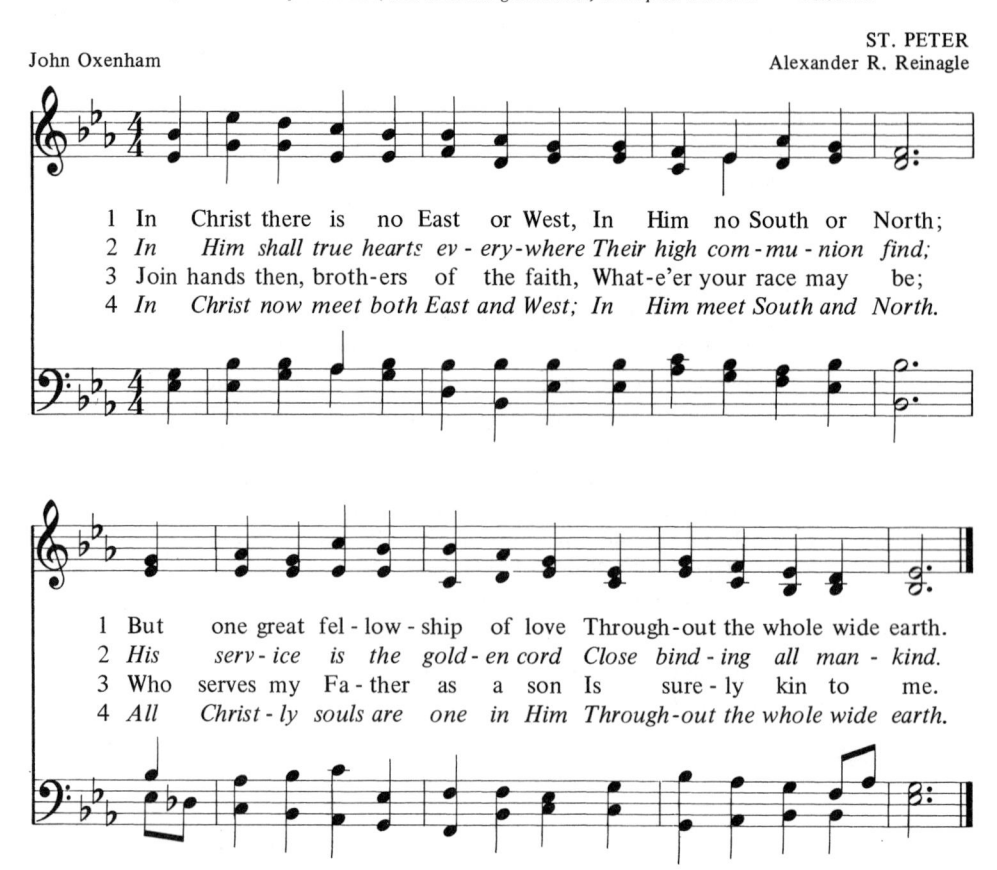

John Oxenham

ST. PETER
Alexander R. Reinagle

1. In Christ there is no East or West, In Him no South or North; But one great fel-low-ship of love Through-out the whole wide earth.
2. In Him shall true hearts ev-ery-where Their high com-mu-nion find; His serv-ice is the gold-en cord Close bind-ing all man-kind.
3. Join hands then, broth-ers of the faith, What-e'er your race may be; Who serves my Fa-ther as a son Is sure-ly kin to me.
4. In Christ now meet both East and West; In Him meet South and North. All Christ-ly souls are one in Him Through-out the whole wide earth.

BROTHERHOOD AND WORLD PEACE

Christ For the World We Sing

Acquaint thyself with Him and be at peace. — Job 22:21

Samuel Wolcott

ITALIAN HYMN
Felice de Giardini

1. Christ for the world we sing; The world to
   Christ we bring With loving zeal—
   The poor and them that mourn, The faint and o-verborne,
   Sin-sick and sorrow-worn, For Christ to heal.

2. Christ for the world we sing; The world to
   Christ we bring With fervent prayer—
   The wayward and the lost, By restless passions tossed,
   Redeemed at countless cost From dark despair.

3. Christ for the world we sing; The world to
   Christ we bring With one accord—
   With us the work to share, With us reproach to dare,
   With us the cross to bear, For Christ our Lord.

4. Christ for the world we sing; The world to
   Christ we bring With joyful song—
   The new-born souls whose days, Reclaimed from error's ways,
   Inspired with hope and praise, To Christ belong. A-men.

BROTHERHOOD AND WORLD PEACE

687 God of Our Fathers

The Lord of hosts is with us, the God of Jacob is our refuge. — Psalm 48:7

Daniel C. Roberts

NATIONAL HYMN
George W. Warren

Trumpets before each stanza

1. God of our fa-thers, whose al-might-y hand
2. *Thy love di-vine hath led us in the past,*
3. From war's a-larms, from dead-ly pes-ti-lence,
4. *Re-fresh Thy peo-ple on their toil-some way,*

1. Leads forth in beau-ty all the star-ry band
2. *In this free land by Thee our lot is cast;*
3. Be Thy strong arm our ev-er sure de-fense;
4. *Lead us from night to nev-er end-ing day;*

1. Of shin-ing worlds in splen-dor through the skies,
2. *Be Thou our rul-er, guard-ian, guide, and stay,*
3. Thy true re-li-gion in our hearts in-crease,
4. *Fill all our lives with love and grace di-vine,*

1. Our grate-ful songs be-fore Thy throne a-rise.
2. *Thy word our law, Thy paths our cho-sen way.*
3. Thy boun-teous good-ness nour-ish us in peace.
4. *And glo-ry, laud, and praise be ev-er Thine!* A-men.

PATRIOTIC

Alternate Last Verse Harmonization

Arranged by Fred Bock

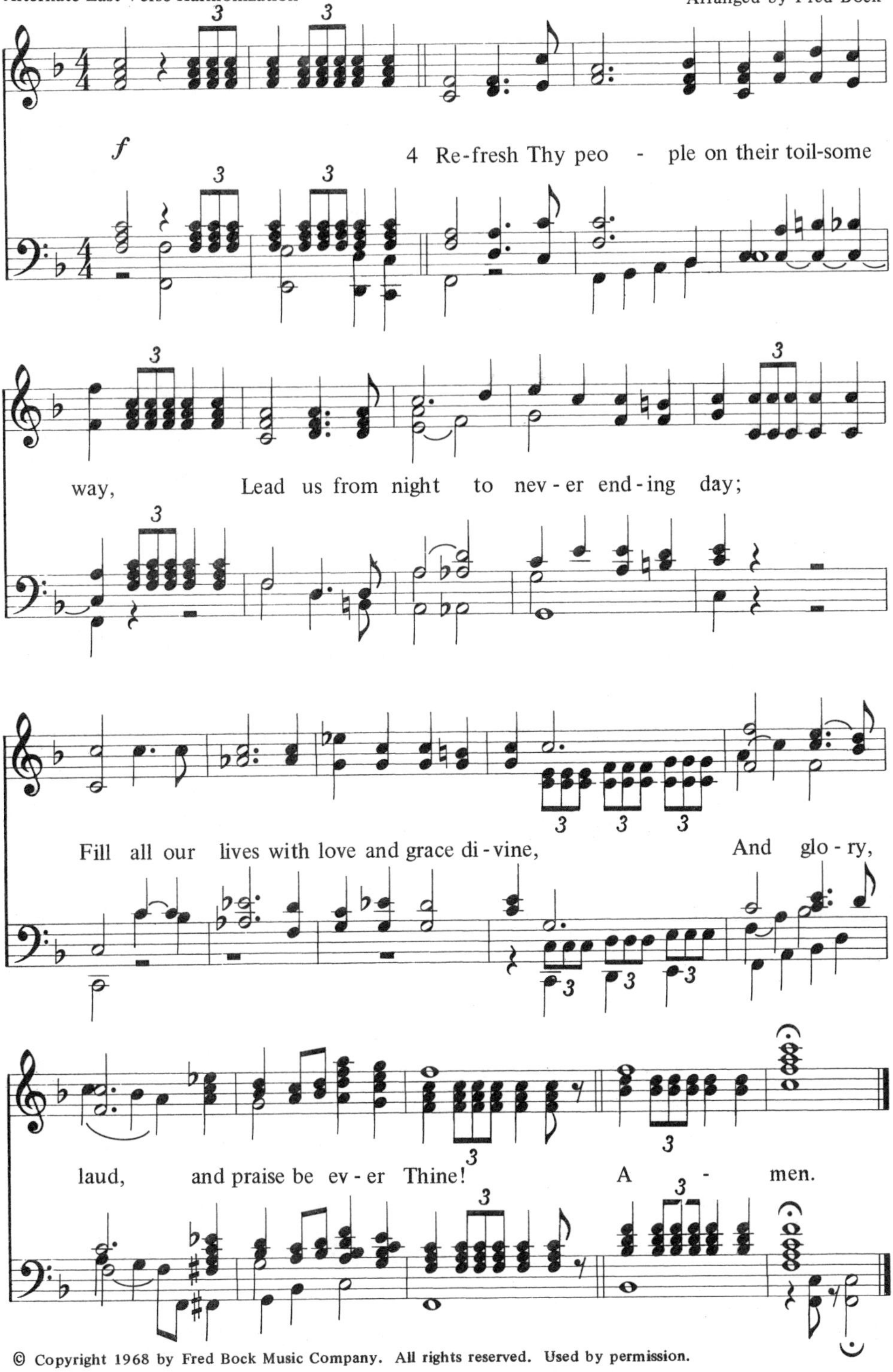

688 The Star-Spangled Banner

...And on Mine arm shall they trust. — Isaiah 51:5

Francis Scott Key

NATIONAL ANTHEM
John Stafford Smith

1. O say, can you see, by the dawn's ear-ly light, What so proud-ly we hailed at the twi-light's last gleam-ing, Whose broad stripes and bright stars, through the per-il-ous fight, O'er the ram-parts we watched, were so gal-lant-ly stream-ing? And the rock-ets' red glare, the bombs burst-ing in air, Gave proof through the night that our flag was still

2. *O thus be it ev-er, when free men shall stand Be-tween their loved homes and the war's des-o-la-tion! Blest with vic-tory and peace, may the heaven-res-cued land Praise the Power that hath made and pre-served us a na-tion! Then con-quer we must, when our cause it is just; And this be our mot-to: "In God is our*

PATRIOTIC

1 there. O say does that star-spangled banner yet wave
2 trust!" And the star-spangled banner in triumph shall wave

1 O'er the land of the free and the home of the brave?
2 O'er the land of the free and the home of the brave?

Before an Election   689

    Lord Jesus, we ask Thee to guide the people of this nation as they exercise their dearly bought privilege of franchise. May it neither be ignored unthinkingly nor undertaken lightyly. As citizens all over this land go to the ballot boxes, give them a sense of high privilege and joyous responsibility.

    Help those who are about to be elected to public office to come to understand the real source of their mandate—a mandate given by no party machine, received at no polling booth, but given by God; a mandate to represent God and truth at the heart of the nation; a mandate to do good in the name of Him under whom this country was established.

    We ask Thee to lead our country in the paths where Thou wouldst have her walk, to do the tasks which Thou hast laid before her. So may we together seek happiness for all our citizens in the name of Him who created us all equal in His sight, and therefore brothers. Amen.

—Peter Marshall

PATRIOTIC

690 America, the Beautiful

*But in every nation He that feareth Him,
and worketh righteousness is accepted by Him.* — Acts 10:35

Katharine Lee Bates

MATERNA
Samuel A. Ward
Descant by Fred Bock

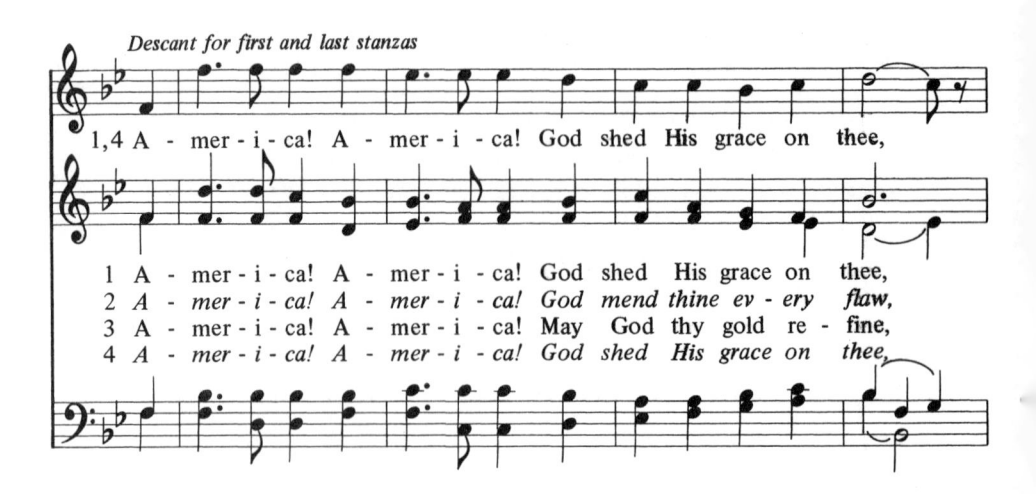

1 O beau-ti-ful for spa-cious skies, For am-ber waves of grain,
2 O beau-ti-ful for pil-grim feet, Whose stern, im-pas-sioned stress
3 O beau-ti-ful for he-roes proved In lib-er-at-ing strife,
4 O beau-ti-ful for pa-triot dream That sees be-yond the years

1 For pur-ple moun-tain maj-es-ties A-bove the fruit-ed plain!
2 A thor-ough-fare for free-dom beat A-cross the wil-der-ness!
3 Who more than self their coun-try loved, And mer-cy more than life!
4 Thine al-a-bas-ter cit-ies gleam, Un-dimmed by hu-man tears!

Descant for first and last stanzas

1,4 A-mer-i-ca! A-mer-i-ca! God shed His grace on thee,

1 A-mer-i-ca! A-mer-i-ca! God shed His grace on thee,
2 A-mer-i-ca! A-mer-i-ca! God mend thine ev-ery flaw,
3 A-mer-i-ca! A-mer-i-ca! May God thy gold re-fine,
4 A-mer-i-ca! A-mer-i-ca! God shed His grace on thee,

© Copyright 1976 by Fred Bock Music Company. All rights reserved. Used by permission.

PATRIOTIC

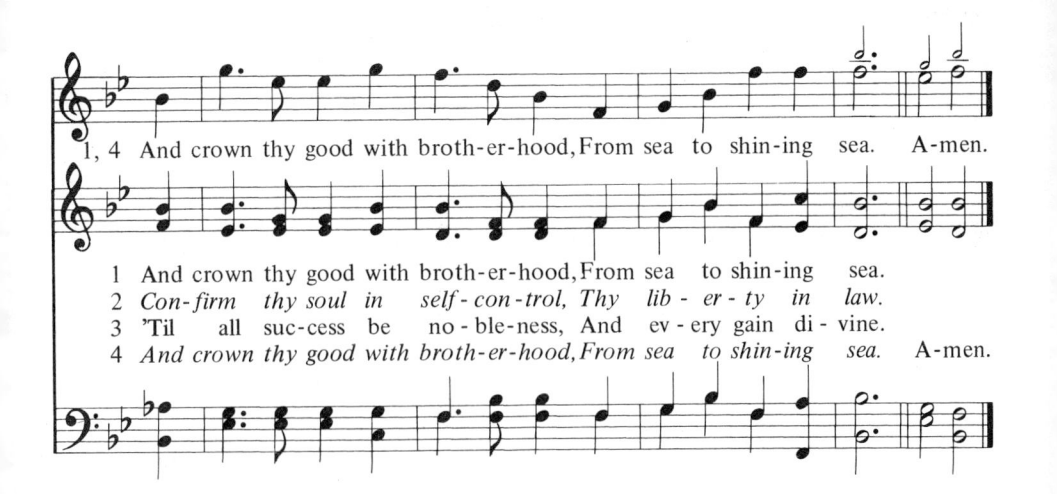

1, 4 And crown thy good with broth-er-hood, From sea to shin-ing sea. A-men.

1 And crown thy good with broth-er-hood, From sea to shin-ing sea.
2 Con-firm thy soul in self-con-trol, Thy lib-er-ty in law.
3 'Til all suc-cess be no-ble-ness, And ev-ery gain di-vine.
4 And crown thy good with broth-er-hood, From sea to shin-ing sea. A-men.

The Social Obligations of a Christian 691

The Bible teaches that the Christian should be law-abiding. The Bible also teaches loyalty to country. A loyalty and love of country does not mean that we cannot criticize certain unjust laws that may discriminate against special groups. The Bible says that God is no respecter of persons. All should have equal opportunities. The government of God is to be our model.

The Bible also teaches that we are to co-operate with the government. Jesus was asked, "Is it lawful to give tribute?" Jesus set the example forever by paying taxes. It takes money to run a government and to maintain law and order. The tax dodger is a civic parasite and an actual thief. No true Christian will be a tax dodger. Jesus said, we are to "render to Caesar the things that are Caesar's." We ought to be more than taxpayers. To be simply law-abiding is not enough. We ought to seek and work for the good of our country. Sometimes we may be called upon to die for it. We are to do it gladly—as unto God. We are to be conscientious in our work as good citizens.

—Billy Graham

PATRIOTIC

692 Battle Hymn of the Republic

If the trumpet give an uncertain sound who shall prepare himself for the battle? — I Corinthians 14:8

BATTLE HYMN OF THE REPUBLIC
American Melody
Introductory fanfare by Roy Ringwald
Descant by Fred Bock

Julia Ward Howe

*Trumpets—
use before first stanza only*

1 Mine eyes have seen the glo-ry of the com-ing of the Lord,
2 *I have seen Him in the watch-fires of a hun-dred cir-cling camps,*
3 He has sound-ed forth the trum-pet that shall nev-er call re-treat,
4 *In the beau-ty of the lil-ies Christ was born a-cross the sea,*

1 He is tram-pling out the vin-tage where the grapes of wrath are stored;
2 *They have build-ed Him an al-tar in the eve-ning dews and damps;*
3 He is sift-ing out the hearts of men be-fore His judg-ment seat;
4 *With a glo-ry in His be-ing that trans-fig-ures you and me;*

1 He hath loosed the fate-ful light-ning of His ter-ri-ble swift sword,
2 *I can read His right-eous sen-tence by the dim and flar-ing lamps,*
3 O be swift, my soul, to an-swer Him, be ju-bi-lant, my feet!
4 *As He died to make men ho-ly let us live to make men free!*

Introductory fanfare © Copyright 1943, Shawnee Press, Inc., Delaware Water Gap, PA 18327. U.S. Copyright renewed 1971. International copyright secured. All rights reserved. Descant © Copyright 1976 by Fred Bock Music Company. All rights reserved. Used by permission.

PATRIOTIC

Descant for Refrain

Glory! Hallelujah! Glory! Hallelujah! Glory! Hallelujah! His truth is marching on!

1 His truth is marching on.
2 *His day is marching on.*
3 Our God is marching on.
4 *While God is marching on.*

Glory! glory! Hallelujah! Glory! glory! Hallelujah! Glory! glory! Hallelujah! His truth is marching on!

PATRIOTIC

693 This Is My Country

... In every nation he that feareth Him, and worketh righteousness is accepted by Him.
— Acts 10:35

Don Raye

MY COUNTRY
Al Jacobs

Unison

This is my country, Land of my birth;

This is my country, Grandest on earth!

I pledge thee my allegiance, America, the bold;

For this is my country to have and to hold!

© Copyright 1940, Shawnee Press, Inc. U.S. Copyright renewed. This arrangement © Copyright 1976, Shawnee Press, Inc. International copyright secured. All rights reserved. Used by permission.

PATRIOTIC

America, Our Heritage

694

Mountains, and all hills, fruitful trees, fowls . . . let them praise the name of the Lord. — Psalm 148:9

Helen Steele

OUR HERITAGE
Helen Steele

1. High tower-ing moun-tains, fields gold with grain, Rich, fer-tile farm-lands, flocks on the plain, Homes blest with peace, with love, with-out fears: This is the her-i-tage we've kept through the years.
2. *Wide roll-ing prai-ries, lakes deep and broad, Can-yons ma-jes-tic, fash-ioned by God, Life lived in peace, con-tent-ed and free:* This is the her-i-tage for-ev-er to be.
3. Stout hearts and true, hold fast what is ours, God give us cour-age through dark-est hours, God give us strength and guide with Thy hand A-mer-i-ca, our her-i-tage, our home-land. A-men.

© Copyright 1943, Shawnee Press, Inc., Delaware Water Gap, PA 18327. U.S. Copyright renewed 1971. © Copyright 1952, 1975, Shawnee Press, Inc. International copyright secured. All rights reserved. Used by permission.

PATRIOTIC

695 My Country, 'Tis of Thee

Blessed is that nation whose God is the Lord. — Psalm 33:12

Samuel F. Smith

AMERICA
Henry Carey
Descant by Mary E. Caldwell

Descant
4 Our fathers' God, to Thee, Author of liberty,

1 My country, 'tis of thee, Sweet land of liberty,
2 *My native country, thee, Land of the noble, free,*
3 Let music swell the breeze, And ring from all the trees
4 *Our fathers' God, to Thee, Author of liberty,*

To Thee we sing: Long may our land be bright With freedom's

1 Of thee I sing: Land where my fathers died, Land of the
2 *Thy name I love. I love thy rocks and rills, Thy woods and*
3 Sweet freedom's song. Let mortal tongues awake; Let all that
4 *To Thee we sing: Long may our land be bright With freedom's*

holy light; Protect us by Thy might, Great God, our King!

1 Pilgrims' pride. From every mountainside Let freedom ring!
2 *templed hills; My heart with rapture thrills Like that above.*
3 breathe partake; Let rocks their silence break, The sound prolong.
4 *holy light; Protect us by Thy might, Great God, our King!*

© Copyright 1976 by Paragon Associates, Inc. All rights reserved.

Amen 696
Louis Bourgeois

A — men.

Twofold Amen 697
Dresden

A - men, A — men.

Threefold Amen 698
Traditional

A — men, A - men, A - men.

Sixfold Amen 699
Paul Sjolund

Moderato sempre cresc. — *mf*
p
A - men, A - men,
pp
Ped.

f rit. *ff*
A - men, A - men, A - men. A — men!

© Copyright 1976 by Paragon Associates, Inc. All rights reserved.

700

Sing unto the Lord a new song – Psalm 33:3

This page has been prepared for future hymnal inserts.

Sing unto the Lord a new song – Psalm 33:3   **701**

This page has been prepared for future hymnal inserts.

702 *Sing unto the Lord a new song* – Psalm 33:3

This page has been prepared for future hymnal inserts.

Indexes

Copyright Acknowledgements

The Scripture passages in this hymnal marked Leslie Brandt are from *Psalms/Now,* © 1973 by Concordia Publishing House. Used by permission.

Those marked (JB) are from *The Jerusalem Bible,* Copyright 1966 by Darton, Longman & Todd, Ltd. and Doubleday & Company, Inc. Used by permission.

Those marked (LB) are from *The Living Bible,* © Copyright 1971 by Tyndale House Publishers, Wheaton, Illinois. Used by permission.

Those marked (NEB) are from *The New English Bible,* ©Copyright 1961, 1970 by The Delegates of the Oxford University Press and the Syndics of the Cambridge University Press. Reprinted by permission.

Those marked (J.B. Phillips) are from *The New Testament in Modern English,* revised edition. Reprinted with permission of MacMillan Publishing Co., Inc. © Copyright J.B. Phillips 1958, 1960, 1972.

Those marked (NIV) are from *The New International Version New Testament,* © Copyright 1973 by the New York Bible Society International. Used by permission.

The passage marked (Psalms in Modern Speech) published by Fortress Press. Used by permission.

Those marked (RSV) are from *The Revised Standard Version of the Bible,* © Copyrighted 1946, 1952, 1971, 1973. Used by permission.

Those marked (TEV) are from *Today's English Version of the New Testament,* © Copyright by the American Bible Society, 1966, 1971. Used by permission.

Those marked (KJV) are from the Authorized King James Version of the Bible.

SOURCES OF READINGS AND PRAYERS

3   © Copyright 1976 by Fred Bock Music Company, Tarzana, California 91356. All rights reserved. Used by permission.
14 © Copyright 1976 by Bryan Jeffery Leech. All rights reserved. Used by permission.
33 Used by permission of Garland Publishing, Inc., New York, New York.
44 From *Contemporary Worship Services* published by Fleming H. Revell Co., © Copyright 1971. Used by permission.
45 From *The Prayers of Peter Marshall,* edited by Catherine Marshall, © Copyright 1954 by Catherine Marshall. Used by permission of McGraw-Hill Book Company.
47 From *Spiritual Depression,* published by Wm. B. Eerdmans Company. © Copyright 1965 by Martin Lloyd-Jones. Used by permission.
54 © Copyright 1967 in *New Songs of Inspiration Number 7.* All rights reserved. Used by permission.
55 © Copyright 1976 by Richard Langford. All rights reserved. Used by permission.
59 From *Amazing Love,* © Copyright 1953 by the Christian Literature Crusade. All rights reserved. Used by permission.
74 © Copyright 1976 by Bryan Jeffery Leech. All rights reserved. Used by permission.
80 From the book, *Positive Thinking for a Time Like This,* © Copyright 1975 by Prentice-Hall, Inc. Published by Prentice-Hall, Inc., Englewood Cliffs, New Jersey.
88 From *The Prayers of Peter Marshall,* edited by Catherine Marshall, © Copyright 1954 by Catherine Marshall. Used by permission of McGraw-Hill Book Company.
90 From *The People, Yes,* © Copyright 1936 by Harcourt Brace Jovanovich, Inc. Renewed 1964 by Carl Sandburg. Reprinted by permission of the publishers.
    © Copyright 1976 by Gloria Gaither. All rights reserved. Used by permission.
97 From *Solzhenitsyn: A Pictorial Autobiography.* Reprinted with the permission of Farrar, Straus & Giroux, Inc., © Copyright 1974 by Farrar, Straus & Giroux, Inc.
103 From *Letters and Papers from Prison.* Revised enlarged edition © Copyright 1953, 1967, 1971 by SCM Press Ltd. Reprinted with permission of MacMillan Publishing Co., Inc.
111 © Copyright 1976 by Pann Baltz. All rights reserved. Used by permission.
113 © Copyright 1976 by Gary W. Demarest. All rights reserved. Used by permission.
119 From *Prayers We Have in Common.* Fortress Press. Used by permission.
126 © Copyright by the American Bible Society 1966, 1971. Used by permission.
139 From *The Mennonite Hymnal,* © Copyright 1969 by Faith and Life Press, Newton, Kansas and Herald Press, Scottsdale, Pennsylvania
141 Reprinted by permission of the United Church Press.
146 From *Contemporary Prayers for Public Worship,* Caryl Micklem, editor. Published by Wm. B. Eerdmans Publishing Company. Used by permission.

154 © Copyright 1976 by Raymond I. Lindquist. All rights reserved. Used by permission.
160 © Copyright 1976 by Gary W. Demarest. All rights reserved. Used by permission.
163 From *Our Song of Hope*. Used by permission of the Reformed Church of America.
167 From *Mere Christianity*, © Copyright 1943, 1945, 1952 by MacMillan Publishing Company, Inc., New York, N.Y. Reprinted with permission of MacMillan Publishing Co., Inc.
188 From *The Prayers of Peter Marshall,* edited by Catherine Marshall, © Copyright 1954 by Catherine Marshall. Used by permission of McGraw-Hill Book Company.
189 From *Markings,* translated by Leif Sjoberg and W.H. Auden. © Copyright 1964 by Alfred A. Knopf Inc., and Faber and Faber, Ltd. Reprinted by permission of Alfred A. Knopf, Inc.
200 © Copyright 1975 by Paragon Associates. From *His Love . . . Reaching.* Used by permission.
218 From "Mr. Jones, Meet the Master", in *Sermons and Prayers of Peter Marshall.* © Copyright 1949, 1950 by Fleming H. Revell Company. Used by permission.
241 From *Thoughts for Everyday Living.* © Copyright 1901 by Charles Scribner's Sons. Copyright renewed 1929 by Katherine T. Babcock.
243 © Copyright 1976 by Gloria Gaither. #1 From *1500 Inspiration Quotes and Illustrations.* © Copyright 1974 by Beacon Hill Publishing Co. of Kansas City and reprinted by Baker Book House, 1975. All rights reserved. Used by permission.
257 From *The Prayers of Peter Marshall* edited by Catherine Marshall, © Copyright 1954 by Catherine Marshall. Used by permission of McGraw-Hill Book Company.
286 © Copyright 1976 by Marilee Zdenek. All rights reserved. Used by permission.
294 From *The Prayers of Peter Marshall,* edited by Catherine Marshall, © Copyright 1954 by Catherine Marshall. Used by permission of McGraw-Hill Book Company.
300 © Copyright 1976 by Raymond I. Lindquist. All rights reserved. Used by permission.
329 From *Daily Celebration,* © Copyright 1971 by Denis Duncan. Published by Word Books, Waco, Texas. All rights reserved. Used by permission.
333 Reprinted from *Lord, Make My Life a Miracle,* a Regal Book. Used by permission of G/L Publications - Copyright 1974 by G/L Publications, Glendale, CA 91209.
346 © Copyright 1976 "The Creative Use of Musical Resources for Worship" by Bruce H. Leafblad. Used by permission.
350 © Copyright 1976 by Gloria Gaither. All rights reserved. Used by permission.
355 © Copyright 1973 by Covenant Press. Used by permission.
364 From *The Church Before the Watching World,* © Copyright 1971 by L'Abri Fellowship, Switzerland. Used by permission of Inter-Varsity Press, USA.
371 From *Let God Love You,* © Copyright 1974 by Word, Inc., Waco, Texas. Used by permission.
380 © Copyright 1976 by Bryan Jeffery Leech. All rights reserved. Used by permission.
383 From *Prayers,* © Copyright 1963 by Sheed & Ward, Inc., New York, N.Y. Used by permission.
391 From *The Prayers of Peter Marshall,* edited by Catherine Marshall, © Copyright 1954 by Catherine Marshall. Used by permission of McGraw-Hill Book Company.
393 From *Folk Psalms of Faith,* © Copyright 1973 by Ray Stedman. Published by Regal Books, a division of G/L Publications, Glendale, CA. 91209.
396 From *Services for Trial Use,* © Copyright 1971 by Charles Mortimer Guilbert as custodian of The Standard Book of Common Prayer. Used by permission.
413 © Copyright 1976 by Howard Childers All rights reserved. Used by permission.
423 © Copyright 1976 by Howard Childers All rights reserved. Used by permission.
424 © Copyright 1976 by Kenneth C. Working. All rights reserved. Used by permission.
431 From *The Holy Spirit and You.* © Copyright 1971 by Logos International, Plainfield, New Jersey. Used by permission.
460 © Copyright 1976 by Bryan Jeffery Leech. All rights reserved. Used by permission.
464 From *The Prayers of Peter Marshall,* edited by Catherine Marshall, © Copyright 1954 by Catherine Marshall. Used by permission of McGraw-Hill Book Company.
475 © Copyright 1976 by Bryan Jeffery Leech. All rights reserved. Used by permission.
484 From *Letters to Malcolm; Chiefly on Prayer.* Published by Harcourt Brace Jovanovich, Inc. © Copyright 1963, 1964. Used by permission. All rights reserved.
487 From *Lord, Be With.* © Copyright 1969 by Concordia Publishing House. All rights reserved. Used by permission.
503 From *Still Higher for His Highest.* © Copyright 1970 by D.W. Lambert. Published by Zondervan by arrangement. Used by permission.
506 From the Prayer on page 151 in *Something Beautiful for God: Mother Teresa of Calcutta* by Malcolm Muggeridge. © Copyright 1971 by The Mother Teresa Committee. By permission of Harper & Row Publishers, Inc.
508 From *Adventures in Prayer.* Text Copyright © 1975 by Catherine Marshall. Published by Chosen Books, Inc. Distributed by Fleming H. Revell Company. Used by permission.
511 © Copyright 1976 by Gary W. Demarest. Used by permission. All rights reserved.
514 Reprint from *C.S. Lewis: Mere Christian* (A Regal Book) by permission of Gospel Light Publications, © Copyright 1973 by G/L Publications, Glendale, CA 91209

517 Reprinted with permission of MacMillan Publishing Co., Inc. From *Letters and Papers from Prison,* revised, enlarged edition. © Copyright 1953, 1967, 1971 by SCM Press, Ltd.
524 © Copyright 1976 by Bryan Jeffery Leech. All rights reserved. Used by permission.
529 From *Our Song of Hope.* By permission of the Reformed Church in America.
532 From *The World Needs Men,* from "In a nutshell." © Copyright by Len Wagner.
533 © Copyright 1976 by Donn D. Moomaw. All rights reserved. Used by permission.
534 From *Power Ideas for a Happy Family.* Copyright © 1972 by Robert Harold Schuller. A Spire Book published by Pillar Books for Fleming H. Revell Company. Used by permission.
536 Reprinted from *The View from the Hearse,* © Copyright 1969, David C. Cook Publishing Co., Elgin, Illinois. Used by permission.
539 From *You Can Be a Great Parent.* Formerly published as *Promises to Peter,* © Copyright 1970 by Charlie W. Shedd and the Abundance Foundation. Published by Word Books, Publisher. All rights reserved. Used by permission.
542 © Copyright 1975 SP Publications, Inc. Wheaton, Illinois. By permission of Victor Books from *For These Fragile Times.*
549 From *Prayer,* © 1976 John T. Benson Publishing Company, 365 Great Circle Road, Nashville, Tennessee 37228. All rights reserved.
561 © Copyright 1976 by Bryan Jeffery Leech. All rights reserved. Used by permission.
566 © Copyright 1972 by Fred Bock Music Company. All rights reserved. Used by permission.
569 © Copyright 1976 by Gloria Gaither. All rights reserved. Used by permission.
570 From *Make Warm Noises,* © Copyright 1971 by Impact Books, a division of John T. Benson Publishing Co. All rights reserved. Used by permission.
573 From *Living the Adventure: Faith and "Hidden" Difficulties.* © Copyright 1975 by Word, Inc., Waco, Texas. All rights reserved. Used by permission.
577 Reprinted from *Love Unlimited,* (a Regal Book) by Bishop Festo Kivengere by permission of Gospel Light Publications, Glendale, CA. © Copyright 1975 by Gospel Light Publications.
582 Lamentations 3:21,22 © Copyright 1976 by John A. Huffman, Jr. Used by permission. All rights reserved.
583 © Copyright 1976 by Gloria Gaither. Used by permission. All rights reserved.
593 © Copyright 1976 by William J. Gaither and Gloria Gaither. All rights reserved. Used by permission.
599 From *All Things Are Possible Through Prayer,* by Charles L. Allen. © Copyright 1958 by Fleming H. Revell Company. All rights reserved. Used by permission.
604 Excerpt from p. 37, *A Doctor's Casebook,* Harper and Row, Jubilee Edition 1976.
610 From *Markings,* translated by Leif Sjoberg and W.H. Auden, Copyright © 1964 by Alfred A. Knopf, Inc., and Faber and Faber, Ltd. Reprinted by permission of Alfred A. Knopf, Inc.
615 Reprinted from *Is Life Really Worth Living?,* by permission of G/L Publications, © Copyright 1974 by G/L Publications, Glendale, California 91209
620 1st Stanza of "I Stand by the Door" from *I Stand By The Door* by Helen Smith Shoemaker. © Copyright 1967 by Helen Smith Shoemaker. By permission of Harper and Row Publishers.
624 © Copyright 1976 by Kenneth C. Working. All rights reserved. Used by permission.
649 © Copyright 1976 by Bryan Jeffery Leech. All rights reserved. Used by permission.
671 From *The Sorrows of God.* © Copyright 1924, Harper & Brothers. Used by permission.
673 By permission of Garland Publishing, Inc.
675 © Copyright 1976 by Bryan Jeffery Leech. All rights reserved. Used by permission.
677 *They'll Know We Are Christians,* Words and music by Peter Scholtes. Copyright © 1966 by F.E.L. Publications, Ltd., 1925 Pontius Avenue, Los Angeles, CA 90025. Performance rights licensed through ASCAP. Further reproduction (even words only) not permitted without F.E.L.'s written permission.
678 From *Ethics.* © Copyright 1955 by MacMillan Publishing Co., Inc. © SCM Press, Ltd., 1955. All rights reserved. Used by permission.
680 From *What Do You Say to a Hungry World?* © Copyright Word Books, Inc. All rights reserved. Used by permission.
684 From *Daily Celebration.* © Copyright 1971 by Denis Duncan. Published by Word Books, Inc.
689 From *The Prayers of Peter Marshall,* edited by Catherine Marshall, © Copyright 1954 by Catherine Marshall. Used with permission of McGraw-Hill Book Company.
691 From *Peace With God.* © 1953 by Billy Graham. Published by Doubleday & Company, Inc. All rights reserved. Used by permission.

NOTE:

Every effort has been made to locate the owners of copyrighted material used in this publication. Upon notification, the Publisher will make proper correction in subsequent printings

Scriptural Index of Readings

Old Testament

420	Exodus 20: 1-7 (Ten Commandments)	449	Psalm 122
578	II Chronicles 7:8-18	449	Psalm 123
478	Psalm 1	388	Psalm 136:1-9, 16-18
553	Psalm 15	438	Psalm 144
41	Psalm 23	3	Psalm 148
8	Psalm 24	375	Psalm 150
346	Psalm 24:3,4	569	Proverbs 3:5
116	Psalm 32	31	Proverbs 3:13-26
426	Psalm 51	569	Proverbs 22:6
482	Psalm 59	531	Proverbs 31:10-21, 23, 25-30
121	Psalm 73:1-3, 21-28	448	Isaiah 6:1-8
490	Psalm 83	196	Isaiah 9:6,7; 11:14
17	Psalm 89	272	Isaiah 52:13-53:12
369	Psalm 90:1-12	569	Isaiah 54:13
375	Psalm 100	111	Jeremiah 29:11
378	Psalm 103:1-5, 19-22	582	Lamentations 3:21,22
11	Psalm 104	99	Lamentations 3:22-33
27	Psalm 110	23	Hosea 14:4b-9
85	Psalm 121	158	Joel 3:1-5

New Testament

173	Matthew 2:1-12	683	I Corinthians 13:1-13
589	Matthew 5:1-12 (The Beatitudes)	290	I Corinthians 15:12-28
243	Matthew 16:13b-16	296	I Corinthians 15:51-58
569	Matthew 18:3-5	63	II Corinthians 4:6-12
211	Matthew 18:3-6	68	II Corinthians 12:1-10
308	Matthew 25:31-46	583	II Corinthians 12:9, 10b
211	Mark 9:35-37	586	Galatians 5:13-6:2
211	Mark 10:14-16	541	Ephesians 3:14-4:6
176	Luke 1:46b-55	612	Ephesians 6:10-20
191	Luke 1:68-79	209	Philippians 2:1-11
186	Luke 2:1-12	492	Philippians 4:6,7
261	Luke 4:14-22	445	Colossians 1:11-20
302	Luke 24:5b-7	233	Colossians 1:15-23
165	John 1:1-14	214	I Timothy 3:16b
20	John 3:14-21	463	Hebrews 12:1-13
271	John 10:14-18	602	James 1:5-8
57	John 14:1-12	90	I Peter 1:6,7
569	John 14:6	90	I Peter 1:13-16
592	John 14:24-30	264	I Peter 1:18-21
152	Acts 2:1-4; 14:22b-24, 36-42	90	I Peter 1:3
660	Acts 17:22-31	380	I John 1:5-7
280	Romans 5:1-11	267	I John 1:6-9
90	Romans 5:2b-5	126	I John 3:1-6
50	Romans 8:28-39	558	I John 4:7-21
90	Romans 8:28a	124, 666	Revelation 7:9-17
156	I Corinthians 2:1-5	237	Revelation 15:3b,4
252	I Corinthians 2:10-16	563	Revelation 22:16, 17
562	I Corinthians 11:17-29		

Alphabetical Index of Authors (readings)

Allen, Charles L.	599
Anonymous	106, 163, 204, 348, 521, 527
Babcock, Maltbie D.	241
Baltz, Pann	111
Barclay, William	329, 684
Bayly, Joseph	536
Bennett, Dennis & Rita	431
Benson, Robert Sr.	54
Bock, Fred	3, 566
Bonhoeffer, Dietrich	103, 517, 678
Brandt, Leslie	11, 17, 27, 426, 438, 448, 482, 490, 553
Brokering, Herbert	487
Browning, Robert	25
Bunyan, John	356
Caswell, Edward	509
Chambers, Oswald	503
Childers, Howard	413, 423
Christensen, James L.	44
Dahlgren, James	355
Demarest, Gary W.	113, 160, 511
Donne, John	90
Gaither, Gloria	90, 200, 243, 350, 569, 570, 583, 593
Gaither, William J.	200, 593
Graham, Billy	691
Guilbert, Charles M.	396
Hammarskjold, Dag	189, 610
Harvey, John W.	410
Hill, Leslie Pinckney	471
Hubbard, David	615
Huff, Ronn	200
Huffman, John A., Jr.	582
Kivengere, Festo	577
Landorf, Joyce	542
Langford, Richard	55
Larson, Bruce	573
Lawrence, Brother	499
Leafblad, Bruce H.	346
Leech, Bryan Jeffery	14, 74, 380, 460, 475, 524, 561, 649, 675
Lewis, C.S.	167, 484, 514
Lindquist, Raymond	154, 300
Lindskoog, Kathryn Ann	514
Lloyd-Jones, Martin	47
Luther, Martin	Page "x"
Marshall, Catherine	508
Marshall, Peter	45, 88, 188, 218, 257, 294, 391, 464, 689
McNair, Jacqueline Hanna	340
Micklem, Caryl	146
Miller, Keith	573
Moomaw, Donn	533
Mooneyham, W. Stanley	680
Moreland, John Richard	245
Muggeridge, Malcolm	243, 506
Ogilvie, Lloyd John	371
Ortlund, Raymond C.	333
Page, Kirby	33, 673
Patrick, Saint	643
Peale, Norman Vincent	80
Phillips, J.B.	302, 562
Quoist, Michel	383
Sandburg, Carl	90
Schaeffer, Francis A.	364
Schuller, Robert H.	534
Shedd, Charlie W.	539
Shoemaker, Samuel	620
Solzhenitsyn, Aleksandr	97
Stedman, Ray	393
Studdert-Kennedy, G.A.	671
Taylor, Kenneth	50, 90, 267, 272, 445, 531, 578
ten Boom, Betsie	59
Tennyson, Alfred Lord	441
Teresa, Mother	506
Tolstoy, Leo	403
Traylor, Champ	549
Tournier, Paul	604
Wagner, Len	532
Wesley, John	640
Working, Kenneth C.	424
Xavier, Francis	509
Yates, Christina	410
Zdenek, Marilee	286

Alphabetical Index of Readings

340	A call to worship	Jacqueline Hanna McNair
14	A celebration for family people	Bryan Jeffery Leech
111	A certain uncertain future	Pann Baltz
403	A confession of faith	Leo Tolstoy
119	A contemporary Te Deum	
"x"	A fair and glorious gift	Martin Luther
396	A general thanksgiving	Standard Book of Common Prayer
74	A pledge of trust	Bryan Jeffery Leech
521	A prayer	Ancient prayer
475	A prayer	Bryan Jeffery Leech
113	A prayer for our world	Gary W. Demarest
55	A prayer for strength	Richard Langford
511	A Stewardship prayer	Gary W. Demarest
139	An affirmation	Mennonite Hymnal
527	Answered prayer	Anonymous
136	Apostle's Creed, The	
97	Assurance	Aleksandr Solzhenitsyn
424	Assurance of pardon	Kenneth Working
589	Beatitudes, The	Matthew 5:1-12
689	Before an election	Peter Marshall
165	Beginning	John 1:1-14
524	Benediction	Bryan Jeffery Leech
378	Bless the Lord	Psalm 103:1-5, 19-22
680	Can this world be fed	W. Stanley Mooneyham
536	Children as a trust	Joseph Bayly
643	Christ be with me	St. Patrick
245	Christ is crucified anew	John Richard Moreland
188	Christmas	Peter Marshall
577	Comparison	Festo Kivengere
136	Credo	The Apostle's Creed
300	Easter	Raymond Lindquist
294	Easter	Peter Marshall
517	Evening prayer	Dietrich Bonhoeffer
45	For loneliness in bereavement	Peter Marshall
196	For unto us	Isaiah 9:6,7; 11:1-4
640	Forgiveness	John Wesley
371	Free from the guilted cage	Lloyd John Ogilvie
599	Freedom of the will	Charles L. Allen
508	Give me a dream	Catherine Marshall
160	Give us your Holy Spirit	Gary W. Demarest
503	Glorifying God in the everyday	Oswald Chambers
50	God is for us	Romans 8:28-39
380	God is light	Bryan Jeffery Leech
25	God, Thou art love	Robert Browning
209	God's nature	Philippians 2:1-11
583	God's power in our weakness	Gloria Gaither
257	Good Friday	Peter Marshall
302	He is risen!	Luke 24:5b-7
388	His love is everlasting	Psalm 136:1-9, 16-18
200	His love . . . reaching	Gloria Gaither, William J. Gaither, Ronn Huff
90	Hope	Compiled by Gloria Gaither
121	How good is God	Psalm 73:1-3, 21-28
189	How proper it is	Dag Hammarskjold
138	I believe in one God	The Nicene Creed
620	I stand by the door	Samuel Shoemaker
286	If we had been there	Marilee Zdenek
448	In the year that King Uzziah died	Isaiah 6:1-8
671	Indifference	G.A. Studdert-Kennedy
582	Jeremiah's hope within hopelessness	John A. Huffman, Jr.

211	Jesus and the children	Matthew 18:3-6, Mark 9:35-37; 10:14-16
47	Joy at all times	Martin Lloyd-Jones
280	Justified by faith	Romans 5:1-11
492	Lasting peace	Philippians 4:6,7
464	Liberation from materialism	Peter Marshall
163	Life in two ages	"Our Song of Hope"
539	Lord, I want to remember	Charlie W. Shedd
506	Make us worthy, Lord	Mother Teresa
532	Manhood	Len Wagner
529	Marriage	"Our Song of Hope"
103	Morning prayer	Dietrich Bonhoeffer
509	My eternal King	Francis Xavier
241	No distant Lord	Maltbie D. Babcock
33	Not by bread alone	Kirby Page
566	One solitary Life	Fred Bock
499	Peace	Brother Lawrence
204	Peace on earth	Anonymous
59	Plans while in prison	Betsie ten Boom
3	Praise Hymn	Psalm 148
348	Praise to God	Anonymous
375	Praises to the Lord	Psalms 100, 150
610	Prayer	Dag Hammarskjold
542	Prayer	Joyce Landorf
460	Prayer	Bryan Jeffery Leech
383	Prayer	Michel Quoist
441	Prayer	Alfred Lord Tennyson
624	Prayer	Kenneth Working
410	Prayer and action	John W. Harvey and Christina Yates
44	Prayer for comfort	James L. Christensen
549	Prayer for unity	Champ Traylor
533	Prayer for the family	Donn Moomaw
431	Prayer of acceptance	Dennis and Rita Bennett
675	Prayer of concern for others	Bryan Jeffery Leech
487	Prayer of dedication	Herbert Brokering
673	Precious in God's sight	Kirby Page
80	Problems	Norman Vincent Peale
41	Psalm 23	
484	Real prayer	C.S. Lewis
573	Renewal	Keith Miller and Bruce Larson
85	Song of Ascents	Psalm 121
272	Substitution	Isaiah 52:13-53:12
593	Take His peace	Gloria Gaither, William J. Gaither
324	Te Deum	Anonymous
570	Thank God for children	Gloria Gaither
561	Thanksgiving	Bryan Jeffery Leech
391	Thanksgiving	Peter Marshall
393	Thanksgiving and praise	Ray Stedman
589	The Beatitudes	Matthew 5:1-12
173	The Birth of Jesus	Matthew 2:1-12
364	The chief end of man	Francis A. Schaeffer
152	The Day of Pentecost	Acts 2:1-4; 14:22b-24, 36-42
463	The example of Jesus Christ	Hebrews 12:1-13
418	The general confession	The Book of Common Prayer
413	The good news of God's forgiveness	Howard Childers
271	The good Shepherd	John 10:14-18
146	The Holy Spirit	Caryl Micklem
218	The humanity of Jesus	Peter Marshall
678	The hungry man and I	Dietrich Bonhoeffer
167	The Incarnation	C.S. Lewis
350	The joy of His presence	Gloria Gaither
356	The love of Christ	John Bunyan
158	The Outpouring of the Spirit	Joel 3:1-5
534	The parent's creed	Robert Schuller
558	The people of God	I John 4:7-21
423	The prayer of confession	Kenneth Working
154	The promise fulfilled	Raymond Lindquist
691	The social obligations of a Christian	Billy Graham
308	The Son of Man in His glory	Matthew 25:31-46
233	The supremacy of Christ	Colossians 1:15-23
604	The tangle of the mind	Paul Tournier
471	The teacher	Leslie Pinckney Hill
615	The temptation to quit	David Hubbard
420	The Ten Commandments	Exodus 20:1-17
41	The Twenty-third Psalm	
54	There has to be a song	Robert Benson
514	True Charity	Kathryn Ann Lindskoog
666	Vision	Revelation 7:9-17
141	We believe in a triune God	United Church of Christ
355	We praise you, Father	James E. Dahlgren
106	We're hungry, Lord	Anonymous compiled by Gloria Gaither
569	Welcoming a child	Peter Marshall
88	When we feel forsaken	
649	Where has all the witness gone?	Bryan Jeffery Leech
243	Who is this man?	Malcolm Muggeridge and Gloria Gaither styled by Bruce H. Leafblad
346	Who shall ascend?	
684	Within the church	William Barclay
531	Womanhood	Proverbs 31: 10-21, 23, 25-30
329	Worship	William Barclay
333	Worship	Raymond C. Ortlund

Scriptural Allusions in Hymns

OLD TESTAMENT:

Reference	Hymn #	Title
Numbers 6:24-26	522	The Lord bless you and keep you
II Chronicles 7:14	575	If My people will pray
Nehemiah 8:10	354	The joy of the Lord
Psalm 23	61	Like a lamb who needs the Shepherd
Psalm 23	66	My Shepherd will supply my need
Psalm 23	40, 42	The Lord's my Shepherd, I'll not want
Psalm 24:7	239	Lift up your heads, ye mighty gates
Psalm 26:8	545	I love your kingdom, Lord
Psalm 46	118	A mighty fortress is our God
Psalm 55:22	53	Cast thy burden upon the Lord
Psalm 72	238	Jesus shall reign, where'er the sun
Psalm 87:3	376	Glorious things of Thee are spoken
Psalm 90	370	O God, our help in ages past
Psalm 92	330	It is good to sing Thy praises
Psalm 98	171	Joy to the world!
Psalm 103	379	Bless His holy name
Psalm 103	379	Bless the Lord, o my soul
Psalm 150	373	Praise the Lord, His glories show
Isaiah 26:3	493	Thou wilt keep him in perfect peace
Isaiah 33:20,21	376	Glorious things of Thee are spoken
Isaiah 40:31	52	They that wait upon the Lord
Isaiah 43:1,2	32	How firm a foundation
Isaiah 54:10	496	Great hills may tremble
Isaiah 54:10	496	Security
Lamentations 3:22, 23	98	Great is Thy faithfulness

NEW TESTAMENT:

Reference	Hymn #	Title
Matthew 6:9-13	440	The Lord's prayer
Matthew 14:19	30	Break Thou the bread of life
Matthew 21:5-11	250	Ride on! Ride on in majesty!
Matthew 21:15,16	248	Hosanna, loud hosanna
Matthew 26:30	565	A hymn of joy we sing
Matthew 28:18-20	674	All power is given unto Me
Matthew 28:18-20	674	Far, far away in sin and darkness
Mark 10:13-15	213	I think when I read that sweet story
Luke 12:49	576	Thou, whose purpose is to kindle
John 3:16	315	For God so loved the world
John 3:16,17	20	God so loved the world
John 13:35	677	They'll know we are Christians by our love
John 13:35	677	We are one in the Spirit
Philippians 2:5-11	351	At the name of Jesus
Philippians 2:13	234	He is Lord
Philippians 2:13	584	God is at work within you
Philippians 4:4	374	Rejoice, the Lord is king
II Timothy 1:12	631	I know Whom I have believed
II Timothy 2:19	32	How firm a foundation
Hebrews 13:5	32	How firm a foundation

707

Topical Index of Hymns

ADVENT (See Christmas)
Christ, whose glory 293
Come, Thou long-expected Jesus 168
Joy to the world! 171
Let all mortal flesh 166
O come, O come, Emmanuel 169
Of the Father's love 172
Thou didst leave 170

ASPIRATION
"Are ye able" 470
Be Thou my vision 468
Eternal life 474
Fill my cup, Lord 481
Fill Thou my life 479
Higher ground 469
I'm pressing on 469
Lord, make me an instrument 474
Make me a blessing 473
May the mind of Christ 483
More about Jesus 477
More love to Thee 476
Nearer, still nearer 485
O, to be like Thee 480
Open my eyes 486
Out in the highways 473
Teach me Your way 472
We are climbing 488

ASSURANCE
Alas, and did my Savior
  (Martyrdom) 274
Alas, and did my Savior (Hudson) 95
All my life long I have panted 100
Anywhere with Jesus 594
At the cross 95
Be still, my soul 77
Blessed assurance 67
Children of the heavenly Father 89
Day by day 102
Dying with Jesus 65
Encamped along the hills 71
Faith is the victory 71
Great is Thy faithfulness 98
He the pearly gates 72
Hiding in Thee 70
I am His and He is mine 590
I am not skilled 94
I am trusting Thee 73
I heard an old, old story 82
I know who holds 96
I've anchored my soul 101
Jesus, I am resting 86
Leaning on the everlasting 87
Let God be God 81
Love divine, so great 72
Moment by moment 65
My God is there 93
My faith has found 75
My faith looks up 84
My hope is built 92
My hope is in the Lord 78
My Shepherd will supply 66
No, not one 221
Now thank we all our God 525
O how He loves you and me 622
O love that will not 404
O safe to the Rock 70
Praise my soul, the King 339
Satisfied 100
Simply trusting every day 79
Standing on the promises 69

The solid Rock 92
There's not a friend 221
They that sow 46
This is my story 67
'Tis so sweet 91
Trusting Jesus 79
Victory in Jesus 82
We search the starlit 93
What a fellowship 87
Yesterday He died for me 76
Yesterday, today and tomorrow 76
Yesterday, today, forever 83

BAPTISM AND DEDICATION
Children of the heavenly Father 89
Christ arose 298
Come, Holy Spirit, Dove divine 559
I think when I read 213
Jesus loves me! 226
O happy day! 647
Take my life 458
This child we dedicate 571
We are God's people 546
Where He leads me 607
Who is on the Lord's side? 409

BIBLE — WORD OF GOD
Break Thou the Bread of life 30
Holy Bible, book divine 34
How firm a foundation 32
Sing them over 29
Standing on the promises 69
Wonderful words of life 29

BROTHERHOOD AND WORLD PEACE
A song of peace 682
Blest be the tie 560
Christ for the world we sing 686
In Christ there is no east 685
Let there be peace on earth 681
Rise up, O men of God! 398
They'll know we are Christians 677
This is my song, O God 682
We are one in the Spirit 677

CHILDREN'S HYMNS
Children of the heavenly Father 89
Fairest Lord Jesus 240
For the beauty 1
Gentle Shepherd 596
I love to tell the story 619
I think when I read 213
I've found a friend 220
In my heart there rings 633
Jesus loves even me 225
Jesus loves me! 226
Jesus loves the little children 15
Jesus, we just want to thank You 461
Let there be peace on earth 683
Let's just praise the Lord 317
Lord, I want to be a Christian 421
O happy day! 647
Open my eyes, that I may see 486
Pass it on 641
Savior, like a shepherd 601
Some children see Him 181
Tell me the old, old story 16
Tell me the stories of Jesus 212
Tell me the story of Jesus 215
The wise may bring their learning 537
There is a green hill 278

Why should He love me? 26
Yesterday, today, forever 83

CHOIR RESPONSES
Alleluia 361
Amens:
  Amen 696
  Twofold Amen 697
  Threefold Amen 698
  Sixfold Amen 699
Cast thy burden 53
Christ, We do all adore Thee 358
God so loved the world 19
Hear our prayer, O Lord 346
Holy, holy 149
Jesus, we just want to thank You 461
Lord, we praise You 367
Peace I leave with you 64
Spirit, now live in me 151
Spirit of the living God 155
Sweet, sweet Spirit 159
The bond of love 544
The Lord bless you 522
We are one in the bond of love 544
Where the Spirit of the Lord is 148

CHORUSES
Alleluia 361
Because He lives 292
Bless His holy name 379
Bless the Lord 379
Come to the water 436
Coming again 305
Father, I adore You 414
Fill my cup, Lord 481
For God so loved the world 315
For those tears I died 436
Get all excited 652
God is at work within you 584
He is Lord 234
His name is wonderful 230
Holy, holy 149
Holy Spirit, flow through me 164
I know a fount 265
I'll be there 130
If my people will pray 575
It only takes a spark 641
Jesus is coming again 305
Jesus, we just want to thank You 461
Joy of the Lord 354
Let's just praise the Lord 317
Lord, we praise You 367
Now I belong to Jesus 637
O how He loves you and me 622
O how I love Jesus 634
Pass it on 641
Precious Lord, take my hand 611
Sweet, sweet Spirit 159
The bond of love 544
The joy of the Lord 354
The longer I serve Him 623
There's a sweet, sweet Spirit 159
They that wait upon the Lord 52
This is my country 694
Through it all 43
To God be the glory 363
To God be the glory (Crouch) 365
Turn your eyes upon Jesus 621
We are climbing 488
We are one in the bond of love 544
When we see Christ 129

Where the Spirit of the Lord is	148
Yesterday He died for me	76
Yesterday, today and tomorrow	76
Yesterday, today, forever	83

CHRISTMAS

All my heart	203
Angels from the realms	190
Angels we have heard	192
As with gladness	202
Away in a manger	185
Away in a manger (Cradle Song)	187
Break forth, O beauteous	207
Child in the manger	198
Come, Thou long-expected	168
Go, tell it	205
Good Christian men	177
Hark, the herald	184
He's still the King of kings	242
How great our joy!	182
I wonder as I wander	183
Infant holy, Infant holy	194
It came upon the midnight	197
Joy to the world!	171
Let all mortal flesh	166
Lo, how a rose	174
Long years ago	201
O come, all ye faithful	193
O come, O come Emmanuel	169
O little town of Bethlehem	178
O sing a song	208
Of the Father's love	172
Redeeming love	199
Silent night, holy night	195
Some children see Him	181
The first noel	179
The star carol	201
Thou didst leave Thy throne	170
We three kings	206
What child is this?	180
While by the sheep	182
While shepherds watched	175

CHURCH, FAMILY OF BELIEVERS

Blest be the tie	560
Built on the Rock	555
Christ is made	557
Come, Holy Spirit, Dove divine	559
Come, we that love the Lord	550
Getting used to the family of God	548
I love Your kingdom, Lord	545
In Christ there is no east	682
Plenty of room	552
The bond of love	544
The Church within us	551
The Church's one foundation	547
The Family of God	543
There's a church within us	551
There's a quiet understanding	556
They'll know we are Christians	677
This child we dedicate	571
We are God's people	546
We are one in the bond of love	544
We are one in the spirit	677

CLOSING HYMNS

A hymn of joy we sing	565
All praise to Thee	518
God be with you	523
Lord, dismiss us	520
Savior, again to Thy dear name	519
The Lord bless you and keep you	522

COMFORT

Be not dismayed	56
Blessed Jesus	39
Burdens are lifted at Calvary	60
Cast thy burden	53
Days are filled	60
God will take care of you	56
He giveth more grace	112
I heard the voice	51
I must tell Jesus	49
I've had many tears	43
In a time of trouble	37
Like a lamb	61
Moment by moment	65
Near to the heart of God	35
No one understands	36
O day of rest and gladness	12
Peace I leave with you	64
Sitting at the feet	58
Sun of my soul	62
Thank God for the promise	110
The great Physician	38
The hiding place	37
The Lord's my Shepherd	40
The Lord's my Shepherd (Brother James' Air)	42
There is a balm	48
There is a place of	35
They that sow	46
They that wait upon the Lord	52
Thou wilt keep Him	493
Thou wilt keep him	43

COMMITMENT AND SUBMISSION

Am I a soldier	411
As with gladness	202
Close to Thee	405
Father, I adore You	414
Give of your best	516
Have Thine own way	400
I surrender all	408
I will serve Thee	397
I've wandered far	406
Jesus calls us	399
Jesus, I come	401
Lead me to Calvary	407
Lord, I'm coming home	406
O Jesus, I have promised	402
O love that will not	404
Out of my bondage	401
Rise up, O men of God!	398
Thou my everlasting	405
Under His wings	412
Who is on the Lord's side?	409

COMMUNION (See also Jesus Christ — Atonement, Crucifixion and Death)

A hymn of joy we sing	565
Beneath the cross	253
Blest be the tie that binds	560
Calvary covers it all	250
Come to Calvary's	276
Here, O my Lord	567
In the cross	251
Jesus, Thy blood	268
Let all mortal	166
Let us break bread	564
O sacred Head	284
When I survey	258

CONCERN FOR OTHERS

Eternal Father	679
For you I am praying	676
I am praying for you	676

I have a Savior	676
Reach out and touch	655
The Savior is waiting	435
They'll know we are Christians	677
We are one in the spirit	677

CONFESSION AND REPENTANCE

At Calvary	415
Cleanse me	425
Come, ye sinners	428
Dear Lord and Father	422
I lay my sins	427
Just as I am	417
Kind and merciful God	419
Lord, I want to be	421
Pass me not	416
Search me, O God	425
Years I spent in vanity	415

CONFIRMATION (See Baptism and Dedication; See also Dedication Services-Children)

CONFLICT (See Loyalty and Courage)

DEDICATION AND DEVOTION

All for Jesus	459
Draw me nearer	455
I am Thine, O Lord	455
I could never outlove	452
I need Jesus	450
I'll live for Him	453
Jesus, the very thought	465
Jesus, Thou joy	451
Jesus, we just want to thank you	461
Living for Jesus	462
My Jesus, I love Thee	456
My wonderful Lord	368
Savior, Thy dying love	279
Take my life	458
Take Thou our minds	467
Take time to be holy	457
Trust and obey	454
We are living	447
What a friend	466
When we walk	454

DEATH (See Funeral Hymns)

DEDICATION SERVICES

Church Building

God whose giving	513
The Church's one foundation	547
We dedicate this temple	568

Children (See also Baptism and Dedication)

Children of the heavenly Father	89
I think when I read	213
Jesus loves me!	226
This child we dedicate	571

Organ

All creatures of our God	347
God whose giving	513

Ordination

Best be the tie	560
Brethren, we have met	321
God is at work within you	584
God, whose giving	513
Have Thine own way	400
Take my life	458
There's a church within	551
They that wait	52

We are God's people	546
We are one in the spirit	677
Your cause be mine	505

DISCIPLESHIP

Come, all Christians	507
Eternal life	474
I could never outlove	452
I'll go where You want	502
It may not be	502
Must Jesus bear	504
Who is on the Lord's side?	409
Your cause be mine	505

EASTER

Because He lives	292
Christ arose	298
Christ the Lord is risen	289
Christ, whose glory	293
God sent His Son	292
He lives	299
He's still the King	242
Hear the bells ringing	301
I know that my Redeemer lives	295
I serve a risen Savior	299
Jesus Christ is risen today	297
Jesus lives and so shall I	288
Let us celebrate	320
Low in the grave	298
The Easter song	301
Thine is the glory	291
Up from the grave	298
Were you there?	287

ENCOURAGEMENT

Burdens are lifted	60
Fear not, little flock	585
God is at work within you	584
God will take care of you	56
He giveth more grace	112
In heavenly love abiding	489
It is no secret	581
Only believe	585

EPIPHANY (See also Christmas)

All my heart today	203
As with gladness	202
Break forth, O beauteous	207
Christ, whose glory	293
Fairest Lord Jesus	240
Go, tell it	205
O sing a song	208
The star carol	201

EVERLASTING LIFE (See also Heaven)

Beyond the sunset	127
Face to face	128
I'll be there	130
In Heaven above	131
Is my name written	125
It will be worth it all	129
It will be worth it all (Gaither)	135
Lord, I care not	125
O that will be glory	132
Oft-times the day	129
Sing the wondrous love	123
Until then	133
When all my labors	132
When I can read	134
When we all get	123
When we see Christ	129

FAMILY AND HOME

A Christian home	538
Blessed Jesus	39
Happy the home	540
In the circle	535
The wise may bring	537

FELLOWSHIP WITH GOD

Face to face	128
He keeps me singing	587
I am His and He is mine	590
I come to the garden	588
I've found a friend	220
In heavenly love	489
In the garden	588
Jesus, the very thought	465
Just a closer walk	591
Leaning on the everlasting	87
Something worth living	638
There's within my heart	633
What a friend	466

FUNERAL HYMNS (See also Comfort)

Abide with me	500
Guide me, O thou	608
He leadeth me	606
I know that my Redeemer lives	295
In Heaven above	131
Jesus lives, and so shall I	288
Near to the heart	35
O love that will not	404
Thank God for the promise	110

GOD — THE FATHER

Be Thou my vision	468
Children of the heavenly Father	89
Day by day	102
Dear Lord and Father	422
Eternal Father, strong to save	679
Father, I adore You	414
God be with you	523
God will take care of you	56
Great is Thy faithfulness	98
If you will only let God	605
Immortal, invisible	319
In Christ there is no East	682
Joyful, joyful we adore Thee	377
Now thank we all our God	525
O love that will not	404
Of the Father's love begotten	172
Praise my soul, the King	339
The God of Abraham	332
The hiding place	37
This is my Father's world	6
To God be the glory	363
To God be the glory (Crouch)	365

GOD'S HAND IN NATURE

Earth and all stars	10
For the beauty	1
God who made the earth	4
God who stretched	9
Great God, we sing	7
How great Thou art	2
Morning has broken	5
My God is there	93
O day of rest	12
O Lord, my God	2
Teach us what we yet	9
This is my Father's world	6
We search the starlit	93
We sing the greatness	338

GOD'S LOVE

Come ye sinners	428
For God so loved	315
God so loved	20
If that isn't love	224
Jesus loves me!	226
Jesus loves the little children	15
Love divine	21
Love sent my Savior	26
Love was when	28
O how He loves you and me	622
O the deep, deep love	24
One day!	22
Redeeming love	199
Tell me the old, old	16
The love of God	18
The wonder of it all	13
Why should He love	26

GRACE, MERCY AND FORGIVENESS

Amazing grace	107
Grace greater than our sin	105
Great God of wonders	104
He giveth more grace	112
Lord Jesus, I long	109
Marvelous grace	105
Rock of Ages	108
Thank God for the promise	110
The love of God	18
There's a wideness	115
Whiter than snow	109
Wonderful grace of Jesus	114

GUIDANCE

All the way my Savior	598
Anywhere with Jesus	594
Gentle Shepherd	596
God leads us along	597
God moves in a	603
Guide me, O Thou	608
He leadeth me	606
I can hear my	607
If you will only let God	605
In shady green	597
Jesus will walk with me	609
Lead on, O King eternal	595
Precious Lord, take my hand	611
Savior, like a shepherd	601
Take Thou my hand	600
Where He leads me	607

HEALING

He touched me	628
I lay my sins	427
Jesus is Lord	235
Jesus, we just want to thank you	461
Rescue the perishing	661
There is a balm	48
There's a wideness	115

HEAVEN (See also Everlasting Life)

Abide with me	500
Face to face	128
For all the saints	614
He the pearly gates	72
In Heaven above	131
It will be worth it all	129
It will be worth it all (Gaither)	135
When I can read	134
When we see Christ	129

HERITAGE

America, our heritage	695
Faith of our fathers	526
God of grace	528
Now thank we	525

HOLY SCRIPTURE (See Bible — Word of God)

HOLY SPIRIT (See also Renewal and Revival)

Blessed quietness	145
Breathe on me	161
Come, Holy Spirit	150
Come, Holy Spirit, Dove divine	559
Come, Holy Spirit, heavenly Dove	144
Fill me now	153
Holy Ghost with light	162
Holy, holy	149
Holy Spirit, flow	164
Hover o'er me	153
Joys are flowing	145
O breath of life	579
Spirit now live in me	151
Spirit of God, descend upon my heart	147
Spirit of the living God	155
Sweet, sweet Spirit	159
The Comforter has come	143
The Spirit of Jesus	157
There's a sweet, sweet Spirit	159
Where the Spirit of the Lord is	148

INNER PEACE (See Peace, Inner)

INSTALLATION (See Dedication Services, Ordination; See also Dedication and Devotion)

INVITATION (See also Confession and Repentance)

Almost persuaded	437
Come to the water	436
Come, ye sinners	428
Even so, Lord Jesus	429
For those tears	436
I surrender all	408
Is your burden heavy?	430
Jesus is calling	434
Jesus is tenderly	434
Let Jesus come	433
Lord, I'm coming home	406
Reach out to Jesus	430
Softly and tenderly	432
The Savior is waiting	435
Thou didst leave Thy throne	170
You said You'd come	436

JESUS CHRIST — ATONEMENT, CRUCIFIXION AND DEATH

Alas! and did my Savior (Martyrdom)	274
Alas! and did my Savior (Hudson)	95
Beneath the cross of Jesus	253
Blessed Redeemer	275
Calvary covers it all	250
Come to Calvary's	276
Come, ye sinners	428
Go to dark Gethsemane	281
I believe in a hill	270
I heard the Savior say	273

I know a fount	265
In the cross of Christ	251
In the hour of trial	122
Jesus paid it all	273
Jesus, priceless treasure	277
Jesus, the Son of God	269
Jesus, Thy blood	268
O sacred Head	284
On a hill far away	256
Savior, Thy dying love	279
The old rugged cross	256
There is a green hill	278
Up Calvary's mountain	275
Were you there?	287
What wondrous love	283
When I survey	258
Worthy the lamb	285
Wounded for me	282

JESUS CHRIST — BIRTH (See Christmas)

JESUS CHRIST — BLOOD

And can it be	260
Are you washed?	259
Have you been to Jesus?	259
I know a fount	265
Jesus, Thy blood	268
Nothing but the blood	266
On a hill far away	256
The blood will never lose	262
The old rugged cross	256
There is a fountain filled	263
What can wash away	266

JESUS CHRIST — CROSS

Beneath the cross	253
Calvary covers it all	250
Down at the cross	255
Glory to His name	255
In the cross of Christ	251
Jesus, keep me near	254
Near the cross	254
On a hill far away	256
The old rugged cross	256
When I survey	258

JESUS CHRIST — FRIEND

I've found a friend	220
Jesus is all the world	627
Jesus is the friend	219
Jesus the very thought	465
Jesus, what a friend	244
No, not one	221
There's not a friend	221
What a friend	466

JESUS CHRIST — HIS LOVE

He left the splendor	224
How marvelous! How wonderful!	223
I am so glad that my Father	225
I stand amazed	223
If that isn't love	224
Jesus, lover of my soul	222
Jesus loves even me	225
Jesus loves me!	226
Redeeming love	199

JESUS CHRIST — HIS NAME

His name is wonderful	230
How sweet the name	229
I will sing of my Redeemer	228
Jesus, the very thought	465
Join all the glorious names	232

Take the name of Jesus	231
There's something about	227

JESUS CHRIST — LIFE AND MINISTRY

I cannot tell	210
I love to tell the story	619
I think, when I read	213
Jesus walked this lonesome	217
O sing a song	208
Strong, righteous man	216
Tell me the stories of Jesus	212
Tell me the story of Jesus	215

JESUS CHRIST — LORDSHIP

Fairest Lord Jesus	240
He is Lord	234
He's still the King of kings	242
Jesus is Lord of all	235
Jesus shall reign	238
Lift up your heads	239
Once our blessed Christ	236
The unveiled Christ	236

JESUS CHRIST—RESURRECTION (See Easter)

JESUS CHRIST — SAVIOR

Fairest Lord Jesus	240
Hallelujah, what a Savior!	246
He's the Savior of my soul	247
I will sing of my Redeemer	228
Jesus, the very thought	465
Jesus, what a friend	244
"Man of sorrows"	246
More love to Thee	476

JESUS CHRIST — SECOND COMING

Christ is coming!	303
Christ returneth!	304
For God so loved the world	315
Glad day! Glad day!	310
Is it the crowning day?	310
It may be at morn	304
Jesus is coming again	305
Jesus is coming to earth again	311
Jesus may come today	310
Let us celebrate	320
Lo, He comes with clouds	306
Marvelous message we bring	305
My Lord, what a morning!	316
Some golden daybreak	312
The King is coming!	313
The market place is empty	313
This could be the dawning	307
What a day that will be	314
What if it were today?	311
When He shall come	309
When we see Christ	129

JESUS CHRIST — TRIUMPHAL ENTRY

All glory, laud and honor	249
Hosanna, loud hosanna	248
Let us celebrate	320
Lift up your heads	239

LONELINESS

God will take care	56
He hideth my soul	120

I've found a friend	220	
Jesus, lover of my soul	222	
No one understands	36	
O, the deep, deep love	24	
The hiding place	37	
The Lord's prayer	440	
They that sow	46	
Through it all	43	

LORD'S SUPPER (See Communion; See also Jesus Christ — Atonement, Crucifixion and Death; Jesus Christ — Blood; Jesus Christ — Cross)

LOYALTY AND COURAGE

All to Jesus	408
Fight the good fight	613
For all the saints	614
I will serve Thee	397
King of my life	407
Lead me to Calvary	407
Onward, Christian soldiers	617
Stand up, stand up	616
Who is on the Lord's side?	409

MARRIAGE

All creatures of our God	347
Great is Thy faithfulness	98
If you will only let God	605
Joyful, joyful	377
Love divine, all loves	27
Now thank we all	525
O God, our help	370
O Master, let me walk	442
O perfect love	530
Praise my soul, the King	339
Rejoice, ye pure	394
The Lord's my Shepherd	40
The Lord's my Shepherd (Brother James' air)	42
The Lord's prayer	440

MISSIONS

All power is given	674
Far, far away	674
Hear the voice of Jesus	669
I'll tell the world	648
Jesus saves!	667
Let your heart	662
Macedonia	668
O breath of life	579
O Zion, haste	658
Once to every man	670
Rescue the perishing	661
Send the light!	663
So send I you	664
The vision of a dying world	668
There's a call comes ringing	663
Through all the world	672
We have heard	667
We've a story to tell	659
Where cross the crowded ways	665

NATION (See Patriotic)

NEW YEAR

Great God, we sing	7
Guide me, O Thou	608
If you will only let God	605
Now thank we all	525
O God, our help	370

OPENING HYMNS (See also Worship and Adoration)

All hail the power (Coronation)	325
All hail the power (Diadem)	326
All hail the power (Miles Lane)	327
Begin my tongue	328
Brethren, we have met	321
Come Christians, join	342
Come, Thou almighty King	341
Come Thou fount	318
For all the saints	614
Holy, holy, holy!	323
Immortal, invisible	319
It is good to sing	330
Let us celebrate	320
O for a thousand tongues	349
O worship the King	336
Praise my soul, the King	339
Praise the Lord, ye Heavens	335
Praise to the Lord, the Almighty	337
Sing praise to God	343
We gather together	387
We praise Thee, O God	334
We sing the greatness	338

PALM SUNDAY (See The Triumphal Entry of Jesus Christ)

PATRIOTIC

America	695
America, our heritage	694
America, the beautiful	690
Battle hymn	692
God of our fathers	687
Mine eyes have seen	692
My country 'tis of thee	695
O beautiful for spacious	690
O say, can you see?	688
The star-spangled banner	688
This is my country	693

PEACE — INNER

Abide with me	500
All will be well	498
Far away in the depths	494
Great hills may tremble	496
In heavenly love abiding	489
It is well with my soul	495
Like a river glorious	497
Peace, perfect peace	491
Security	496
The Savior is waiting	435
Thou wilt keep him	493
Through the love of God	498
'Til the storm passes by	501
When peace, like a river	495
Wonderful peace	494

PRAYER AND INTERCESSION

Dear Lord and Father	422
I am praying for you	676
I need Thee every hour	443
In the hour of trail	122
Kind and merciful God	419
O Master, let me walk	442
Our Father, who art	440
Prayer is the soul's	446
Speak, Lord, in the stillness	444
Sweet hour of prayer	439
The Lord's prayer	440

REFUGE

A mighty fortress	118
A shelter in the time	117
A wonderful Savior	120
Anywhere with Jesus	594
He hideth my soul	120
In the hour of trial	122
The hiding place	37
The Lord's our Rock	117

RENEWAL AND REVIVAL

Dear Lord and Father	422
God of grace	528
If my people	575
O breath of life	579
Renew Thy church	572
Revive us again	574
Search me, O God	425
Spirit, now live in me	151
There shall be showers	580
Thou, whose purpose	576
We praise Thee, O God	574

SALVATION (See Invitation; Confession and Repentance)

SPIRITUALS

Go, tell it	205
Jesus walked this lonesome valley	217
Just a closer walk	591
Let us break bread	564
Lord, I want to be a Christian	421
My Lord, what a morning!	316
There is a balm	48
Were you there?	287

STEWARDSHIP (see also Thanksgiving; Discipleship)

Give of your best	516
Glorious is Thy name	510
God, whose giving	513
Little is much	512
Now thank we all	525
Take my life	458
We give Thee but Thine	515

TESTIMONY, WITNESS AND EVANGELISM

At Calvary	415
Christ, for the world	686
Come, every soul	629
Come we that love the Lord	550
Earthly friends may prove	651
Fill my cup, Lord	481
Get all excited	652
Have you any room	654
He lifted me	653
He touched me	628
He's everything to me	632
Heaven came down	657
I have a song	633
I have a song I love	644
I know not why	631
I know whom I have believed	631
I love to tell	619
I will sing the wondrous	618
I'd rather have Jesus	650
I'll tell the world	648
If I gained the world	642
In loving kindness	653
In my heart	633
In the stars His handiworks	632
It only takes a spark	641

It took a miracle	626	Down at the cross	255	Doxology	382, 384
Jesus is all the world	627	Glory to His name	255	For all the saints	614
Jesus is calling	434	In the cross of Christ	251	Glorious Things of Thee	376
Jesus my Lord will love me	637	Jesus, keep me near	254	God the Omnipotent	353
Jesus never fails	651	Near the cross	254	Hallelujah, what a Savior!	246
Jesus saves!	667	On a hill far away	256	Holy God, we praise	385
Let God be God	81	The old rugged cross	256	Holy, holy, holy!	323
Lord, speak to me	625	When I survey	258	How can I say thanks?	365
Now I belong to Jesus	637			How great Thou art	2
O breath of life	579	TRINITY		I stand amazed	223
O for a thousand tongues	349	Gloria Patri	142	I will praise Him!	359
O happy day!	647	Glory be to the Father	142	Immortal, invisible	319
O how He loves you and me	622	Holy, holy, holy!	323	It is good to sing	330
O, how I love Jesus	634	Hymn to the Trinity	140	Joy of the Lord	354
O soul, are you weary	621	Praise Ye, the Triune	137	Joyful, joyful	377
Only trust Him	629			Let us celebrate	320
Pass it on	641	TRIUMPHAL ENTRY (See Jesus Christ - Triumphal Entry)		Let's just praise	317
Reach out and touch	655			Lord, we praise You	367
Redeemed	646			My Savior's love	223
Rescue the perishing	661	UNITY AND FELLOWSHIP OF BELIEVERS (See Church – Family of Believers)		My tribute	365
Room at the cross	645			My wonderful Lord	368
Shackled by a heavy burden	628			O could I speak	344
Since I have been redeemed	644			O day of rest	12
Since Jesus came into	639	WEDDINGS (See Marriage)		O for a heart	357
Something beautiful	656			O for a thousand tongues	349
Something worth living for	638	WORLD PEACE (See Brotherhood and World Peace)		O God, our help	370
Tell me the story of Jesus	215			O worship the King	336
The cross upon which Jesus	645			Praise be to Jesus	366
The light of the world	636	WORSHIP AND ADORATION		Praise God from whom	382, 384
The longer I serve Him	623			Praise, my soul, the King	339
There is a name I love	634	All creatures of our God	347	Praise the Lord, His glories	373
There is sunshine	630	All hail the power (Coronation)	325	Praise the Lord: ye Heavens	335
There's room at the cross	645	All hail the power (Diadem)	326	Praise the Savior, ye who	362
Turn your eyes upon Jesus	621	All hail the power (Miles Lane)	327	Praise ye the Father for His lovingkindness	136
We're marching to Zion	550	All people that on earth	381		
What a wonderful change in my life	639	All praise to Him who reigns above	352	Praise ye the triune	136
				Praise to the Lord	337
Why do I sing about Jesus?	635	Alleluia	361	Rejoice, the Lord	374
		At the name of Jesus	351	Sing praise to God	343
THANKSGIVING		Begin, my tongue	328	Sometimes "Alleluia"	331
Come, ye thankful people	392	Bless His holy name	379	The God of Abraham	332
Let all things now living	389	Bless the Lord	379	To God be the glory	363
O let your soul now be filled	390	Blessed be the name	352	To God be the glory (Crouch)	365
Rejoice, ye pure in heart	394	Brethren, we have met	321	We gather together	387
Sometimes "Alleluia"	331	Christ has for sin	372	We praise Thee, O God	334
Thanks to God	386	Christ, we do all	358	We sing the greatness	338
We gather together	387	Come, Christians, join	342	What a wonderful Savior	372
We plow the fields	395	Come, Thou Almighty King	341	When I saw the	359
Beneath the cross	253	Come, Thou Fount	318	When morning gilds	322
		Crown Him with many crowns	345	You servants of God	360

Alphabetical Index
of Hymn Titles and First Lines

709

A Christian home	538	FINLANDIA
A hymn of joy we sing	565	SCHUMANN
A mighty fortress is our God	118	EIN' FESTE BURG
A shelter in the time of storm	117	SHELTER
A song of peace	682	FINLANDIA
A wonderful Savior is Jesus my Lord	120	HE HIDETH MY SOUL
Abide with me	500	EVENTIDE
Alas! and did my Savior bleed	274	MARTYRDOM
Alas! and did my Savior bleed	95	HUDSON

All creatures of our God and King	347	LASST UNS ERFREUEN
All for Jesus	459	CONSTANCY
All glory, laud and honor	249	ST. THEODULPH
All hail the power of Jesus' name	325	CORONATION
All hail the power of Jesus' name	326	DIADEM
All hail the power of Jesus' name	327	MILES LANE
All my heart today rejoices	203	WARUM SOLLT ICH
All my life long I had panted	100	SATISFIED
All people that on earth do dwell	381	OLD 100th
All power is given unto Me	674	GO YE
All praise to Him who reigns above	352	BLESSED BE THE NAME
All praise to Thee, my God	518	TALLIS' CANON
All the way my Savior leads me	598	ALL THE WAY
All to Jesus I surrender	408	SURRENDER
All will be well	498	AR HYD Y NOS
Alleluia	361	ALLELUIA
Almost persuaded	437	ALMOST
Am I a soldier of the cross?	411	ARLINGTON
Amazing grace! How sweet the sound	107	AMAZING GRACE
Amens:		
Amen	696	
Twofold	697	
Threefold	698	
Sixfold	699	
America	695	AMERICA
America, our heritage	694	OUR HERITAGE
America, the beautiful	690	MATERNA
And can it be that I should gain?	260	SAGINA
Angels from the realms of Glory	190	REGENT SQUARE
Angels we have heard on high	192	GLORIA
Anywhere with Jesus I can safely go	594	SECURITY
"Are ye able," said the Master	470	BEACON HILL
Are you washed in the blood?	259	WASHED IN THE BLOOD
As with gladness men of old	202	DIX
At Calvary	415	CALVARY
At the cross	95	HUDSON
At the name of Jesus	351	KING'S WESTON
Away in a manger	185	AWAY IN A MANGER
Away in a manger (Cradle song)	187	CRADLE SONG
Battle hymn of the Republic	692	BATTLE HYMN OF THE REPUBLIC
Be not dismayed	56	GOD CARES
Be still my soul	77	FINLANDIA
Be Thou my vision	468	SLANE
Because He lives	292	RESURRECTION
Begin, my tongue, some heavenly theme	328	MANOAH
Beneath the cross of Jesus	253	ST. CHRISTOPHER
Beyond the sunset	127	SUNSET
Bless His holy name	379	BLESS THE LORD
Bless the Lord, O my soul	379	BLESS THE LORD

Blessed assurance, Jesus is mine	67	ASSURANCE
Blessed be the name	352	BLESSED BE THE NAME
Blessed Jesus	39	BLESSED JESUS
Blessed quietness	145	BLESSED QUIETNESS
Blessed Redeemer	275	REDEEMER
Blest be the tie that binds	560	DENNIS
Break forth, O beauteous heavenly light	207	ERMUNTRE DICH
Break Thou the bread of life	30	BREAD OF LIFE
Breathe on me, breath of God	161	TRENTHAM
Brethren, we have met to worship	321	HOLY MANNA
Built on the rock	555	KIRKEN
Burdens are lifted at Calvary	60	BURDENS LIFTED
Calvary covers it all	250	CALVARY COVERS IT
Cast thy burden upon the Lord	53	CAST THY BURDEN
Child in the manger	198	BUNESSAN
Children of the heavenly Father	89	TRYGGARE KAN INGEN VARA
Christ arose	298	CHRIST AROSE
Christ for the world we sing	686	ITALIAN HYMN
Christ has for sin atonement made	372	BENTON HARBOR
Christ is made the sure foundation	557	REGENT SQUARE
Christ is coming!	303	BRYN CALFARIA
Christ returneth!	304	CHRIST RETURNETH
Christ the Lord is risen today	289	EASTER HYMN
Christ, we do all adore Thee	358	ADORE THEE
Christ, whose glory fills the skies	293	LUX PRIMA
Cleanse me	425	MAORI
Close to Thee	405	CLOSE TO THEE
Come, all Christians, be committed	507	BEACH SPRING
Come, Christians, join to sing	342	MADRID
Come, every soul by sin oppressed	629	MINERVA
Come, Holy Spirit	150	COME, HOLY SPIRIT
Come, Holy Spirit, Dove divine	559	MARYTON
Come, Holy Spirit, heavenly Dove	144	GRAFENBERG
Come, Thou almighty King	341	ITALIAN HYMN
Come, Thou fount of every blessing	318	NETTLETON
Come, Thou long-expected Jesus	168	HYFRYDOL
Come to Calvary's holy mountain	276	HOLY MOUNTAIN
Come to the water	436	CHILDREN OF THE DAY
Come, we that love the Lord	550	MARCHING TO ZION
Come, ye sinners, poor and needy	428	BEACH SPRING
Come, ye thankful people, come	392	ST. GEORGE'S WINDSOR
Coming again	305	COMING AGAIN
Crown Him with many crowns	345	DIADEMATA
Day by day and with each passing moment	102	BLOTT EN DAG
Days are filled with sorrow and care	60	BURDENS LIFTED
Dear Lord and Father of mankind	422	REST
Down at the cross	255	GLORY TO HIS NAME
Doxology	382, 384	OLD 100th
Draw me nearer	455	I AM THINE
Dying with Jesus, by death reckoned mine	65	WHITTLE

Earth and all stars   10   DEXTER
   Earthly friends may prove untrue   651   JESUS NEVER FAILS
   Encamped along the hills of light   71   FAITH IS THE VICTORY
   Eternal life   474   ETERNAL LIFE
   Eternal Father, strong to save   679   MELITA
   Even so, Lord Jesus, come   429   LORD JESUS, COME

Face to face   128   FACE TO FACE
   Fairest Lord Jesus   240   CRUSADER'S HYMN
   Faith is the victory   71   FAITH IS THE VICTORY
   Faith of our fathers   526   ST. CATHERINE
   Far away in the depths of my spirit tonight   494   WONDERFUL PEACE
   Far, far away in sin and darkness   674   GO YE
   Father, I adore You   414   MARANTHA
   Fear not, little flock   585   ONLY BELIEVE
   Fight the good fight   613   PENTECOST
   Fill me now   153   FILL ME NOW
   Fill my cup, Lord   481   FILL MY CUP
   Fill Thou my life, O Lord my God   479   RICHMOND
   For all the saints   614   SINE NOMINE
   For God so loved the world   315   GOD LOVED THE WORLD
   For the beauty of the earth   1   DIX
   For those tears I died   436   CHILDREN OF THE DAY
   For you I am praying   676   INTERCESSION

Gentle Shepherd   596   GENTLE SHEPHERD
   Get all excited   652   GET ALL EXCITED
   Getting used to the family of God   548   TOGETHER
   Give of your best to the Master   516   BARNARD
   Glad day! Glad day!   310   GLAD DAY
   Gloria Patri   142   GLORIA PATRI
   Glorious is Thy name, most holy   510   HOLY MANNA
   Glorious things of Thee are spoken   376   AUSTRIAN HYMN
   Glory be to the Father   142   GLORIA PATRI
   Glory to His name   255   GLORY TO HIS NAME
   Go, tell it on the mountains   205   GO TELL IT ON THE MOUNTAINS

   Go to dark Gethsemane   281   REDHEAD NO. 76
   God be with you 'til we meet again   523   GOD BE WITH YOU
   God is at work within you   584   TOPEKA
   God leads us along   597   GOD LEADS US
   God moves in a mysterious way   603   DUNDEE
   God of grace and God of glory   528   CWM RHONDDA
   God of our fathers   687   NATIONAL HYMN
   God sent His Son   292   RESURRECTION
   God so loved the world   20   STAINER
   God the Omnipotent   353   RUSSIAN HYMN
   God, who made the earth and heaven   4   AR HYD Y NOS

God, who stretched the spangled heavens	9	HYMN TO JOY
God, whose giving knows no ending	513	NETTLETON
God will take care of you	56	GOD CARES
Good Christian men, rejoice	177	IN DULCI JUBILO
Grace greater than our sin	105	MOODY
Great God of wonders	104	WONDERS
Great God, we sing Your mighty hand	7	GERMANY
Great hills may tremble	496	BERGEN MA VIKA
Great is thy faithfulness	98	FAITHFULNESS
Guide me, O Thou great Jehovah	608	CWM RHONDDA

*H*allelujah, what a Savior! — 246 — HALLELUJAH! WHAT A SAVIOR!

Happy the home when God is there	540	ST. AGNES
Hark! the herald angels sing	184	MENDELSSOHN
Have you any room for Jesus?	654	ANY ROOM
Have you been to Jesus?	259	WASHED IN THE BLOOD
Have Thine own way, Lord	400	ADELAIDE
He giveth more grace	112	HE GIVETH MORE GRACE
He hideth my soul	120	HE HIDETH MY SOUL
He is Lord	234	HE IS LORD
He keeps me singing	587	SWEETEST NAME
He leadeth me, O blessed thought	606	HE LEADETH ME
He left the splendor of Heaven	224	LOVE
He lifted me	653	HE LIFTED ME
He lives	299	ACKLEY
He the pearly gates will open	72	PEARLY GATES
He touched me	628	HE TOUCHED ME
He's everything to me	632	WOODLAND HILLS
He's still the King of kings	242	KING OF KINGS
He's the Savior of my soul	247	SAVIOR OF MY SOUL
Hear the bells ringing	301	EASTER SONG
Hear the voice of Jesus calling	669	RIPLEY
Heaven came down and glory filled my soul	657	HEAVEN CAME DOWN
Here, O my Lord, I see Thee face to face	567	PENITENTIA
Hiding in Thee	70	HIDING IN THEE
Higher ground	469	HIGHER GROUND
His name is wonderful	230	MIEIR
Holy Bible, book divine	34	ALETTA
Holy Ghost, with light divine	162	MERCY
Holy God, we praise Thy name	385	GROSSER GOTT
Holy, holy	149	HOLY, HOLY
Holy, holy, holy! Lord God almighty!	323	NICAEA
Holy Spirit, flow through me	164	MILLS
Hosanna, loud hosanna	248	ELLACOMBE
Hover o'er me, Holy Spirit	153	FILL ME NOW
How can I say thanks?	365	MY TRIBUTE
How firm a foundation	32	FOUNDATION
How great our joy!	182	JUNGST
How great Thou art	2	O STORE GUD
How marvelous! How wonderful!	223	MY SAVIOR'S LOVE

How sweet the name of Jesus sounds	229	ST. PETER
Hymn to the Trinity	140	HYMN TO THE TRINITY

I am His and He is mine	590	EVERLASTING LOVE
I am not skilled to understand	94	EWHURST
I am praying for you	676	INTERCESSION
I am so glad that my Father in Heaven	225	GLADNESS
I am Thine, O Lord	455	I AM THINE
I am trusting Thee, Lord Jesus	73	BULLINGER
I believe in a hill called Mount Calvary	270	MOUNT CALVARY
I can hear my Savior calling	607	NORRIS
I cannot tell	210	LONDONDERRY AIR
I come to the garden alone	588	GARDEN
I could never outlove the Lord	452	NEVER OUTLOVE
I have a Savior, He's pleading in Glory	676	INTERCESSION
I have a song I love to sing	644	OTHELLO
I have a song that Jesus gave me	633	HEART MELODY
I hear the Savior say	273	ALL TO CHRIST
I heard an old, old story	82	HARTFORD
I heard the voice of Jesus say	51	VOX DILECTI
I know a fount	265	I KNOW A FOUNT
I know not why God's wondrous grace	631	EL NATHAN
I know that my Redeemer lives	295	DUKE STREET
I know who holds tomorrow	96	I KNOW
I know whom I have believed	631	EL NATHAN
I lay my sins on Jesus	427	CRUCIFIX
I love to tell the story	619	HANKEY
I love Your kingdom, Lord	545	ST. THOMAS
I must tell Jesus	49	ORWIGSBURG
I need Jesus	450	I NEED JESUS
I need Thee every hour	443	NEED
I serve a risen Savior	299	ACKLEY
I stand amazed in the presence	223	MY SAVIOR'S LOVE
I surrender all	408	SURRENDER
I think when I read that sweet story of old	213	SWEET STORY
I will praise Him!	359	I WILL PRAISE HIM
I will serve Thee	397	SERVING
I will sing of my Redeemer	228	MY REDEEMER
I will sing the wondrous story	618	WONDROUS STORY
I wonder as I wander	183	I WONDER
I'd rather have Jesus	650	I'D RATHER HAVE JESUS
I'll be there	130	I'LL BE THERE
I'll go where You want me to go	502	I'LL GO
I'll live for Him	453	DUNBAR
I'll tell the world that I'm a Christian	648	TUCKER
I'm pressing on the upward way	469	HIGHER GROUND
I've anchored my soul	101	GOOD SHIP
I've found a friend, O such a friend	220	FRIEND
I've had many tears and sorrows	43	THROUGH IT ALL
I've wandered far away from God	406	COMING HOME
If I gained the world	642	TRUE RICHES

If my people will pray	575	CHRONICLES
If that isn't love	224	LOVE
If you will only let God guide you	605	NEUMARK
Immortal, invisible, God only wise	319	ST. DENIS
In a time of trouble	37	HIDING PLACE
In Christ there is no East or West	685	ST. PETER
In Heaven above	131	HAUGE
In heavenly love abiding	489	SEASONS
In loving-kindness Jesus came	653	HE LIFTED ME
In my heart there rings a melody	633	HEART MELODY
In shady green pastures	597	GOD LEADS US
In the circle of each home	535	BEL AIR
In the cross of Christ I glory	251	RATHBUN
In the garden	588	GARDEN
In the hour of trial	122	PENITENCE
In the stars His handiwork I see	632	WOODLAND HILLS
Infant holy, Infant lowly	194	W ZLOBIE LEZY
Is it the crowning day?	310	GLAD DAY
Is my name written there?	125	IS MY NAME
Is your burden heavy?	430	REACH OUT TO JESUS
It came upon the midnight clear	197	CAROL
It is good to sing Thy praises	330	ELLESDIE
It is no secret	581	IT IS NO SECRET
It is well with my soul	495	VILLE DU HAVRE
It may be at morn	304	CHRIST RETURNETH
It may not be on the mountain's height	502	I'LL GO
It only takes a spark	641	PASS IT ON
It took a miracle	626	MONTROSE
It will be worth it all (Rusthoi)	129	WHEN WE SEE CHRIST
It will be worth it all (Gaither)	135	WORTH IT ALL
Jesus calls us o'er the tumult	399	GALILEE
Jesus Christ is risen today	297	LLANFAIR
Jesus, I am resting, resting	86	TRANQUILITY
Jesus, I come	401	JESUS I COME
Jesus is all the world to me	627	ELIZABETH
Jesus is calling	434	CALLING TODAY
Jesus is coming again	305	COMING AGAIN
Jesus is coming to earth again	311	WHAT IF IT WERE TODAY
Jesus is Lord of all	235	LORD OF ALL
Jesus is tenderly calling you home	434	CALLING TODAY
Jesus is the friend of sinners	219	FRIEND OF SINNERS
Jesus, keep me near the cross	254	NEAR THE CROSS
Jesus lives, and so shall I	288	JESU, MEINE ZUVERSICHT
Jesus, lover of my soul	222	ABERYSTWYTH
Jesus loves even me	225	GLADNESS
Jesus loves me! this I know	226	JESUS LOVES ME
Jesus loves the little children	15	CHILDREN
Jesus may come today	310	GLAD DAY
Jesus my Lord will love me forever	637	ELLSWORTH
Jesus never fails	651	JESUS NEVER FAILS
Jesus paid it all	273	ALL TO CHRIST

Jesus, priceless treasure	277	JESU, MEINE FREUDE
Jesus saves!	667	JESUS SAVES
Jesus shall reign where'er the sun	238	DUKE STREET
Jesus, the son of God	269	SWEET WONDER
Jesus, the very thought of Thee	465	ST. AGNES
Jesus, Thou joy of loving hearts	451	QUEBEC
Jesus, Thy blood and righteousness	268	GERMANY
Jesus walked this lonesome valley	217	LONESOME VALLEY
Jesus, we just want to thank You	461	THANK YOU
Jesus! what a friend for sinners	244	HYFRYDOL
Jesus will walk with me	609	JESUS WILL WALK WITH ME
Join all the glorious names	232	DARWALL'S 148th
Joy of the Lord	354	HOUSTON
Joy to the world!	171	ANTIOCH
Joyful, joyful. we adore Thee	377	HYMN TO JOY
Joys are flowing like a river	145	BLESSED QUIETNESS
Just a closer walk with Thee	591	CLOSER WALK
Just as I am, without one plea	417	WOODWORTH

*K*ing of my life, I crown Thee now   407   LEAD ME TO CALVARY
   Kind and merciful God   419   ELFAKER

*L*ead me to Calvary   407   LEAD ME TO CALVARY

Lead on, O King eternal	595	LANCASHIRE
Leaning on the everlasting arms	87	SHOWALTER
Let all mortal flesh keep silence	166	PICARDY
Let all things now living	389	ASH GROVE
Let God be God	81	CARLA
Let Jesus come into your heart	433	Mc CONNELSVILLE
Let there be peace on earth	681	WORLD PEACE
Let us break bread together	564	LET US BREAK BREAD
Let us celebrate the glories of our Lord	320	BELLAMY
Let your heart be broken	662	BJORKLUND MAJOR
Let's just praise the Lord	317	LET'S JUST PRAISE THE LORD
Lift up your heads, ye mighty gates	239	TRURO
Like a lamb who needs the Shepherd	61	LIKE A LAMB
Like a river glorious	497	WYE VALLEY
Like the woman at the well	481	FILL MY·CUP
Little is much when God is in it	512	LITTLE IS MUCH
Living for Jesus	462	LIVING
Lo! He comes with clouds descending	306	REGENT SQUARE
Lo, how a rose e'er blooming	174	ES IST EIN ROS'
Long years ago	201	STAR CAROL
Lord, dismiss us with Your blessing	520	SICILIAN MARINERS
Lord, I care not for riches	125	IS MY NAME
Lord, I want to be a Christian	421	I WANT TO BE A CHRISTIAN
Lord, I'm coming home	406	COMING HOME
Lord Jesus, I long to be perfectly whole	109	FISCHER
Lord, make me an instrument of Thy peace	474	ETERNAL LIFE
Lord, speak to me	625	CANONBURY
Lord, we praise You	367	LORD WE PRAISE YOU

Love divine, all loves excelling	21	BEECHER
Love divine, so great and wondrous	72	PEARLY GATES
Love sent my Savior to die in my stead	26	LOVE ME
Love was when	28	DALSEM
Loved with everlasting love	590	EVERLASTING LOVE
Low in the grave He lay	298	CHRIST AROSE

Macedonia

	668	ALL SAINTS' NEW
Make me a blessing	473	SCHULER
"Man of sorrows," what a name!	246	HALLELUJAH! WHAT A SAVIOR!
Marvelous grace of our loving Lord	105	MOODY
Marvelous message we bring	305	COMING AGAIN
May the mind of Christ, my Savior	483	ST. LEONARDS
Mine eyes have seen the glory	692	BATTLE HYMN OF THE REPUBLIC
Moment by moment	65	WHITTLE
More about Jesus	477	SWEENEY
More love to Thee, O Christ	476	MORE LOVE TO THEE
Morning has broken	5	BUNESSAN
Must Jesus bear the cross alone?	504	MAITLAND
My country, 'tis of thee	695	AMERICA
My faith has found a resting place	75	NO OTHER PLEA
My faith looks up to Thee	84	OLIVET
My God is there controlling	93	EWHURST
My hope is built	92	SOLID ROCK
My hope is in the Lord	78	WAKEFIELD
My Jesus, I love Thee	456	GORDON
My Lord, what a morning!	316	STARS FALL
My Savior's love	223	MY SAVIOR'S LOVE
My Shepherd will supply my need	66	RESIGNATION
My tribute	365	MY TRIBUTE
My wonderful Lord	368	WONDERFUL LORD

Near the cross

	254	NEAR THE CROSS
Near to the heart of God	35	McAFEE
Nearer still nearer	485	MORRIS
No, not one	221	NO NOT ONE
No one understands like Jesus	36	ARIZONA
Nothing but the blood	266	PLAINFIELD
Now I belong to Jesus	637	ELLSWORTH
Now thank we all our God	525	NUN DANKET

O beautiful for spacious skies

	690	MATERNA
O breath of life	579	BLOMQVIST
O come, all ye faithful	193	ADESTE FIDELES
O come, O come, Emmanuel	169	VENI EMMANUEL
O could I speak the matchless worth	344	ARIEL
O day of rest and gladness	12	MENDEBRAS
O for a heart to praise my God	357	RICHMOND
O for a thousand tongues to sing	349	AZMON

O give us homes built firm upon the Savior	538	FINLANDIA
O God, our help in ages past	370	ST. ANNE
O happy day!	647	HAPPY DAY
O how He loves you and me	622	HE LOVES YOU AND ME
O how I love Jesus	634	O HOW I LOVE JESUS
O Jesus, I have promised	402	ANGEL'S STORY
O little town of Bethlehem	178	ST. LOUIS
O let your soul now be filled with gladness	390	RANSOMED SOUL
O Lord, my God, when I in awesome wonder	2	O STORE GUD
O love that will not let me go	404	ST. MARGARET
O Master, let me walk with Thee	442	MARYTON
O perfect love	530	O PERFECT LOVE
O sacred Head, now wounded	284	PASSION CHORALE
O safe to the rock	70	HIDING IN THEE
O say, can you see?	688	NATIONAL ANTHEM
O sing a song	208	KINGSFOLD
O soul are you weary and troubled?	621	LEMMEL
O that will be glory for me	132	GLORY SONG
O the deep, deep love of Jesus	24	EBENEZER
O to be like Thee!	480	CHRISTLIKE
O worship the King	336	LYONS
O Zion, haste, thy mission high fulfilling	658	TIDINGS
Of the Father's love begotten	172	DIVINUM MYSTERIUM
Oft-times the day seems long	129	WHEN WE SEE CHRIST
On a hill far away	256	RUGGED CROSS
Once our blessed Christ of beauty	236	UNVEILED CHRIST
Once to every man and nation	670	EBENEZER
One day!	22	ONE DAY
Only believe	585	ONLY BELIEVE
Only trust Him	629	MINERVA
Onward Christian soldiers	617	ST. GERTRUDE
Open my eyes, that I may see	486	OPEN MY EYES
Our Father, who art in Heaven	440	MALOTTE
Out in the highways and by-ways of life	473	SCHULER
Out of my bondage, sorrow and night	401	JESUS I COME
Pass it on	641	PASS IT ON
Pass me not, O gentle Savior	416	PASS ME NOT
Peace I leave with you	64	PEACE I GIVE
Peace, perfect peace	491	PAX TECUM
Plenty of room in the family	552	PLENTY OF ROOM
Praise be to Jesus	366	PRAISE BE TO JESUS
Praise God, from whom all blessings flow	382, 384	OLD 100th
Praise, my soul, the King of Heaven	339	LAUDA ANIMA
Praise the Lord, His glories show	373	LLANFAIR
Praise the Lord! ye heavens, adore Him	335	FABEN
Praise the Savior, ye who know Him!	362	ACCLAIM
Praise to the Lord, the Almighty	337	LOBE DEN HERREN
Praise ye the Father, for His loving-kindness	136	FLEMMING
Praise ye, the triune God	136	FLEMMING
Prayer is the soul's sincere desire	446	SINCERE DESIRE
Precious Lord, take my hand	611	PRECIOUS LORD

Reach out and touch	655	REACH OUT
Reach out to Jesus	430	REACH OUT TO JESUS
Redeemed	646	REDEEMED
Redeeming love	199	REDEEMING LOVE
Rejoice, the Lord is King!	374	DARWALL'S 148th
Rejoice, ye pure in heart	394	MARION
Renew Thy church, her ministries restore	572	ALL IS WELL
Rescue the perishing	661	RESCUE
Revive us again	574	REVIVE US AGAIN
Rise up, O men of God!	398	FESTAL SONG
Rock of ages, cleft for me	108	TOPLADY
Room at the cross	645	STANPHILL

Satisfied	100	SATISFIED
Savior, again to Thy dear name	519	ELLERS
Savior, like a shepherd lead us	601	BRADBURY
Savior, Thy dying love	279	SOMETHING FOR JESUS
Search me, O God	425	MAORI
Security	496	BERGEN MA VIKA
Send the light!	663	McCABE
Shackled by a heavy burden	628	HE TOUCHED ME
Silent night, holy night	195	STILLE NACHT
Simply trusting every day	79	TRUSTING JESUS
Since I have been redeemed	644	OTHELLO
Since Jesus came into my heart	639	McDANIEL
Sing praise to God who reigns above	343	MIT FREUDEN ZART
Sing the wondrous love of Jesus	123	HEAVEN
Sing them over again to me	29	WORDS OF LIFE
Sitting at the feet of Jesus	58	COMFORT
So send I you	664	SO SEND I YOU
Softly and tenderly	432	THOMPSON
Some children see Him	181	SOME CHILDREN
Some golden daybreak	312	DAYBREAK
Something beautiful	656	SOMETHING BEAUTIFUL
Something worth living for	638	SOMETHING MORE
Sometimes "Alleluia"	331	SOMETIMES ALLELUIA
Speak, Lord, in the stillness	444	QUIETUDE
Spirit now live in me	151	LOIS
Spirit of God, descend upon my heart	147	MORECAMBE
Spirit of the living God	155	LIVING GOD
Stand up, stand up for Jesus	616	WEBB
Standing on the promises of God	69	TURLOCK
Strong, righteous man of Galilee	216	MELITA
Sun of my soul	62	HURSLEY
Sweet hour of prayer	439	SWEET HOUR
Sweet, sweet Spirit	159	SWEET, SWEET SPIRIT

Take my life and let it be consecrated	458	HENDON
Take the name of Jesus with you	231	PRECIOUS NAME

Take Thou my hand, O Father	600	SO NUMM DENN
Take Thou our minds, dear Lord	467	HALL
Take time to be holy	457	LONGSTAFF
Teach me Your way, O Lord	472	COMACHA
Teach us what we yet may be	9	HYMN TO JOY
Tell me the old, old story	16	EVANGEL
Tell me the stories of Jesus (I love to hear)	212	STORIES OF JESUS
Tell me the story of Jesus, write on my heart	215	STORY
Thank God for the promise of Spring	110	SPRINGTIME
Thanks to God for my Redeemer	386	TACK O GUD
The blood will never lose its power	262	THE BLOOD
The bond of love	544	BOND OF LOVE
The Church within us	551	THE CHURCH WITHIN US
The Chruch's one foundation	547	AURELIA
The Comforter has come	143	COMFORTER
The cross upon which Jesus died	645	STANPHILL
The Easter song	301	EASTER SONG
The family of God	543	FAMILY OF GOD
The first Noel	179	THE FIRST NOEL
The God of Abraham praise!	332	LEONI
The great Physician	38	GREAT PHYSICIAN
The Haven of rest	101	GOOD SHIP
The hiding place	37	HIDING PLACE
The joy of the Lord	354	HOUSTON
The King is coming!	313	KING IS COMING
The light of the world is Jesus	636	LIGHT OF THE WORLD
The longer I serve Him	623	THE SWEETER HE GROWS
The Lord bless you and keep you	522	BENEDICTION
The Lord's my Shepherd, I'll not want	40	CRIMOND
The Lord's my Shepherd, I'll not want	42	BROTHER JAMES' AIR
The Lord's our rock, in Him we hide	117	SHELTER
The Lord's prayer	440	MALOTTE
The love of God	18	LOVE OF GOD
The market-place is empty	313	KING IS COMING
The old rugged cross	256	RUGGED CROSS
The Savior is waiting	435	CARMICHAEL
The solid Rock	92	SOLID ROCK
The spirit of Jesus is in this place	157	SPIRIT OF JESUS
The star carol	201	STAR CAROL
The star-spangled banner	688	NATIONAL ANTHEM
The unveiled Christ	236	UNVEILED CHRIST
The vision of a dying world	668	ALL SAINTS' NEW
The wise may bring their learning	537	FOREST GREEN
The wonder of it all	13	WONDER OF IT ALL
There is a balm in Gilead	48	BALM IN GILEAD
There is a fountain filled with blood	263	BELMONT
There is a green hill far away	278	GREEN HILL
There is a name I love to hear	634	O HOW I LOVE JESUS
There is a place of quiet rest	35	McAFEE
There is sunshine in my soul today	630	SUNSHINE
There shall be showers of blessings	580	SHOWERS OF BLESSING
There's a call comes ringing	663	McCABE

There's a church within us, O Lord	551	THE CHURCH WITHIN US
There's a sweet, sweet Spirit in this place	159	SWEET, SWEET SPIRIT
There's a quiet understanding	556	QUIET UNDERSTANDING
There's a wideness in God's mercy	115	WELLESLEY
There's not a friend like the lowly Jesus	221	NO NOT ONE
There's room at the cross for you	645	STANPHILL
There's something about that name	227	THAT NAME
There's within my heart a melody	633	SWEETEST NAME
They that sow in tears	46	THEY THAT SOW IN TEARS
They that wait upon the Lord	52	TEACH ME LORD
They'll know we are Christians by our love	677	ST. BRENDAN'S
Thine is the glory	291	JUDAS MACCABEUS
This child we dedicate to Thee	571	FEDERAL STREET
This could be the dawning of that day	307	DAWNING
This is my country	693	MY COUNTRY
This is my Father's world	6	TERRA BEATA
This is my song, O God of all the nations	682	FINLANDIA
This is my story, this is my song	67	ASSURANCE
Thou didst leave Thy throne	170	MARGARET
Thou my everlasting portion	405	CLOSE TO THEE
Thou, whose purpose is to kindle	576	HYFRYDOL
Thou wilt keep him in perfect peace	493	PERFECT PEACE
Through all the world	672	CONRAD
Through it all	43	THROUGH IT ALL
Through the love of God, our Savior	498	AR HYD Y NOS
'Til the storm passes by	501	LISTER
'Tis so sweet to trust in Jesus	91	TRUST IN JESUS
To God be the glory	363	TO GOD BE THE GLORY
To God be the glory (Crouch)	365	MY TRIBUTE
Trust and obey	454	TRUST AND OBEY
Trusting Jesus	79	TRUSTING JESUS
Turn your eyes upon Jesus	621	LEMMEL
Under His wings	412	HINGHAM
Until then	133	UNTIL THEN
Up Calvary's mountain	275	REDEEMER
Up from the grave He arose	298	CHRIST AROSE
Victory in Jesus	82	HARTFORD
We are climbing Jacob's ladder	488	JACOB'S LADDER
We are God's people	546	SYMPHONY
We are living, we are dwelling	447	BLAENHAFREN
We are one in the bond of love	544	BOND OF LOVE
We are one in the Spirit	677	ST. BRENDAN'S
We dedicate this temple	568	AURELIA
We gather together	387	KREMSER
We give Thee but Thine own	515	SCHUMANN
We have heard the joyful sound	667	JESUS SAVES
We plow the fields and scatter the good seed	395	WEIR PLTUGEN
We praise Thee, O God	574	REVIVE US AGAIN

We praise Thee, O God, our Redeemer	334	KREMSER
We search the starlit Milky Way	93	EWHURST
We sing the greatness of our God	338	ELLACOMBE
We three Kings of Orient are	206	KINGS OF ORIENT
We're marching to Zion	550	MARCHING TO ZION
We've a story to tell to the nations	659	MESSAGE
Were you there?	287	WERE YOU THERE
What a day that will be	314	WHAT A DAY
What a fellowship, what a joy divine	87	SHOWALTER
What a friend we have in Jesus	466	ERIE
What a wonderful change in my life	639	McDANIEL
What a wonderful Savior	372	BENTON HARBOR
What can wash away my sin?	266	PLAINFIELD
What child is this, who, laid to rest?	180	GREENSLEEVES
What if it were today?	311	WHAT IF IT WERE TODAY
What wondrous love is this	283	WONDROUS LOVE
When all my labors and trials are o'er	132	GLORY SONG
When He shall come	309	PEARCE
When I can read my title clear	134	PISGAH
When I saw the cleansing fountain	359	I WILL PRAISE HIM
When I survey the wondrous cross	258	HAMBURG
When morning gilds the skies	322	LAUDES DOMINI
When peace, like a river	495	VILLE DU HAVRE
When we all get to Heaven	123	HEAVEN
When we see Christ	129	WHEN WE SEE CHRIST
When we walk with the Lord	454	TRUST AND OBEY
Where cross the crowded ways of life	665	GERMANY
Where He leads me	607	NORRIS
Where the Spirit of the Lord is	148	THERE IS PEACE
While by the sheep	182	JUNGST
While shepherds watched their flocks	175	CHRISTMAS
Whiter than snow	109	FISCHER
Who is on the Lord's side?	409	ARMAGEDDON
Why do I sing about Jesus?	635	KETCHUM
Why should He love me so?	26	LOVE ME
Wonderful grace of Jesus	114	WONDERFUL GRACE
Wonderful peace	494	WONDERFUL PEACE
Wonderful words of life	29	WORDS OF LIFE
Wondrous love	283	WONDROUS LOVE
Worthy the Lamb	285	WORTHY
Wounded for me	282	FOR ME
Years I spent in vanity and pride	415	CALVARY
Yesterday He died for me	76	YESTERDAY-TODAY-TOMORROW
Yesterday, today and tomorrow	76	YESTERDAY-TODAY-TOMORROW
Yesterday, today, forever	83	NYACK
You said You'd come and share all my sorrows	436	CHILDREN OF THE DAY
You servants of God, your Master proclaim	360	HANOVER
Your cause be mine, great Lord divine	505	RICHMOND BEACH